THE FIRST FOUR

THE FIRST FOUR

The Gospel Writers Give Good News
to the Youth of the Twenty-First Century

BILL PRICE

RESOURCE *Publications* • Eugene, Oregon

THE FIRST FOUR
The Gospel Writers Give Good News to the Youth of the Twenty-First Century

Copyright © 2025 Bill Price. All rights reserved. Except for brief quotations in critical publications or reviews, no part of this book may be reproduced in any manner without prior written permission from the publisher. Write: Permissions, Wipf and Stock Publishers, 199 W. 8th Ave., Suite 3, Eugene, OR 97401.

Resource Publications
An Imprint of Wipf and Stock Publishers
199 W. 8th Ave., Suite 3
Eugene, OR 97401

www.wipfandstock.com

PAPERBACK ISBN: 979-8-3852-4935-0
HARDCOVER ISBN: 979-8-3852-4936-7
EBOOK ISBN: 979-8-3852-4937-4
VERSION NUMBER 05/13/25

Scripture taken from the ESV* Bible (The Holy Bible English Standard Version*) Text Edition: 2016. Copyright © 2001 by crossway, a publishing ministry of Good News Publishing. The ESV* text has been reproduced in cooperation with and by permission of Good News Publishers. Unauthorized reproduction of this publication is prohibited. All rights reserved.

Scripture taken from The King James Version. Public Domain.

Scripture taken from the New King James Version* Copyright © 1982 by Thomas Nelson. Used by permission. All rights reserved.

Scripture taken from the Holy Bible, New Living Translation, copyright © 1996, 2004, 2015 by Tindale House Foundation. Used by permission of Tyndale House Publications, Inc. Illinois 60188. All Rights reserved,

To Hester—Who has been by my side from the beginning

and

To Julie—For saying that I need to keep writing

CONTENTS

Gospel I: I Am Levi

Part 1   From a Cheater to a Preacher | 3
Part 2   The Genealogy was Written First | 7
Part 3   The Birth | 9
Part 4   Baptism and Temptation | 12
Part 5   Jesus Taught Us How to Pray and He did miracles | 15
Part 6   Not Accepted By All | 18
Part 7   Jesus Is God But Was Rejected By His Own | 22
Part 8   The Death of the Baptist, More Miracles, and Walking on Water | 26
Part 9   Who Am I? | 29
Part 10   Hosanna to the Son of David | 35
Part 11   The Great Commandment and the End | 38

Gospel II: The Good News According To Me, Mark

Part 1   Introduction | 49
Part 2   The Prophets Tell of John the Baptist | 51
Part 3   Finding Disciples, Healing, and Preaching | 53
Part 4   The Pharisees Follow and Begin to Plot | 56
Part 5   Picking the Twelve and Explaining Who His Brothers Were | 58
Part 6   Jesus Uses Parables | 60
Part 7   "The Sower sows the word." | 61
Part 8   The Demons and the Swine | 63

CONTENTS

Part 9   Who Touched Me? | 65
Part 10 Not Being Accepted and Sending Out the Twelve | 67
Part 11 The Death of the Baptist | 68
Part 12 The Miracle of the Loaves and Walking on Water | 69
Part 13 Making Enemies of Unbelievers | 71
Part 14 Miracle After Miracle | 73
Part 15 Beware the Leaven of the Pharisees | 75
Part 16 Transfigured | 77
Part 17 Why Can't We Do It? | 79
Part 18 Marriage and Children | 81
Part 19 How to Get to Heaven | 82
Part 20 The Son of Man Will Suffer | 83
Part 21 The Fig Tree and the Money Changers | 85
Part 22 The Chief Priests, Scribes, and Pharisees | 86
Part 23 The End Times | 89
Part 24 Passover, the Last Supper, the Garden | 91
Part 25 False Accusations and Death | 94
Part 26 "The King of the Jews" | 96

Gospel III: The Gospel According to Luke

Part 1   . . . Because I Care | 101
Part 2   Mary and Elizabeth | 103
Part 3   The Birth of the King | 105
Part 4   John the Baptist | 107
Part 5   Jesus in the Wilderness | 109
Part 6   Not Accepted By His Own | 110
Part 7   Miracles and Choosing His Disciples | 112
Part 8   Why Be With the Sinners? | 115
Part 9   The Lord of the Sabbath | 116
Part 10 The Centurion's Servant and the Dead Young Man | 118
Part 11 The Woman Who Washed the Feet of Jesus | 120
Part 12 The Parable of the Seeds | 122
Part 13 The Demon Legion and the Swine | 124
Part 14 Jairus and His Daughter | 126

CONTENTS

Part 15 The Transfiguration, the Demon, and the Child | 129
Part 16 The Many Followers and My Neighbor | 131
Part 17 The Meaning of Prayer | 133
Part 18 Some Reject, Some Want Proof, and Some Believe | 135
Part 19 Dining with the Pharisee | 137
Part 20 Another Supper with Pharisees | 140
Part 21 Tax Collectors, Sinners, and the Prodigal | 142
Part 22 The Unjust Steward | 144
Part 23 The Fulfilled Law | 146
Part 24 Forgiveness, Faithfulness, Humbleness | 148
Part 25 Prayer Faith and Eternal Life | 150
Part 26 Traveling toward Jerusalem | 152
Part 27 The Authority Questioned—The Savior Hated | 155
Part 28 The End and the Return | 157
Part 29 Passover and the Last Supper | 159
Part 30 Betrayed Mocked and Killed | 162
Part 31 The Resurrection | 166
Part 32 Conclusion | 168

Gospel IV: The Beloved Disciple—I'm John, and I'm All about the Love

Part 1   The Words of the First Four | 171
Part 2   I'm Different from the Others | 175
Part 3   Relationship with Jesus | 177
Part 4   Relationship with Peter | 179
Part 5   The Word Became Flesh | 181
Part 6   Five Types of Love | 185
Part 7   Understanding Tripartite | 193
Part 8   The "I Am That I Am" and the "I Am" | 198
Part 9   The Five Parts of My Gospel | 203
Part 10 My Letter to You with Love | 229
Part 11 Final: What Do I Do Next? | 231

Appendix: For Your Consideration | 233
Bibliography | 235

Gospel I

I AM LEVI

Part 1

FROM A CHEATER TO A PREACHER

I am Levi and I would like to introduce myself and explain things I observed while my world was in turmoil. I was the writer of Matthew, the first synoptic Gospel in the New Testament. My fellow followers of Jesus, Mark and Luke, also wrote Gospels. The three of our writings are telling about the events we encountered and are pretty much the same. Our point of view is equal to each other and we often write the same words and expressions, because we lived it. After all. That is what synoptic means. We all recorded a synopsis of the life, death, and resurrection of Jesus, the Christ.

I Wrote the first book to explain how one person can change the entire Earth. Mine does differ from the others originally because I wrote it for the Jewish people who had become followers of Jesus. I often thought they should not lose the customs our people had followed for thousands of years. I believed that our traditions should not be forgotten by these new gentiles.

I am however getting ahead of myself. I wish to go back to the time I met this Jesus. As I have told you, my name was Levi and I am not afraid to tell you I was a cheat and a thief when it came to my own people, the Jews. I had been hired as a tax collector by the Romans, under the hierarchy of Herod Antipas, and I conducted my business in the city of Capernaum.[1] I'll admit it was pretty easy to make a pretty penny in my business. I guess that's why people hated me so. I was, however, just doing my Job as it had been done long before I took the job. I paid Rome first for all the taxes owed by my fellow citizens and travelers. After I paid, I collected what I wanted

---

1. Doug Culp, "Matthew: From tax collector to apostle," FAITH Catholic, Sept. 20, 2022, https://dioceseofraleigh.org/news/matthew-tax-collector-apostle.

GOSPEL I: I AM LEVI

and that practice would more than compensate me for any money lost by paying the Romans. I was great with numbers and figures. I was also great at charging more than each person owed, so I was making a pretty good living.

There was one fall back to the job, though. As I mentioned, I was a hated man who was driven by a greedy heart. No one ever questioned my figures and they all paid me what I told them they owed, I had the support of the Roman soldiers, so no one ever complained, well at least not to me.

All of that changed one day while I was collecting at the customs house in Capernaum. I was going about my business when this man came to me as I sat in my tax booth. He was a kind gentle looking man whose eyes pierced my very soul. I had heard the stories about this preacher and teacher. I had listened to those who had gone to John the Baptist. He had told them that they must repent, for the Kingdom of God was at hand. John explained that his job was only to prepare God's people for the Messiah. It was at least thought, by many of us, that The Son of God had been born and John stated that this man was Jesus.

This man named Jesus was talking to many and was bringing a new message about those valued by the Kingdom of Heaven. As I sat pondering my job, filled with numbers and facts and what I could get for myself, I kept thinking about the things that this Jesus had said. I later recorded these things so that I could share them with the world.

I once heard that He declared those who were poor in spirit were blessed. My friends, which were few and far between, and I knew exactly what this man meant. Being poor in spirit was the realization that you are full of sin and there is nothing you can do to make yourself acceptable in the sight of God. Only by accepting the messiah would you be saved. Those who are poor in spirit know it is faith alone that makes one acceptable.

Next, I heard that He had said blessed are those who mourn, for they will see comfort. If someone experiences true deep grief, then they would understand the spiritual message here. This man seemed to explain that grief was more than the sadness we feel when we lose something or when a loved one dies. People mourn over grief, yes, but He was teaching about the grief we should have because of our sin which truly hurts God. If we know we grieve spiritually, we know we will see comfort in Heaven.

Jesus also told the crowd that those who seek out and hunger for rightness will find satisfaction. If you have ever gone hungry, you will know how great it Is to be fed a good meal. The Son of God, however was telling those who listened how important it was to hunger for the need to be like Jesus. If people hunger or thirst for righteousness, satisfaction will be given. It may not appear here, on this earthly plane, but satisfaction will happen in Heaven.

When this Messiah explained that those who show mercy will also receive mercy, they understood. Show compassion to those in need and God will bless you. That was rather simple, even though the average person would not think this trait was necessarily in their time, because Israel was now occupied by the Romans and the Romans were hated. If a Roman had a problem with a jew and needed gratification, I guarantee mercy would not be given. The Savior of God's people, however, had a different message though and His people needed to show mercy even to the Romans.

Blessed are the pure in heart, for they will see God, was the next trait Jesus spoke of. Being pure, being without guilt, or being blameless is a trait that can be possessed by no one. Every person falls because of original sin and faces death. That is the fault of the first humans created by God. Every Jew knew that the wages of sin had to be atoned for. There had to be a sacrifice to be given forgiveness. Purity of heart, in the words of this teacher named Jesus, though, meant that one could have no hidden agendas or be hypocritical when it came to the purity of the soul. Those who were truly pure, would see God.

Peace in our time seemed to be impossible, yet Jesus said that the peacemakers were children of God. Jesus was the Prince of Peace and He wanted others to follow His example. The Kingdom of Heaven belongs to those who would be peacemakers. After all, it would be Jesus who would lay down His life to make peace between mankind and God. Jesus would sacrifice Himself to bring us to God eternally.

There is one problem for those who would follow the things Jesus was teaching. These believers would be persecuted for their beliefs. They would eventually be hunted down by those who sought power over others. They would face prison, torture, and death just because the chose to follow the Messiah. Jesus, however, told them they would be blessed for being persecuted for the sake of righteousness, These people would receive the kingdom of heaven.

The man who said all of these things was now looking at me, When He spoke I practically froze. He simply said, "Follow me." I rose and did exactly that. I followed Him and became known as Matthew. I became a disciple and my first act was to invite Him and others to dine with me. I

GOSPEL I: I AM LEVI

prepared a feast and Jesus came. He and others came to my house. The Pharisees used this to discredit Jesus. They spoke loudly saying, "How can this man eat with tax collectors and sinners. They're regulations forbade Rabbis and Pharisees from eating with sinners, so they could not understand this Messiah.

I didn't care anymore what others said or thought. I think I was chosen by my Lord because of my accurate record keeping and my attention to details. I was a keen observer and had a great memory. This would help me as I began to write about the Savior of the world.

Part 2

THE GENEALOGY WAS WRITTEN FIRST

As I told you, my name was Levi. I got my new name, Matthew, after I decided to follow the Man who came to me and told me to follow Him. I became an Apostle of The Lord, Jesus, The Christ, and I was a new man. I could never go back to the sinful life I had lived. Even your pope Benedict, from your time, understood my changes. He said, "In the figure of Matthew, the Gospels present to us a true and proper paradox: those who seem to be the farthest from holiness can even become a model of the acceptance of God's mercy and offer a glimpse of its marvelous effects in their own lives."

Since Matthew means "Gift of Yahweh (Gift of God)," that's who I became. To understand why my name changed, you need to understand the gift of God. You see, I knew that Jesus was the Messiah, He was the Son of God, whose coming was foretold by the Prophets of God, found in the Tora and Old Testament. Because I absolutely and immediately believed this, I began my Gospel by explaining the Genealogy of the one who would be the Savior of the Jews. After all, I was good at this. I did believe in accurate records and using the great memory God had given me.

To begin, I must explain why my list of ancestors is different than others. You see, I skipped some Generations to focus on the direct lineage of Jesus. I needed to show people that Jesus was who He said He was. I used this common ancient practice of structure to make it easier for people to understand Jesus was "the Son of David". He was a direct descendent of King David as well as Abraham. I was simply making a point here.

It was Jermiah who told us, in chapter 23 and verses 5-6, "The days are coming, declares the Lord, when I will raise up for David a righteous

GOSPEL I: I AM LEVI

Branch. A King . . . who will reign wisely and do what is just and right in the land. In his days Judah will be saved and Israel will live in safety This is the name by which he will be called: The Lord Our Righteous Savior. It was Jesus that came from the House of David, the son of Jesse. All of the other names I will leave to you to read in my Gospel.

I will admit that I was, firstly, writing for the Jews. I have received, how do you say it, a lot of slack for historians, Many have tried to express that Luke's account of the ancestry and my account are different, therefore are untrue. Nothing could be further from the truth. Luke, in his Gospel account, used David's son Nathan and followed his descendants to Jesus. I used King Davids son Solomon and followed his descendants and they both lead to the same person. That was the child born of Mary and Joseph, Jesus the Messiah.

Part 3

THE BIRTH

Anyway, Mary became the mother of Jesus by the Holy Spirit, for she had known no man. Mary had been promised to Joseph and were to be married. So many people find this so hard to believe, but they must remember we are talking about the creator of the universe here. Joseph was an honorable man and a just man who didn't want to make this miracle a public thing.

Knowing the law, Mary would have been stoned to death if the public knew. The only thing Mary could say was what an angel had told her. Everyday people in my time, would not have believed her, but Joseph soon had a similar story. Mary's son was to be the Son of God, the Messiah, and he was to take her as his wife without any fear.

The Angel told Joseph that he was to name this child Jesus because He would save all people from their sin. Of course, this was going to happen and it would fulfill the prophecy which had stated, "Behold, a virgin shall be with child, and shall bring forth a son, and they shall call his name Emmanuel, which being interpreted is, God with us." This is found in Isaiah 14. Joseph rose up and obeyed the Angel and took Mary as his wife.

Jesus was born in Bethlehem during the reign of Herod the King. Wise men from the east came because of the sign in the heavens that told them a king was to be born. They went to Herod and asked where this King of the Jews was. They explained that they had seen his star in the east, and had come to worship him.

Since Harod was a jealous and self-centered King, he was troubled by this. I believe he was afraid someone was going to take over his position and he wasn't about to put up with that. He gathered all the chief priests and scribes together, and demanded that they tell him where this Christ was to be born.

They told him it had been written by the prophet Micah and it said, "And thou Bethlehem, in the land of Judaea, art not the least among the princes of Juda: for out of thee shall come a Governor, that shall rule my people Israel."

Herod was a great builder, but he was also an evil tyrant. He had killed his father and some of his wives and he was not about to let a child usurp his throne.

He asked the wise men to go and worship this child and, in return, come back and tell him where the baby was. He said he wanted to worship this new king also.

The wise men found Jesus and they rejoiced, filled with joy. They presented Him with gifts fit for a King: gold, and frankincense and myrrh, These gifts were standard gifts which were to be offered to honor any king. Gold was a precious metal showing that one was worthy to be a king. Frankincense was a perfume that was a symbol of the divinity of Jesus, Myrrh was an oil which may have foretold of the anointing He was to receive when He became a sacrifice for the sins of the world.

The wisemen were warned by God, after they had seen the Christ, to depart in another direction; they were not to return to Herod. When they left they listened and went to their homes by a different route,

It was then when an Angel came to Joseph and said to him that he should arise and take the young child and his mother and flee into Egypt, He was warned to stay there until the Angel of the Lord said he could return. The explanation was given that Herod wanted to kill their son. Joseph did as he was told. I remember, from my lessons that the prophet Hosea (Hosea 11:1) said, "Out of Egypt have I called my son."

Herod was so angry when the wisemen did not return, He ordered all the children of Bethlehem and all the children in the surrounding areas, two years and under, to be killed. The soldiers of Herod followed his orders and all of Israel mourned.

Again, I remembered my history and the prophet who had foretold, "In Rama was there a voice heard, lamentation, and weeping, and great mourning, Rachel weeping for her children, and would not be comforted, because they are not." They were all dead.

When Harod the Great finally died, Mary and Joseph were told by an Angel that it was safe to return. Jesus had been brought back from Egypt.

THE BIRTH

Because of another angelic visit, Joseph took his family to live in Nazareth. There were many prophets in the old Testament who suggested this would occur and it did come to pass.

Part 4

BAPTISM AND TEMPTATION

I STARTED BY SHOWING that the man I followed came from the House of David and was born of Mary. I must now explain what happened to Jesus just before He began His mission. In his early years, He led an obscure life being raised to help His father, Joseph, as a carpenter. He did, at the age of twelve, follow His parents to Jerusalem to celebrate Passover. My brother in Christ, Luke, wrote about this in his Gospel. I believe it is important to show you his words because not much was written before Jesus sought out John the Baptist. The words that you will see are the words stated by Jesus Himself. I hope that makes it a bit clearer for you.

> Every year Jesus' parents went to Jerusalem for the Festival of the Passover. When he was twelve years old, they went up to the festival, according to the custom. After the festival was over, while his parents were returning home, the boy Jesus stayed behind in Jerusalem, but they were unaware of it. Thinking he was in their company, they traveled on for a day. Then they began looking for him among their relatives and friends. When they did not find him, they went back to Jerusalem to look for him.
>
> After three days they found him in the temple courts, sitting among the teachers, listening to them and asking them questions. Everyone who heard him was amazed at his understanding and his answers. When his parents saw him, they were astonished. His mother said to him, "Son, why have you treated us like this? Your father and I have been anxiously searching for you."
>
> "Why were you searching for me?" he asked. "Didn't you know I had to be in my Father's house?" But they did not

BAPTISM AND TEMPTATION

understand what he was saying to them. Then he went down to Nazareth with them and was obedient to them. But his mother treasured all these things in her heart. And Jesus grew in wisdom and stature, and in favor with God and man. (Luke 2:41–52 NIV)

When Jesus was thirty, He began the work His Father in Heaven had given. He left His home in Nazareth of Galilee and traveled to see John at the river Jordan. One day, Jesus came to John the Baptist and said that He wanted to be baptized. Standing in the Jordan river, John told Jesus that it was he who needed to be baptized by Jesus but, the Messiah replied, "Let it be so now; it is proper for us to do this to fulfill all righteousness." Then John consented (Matthew 3:15 NIV) and Jesus was baptized.

When Jesus was baptized the Heavens opened up and a voice was heard saying, "This is my beloved Son, in whom I am well pleased." I believe that the facts here speak for themselves. Jesus came from David and He fulfilled the prophecy.

After that, Jesus was led into the wilderness because He was about to be tempted by Satan. We all remember the first Adam was tempted by Satan and he failed. Because of this sin, mankind would now suffer death. God is perfect and sin goes against His will. God and sin cannot exist together. As far as light is from the dark, God is from sin. In the old Testament, God's people would need a sacrifice to please God and remove their sin. All humans are tempted by sin and all humans fail. This was the nature of man caused by the first Adam.

Jesus was the Second Adam, at least that is what my friend Paul called Him when he wrote, So it is written: "The first man Adam became a living being"; the last Adam, a life-giving spirit. The spiritual did not come first, but the natural, and after that the spiritual. The first man was of the dust of the earth; the second man is of heaven. As was the earthly man, so are those who are of the earth; and as is the heavenly man, so also are those who are of heaven. And just as we have borne the image of the earthly man, so shall we bear the image of the heavenly man" (1 Cor. 15:45–49 NIV).

Paul was going into more detail than I wish to present here. I am merely saying that Jesus was the second Adam in that He was about to be tempted by Satan. First, the Holy Spirit led Jesus into the wilderness. He would remain there for 40 days. While in the wilderness, Satan appeared to Him and said, "If you are the Son of God, tell these stones to become bread." Jesus answered, "It is written: 'Man shall not live on bread alone, but on every word that comes from the mouth of God." (Matthew 4: 3–4 NIV)

GOSPEL I: I AM LEVI

Jesus was quoting the Old Testament in Deuteronomy 8:3: "He humbled you, causing you to hunger and then feeding you with manna, which neither you nor your ancestors had known, to teach you that man does not live on bread alone but on every word that comes from the mouth of the Lord." This temptation failed.

Next, the Devil not being satisfied took Him to the holy city and had him stand on the highest point of the temple. "If you are the Son of God," he said, "throw yourself down. For it is written: '"He will command his angels concerning you, and they will lift you up in their hands, so that you will not strike your foot against a stone."

Jesus answered him, "It is also written: 'Do not put the Lord your God to the test'" (Matthew 4:7 NIV) It is no coincidence that Deuteronomy 6:16 says: "Ye shall not tempt the LORD your God, as ye tempted him in Massah." Again Jesus did not fall into temptation.

Again, the devil took him to a very high mountain and showed him all the kingdoms of the world and their splendor. "All this I will give you," he said, "if you will bow down and worship me." Jesus said to him, "Away from me, Satan! For it is written: 'Worship the Lord your God, and serve him only." (Matthew 4:10 NIV) In Deuteronomy 6:13 it was written: "Thou shalt fear the LORD thy God, and serve him, and shalt swear by his name." Jesus, being God in the flesh, beat the Devil, He had done what the first Adam could not do! Satan left Him and the Angels of God attended to Him.

Soon, he left the wilderness to start His mission, From that point on, Jesus began to preach and teach. He had said and I have recorded His words in my Gospel Chapter 4 verse 17: "Repent, for the Kingdom of God is at hand." (Matthew 4:17) As he traveled He called men to follow Him. Peter and Andrew, James and John were the first four. He stated that He was going to take these fisherman and turn them into fishers of men.

He took them with Him as He went His reputation grew. He was teaching, preaching, healing the sick, driving out demons, and curing the lame. It didn't take long before He was being followed by a multitude of people, hanging on His every word. I told you earlier about the sermon he gave concerning the beatitudes. I had decided to follow this man because I knew, without a doubt, that He was God's Son.

Part 5

JESUS TAUGHT US HOW TO PRAY AND HE DID MIRACLES

AFTER JESUS HAD TAUGHT who would be blessed, He was asked how we should pray? After all, it was on this mountain that Jesus said that they should ask and it would be given to them, They should seek and they will find, and if they knock, the door will be opened to them. It was important, too, that He taught them to pray by saying:

> "This, then, is how you should pray: Our Father in heaven, hallowed be your name, 10 your kingdom come, your will be done, on earth as it is in heaven. 11 Give us today our daily bread. 12 And forgive us our debts, as we also have forgiven our debtors. 13 And lead us not into temptation, but deliver us from the evil one." (Matthew 6:9-13)

Since then, you have added "For yours is the Kingdom and the Power and the Glory forever. AMEN" I actually see nothing wrong, but since believing in being exact, I wanted to quote what our Lord said—only.

You see, I know Jesus wanted us to love. It isn't that hard to understand. If we as humans know how to treat our children with love, how much more is God capable of? Even though He spoke of love, He also gave the people a warning. He told them not everyone who says they know Jesus will be allowed in Heaven. Whatever we do to the least of our brothers we do to Him.

He asked us to build our house on a rock instead of on sand. The house built on a rock could withstand anything that came against it. A house built

GOSPEL I: I AM LEVI

on sand would not stand, but would be destroyed. Of course, He meant our faith should be built on Him and the firm foundation of which He taught.

Now, the multitude, gathered there to hear Him, were astonished at His words. He wasn't talking to them like the Priests and Scribes found in the Temple. He spoke and when He did, it was with authority.

When He came down from the mountain, to once again travel and teach, the people came with Him. Along the way, a leper, who worshiped Him, came to Jesus and asked, "Lord, if you are willing, can you make me clean?"

Jesus answered, "I am willing. Be clean." (Matthew 8:3). Immediately he was healed.

As He traveled and was about to arrive in Capernaum, a Centurion of Rome came to Him and asked Jesus to please heal his servant who had been paralyzed. Jesus told the centurion that he would go with him. "Lord, I am not worthy," he said to Jesus, "that you should come under my room. But only speak a work, and my servant will be healed." He explained to Jesus how he was a man with many soldiers under him. He had authority and when he gave an order, he knew it would be followed. He didn't have to be there. He felt the same about Jesus.

When Jesus heard this, He spoke. "Assuredly, I say to you, I have not found such great faith, not even in Israel. And I say to you that many will come from the east and west and sit down with Abraham, Issac, and Jacob in the Kingdom of Heaven . . . Go your way and as you believed, so let it be done for you." (Matthew 8:10), The Centurion's servant was healed at that very moment.

I need to stop for a second and explain one thing. I know that you understand there are many versions of the Gospels. During the rest of my story to you I will be using the New King James Version (NKJV) when I quote the Savior. It's not that one is better than the other, it's just the one I chose. With your permission, I will simply use the chapter and verse because you know the work is mine. Now where was I?

Jesus then came to Peter's house, and they found that Peter's mother had a fever. Jesus touched her hand, and she was healed. Later that day the people brought to Him many who was demon possessed. He cast out the demons with a word, and healed all of them who were sick. I write this again to show the fulfilled prophecy, which was spoken by Isaiah: "He Himself took our infirmities and bore our sickness."

JESUS TAUGHT US HOW TO PRAY AND HE DID MIRACLES

When he saw the great multitude of people, Jesus decided to depart for a while. As He and His disciples were on a boat; A storm came upon them. The waves were so big, it almost capsized the boat. Jesus, however, was asleep. The disciples, being afraid, went to Him and woke Him saying that they were about to perish. They pleaded for Him to save them.

Jesus said to them, in 8:26, "Why are you fearful, O you of little faith?" He simply rose and rebuked the wind and instantly there was a great calm. The men marveled and stated how unbelievable it was that even the wind and the sea obeyed Him

Part 6

NOT ACCEPTED BY ALL

When they arrived at the other side of the sea, in Gergesenes, two men came out of tombs toward Jesus. They were demon possessed and so fierce, that no dared pass them. They shouted at Jesus and said, "What have we to do with you, Jesus, You Son of God. Have you come here to torment us before the time?"

I personally think the demons were stating here the power that The Christ had over them. He was the authority and had the power to judge them and punish them. When they spoke the words, "before the time" they were talking about Judgment Day and He was there to judge them before that day. They knew they were about to be driven out of these men who they possessed. In the distance they heard a group of swine eating. They asked Jesus, that if He were going to cast them out, that they be cast into the swine. Jesus commanded with one word. "Go!" (8–32)

The demons went into the swine, and ran down to the sea and were drowned. The owners of the swine went into the town, telling everyone what had happened, When the people came to Jesus they begged him to leave their region. You must understand that these men were heathen, and saw Jesus as a destroyer instead of a savior. He and the disciples departed back to the sea and crossed back to their own land.

When Jesus returned, naturally there were crowds that would gather to hear Him preach and to see Him perform Miracles. They brought to Jesus a paralyzed man lying on his bed. When Jesus saw the faith that the people had, He said, "Son, be of good cheer; your sins are forgiven you."

NOT ACCEPTED BY ALL

Some of the scribes there, well, kind of freaked out. They called Jesus a blasphemer. Today, you might call him a traitor to his religious cause. Jesus, however knew their thoughts.

He spoke to them, saying, "Why do you think evil in your hearts? For which is easier to say, Your sins are forgiven you, or to say, Arise and walk? But that you may know that the Son of man has power on earth to forgive sins"—looking at the man he continued, "Arise, pick up your bed and go to your house." (9:4–6)

And he rose up and went to his house. The many people witnessing this marveled and worshiped Him saying "Glory to God, who has given such power to man."

I have explained this before but it is so important that you understand. Remember when the Pharisees saw the disciples, and Jesus sitting and eating with me, the other tax collector and, well basically, sinners. They had asked us why their teacher would eat with such horrible human beings. Of course, Jesus knew what they had asked and he spoke to them.

"Those who are well have no need for a physician, but those who are sick do." Go and learn what this means: I desire mercy and not sacrifice, for I did not come to call the righteous, but sinners to repentance." (9:12–13)

The Pharisees and the Baptist's disciples asked another question of Jesus, at that time. They wanted to know why they and the Pharisees were required to fast often, but, we, the disciples of Jesus did not.

Jesus told them that the friends of the bridegroom won't be sad when they are with the bridegroom. But the day will come when the bridegroom will be taken from them. Then they will fast. Jesus also told them that no one would put new un-shrunk cloth on an old garment because it may shrink and would just tear again. Actually, it would become a worse tear. He also told them that no one would put new wine in old wineskins, because that, too, would tear and the wine would be lost.

Obviously, he was foretelling the fact that He would one day be taken away from us. But He was also explaining by use of a parable. The old garment signifies the life of a sinful man, like I, Levi, used to be. The new garment is a life of holiness, the new Matthew. The patch, however, may represent such old sacrificial laws that are now done because they have always been done, such as fasting. They have been repeated so much, they have lost their meaning.

By telling about the new wine and old wineskins, Jesus is displaying the actions of the Pharisees. They are following old tradition and live by old

GOSPEL I: I AM LEVI

principles. Jesus is presenting "New Wine" by calling sinners to repent and become new creatures in Christ, Jesus.

While teaching all these things, a ruler came and worshiped Him. He told Jesus that his daughter had just died, but if He would lay His hand on her, she would live again. Jesus and the rest of us got up and went with him.

On the way, a woman who had been bleeding on and off for twelve years touched the hem of Jesus's garment. She had said to herself that if she merely touched His garment, she would be well.

Jesus felt this and turned to her saying, "Be of good cheer, daughter. Your faith has made you well." (9:22) And Jesus continued on to the house of the ruler.

When Jesus came into the house, He saw the family and friends crying. He said to them, "Make room, for the girl is not dead, but just sleeping." (9:24). The crowd ridiculed Him and they were put outside.

Because of Jesus, two blind men saw, for they believed, and a man who was mute, after Jesus cast out a demon that possessed him, was able to speak. Jesus was healing and winning souls, but the Pharisees told the crowds that he was doing this because of the power of evil. How untrue! Jesus continued teaching and preaching about the Kingdom of Heaven. He constantly healed people of every sickness they possessed. Jesus Commissioned The Disciples.

When He saw that there were so many lost people searching for a shepherd, He had compassion for them. He told us, the disciples, "The harvest is truly plentiful, but the laborers are few." (9:37). With new power, given to us by Jesus, He decided He would be sending us to all the towns of Israel. He gave us power to cast out demons and power to heal the sick in His name. All twelve of us did as He commanded,

Before I continue, Let me tell you the names of the twelve. There was Simon, who was called Peter and his brother Andrew. There was James, the son of Zebedee and John, his brother, Also among them was Philip and Bartholomew, and me, Matthew. There was James, the son of Alphaeus, Simon the Canaanite, and Thaddaeus. Then, there was Judas, the one who would betray Jesus.

Jesus was going to send all twelve of us out to preach that the Kingdom of God was at hand and he told us to heal the sick, He said we should go to those who would accept us and if someone or some city would not accept us or our words, then we should leave and shake the dust of that city from us feet. That city, when it came to judgment, would not fare as well as

NOT ACCEPTED BY ALL

Sodom and Gomorrah. We remember the evil that was found in Lot's time and understood what we were about to face.

Jesus said, "Behold, I send you out as sheep in the midst of wolves. Therefore, be wise as serpents and harmless as doves." (10:16). Jesus told us that we would face hardships and people who would hate us because we were His disciples. He said they would want to do harm to us, but we would surely be provided for by God. He said that we should not be afraid. He informed us that if anyone confesses Him before man, He would also confess then to His Father in Heaven.

Part 7

JESUS IS GOD BUT WAS REJECTED BY HIS OWN

When Jesus finished commanding the twelve of us, He went to preach in our cities. John the Baptist, who was in prison, sent his own disciples to ask Jesus if he was the Messiah. Jesus told those disciples to go and tell John the things they had seen and heard. The sick had been healed, the blind saw, the lame walked, the deaf heard, and dead were raised up and the poor had the gospel preached to them. When they had departed, Jesus spoke to the crowds about John the Baptist. He called John more than a prophet and said that he was a messenger doing the work of Elijah.

Jesus, then, stated that he had no compassion for all the towns where he had preached and where the people had not repented. He stated that cities from the past who had sinned against God, would be better off on judgment day than those who rejected Him now. Yet, Jesus still asked then to accept Him. He said, "Come to me all you who labor, and are heavy laden, and I will give you rest." (11:28)

One Sabbath, we were going through a grain field with Jesus. We were hungry, so we picked some of the grain and ate it. The Pharisees saw this and said that the disciples were sinning because they were doing something that was unlawful in the land of Israel. Jesus rebuked them saying they did not understand that these men were blameless because they obey Him, who is greater than even the Temple. In other words, Jesus was telling them that He was God, for the only thing greater than the Temple, for a Jew, was God, Himself. Jesus told them, "For the Son of Man is Lord, even of the Sabbath." (12:8)

Jesus then went into their Synagogue, where He met a man with a deformed hand. The Pharisees watched Jesus and said He would be sinning if He healed a man on the Sabbath. Jesus asked them, "What man is there among you who has one sheep, and if it falls into a pit on the Sabbath, will not lay hold of it and lift it out? Of how much more value then, is a man than a sheep. Therefore, it is lawful to do good on the Sabbath." (12:11,12).

Jesus took the man's hand and healed it and the Pharisees started plotting as to how they could destroy Him. So, Jesus left, followed by many people. There were those who brought a man to Him who was both blind and mute because of a demon. The multitudes were amazed when Jesus healed the man. The Pharisees, however, told the crowd that Jesus used the Devil to cast out demons.

Jesus replied, "Every Kingdom divided against itself is brought to desolation and every house that is divided against itself cannot stand." (12:25). He told them, basically, Satan could not cast himself out.

He stated to them that His power was given to Him by God the Father. He also said to them that if they were not for Him, they were against Him and they would be judged or redeemed by the words they spoke.

The scribes and the Pharisees then asked Him to show them a sign. Jesus responded by telling them that it was an evil and sinful generation that needed signs to convince them. And no sign would be given to them except the one shown by the story of Jonah. Jonah spoke to Nineveh and they repented and were saved, but Jesus said He was greater than even Jonah. Jesus assured them that a generation like these scribes and Pharisees would surely be condemned.

Now while Jesus was speaking, his mother and brothers came to Him. The people told Him that they were there, but He asked, "Who is my mother and who are my brothers?" He stretched out His hand and continued. "Here are my mother and my brothers, for whoever does the will of my Father is my brother and sister and mother." (12:48–50)

On that same day Jesus went out to the sea. There was such a crowd following, that Jesus got into a boat to teach them. He began with parables. He described a Sower who went out to sow. Some of the seeds he was sowing fell by the wayside and the birds came and ate them. Some of the seeds had fallen on rocks. Now maybe they started to grow, but the sun and the heat soon dried them out. The ones that fell among the thorn bushes, were choked out and never grew. Some, however, fell on fertile soil. Those seeds grew and yielded a great crop.

We asked Jesus why He was using stories and parables and he Explained, "It has been given to you to know the mysteries of the Kingdom of Heaven, but to them it has not been given . . . Therefore I speak to them in parables because seeing they do not see, and hearing they do not hear, nor do they understand. And in them the prophecy of Isaiah is fulfilled." (13:11–13).

This prophecy of Isaiah says: "Hearing, you will hear and not understand, and seeing, you will see and not perceive." The prophecy goes on to explain that He must speak this way so many will understand and he would be able to heal them.

Jesus told us that whenever people do not understand, the devil can come in and he steals his heart. This explained the first parable of the seeds thrown by the wayside, and stolen by the birds. The explanation continued by showing that the seeds which fell on the rocks are like people who receive the word and are joyful. Their seed, however, is not well rooted. Soon, the troubles of the world and persecution make him stumble. Those seeds thrown to the thorns, is likened to the man who hears the word, but the riches of the world deceives him, and he chokes. The man who receives the good seed in the good soil, is the man who will hear, understand, and bear fruit.

Jesus told another parable, showing that the Kingdom of Heaven was like the man who sowed good wheat seed in good soil. While he was sleeping, an enemy came and sowed Tares (weeds that look like wheat, but are worthless) among the wheat. The servants went to their master and told him, asking if they should go and pull the weeds. He told them not to pull them, because they might also loosen the wheat, destroying the crops. He said to let it grow until the harvest and then the reapers would divide the good from the bad. It is then we will gather the weeds and burn them, saving only the wheat for the barn. In other words, those who believe and grow in Christ, even when attacked by the Devil who sows evil, will be separated from others who have followed evil. They are bound for eternal life while the evil face eternal fire.

The third parable dealt with the mustard seed. This seed is the smallest in the world, yet produces a greater plant than any other herb. This parable showed the people that the beginnings of the Christian faith would be small, but would grow into that which is useful and greater than anything else.

JESUS IS GOD BUT WAS REJECTED BY HIS OWN

The next parable was of the leaven (a substance used to produce fermentation in dough for making bread), It taught the people that the word of God and the spirit work gradually and silently, hardly being seen as it works. Yet there is a great change which happens to alter the soul of man. Jesus told these four parables to the multitude that it might fulfill yet another prophecy found in Psalms 78:2 which said, "I will open my mouth in parables; I will utter things kept secret from the foundation of the world." He then sent the people away. His disciples came to Him and asked that He explain the meanings of the parables.

He answered saying, "He who sows the good seed is the Son of Man. The field is the world and the seeds are the sons of the kingdom. The Tares are the sons of the wicked one. The enemy who sows them is the devil. The Harvest is the end of the age, and the reapers are the Angels." (13:37–39).

Jesus was saying that at the end of the age The Son of Man will send his Angels to gather all of mankind. Those who did not accept His word and salvation would be gathered up and cast into the fire with the evil one. The outcry and wailing will be great, but too late. He added, "Then the righteous will shine forth as the sun in the Kingdom of their Father. He who has ears to hear, let him hear." (13:43).

We, the disciples listened to Jesus as he stated the importance of these parables. He expressed that the Kingdom of Heaven was like a treasure found and hidden in a field by a man. It is then that the man who found the treasure sells everything he has and buys that exact field. Jesus stressed that Heaven was also like a jeweler seeking beautiful pearls, but he found one so precious that he sold everything to buy that one pearl. Heaven is also like a dragnet, which is cast into the sea and is filled with everything found in that sea. The fisherman will keep the good and throw the bad away. That is the way it will be on judgment day. The angels will throw away the wicked just like the bad things that were found in the net.

When Jesus finished clarifying the meanings of the parables, He left and went to His own country. He began preaching in the synagogue. The people there heard Him and said, "When did this man get this wisdom and these mighty works. Is He not the carpenter's son? Is not his mother called Mary? His brothers James, Joses, Simon, and Judas? And his sisters, are they not all with us? They were greatly offended by him. Jesus said to them, "A prophet is not without honor except in his own country and in his own house." (13:57). The Lord did not do many works there, because they refused to believe in Him.

Part 8

THE DEATH OF THE BAPTIST, MORE MIRACLES, AND WALKING ON WATER

Now, Herod heard about Jesus and thought that He may be John the Baptist come back to life. That must be why this Man possessed such power. He had to say, "come back to life" because it was he who had put John to death. John had constantly told Herod how he living in sin because he had married his brother's wife. Herod wanted to put John to death before, but was afraid of the people who thought John was a prophet. Herod's wife plotted with her own daughter to have John beheaded. Herod loved to see his wife's daughter dance and said, at his birthday celebration, he would give her anything if she would dance for him. She did and then asked for the head of the Baptist on a platter. Herod was upset, but had to give her what she wanted, because he had sworn an oath to her. When Jesus heard of this, He left and went to a deserted place.

    Jesus wasn't alone for long. A multitude found him and he, feeling compassion, began healing them and teaching them. He preached and healed late into the evening. Because it was late, some disciples told Jesus it was time to send them away. But Jesus had another idea. He told us we should feed all of them. We expressed that they only had five loaves of bread and two fish. The Lord told them to bring it to Him. Jesus prayed and blessed the food we had and He told us to start handing it out to the five thousand people there. To our amazement the food multiplied, feeding everyone, with twelve baskets of bread and fish left over. Many of the people heard and believed that day.

THE DEATH OF THE BAPTIST

After this, the people went their way to their own homes. Jesus told us to get on the boat that was by the shore. He asked us to meet Him on the other side of the sea. Jesus, being alone, went up into the mountain to pray.

By now, however, the boat was in the middle of the sea. It was being tossed by the waves because of a great wind. We saw Jesus coming to us, walking on water. When we saw this, thinking it was a ghost, we were filled with fear and cried out.

Jesus immediately spoke, saying, "Be of good cheer. It is I; do not be afraid." (14:27).

Peter answered Him and said, "Lord, if it is you, command me to come to you on the water."

So, Jesus called to him, saying, "Come." (14:29) and Peter did. He was walking on the water toward Jesus. I guess he realized he was actually walking on water on a windy sea and he became afraid. He started sinking and called to Jesus to save him. Jesus stretched out his hand and caught Peter, saving him. Jesus said, "O you of little faith, why did you doubt?" (14:31).

When they got to the boat, where the rest of us were, the wind calmed. Those in the boat then worshiped Him, calling him the Son of God. Soon we reached the shore of Gennesaret and the people recognized Jesus and came to Him with all those who were sick, asking Him to heal them. They begged Him to allow them to touched the hem of His garment, because that would be enough. All of the people who touched his hem, were healed. Hypocrites!

The Pharisees again came to Jesus and asked for a sign, to prove Himself to them. The Lord answered them saying, "When it is evening you say it will be fair weather , for the sky is red; and in the morning it will be foul weather today, for the sky is red and threatening." (16:2–3). Now what could reading the weather, have to do with signs?

They He spoke with full authority. "Hypocrites! You know how to discern the face of the sky, but you cannot discern the signs of the times." (16:3). He called them a wicked and adulterous generation. He told them they would receive no sign.

Jesus told us to beware the leaven of the Pharisees and the Sadducees because these two were the ruling class of the Jews. The Sadducees believed only in the word of God, written down by Moses, While the Pharisees accepted that and also used oral tradition as authoritative doctrine.

GOSPEL I: I AM LEVI

Now, when Jesus told us to beware of the Leaven of these rulers, we disciples began wondering if Jesus was talking about bread they should have bought.

Jesus spoke to us and said, "How is it that you do not understand that I did not speak to you about bread?" (16:11). Remembering then the miracle of the loaves and fish, the disciples understood that their Lord was talking about the wrong teachings of the Jewish rulers.

Part 9

WHO AM I?

WHEN THEY HAD COME into Philippi, Jesus asked all of His disciples who the people said He was. We told Him that some called Him John the Baptist, while others said He was Elijah or Jeremiah. Some said He was just a prophet.

Jesus looked to us and asked, "But who do you say that I am?" (16:15).

Simon Peter answered quickly, "You are the Christ. The Son of the living God. " Jesus then blessed Peter, telling him that flesh and blood had not revealed this to him, but it was His Father in Heaven.

The Christ continued, "You are Peter, and on this rock, I will build my church, and the gates of Hades shall not prevail against it . . . I give you the keys to the kingdom of heaven, and whatever you bind on Earth will be bound in Heaven and whatever you loose on Earth will be loosed in Heaven," (16:18–19)

Now Mark and Luke did not write that Peter said, "Jesus was the Son of the Living God" when they recorded this part of our journey. Many of your critics point that out, as if that makes a difference. They should look at the rest of their Gospel, where they are eager to tell others who Jesus really is. Just because we all wrote differently, doesn't make it untrue!

Anyway, Jesus said that He was in the process of establishing His church in the world. That this new church would not end, but exist until He Himself returned at the end of the age. He explained that Hell itself could not triumph over it. He, in fact, was explaining to us that by giving us the keys to the Kingdom of Heaven, He meant that he was imparting to us the knowledge of how to enter the kingdom and the power to lead others to it.

GOSPEL I: I AM LEVI

Jesus then told us that we should tell no one that He was Jesus the Christ, at least for now.

Our Lord turned to us and started explaining how He was going to go to Jerusalem, be persecuted, and suffer. He described, too, that He was going to die, but was also going to rise up in three days. Peter was a bit upset and took Jesus aside and told Him that he was in no way going to have to do this.

Jesus turned to Peter and said, "Get behind me Satan! You are an offense to me, for you are not mindful of the things of God, but the things of men." (16:23).

He then turned to the rest of us and said, "If anyone desires to come after me, let him deny himself, and take up his cross, and follow me. For whoever desires to save his life will lose it, but whoever loses his life for my sake, will find it. For what profit is it to a man if he gains the whole world, and loses his own soul." (16:24–25). He finished by stating that we would be rewarded according to our works.

I do not want people now thinking that Jesus was saying that Peter was Satan. I am sure He was not, for the Hebrew name Jesus actually used meant adversary. I think He was merely stating that Jesus had to do what He had come to the world to do. It wasn't Peter who offended Him, but the words the adversary was using.

Six days later, Jesus told James, Peter, and John to go with him to the top of the mountain. The three disciples watched Jesus as His face began to shine like the sun. His clothes became vibrantly white. Suddenly two others appeared next to Jesus and began talking to Him. It was Moses and Elijah.

As they were talking, Peter said to the Lord that it was so good that they got the chance to see this vision, that they should build three tabernacles. One for Elijah, one for Moses, and one for Jesus. As he was speaking, a cloud appeared over top of them and they heard the voice of God saying, "This is my beloved Son, of whom I am well pleased. Hear Him!"

When Peter, James, and John heard this, the fell to the ground in fear. But Jesus came to them, touched them, and said, "Arise and do not be afraid." (17–17).

When the three looked up, there was no one else there with them, but Jesus. He walked with His disciples, down the mountain, telling them not to say a word to anyone about what they had seen "... until the Son of Man is risen from the dead."

WHO AM I?

As the four were walking, the disciples asked Jesus why the scribes had taught that Elijah should come before the son of man? Jesus stated that Elijah had already come, was not recognized, and had suffered at their hands.

"Likewise," Jesus said, "the Son of Man is also about suffer at their hands." (17:12). Then the three disciples understood that Jesus was speaking about John the Baptist.

When the four finally reached the rest of the disciples and the other people, a man came to Jesus and asked Him to heal his son who suffered from epilepsy. He explained how his son had often tried ending his own life by throwing himself into the water or into fire. He pointed out to Jesus that he had taken his son to the disciples to be healed, but they could not heal the child.

When Jesus heard this, he healed the child. Turning to His disciples, he expressed the reason they were unable to perform this miracle. After the boy was healed, the twelve asked Jesus why they were unable to do it?

Jesus admonished them saying, "Because of your unbelief; for assuredly, I say to you, if you have faith as a mustard seed, you will say to this mountain, 'move from here to there' and it will move and nothing will be impossible for you." (17:20)' But, that would take plenty of prayer and fasting.

When they were done, Jesus and His followers went to Galilee. Jesus began explaining what was about to happen to Him. He told them that the time was near, when he would be betrayed and crucified. He continued, though, by specifying that He would also be raised up from the dead on the third day. The disciples were extremely sorrowful at these words, and at the same time filled with amazement.

Leaving Galilee, they journeyed to Capernaum. There Peter was asked by the Temple tax collectors if his master had paid the Temple tax. Peter told Jesus that he had been questioned and Jesus asked if the collectors took money from strangers, or their own sons. Peter said that the sons did not pay. The Christ stressed that the sons of the church should not pay either, but He however would pay the tax. Jesus told Peter to go to the sea and catch a fish. When he did, he would find a coin in its mouth. That would be the money needed for the collectors. Once again, God provided yet another miracle.

The disciples came to Jesus with a question. "Who then is the greatest in the Kingdom of Heaven?" Jesus replied, "Assuredly I say to you, unless you are converted and become as little children, you will by no means enter the Kingdom of Heaven." (18:3).

GOSPEL I: I AM LEVI

Jesus added that one must be as humble as a child to be the greatest in Heaven, If, therefore, someone causes one of His children who believes in Him to sin, it would be better if this person were drowned in the sea. Jesus also explained that if a part of them (like a hand for example) caused them to sin, they should cut it off. It would be better to be maimed and go to Heaven, than to be whole and end up in eternal Hell fire. To further their understanding, he pointed out that even if an eye causes one to sin, it should be plucked out. It's better to be in Heaven with one eye than damned with two. Did He literally mean one should cut of his hand or pluck out his own eye? Not at all. He was using this as a metaphor. In other words, If you do something that is a sin toward God, stop it. It not worth an eternal life without God.

You see, Jesus came into this world to save His children not to condemn them. He was, indeed, like a good shepherd. If, for example a man had one hundred sheep and one of them was lost, the good man would leave the ninety-nine others and look to save the one that had gone astray. The good shepherd would be so glad for that one sheep because he was lost, but then saved again. Jesus finished by asserting, ". . . It is not the will of your Father who is in Heaven that one of these little ones perish." (18–14).

The Master's lesson, then, was that if a brother in Christ were to sin against any one of them, they should bring it to the attention of the sinner. If the sinner would not repent, then they should inform the rest of the Church. If the sinner still refused to repent, they were to treat him like a heathen (a non-believing gentile) or an unrepentant tax collector.

Peter then asked the Master how many times should a man be forgiven, as much as seven times? Jesus replied, "I do not say to you, up to seven times, but up to seventy times seventy." (18:22). This, I think is what His Father in Heaven wants us all to do—forgive so that we are forgiven and gain Eternal Life.

After leaving Galilee, Jesus and the twelve went to Judea beyond the Jordan, healing the many people who followed. The Pharisees also came to Jesus because they were once again testing Him. They asked if it was lawful for a man to divorce his wife for any reason. Of course, they knew that Moses had said it was permitted to divorce.

Now, Jesus answered them saying it was not permitted. He continued, ". . . For this reason, (God had created a man and a women) a man shall leave his father and mother and be joined to his wife and the two shall become one flesh. Therefore, what God has joined together, let no man separate." (19:5–6).

WHO AM I?

The Pharisees figured they had caught Jesus in a mistake, which the Son of God could not make. "Why then," They asked, "did Moses command to give a certificate of divorce?"

"Moses, because of the hardness of your Hearts," Jesus stated with authority. "permitted you to divorce your wives, but from the beginning it was not so" (19:9).

I know that Jesus did not allow them to try to catch Him up in semantics. He knew their thoughts and their hearts, but He was the truth. Jesus was telling them all that divorce leads to adultery. We are all human and make mistakes, but Jesus was explaining what God had planned for us, not what man planned.

It was a little later, that people began to bring little children to Jesus so that He might bless them and pray. The disciples told them that they should not be bothering their Lord. But, Jesus said, "Let the little children come to me and do not forbid them; for of such is the Kingdom of Heaven" (19:14). He laid hands on them and prayed for them, proving that Jesus loves the little children.

This showed me, personally, and the other eleven, that having a childlike (Not childish) belief was what was needed for salvation and eternal life, for the childlike heart is pure. You see, being childish is a trait that no one likes. It is the act of immaturity and sometimes silliness to an extreme. Being childlike, though, is having possessing an innocence and showing trust in someone else, The latter is what Jesus was describing.

When Jesus left the children, a rich man came to him asking him how someone gets into Heaven and has eternal life. Jesus told him, "Keep the commandments. You shall not murder. You shall not commit adultery. You shall not steal . . . You shall love your neighbor as yourself" (19:17–19).

The man stated that he had keep the commandments ever since he was a young boy. He asked what else was needed. Jesus said that he should sell everything he owned, and give all the money to the poor. After that he should be willing to follow the Christ. Now when this man being very rich, heard what Jesus had said to him, he left full of sadness.

Jesus turned to the twelve of us and taught us saying, ". . . I say to you, it is easier for a camel to go through the eye of a needle than for a rich man to enter the Kingdom of God" (19:24). I thought about this and realized that if someone values their earthly possessions more than eternity, then it would be hard for them to give up everything to follow the Savior, However

GOSPEL I: I AM LEVI

Jesus isn't saying that a rich man can never get into Heaven, He merely states that it is hard. The choice is ours.

I repeat, it is not that a person with lots and lots money can't get into Heaven, but if that money is his god (of he loves the money more than God) he is not going to enter. Anyway Jesus continued guaranteeing us, because we followed Him, we would be rewarded. He finished by assuring us that ". . . the last will be first and the first last. For many are called, but few chosen" (20:16).

It was then that Jesus told the twelve of us that we were all going to Jerusalem. He again told us He would be betrayed and that the chief priests and the scribes would arrest Him and condemn Him to death. He told us that they would hand Him over to the gentiles and they would scourge Him, mock Him, and crucify Him. BUT, on the third day He would rise again.

The mother of Zebedee's sons, James and John, asked if Jesus would grant that her sons would be able to sit on the right and left side of Him when He came to His Kingdom. I guess it's hard to put blame here because she wanted the best for her boys. But, Jesus told her that she didn't know what she was asking, for what she ask was not the Lord's to give, but it was for those for whom it was prepared by His Father.

I think the other disciples were a little upset about what was asked, but we were called over to Jesus and we let it go. Jesus communicated to us that if we desired to be great, we must first be a servant. After all, Jesus himself had come to serve, not to be served. He had come to give his life as a ransom for many people. We are held captive on this earth because of sin. To free us from that, the ransom would have to be sacrifice, and Jesus, even though we didn't understand it all then, was to be that sacrifice.

On the way to Jerusalem, Jesus was stopped by two blind men. They must have really believed Jesus could heal them, because they asked twice, "Have mercy on us, Oh Lord, Son of David. Have mercy on us, Oh Lord, Son of David."

Jesus stopped and asked, "What do you want me to do for you?" (20:32).

Without hesitation, they said, "Lord, that our eyes may be opened." Jesus felt compassion for them and touched their eyes, healing them. The two, with joy, followed Jesus. Can you imagine how the blind would feel if God gave them sight? No wonder they followed. But, those who do not see that Jesus as who He said He was are blind. The joy comes when their eyes are opened and they follow.

Part 10

HOSANNA TO THE SON OF DAVID

Near Jerusalem, at the Mount of Olives, Jesus sent two disciples to go into the village. There they would see a donkey tied up and there would also be a colt with her. Bring them to me, but if anyone asks you what you are doing, then tell them it is for the Lord. He will let them go with you.

Now this was done to fulfill the prophecies of both Zechariah and Isaiah. (Yes, I am still referring to prophecy again to prove to you who Jesus was.) The two prophets stated, "Tell the daughter of Zion, behold your King is coming lowly and sitting on a donkey, a colt, the foal of a donkey." and "The Lord has made proclamation to the ends of the earth: Say to Daughter Zion, See, your Savior comes!" (Zechariah 9:9 and Isaiah 62:11).

The two brought the donkey and foal and Jesus sat upon it, riding into Jerusalem. As he came, people honored him by placing their garments and palm branches on the ground before Him. The multitude cried out, shouting, "Hosanna to the Son Of David. Blessed is He who comes in the name of the Lord. Hosanna in the highest" (21:9).

Many followed Jesus to the Temple. When He arrived, he saw the merchants selling animals that were to be used for sacrifice. Jesus became angry. He overturned the tables where the money changers, were sitting and the chairs of the people selling doves. "It is written," Jesus shouted, "My house shall be called a house of prayer, but you have made it into a den of thieves" (21:13).

While He was there, though, the blind and the lame came to Him and He still healed them. The chief Priests and scribes saw the miracles and heard children shouting "Hosanna to the Son of David." They were outraged and asked Jesus if he heard what these children were saying. I think I might have seen a slight smile on His face as he spoke, but it might just be me.

"Have you never read: Out of the mouth of babes and nursing infants, you have perfected praise?" (21:16). Jesus turned around and left after He spoke.

He went to Bethany and decided to spend the night and in the morning, he felt hungry. He went up to a fig tree that bore no fruit. Jesus said, that one tree would never bear fruit again. Immediately the tree withered. We asked Jesus how the tree died so quickly, and he told us that if we have faith we would be able to do the same and even more. He said, "Whatever things you ask in prayer, believing, you will receive" (21:22).

After that, Jesus went back to the temple. The priests and elders were waiting for Him there and confronted Him asking where He got the authority to do the things He could do. Jesus answered their question with one of His own. He told them that if they could answer His question, then He would answer theirs. "The Baptism of John, was it from Heaven or from Man?" (21:25).

Now the leaders knew if they said Heaven, Jesus could ask them why they didn't believe him. If they answered man, the crowd would be against them, for they all considered John a prophet. They answered that they did not know. Jesus, in turn, said that He wouldn't answer their question either.

Jesus did tell them a story. He said that a man had two sons. He went to the first and asked him to go and work in the fields. The son said "no." After considering what he had done, he went to the fields and worked anyway. Now the second son was asked to go work in the fields and he told his father, "yes." He, however did not go. Jesus looked at them and asked, "which of the two did the will of his father?" (21:31). Even though they told Him the first son did right, Jesus told the chief priests and scribes, that ". . . tax collectors and harlots will enter the Kingdom of God before you will" (21:31). "For John came to you in the way of righteousness, and you did not believe him. But, tax collectors and harlots did believe him, and when you saw it, you did not relent and believe him" (21:32).

Then Jesus told another parable. There was a vineyard owner who rented out his land to vine dressers. These were men who tended or cultivated grape vines. The owner left and went into a far country. When he returned, he sent three servants to collect the fruit from the vine dressers. They saw the three coming and beat one, killed the second, and stoned the last servant. The owner then sent more servants and they were killed, too. Finally, He sent his own son. The vine dressers said they should kill him, also, and just take the fields. Jesus asked them, "When the owner of the vineyard comes, what will he do to those vine dressers?" (21:40).

They said to Him that he should destroy those wicked men and hire others who would give him the grapes when they were ready to be pressed.

Jesus rebuked them saying, "Have you never read the scriptures? 'The stone which the builders rejected, has become the corner stone. This was the Lord's doing and it is marvelous in our eyes.' (Psalm 118) Therefore I say to you, the Kingdom of God will be taken from you and given to a nation bearing the fruits of it" (21:42–43).

What Jesus was saying was that He was the cornerstone that some had rejected and now He was the foundation on which the message of salvation was built upon. Now, because these holy people of the temple refused to accept Jesus, they would not see the Kingdom of God. The priests, knew exactly what Jesus was talking about them and they wanted to arrest Him, but they were afraid of the crowd because the people considered Jesus a prophet.

Part 11

THE GREAT COMMANDMENT AND THE END

MANY PARABLES WERE GIVEN, trying to get the people to understand what Jesus was telling them. It was not easy for us either. We disciples are human. We did however, have a leg up, as it were, on others. We were with the Lord on a daily basis, and I think I was finally getting it. Jesus was saying that God had sent John, and man killed him. Now God had sent Jesus, His own Son, and even He was to die. Jesus was also telling us that many of us were called, but few were chosen. There were many who rejected Jesus and there were a few who were willing to follow Him. Anyway, back to my story.

The Pharisees were trying to trap Jesus, so they asked Him if it was lawful to pay tax to Caesar? Jesus knew it was a trick, so he asked them for a coin and to tell Him whose face was on that coin. They told Him it was the face of Caesar. Jesus answered, "Render therefore to Caesar the things that are Caesar's, and to God the things that are God's" (22:21).

The Sadducees and the Pharisees continued to try to trip up Jesus and they failed every time. One of the lawyers, testing Jesus, asked Him what the greatest Commandment was. First, Jesus stated what was written also in Deuteronomy. "You shall love the Lord your God with all your heart, with all your soul, and with all your mind. This is the first and great commandment. And the second is like it. You shall love your neighbor as yourself. On these two Commandments hang all the law and the prophets" (22:37–40).

Jesus then asked the Pharisees who the Christ was. Whose son was He? They answered that He was David's son. Jesus quoted the psalms where

THE GREAT COMMANDMENT AND THE END

it said that David called the Christ, the Messiah, Lord. He silenced the Pharisees then, stating that if David called the Christ Lord, how then could he be his son? From then on, No one questioned Jesus.

Jesus criticized the rulers of the Jewish people. He said that they sit in the seat of Moses, telling the children of God what they should do. Then, thinking they are better than others, don't do what they teach. They demand hard work from the people, but do nothing themselves. The things they do, are only done so that they get praises from the crowds. They are hypocrites. Their long prayers are a pretense, and they showed themselves as busy converting souls to their religion and not for the glory of God. They are blind to the ways of God. They are more than willing to tithe their spices, but they forget the more important parts of the law, such as justice, mercy and faithfulness. They should do both. The scribes and Pharisees are like tombs, They look so wonderful on the outside, but contain only the dead. On the outside they are high and mighty, like righteous men. On the inside they are lawless. These leaders build tombs to the prophets, saying they would have died with them if they were in that time period. Jesus, however said that they were more like the descendants of those who killed the prophets.

I write all of this because I told you at the beginning, I was a changed man. I was an evil doer, a tax collector, but now I follow Jesus, the Messiah. I know that some say Jesus was harsh, but I say Jesus was being truthful. These men would rather receive the praise and worship from the people than accept the Messiah even though some may have actually thought that Jesus could be the Christ. I believe that Jesus wanted all to come under His protection, but knew, even then, what was about to happen. He knew His people were to suffer heavily until they finally recognize Him when He returns. At the return in the last days, they will hail Jesus as the Messiah, and receive him whom their fathers killed as the merciful Savior.

Jesus left the temple and as He did, the disciples pointed out all the buildings of the Temple. And Jesus said to them, "Do you see all these things? Assuredly, I say to you, not one stone shall be left here upon another. . . " (24:2). The twelve of us asked our Lord when this was going to happen. When was the end of the age; when would He would return? Jesus answered us by pointing out the fact that we should not be deceived. He testified that before He returns, others would come, pretending that they were the Christ. They will deceive many and then you will hear of wars and rumors of wars. He did console us a bit by indicating that we should not be troubled or afraid, because all of this must happen before His return.

GOSPEL I: I AM LEVI

He stated that one nation would rise against another, and there will be famine, pestilence, and earthquakes in various and unique places. He detailed, for us, the fact that people would want to harm us or kill us for His name sake. They would hate each other and us and be offended to the point of betraying each other. Jesus told us that false prophets would arise and deceive many and lawlessness would turn love cold. He, however, who persists and abides to the end will be saved. The Gospel of the kingdom will be preached to the entire world and to all the nations. Then, the end would come.

Jesus said that when we see the Abomination of desolation, flee from it. Now, Jesus did not define the abomination of desolation, but because I knew the Old Testament and the scriptures, I think I can define the term for you. You see, Daniel used the term. As a matter of fact, he used it three times. In the Hebrew language and the Greek, the word abomination describe anything that is associated with idolatry or means the defiling of something. It is connected with pagan or false idols. Desolation is describing a place that is devastated or uninhabitable. So, Jesus was telling us that a time would be coming that would be devastating to the believers in Christ Jesus. You see, if those day are not limited, no one on earth would be saved, so that is why Jesus will be returning.

When He does return, there will be a sign in the clouds. The sun will be darkened and the moon will not give light. The stars will fall from the heavens and Heaven, itself, will shake. Then all people will see the Son of Man coming in the clouds, in all His glory. He will gather all of His chosen ones. This is what is called the second coming. It is the time that Jesus comes and defeats Satan, He will then take His place as the true King of the world.

We wanted to know more, so Jesus told us a parable about a fig tree. He said, "When its branch has already become tender and puts forth leaves, you know that summer is near. So, you also, when you see these things, know that it is near, even at the doors" (24:32–35). We understood that we would know by the signs. It would be days just as Noah saw when He was alive.

It is separate and distinct from what many call the rapture. I believe the rapture comes first. And I tried to explained this in my Gospel chapter 24:40–41. Our Lord told us that Heaven and Earth would pass away, but his words would never pass away. He spoke as a matter of fact. when he told us that no one would know the exact time of His return except His Father, but we should all be prepared. It could happen that two men may be standing in the middle of a field, and one would disappear and one would remain. Two

THE GREAT COMMANDMENT AND THE END

women may be making bread and one would be taken and the other would be left behind. Many will not be ready, and there will be great sadness and weeping and gnashing of teeth. Jesus would take true believers from the earth, but He would not set foot on the ground just yet.

Jesus taught us that wise disciples remain vigilant for Jesus' return, so Jesus told us more parables to solidify our understanding of His second coming. The first was about the women waiting for the bridegroom. There were ten of them and five had lanterns with extra oil, and five did not bring extra oil. The bridegroom had been held up for some unknown reason and the ten women, waiting for him, slept. When the bridegroom was approaching, the five women who had not brought extra oil, ran out of light. They were told to go and buy some, because the five who had extra oil had enough for them only. The first five went to buy extra oil and while they were gone, the bridegroom arrived.

He took the women who were prepared, and went to the wedding, shutting the door behind them. When the other five got back, they went to the door and asked their Lord if they could enter. He simply stated that he didn't know them, so they could not come in. Jesus told us again to be prepared, for we didn't know the day or the hour of His return.

The second parable concerned how the Kingdom of Heaven was like a master who was about to travel. He called his servants to him and gave them talents. (In my day, a talent was money) To the first, he gave five talents. To another he gave two talents and the third got one. The master knew and he had given to each according to his own ability. The servant who had received five talents traded wisely and doubled his talents. The second did the same and ended up with four talents. The servant, however, with the one talent went and buried it so he would not lose it.

When the master returned the servants who had doubled what they had been given were called good and faithful. They were told to enter into the joy of their Lord and that they would be given even more responsibility. The servant given one talent, and hiding it, was rebuked, called lazy, and wicked. He had not added to his talents and what he had was taken from him. The problem wasn't that the servant with one talent saved the one talent, the problem was that he didn't do anything with it. I, Matthew will tell you, If the Lord gives you something, build it up and use it for the good of your Lord.

Jesus then told us that all nations would come before the Lord and He would divide them like a Shepard divides the sheep from the goats. He

GOSPEL I: I AM LEVI

would put the sheep on His right and the goats on the left. The King would then tell those on His right to come to Him because when He was hungry, they fed Him and when He was thirsty, they gave Him a drink. When He was naked, they clothed Him and even as a stranger, they gave Him shelter.

Now, those on His right said they had never seen Him to be able to do all those things. Jesus, however, did tell us He would say, "Assuredly I say to you, inasmuch as you did it to the least of these, my brethren, you did it to me" (25:45). To those on the left, you can guess what was done. Jesus said, "Depart from me, you cursed, into the everlasting fire prepared for the devil and his angels" (25:46).

Why, you may ask? When Jesus was hungry, thirsty, naked, or a stranger in need, those on His left had done nothing for Him. They did try to say they had never seen Him so they could not do these things for Him, but that is when He said how you treat others is exactly how you would treat me. Now the evil will receive their judgment and the righteous will be received into eternal life.

After Jesus taught the twelve of us, He reminded us that in two days Passover would be here. He said to us that ". . . The son of Man will be delivered up to be crucified" (26:2). It was then that the chief priests, the scribes, and the elders of the people got together and plotted to kill Jesus. Our Master and we were in Bethany, at the house of Simon the leper. A woman came to Jesus and anointed Him with expensive oil. Some of the disciples saw this and asked why she was wasting this. It could be sold and the money given to the poor. Jesus said, "Why do you trouble this woman, for she has done a good work for me" (26:11). He explained his answer to us telling us that she was preparing Him for burial and by doing this she would be remembered every time the Gospel is preached to the world.

I can tell you that I had no idea, but Judas had gone to the chief priests and asked what they would give him if he delivered Jesus to them. They handed him thirty pieces of silver and made plans on how he would betray Jesus. The rest of us began to prepare for the feast we went into the city and found a room where Jesus could celebrate the Feast of Unleavened Bread. When we were all there Jesus told us that one of us would betray Him. Each of us, filled with sadness, began to ask, "Lord, is it I"

Jesus answered, "He who dips his hand in the tray with me will betray me. The Son of Man indeed, goes just as it was written of Him, but woe to the man by whom the Son of Man is betrayed. It would have good for that man if he had not been born" (26:23–24).

THE GREAT COMMANDMENT AND THE END

Now Judas asked Jesus, "Is it I?" Jesus replied, "You have said it" (26:25).

And as we were eating, Jesus broke bread and blessed it, giving it to us and saying, "Take, eat. This is my body" (26:26). Then He took to cup and gave thanks and gave it to us saying, "Drink from it, all of you, For this is the blood of my new covenant, which is shed for many and for the remission of sin" (26:27–28).

Jesus told us He would not ever drink this again until he did it in Heaven with us. Then we sang a hymn and walked to the Mount of Olives. It was there Jesus told all of us that we would all stumble because of the things which were about to happen. Having knowledge of the Scripture, as I have said, I knew what Jesus was quoting, for it is written in Zechariah 13:7 "I will strike the Shepard and the sheep will scatter."

Peter told Jesus that he would never be made to stumble. I heard our Lord tell Peter that before the rooster crows, he would deny Jesus three times. Peter told Him that even if he had to die with the Master, he would not deny Jesus. As a matter of fact, we all said that to Jesus.

Jesus went to the Garden of Gethsemane to pray. He asked Peter and the two sons of Zebedee to accompany Him, while the rest of us sat a little ways off. We could tell Jesus was depressed and sorrowful, but none of us fully understood at that time.

Jesus began to pray, "Oh Father, if it is possible, let this cup pass from me; nevertheless not as I will but as you will" (26:39).

Peter and the others, being tired, fell asleep, and Jesus asked them to stay awake. He went back to prayer, but again Peter and the others could not stay awake. Jesus came to them and told them that the hour was at hand. It was time and He would be betrayed.

It was at that time that Judas came to Jesus, having already told the chief priests that whomever he kissed would be the one that they should seize. Judas then betrayed the Christ with a kiss. When the multitude with swords and clubs took Jesus, Peter drew his sword and cut off the ear of the servant of the high Priest. Jesus told Peter not to use the sword or to fight them, for all of this must happen for the scriptures to be fulfilled. It was then that all the disciples fled.

Those who had taken Jesus brought His before Caiaphas, where the chief priests, the elders, and all of the council looked at false testimony in order to put Him to death. They questioned Jesus, but He remained quiet.

GOSPEL I: I AM LEVI

The high priest came up to Jesus and demanded, "I put you under oath by the living God. Tell us if you are the Christ" (26:63). Jesus said to him, "It is as you said. Nevertheless, I say to you hereafter you will see the Son of Man sitting at the right hand of the Power and coming on the clouds of Heaven" (26:64).

The high priest tore his clothes and shouted that Jesus had spoken blasphemy. The accusers said that Jesus needed to be put to death. They started to mock and ridicule Jesus. They struck Him and spat on Him.

At the same time, Peter was outside in the courtyard and a servant girl saw him, asking if he was one of those with Jesus, and Peter said that he didn't know what she was talking about. Peter went out of the gate and another girl spotted him, asking if he was with Jesus. Peter answered that he did not know the man. A little later others came up to him and said that surely, he was one of them. Peter began to curse and swear, saying he didn't know this man. At that second, the rooster crowed and Peter remembered what Jesus had said to him. Peter went out and began to cry uncontrollably.

The next day the priests and scribes delivered Jesus to Pontius Pilate. At the same time Judas felt sorry and despondent and tried to return the money to the chief priest saying he had sinned and betrayed innocent blood. He threw the money back into the temple, and went out and hanged himself. The priests used the money for the burial of the poor, yet again fulfilling the prophecy of Jeremiah, who had said, "... and they took the thirty pieces of silver, the value of Him who was priced, whom they the children of Israel priced, and gave them for a potters field. . . " (27:6-7).

Now Jesus stood before the governor, Pilate, and he asked Jesus if He were the King of the Jews and Jesus replied, "It is as you say" (27:11). During the rest of the trial, Jesus said nothing to defend himself. Pilate went to the Jews and reminded them that because of their Passover, Pilate could release one prisoner. He asked the Jewish people who they wanted released and they shouted that they wanted Barabbas. When Pilate asked them what he was to do with this Christ, to People shouted, crucify Him! It was then that he scourged Jesus and gave him up to be crucified.

The soldiers of the Governor took Jesus and stripped Him, putting a scarlet robe on Him. They twisted a crown of thorns and shoved it on His head. They mocked Him shouting, "Hail, King of the Jews." They spat on Him and took the reed they had given Him as a king's scepter, and hit Him in the head with it. They then took Him to the "Place of the Skull" to crucify Him. They took His garments and cast lots for them, fulfilling

THE GREAT COMMANDMENT AND THE END

the prophecy spoken in Psalm 22:18: "They divided my garments among them and for my clothing, they cast lots." They placed a sign over His head that read: THIS IS JESUS THE KING OF THE JEWS. Then two robbers were crucified with Him, one to His right and the other on His left. Those who passed by, blasphemed Him, laughing and saying, "You who said you would destroy the Temple and build it again in three days, save yourself." They mocked Him saying that He was able to save others, but could not save Himself.

From the sixth hour to the ninth hour there was darkness over the land and at the ninth hour Jesus said, "Eli, Eli lama Sabachthani." That is: "My God, My God, why have you forsaken me?" (27:46).

Some there thought He was calling for Elijah. One of them took a sponge filled with sour wine, offering Him a drink. The others said to leave Him alone, so they could see if Elijah would appear. And Jesus then cried out and gave up His Spirit. At that exact time, the Temple veil was torn in two and there was an earthquake and the rocks were split. There was a Centurion with the others who said, as the ground shook, "Truly this was the Son of God" (27:54).

Joseph of Arimathea, a follower of Jesus, went to Pilate and asked if he could bury the body of Christ. He took the body, wrapped it in linen, laid it in a tomb, and sealed it with a giant stone. The chief priests and the Pharisees then asked Pilate to guard the tomb, for they remembered that Jesus had claimed He would rise on the third day. They said the tomb needed guarding because the disciples would come, steal the body, and claim that Jesus had risen from the dead. Pilate sent guards to the tomb, sealed it, and made it secure.

After the Sabbath, Mary Magdalene and another Mary went to the tomb. There was a great earthquake, because an angel came down, rolled away the stone and sat upon it. His face shown like lightning and his clothing were as white as snow. The guards shook with fear and fell down like dead men.

The angel told the women that he knew who they were looking for and that Jesus was not there, for He had risen. He told them to go to the disciples and say that Jesus rose from the dead and He would see them in Galilee. The women were filled with Joy and started to go tell the disciples.

When they started to leave, Jesus appeared to them telling them, "Do not be afraid. Go and tell my brethren to go to Galilee, and there they will see me" (28:10). Now the Pharisees, hearing what the soldiers reported,

GOSPEL I: I AM LEVI

paid the soldiers to say the Disciples had stolen the body, while we slept. This report is used, even today, by the non-believers. However, knowing the romans and their methods, if the soldiers had really fallen asleep, they would have been killed for doing so.

The eleven of us who were left, went to the place where Jesus had told us to meet Him. When we saw Him, we worshiped Him. Jesus came and spoke to us saying, "All authority has been given to me in Heaven and on earth. Go therefore, and make disciples of all nations, baptizing them in the name of the Father and of the Son and of the Holy Spirit teaching them to observe all things that I have commanded you; and lo, I am with you always, even to the end of the age" AMEN (28:18–20).

Now I, Matthew, have written all of this to tell you what I testify to as the truth and the fulfillment of all scripture. I know that God can use anyone to help Him spread the good news. Maybe you think you are not good enough, or not smart enough, to be a follower of Jesus. He is looking for people who are dedicated and I have to tell you that I believe the highest calling you can have is in the service of God.

It is my suggestion that you don't listen to all your friends in this world, who tell you to live for the moment, for nothing can be better for you than to follow Jesus. You see, I have seen and I believe that I have proven through word and scripture that Jesus is God and so I say, God bless you.

Gospel II

THE GOOD NEWS ACCORDING TO ME, MARK

Part 1

INTRODUCTION

My name is Mark, and I was once about to be lunch for a lion and a lioness—almost. Let me explain. You see, my father, Aristobulus, and I went out to the Jordan. While we were walking, a lion and a lioness stalked us. My father told me to run, because he was old and could not outrun the lions. He said he would sacrifice himself to save me. I, being a follower of the Christ, knew that the Son of God was with us. I believed that through all things, He would protect us, and I began to pray. I asked for Jesus to save us. It was at that exact time, that the lion and lioness fell dead. My father, seeing this, changed his life at that very moment and he decided to follow the teachings of Jesus.[1] I am, though, getting ahead of myself.

I said my name was Mark. Actually, I was born John Mark, Son of Mary and Aristopolus, but when I changed, like many of us, so did my name. I was not one of the twelve original disciples that walked with Jesus, but I became a Christian because of the one called Peter who often came to my mother's house and because of the things I had seen, growing up. In the Book of Acts 14:5, Luke writes about me and my brothers in Christ, because I was their assistant.

As I grew up, I learned the family trade. I was a worker of leather.[2] Because of this you will find that I have a way of writing that pieces the

---

[1]. Tony Burke, "Life of Mark," *e-Clavis: Christian Apocrypha*, September 2024, https://www.nasscal.com/e-clavis-christian-apocrypha/life-of-mark/.

[2]. Hilda Scott, "What Was Mark's Occupation in the Bible," *The Holy Script*, Feb. 12, 2024, https://www.theholyscript.com/what-was-marks-occupation-in-the-bible.

GOSPEL II: THE GOOD NEWS ACCORDING TO ME, MARK

story together as something made of leather would be pieced together. I am so used to taking little pieces and forming them into something of worth.

Anyway, My mother was Mary and we lived in Bethany. My house was an important gathering spot Jesus visited on occasion, and there lies the reason I know Him. I happened to be one who saw Jesus turn the water into wine. My house was also used during the Last Supper and was the meeting place of many early believers. When the disciples saw Jesus after the resurrection, they were in my house.[3] I also was there when our Lord ascended into Heaven. Finally, my mother's brother and I were one of the seventy disciples, who were sent out by Jesus to tell all the world about the Son of God and the Gospel, or Good News.

One embarrassing moment in my life was when I saw Jesus betrayed. I was the young boy in a blanket, at the garden where Jesus was arrested. I was almost captured, but all the romans got was the blanket. I escaped naked as a jaybird.[4]

Fifteen years after the ascension, I went to Egypt to tell them, too, about the good news of Jesus of Nazareth. I founded the Church of Alexandria and became the first bishop. I, too, was the founder of Christianity in Africa.[5] It is this gospel that I now tell you. My message, I guess, can be sown up in one verse. ". . . The Son of Man did not come to be served, but to serve and to give His life, a ransom of many."

---

[3]. Mark Nickens, "Mark's House: Early Gathering Place for Christians," Study the Church, 2010, http://studythechurch.com/articles/early-church/marks-house. Plus: It was probably the site of the Last Supper.

[4]. Ryan Nelson, "Who Was John Mark? The Beginner's Guide," *Overview Bible*, Apr 17, 2019, https://overviewbible.com/john-mark/.

[5]. Dr. Pat's Orthodox Super Sunday School Curriculum, "Egypt: St. Mark of Alexandria," 2020, https://orthodoxsundayschool.org/church-history/10-12-years-old/egypt-st-mark-alexandria.

Part 2

THE PROPHETS TELL OF JOHN THE BAPTIST

Let Me begin my story of the man I knew as Jesus, the Messiah. Now I wasn't one of the original twelve disciples, but I have first-hand knowledge of the one we call The Christ. I remember quite a lot from my youth, but what I write I have learned from Peter, the Rock, on which Jesus built His church.

The beginning of my Gospel deals with the prophecy of Isaiah, who said, "Behold I send my messenger before your face, Who will prepare your way for you. The voice of one crying in the wilderness: Prepare the way of the Lord; make His path straight." (Mark 1:2 NKJV) It was John the Baptist who was preaching this to those who wished to repent. The people of Judea and those from Jerusalem had come to John to be baptized and confess their sins. To make it a bit easier for all, I have used the New King James Version (NKJV) and all of my quote come from my Gospel. It will be easier for all if I omit Greek, Latin, and Hebrew.

First, John the Baptist was a simple man of God. His only clothes were made of camel hair and a leather belt to hold it. He ate locusts and honey, because he needed nothing else but to tell the people that one was coming that would be greater than he. You see, John would shout out, "I indeed baptize you with water, but He will baptize you with the Holy Spirit."

Now it came to pass, (I love this way of talking) that Jesus from Nazareth of Galilee, came to be baptized by John. John observed Jesus as He was coming up out of the river, and saw a dove descending upon Jesus. He also

GOSPEL II: THE GOOD NEWS ACCORDING TO ME, MARK

heard a voice that came from Heaven, itself, saying, "You are my beloved Son of whom I am well pleased."

Instantly, Jesus went into the wilderness and He stayed there for forty days, while He was being tempted by Satan. While He was there though, the Angels of God ministered to Him.

Now when John was put in prison, Jesus came and began preaching the good news of the Kingdom of God. Jesus said, "The time is fulfilled and the Kingdom of God is at hand. Repent and believe in the Gospel."

Part 3

FINDING DISCIPLES, HEALING, AND PREACHING

As Jesus was walking by the sea of Galilee, He saw two fishermen, Simon and his brother Andrew. Jesus called to them, "Follow Me, and I will make you become fishers of men." They dropped their nets, left their fishing, and followed Jesus.

When he traveled a bit farther, He saw James, the son of Zebedee, along with his brother John fixing their nets. They, too, left what they were doing and followed this man. All of them followed Jesus to the synagogue in Capernaum, where He began to preach because it was the Sabbath. They were astounded at the way He spoke because He taught with certainty and authority.

In the synagogue, on that particular day was a man who was possessed by unclean spirits. He shouted at Jesus "Let us alone! What have we to do with you, Jesus of Nazareth? I knew who you are—The Holy One of God!"

Jesus rebuked him saying, "Be quiet and come out of him."

The man convulsed and cried out. and the evil spirit came out of him. Everyone there was filled with amazement and started questioning who this man was. They spoke among themselves and asked where this Man got this kind of authority, for even the unclean spirits obey Him. It was then that the word spread throughout Galilee of Jesus and His power.

As soon as they left the synagogue, Jesus, Andrew, James, and John went to the house of Simon. Simon's wife's mother (his mother-in-law) was

GOSPEL II: THE GOOD NEWS ACCORDING TO ME, MARK

sick with fever. When Jesus saw her, he reached out His hand and held hers. She instantly became well. From that day, she decided to serve Jesus.

As the sun was setting, people from all over came to Him, bringing those who were sick and those who were filled with evil spirits. The whole city seemed to be at Simon's door watching this man Jesus. The Son of God then began healing the sick and driving the demons out of those who had been possessed. The spirits who were cast out could not speak, because they knew who Jesus was.

In the morning before sunrise, Jesus went out of the house to a place where He could be alone. to pray. His followers found Him and said that everyone had been looking for Him. He looked at them and simply said, "Let us go into the next towns, that I may preach there also, because for this purpose I have come forth."

He was unceasing in His preaching at all of the synagogues throughout Galilee, and He also continued casting out demons wherever He went. In one place, a leper came to Him and said, "If you are willing, you can make me clean."

Jesus was filled with compassion and moved by this man's faith. The Lord reached out and touched the leper, saying, "I am willing; be cleansed." As soon as He spoke the words, the leper was healed. Jesus told the man to say nothing to anyone about what had just happened. This man, however did not listen and began telling everyone who would listen. It would have become so crowded and overwhelming, that Jesus went outside the city to a deserted place. There was a multitude of people, however, that followed Him, coming from every direction.

After some days, Jesus returned to Capernaum, and the people heard that He was there. They came to the house, where Jesus was, and the crowd was so big that no one else could fit through the door. He preached to them and as He did, a paralyzed man, carried by four others, tried to get in. There were so many there, they could not enter. The four men uncovered the roof, carried the paralytic to the roof and lowered him with rope so he could be healed. When Jesus saw their faith, He said to the man, "Son, your sins are forgiven you."

Some of the scribes from the synagogue were there and asked, "Why does this man Blaspheme? Who can forgive sins, but God alone?"

Jesus looked at them and stated, "Why do you reason about these things in your heart? Which is easier to say to the paralytic, Your sins are forgiven you, or to say, Arise, take up your bed and walk. But that you know

FINDING DISCIPLES, HEALING, AND PREACHING

that the Son of Man has power on earth to forgive sins," Jesus turned to the paralyzed man and continued. "I say to you, arise, take up your bed, and go to your home."

The man then picked up his bed and walked out. The crowd was astonished and started glorifying God telling each other they had never seen the likes of this.

Part 4

THE PHARISEES FOLLOW AND BEGIN TO PLOT

Jesus then went down by the sea and a multitude of people followed and He preached to them. As he was passing by, He saw a man named Levi. Sitting at his tax office. Jesus said to him, "Follow me."—and he did.

Jesus happened to go to Levi's house for diner, and there with him were many tax collectors and other sinners. When the scribes and the Pharisees saw this, they asked the disciples, "How can Jesus eat with tax collectors and sinners?"

Even though Jesus didn't hear, He knew what had been asked. Jesus spoke. "those who are well, have no need of a physician, but those who are sick. I did not come to call the righteous, but sinners, to repentance."

When they saw that Jesus and the disciples were not fasting, they asked why the disciples of John the Baptist and the Pharisees fasted, but the disciples of Jesus didn't.

Jesus said to them, "Can the friends of the bridegroom fast when the bridegroom is with them? As long as they have the bridegroom with them, they cannot fast. But the days will come when the bridegroom will be taken from them, and they will fast in those days."

Jesus continued by explaining how no one would sew a piece of unshrunk cloth on an old article of clothing. The new would pull away from the old and cause a bigger tear. He also suggested that no one would want to put new wine in an old worn-out wine skin, because it would leak and one

THE PHARISEES FOLLOW AND BEGIN TO PLOT

would lose the new wine. New wine requires new wine skins. I think they were scratching their heads a bit after this.

On another occasion, Jesus and His disciples were in a grain field. The disciples began picking the grain and eating. Now you can probably guess, the Pharisees were watching. They asked Jesus why His followers did not obey the Law of the Sabbath. Jesus reminded them of David and how he took the bread of the Priests, even though it was against Jewish Law. He ate it and gave it to the people.

Jesus added, "The Sabbath was made for man and not man for the Sabbath. Therefore, the Son of Man is Lord of the Sabbath." The Pharisees were getting upset at this point.

Jesus again went to preach in the synagogue. A man was there who had a disfigured hand. The leaders in the Synagogue watched Jesus closely. They wanted to accuse Him for working on the Sabbath—if he healed this man. Jesus told the man with the disfigurement to come forward. He asked the Priests and the Pharisees if it were lawful to do good on the Sabbath, but they did not speak. Jesus looked at them with a bit of anger, because their hearts had hardened.

Jesus said, "Stretch out your hand." and as he did the man's hand was made whole. The Pharisees immediately went out and began to plot against the Lord. They met with the Herodians: a Jewish political party who supported the dynasty of Herod. They both wanted to destroy Jesus.

Part 5

PICKING THE TWELVE AND EXPLAINING WHO HIS BROTHERS WERE

Jesus, however, went to the Sea of Galilee. There he was approached by many people from Galilee and Judea. They came from Jerusalem, Tyre, and from beyond the Jordan. Everyone who heard of the many things He had done also came. Jesus told the disciples to prepare a boat for Him, by the shore, so He would not be crushed by the crowd. He healed many and delivered many from demons who shouted when He cast them out, "You are the Son of God." He, though, silenced them, not wanting them to make Him known at that time.

After this time, Jesus went into the mountains and appointed the twelve, so that they would follow Him, learn from Him, and be sent out to teach others about Him. He gave to them power to heal the sick and cast out demons. He chose Simon, and then gave him the name Peter. He also chose James and John, the sons of Zebedee. He called them the sons of thunder. Andrew, Philip, Bartholomew, and Matthew were chosen, too. He also selected Thomas, James the son of Alphaeus, Thaddaeus, and Simon the Canaanite. Finally, He picked Judas Iscariot, the one who would eventually betray Him.

Now when the people of His own land heard about Jesus and all the things He was doing, they went out to him, to lay hold of Him, because they thought He had lost His mind. The scribes were telling the people that

PICKING THE TWELVE

He had the Devil in Him allowing Him to cast out demons. So, He called them out.

Jesus said, "How can Satan cast out Satan? If a Kingdom is divided against itself, that Kingdom cannot stand. And if a house is divided against itself, that house cannot stand. And if Satan is risen up against himself, and is divided, he cannot stand, but has an end. No one can enter a strong man's house and plunder his goods, unless he first binds the strong man. And then he will plunder his house. Assuredly I say to you, all sins will be forgiven the sons of men, and whatever blasphemies they may utter; but he who blasphemes against the Holy Spirit never has forgiveness, but is subject to eternal condemnation."

It was then that His mother and brothers came to Him. The people told Jesus that they were calling for Him, but He answered them by asking them who His mother and brothers were. He looked at the crowd, pointed at them, and said, "Here are my mother and brothers! For whoever does the will of God is my mother and my sister and brother."

Part 6

JESUS USES PARABLES

Jesus went to the sea again and began to teach. To help with understanding, He spoke using parables. He began with the story concerning the farmer who was planting seeds. Some of the seeds being sown fell by the wayside and the birds came and ate them. Some fell on rocks and stones, and didn't root, so, when the sun beat down on the sprouts, and they dried up. There would not be much growth there. Some of the seeds grew, but they were in the thorny patch and they were choked out by the thorny weeds. The seeds that fell on the good earth, grew into the most wonderful crop, producing greatly. Jesus told the crowd, that "He who has ears to hear, let him hear."

Later, the disciples were alone with Jesus and they asked Him to tell them what the parable meant. Jesus stressed how important it was that they had been given the gift of understanding concerning the Kingdom of Heaven. This was something someone in the crowd, who gathered to hear Him, could not grasp yet.

He then indicated that they needed to understand this parable. How else would they understand all the other parables He would use later? How, too, would they be able to use parables when they were teaching about the word? He began informing them of the meaning.

Part 7

"THE SOWER SOWS THE WORD."

Jesus continued, "And these are the ones by the wayside where the word is sown. When they hear, Satan comes immediately and takes away the word that was sown in their hearts. These likewise are the ones sown on stony grounds who, when they hear the word immediately receive it with gladness; and they have no root in themselves and so only endure for a time. Afterward, when tribulation or persecution arises for the words sake, they stumble."

Next, Jesus pointed out the seeds in the thorns. He reasoned as He spoke, that these were "ones who hear the word, and the cares of the world, the deceitfulness's of riches, and the desire for other things entering in, choke the word and it becomes unfruitful."

Jesus expressed the importance of the ones sown on good ground as, "those who hear the word, accept it, and bear fruit, some thirtyfold, some sixty, some a hundred"

The Lord asked the twelve if it were fit to take a lamp and hide it under a basket or a bed. He stressed the importance of not hiding anything or keeping things secret that should come to the light. He told them that they must understand His parables and keep them in their memory because they may need to use the words later. Jesus encouraged them to carefully heed the words they heard from Him and, like students, understand them so that they would be able to teach His word in the future. If they did, then their knowledge of the mysteries of the gospels, principles, and the kingdom would increase. He ended by telling them that the Kingdom of God was ". . . like a mustard seed which, when it is sown on the ground, is

GOSPEL II: THE GOOD NEWS ACCORDING TO ME, MARK

smaller than any other seed on earth; but when it is sown it grows up and becomes greater than all herbs, and shoots out large branches, so the birds in the air may nest under its shade." So, Jesus used many parables and the disciples heard them and understood.

Part 8

THE DEMONS AND THE SWINE

On that same day Jesus and His disciples got into a boat to go to the other side, in the land of the Gadarenes. As they were traveling, a great windstorm came up and water started to fill the boat. Jesus was sleeping, at the time, so the disciples woke him, because they were afraid. They were shouting that they were about to perish. Jesus arose and commanded the wind and said to the water,

"Peace, be still."

That was all it took. The storm just stopped and it was once again calm. But Jesus turned to his disciples and said, "Why are you so fearful? How is it that you have no faith?"

They were still fearful and said among themselves, "Who can this be, that even the wind and the sea obey Him?"

They came to the shore of Gadarene and got out of the boat. As they arrived, they were practically attacked by a man with unclean spirits possessing him. This man actually lived in the tombs. In the past had been shackled with irons and chains, but because of the demons, he was strong and constantly broke them, so they were no longer used. He was always running in the mountains and the tombs, cutting himself with stones constantly.

When He saw Jesus, He ran to Him and screamed, "What have I to do with you, Jesus, Son of the most high God? I implore you by God that you not torment me."

Jesus commanded, "Come out of the man, unclean spirit. What is your name."

GOSPEL II: THE GOOD NEWS ACCORDING TO ME, MARK

And he answered, "My name is Legion, for we are many." The demons continued by asking Jesus not to throw them out of the country. Instead, they asked that Jesus cast them into a herd of swine, who were nearby.

Jesus did just that, and the swine, numbering about two thousand, ran down the Hill, jumped into the sea, and were drowned. Those there, who took care of the swine, were afraid and ran to the city to tell others what they had witnessed.

The people of the city and the country came to Jesus and saw what had occurred. They were angry and asked Jesus and His disciples to leave their land. All except the man who had been possessed. He asked Jesus if he could come with them, but Jesus said, "Go home to your friends and tell them what great things the Lord has done for you, and how he has had compassion on you." The man did as Jesus asked and told many what the Son of God had done to save him. Jesus and the twelve then left.

Part 9

WHO TOUCHED ME?

When they arrived, back on the other side of the sea, there were a multitude of people waiting on the shore, to see Jesus. Among them was a leader of the synagogue named Jairus. When he saw the Christ, he fell at His feet. He told Jesus that his daughter was near death and asked Him to come and lay his hands on her so that she would be healed. Jesus said that he would come, and many people followed swarming Jesus.

There was, among the crowd, a certain woman who had been sick. She had a flow of blood that had not stopped for twelve years. She had done many things the physicians had demanded of her, but nothing had cured her. She had spent all that she had to get better, but was only getting worse every day.

As Jesus passed her, she reached out and touched the hem of His garment, for she had said to herself, "If I only touch His clothes I will be healed." Immediately her bleeding stopped and she was well. Jesus felt that someone had touched Him and knew some power had gone from Him and a healing had taken place.

He asked His disciples, "Who touched My clothes?"

And the twelve said basically everyone who was in the crowd had touched Him. They were a bit confused and asked why He has said this. Jesus looked around the crowd. Seeing this, the woman who had touched Him came to Him and explained why she had done it.

Jesus spoke to her saying, "Daughter, your faith has made you well. Go in peace and be healed of your affliction."

GOSPEL II: THE GOOD NEWS ACCORDING TO ME, MARK

Then He continued on with Jairus to heal his daughter, but when they arrived, Jesus saw many crying and in sorrow. They had said He was too late and the girl had died.

Jesus spoke to them and asked, "Why make this commotion and weep? The child is not dead, but sleeping."

The crowd of people there ridiculed Him and He told them to leave as He went to the girl. He took the girl by the hand, and said, "Little Girl, I say to you, arise." And, at that very second, she did. Now the family and friends were amazed, but Jesus told them not to tell anyone, but to feed the girl, because she would be hungry.

Part 10

NOT BEING ACCEPTED AND SENDING OUT THE TWELVE

Jesus led His disciples to His own land and began teaching in the synagogue. Many of the people there heard Him speak and asked among themselves where He had gotten this power to do the things He had done. Many had asked if this was the carpenter's son, the son of Mary, who they had seen grow up in their own city. The people, there, were offended by their former neighbor, and all Jesus could say was, "A prophet is not without honor, except in his own country, among his own relatives, and in his own house."

While Jesus was there, not much could be done. He did lay hands on a few sick people, healing them and walked throughout some of the small villages, teaching there. He did call his disciples to Him and began sending them out two by two, giving them power over unclean spirits. He told them they were not to take anything with them on their journey, except a staff.

They did not take bread, bags, or money with them and they took no more than one tunic. With sandals on they feet, thy went out to preach repentance to the people. Jesus said to them, when they parted, "In whatever place (whatever town) you enter a house, stay there till you depart from that place. And whoever will not receive you nor hear you, when you depart from there, shake of the dust under your feet as a testimony against them. Assuredly I say to you, it will be more tolerable for Sodom and Gomorrah in the day of judgment than for that city." They went out preaching, casting out demons, and healing in the name of the Messiah.

Part 11

THE DEATH OF THE BAPTIST

King Herod had heard all about the disciples Master and the things He had accomplished. He began asking who this Jesus was. He said that maybe it was John the Baptist come back to life, giving power to this man. Others called Jesus Elijah or a prophet, or something like a prophet. But Herod insisted that it was John the Baptist raised from the dead.

He should have known all about John and probably had a guilty conscience. He, after all, was the one who arrested John and placed him in prison. John had called Herod unlawful and a sinner because he had married Herodias, his brother's wife. Herodias hated John for this and wanted him dead at any cost. The opportunity came during Herod's birthday. The leaders of Galilee, the nobles, high officers, and the chief men, were all in attendance at Herod's feast.

When the daughter of Herodias came in and danced for the crowd, Herod was so pleased that he swore an oath to give her anything she asked, even if she asked for half of his kingdom. After plotting with her mother she told Herod that she wanted the head of the Baptist on a platter.

Herod was saddened and sorry that he had sworn an oath, but he did what she asked and had John the Baptists beheaded. When his disciples heard what had happened, they came and buried John. It was easy, then, for Herod to believe that this man, Jesus, was indeed the Baptist who had risen from the dead.

Part 12

THE MIRACLE OF THE LOAVES AND WALKING ON WATER

The twelve apostles came back to Jesus and described the things they had been doing. They pointed out to Him what they had taught and what they had done for the people. Jesus said they should go with Him to a deserted place and rest. They started to leave and headed for a boat left on the shore, but the people saw them and come in throngs from all over to hear Jesus. When He saw them, he felt compassion because they were, to Him, like sheep without a shepherd. He began teaching them many things and stayed with them late into the evening. The disciples asked Jesus to let them go their way, because it was late and there was no food for them there.

Jesus looked at the twelve, and said, "You give them something to eat."

The disciples asked if they should go all the way into the town and buy food. The would not have enough money. Then, Jesus asked them how many loaves they had. They went and checked and came back reporting that they only had fives loaves and two fish. Jesus had the people sit in groups of fifty and one hundred, for there were five thousand present. When He took the bread and the two fish, He lifted His eyes toward Heaven and blessed the loaves and the fish and then handed them to the disciples. They became a part of the miracle as they began handing out the food. There was enough for everyone, with twelve baskets full left over when all had their fill.

When they were done, Jesus commanded His disciples get on the boat and cross to the city of Bethsaida, while He went to the mountain to pray. As He was praying, Jesus could see the disciples' boat in the distance, being

GOSPEL II: THE GOOD NEWS ACCORDING TO ME, MARK

tossed by a rough sea. A storm had come upon them and they were frightened. Jesus went to them, walking on water, and they were even more afraid because they thought He was a ghost.

He said to them, "Be of good cheer. It is I; do not be afraid." He came into the boat and the sea became calm. They continues until they came to Gennesaret. The multitude recognized Jesus and His disciples and came to Him. He spent His time there traveling from town to town and village to village, healing and teaching them the word.

Part 13

MAKING ENEMIES OF UNBELIEVERS

THE PHARISEES AND THE scribes came to Him complaining once again how His disciples did not follow Jewish Law—even the lesser of the Laws. Oh my, the twelve were seen eating without washing their hands first. Now this may sound like such a little thing, but the Pharisees and scribes knew the Law told them not to eat bread that had been defiled (touched by unwashed hands). The disciples were doing just that and the rulers and leaders would never be caught doing what they had witnessed. They came to Jesus and asked why his followers did not comply with the traditions of the elders.

Jesus answered them. "Well did Isaiah prophesy of you hypocrites, as it is written: 'This people honors me with their lips, but their heart is far from me. And in vain they worship me, teaching as doctrines the commandments of men.' For laying aside the Commandments of God, you hold the tradition of men . . ."

Jesus continued rebuking them, telling them they were arrogant and pompous, and recounting the times they weren't following God's Commandments themselves. He mentioned all the times they caused others to break the Laws, making the Laws of God ineffective.

Jesus then called to the crowd and began teaching, "Hear me everyone and understand. There is nothing that enters a man from outside which can defile him; but the things which come out of him, those are the things that defile a man. If anyone has ears to hear, let them hear."

Jesus then went into a friend's house with His disciples and they asked Him to explain what He had told the crowd. Jesus informed them that they needed to start understanding. He explained that a man cannot be defiled

GOSPEL II: THE GOOD NEWS ACCORDING TO ME, MARK

because he puts something into his stomach. What, however, comes out of a man, comes from his heart and if it is not pure, than that will defile him. All the evil and sinning that men do come from inside them.

Part 14

MIRACLE AFTER MIRACLE

Jesus went to Tyre and Sidon next, thinking he would escape the crowds for a while in the house of a friend. When He was there, a woman who had a daughter possessed by an unclean spirit fell at His knees. This woman was a Greek and begged Jesus to help her daughter.

Jesus said to her "Let the children be filled first, for it is not good to take the children's bread and throw it to the little dogs." Now this may sound harsh in your time, but you must remember Jesus, being Jewish, wanted to help His chosen people first.

Now this Greek woman understood that and answered by telling Jesus that even the dogs under the table can eat the crumbs dropped by the children. So even the Gentiles are deserving of compassion from the Lord.

Being touched by her words, Jesus said, "For this saying, go your way; the demon has gone out of your daughter." and when the woman got home, she found that her daughter was well again.

Jesus then left, once again, for the Sea of Galilee. On His way men brought Him a man who was deaf and also had a speech impediment. And they begged Him to lay hands on this man. Jesus put His fingers into the man's ears and shouted, "Be opened." Immediately the man heard and could speak plainly. Jesus commanded them not to tell anyone, but the more He told them not to say anything, the more they reported to others.

Jesus always found Himself in front of a multitude of people, teaching them about the Kingdom of God. On another occasion, he was surrounded by about four thousand people who had been following Him for days. Jesus felt compassion for these people and did not want to send them on their

GOSPEL II: THE GOOD NEWS ACCORDING TO ME, MARK

way without giving them food, afraid many would faint on their way home. Once again, The Christ took seven loaves of bread and fish and fed the four thousand. When all four thousand had their fill, He sent them on their way.

Part 15

BEWARE THE LEAVEN OF THE PHARISEES

JESUS GOT INTO A boat with His disciples and went to Dalmanutha. When they had reached the shore, the Pharisees came out to argue with Him, demanding that He give them a sign.

"Why does this generation seek a sign?" Jesus asked. "Assuredly, I say to you, no sign shall be given to this generation."

It was then that Jesus left them and, with His disciples, got back into the boat. Jesus charged His twelve followers to beware of the leaven of these Pharisees and the leaven of Herod. The disciples look at each other and questioned what Jesus had meant. They then remembered they only had one loaf of bread left for this trip. They thought that maybe Jesus was referencing that fact that they didn't have enough bread.

Jesus spoke to them. "Why do you reason, because you have no bread? Did you not perceive nor understand? Is your heart still hardened?" Jesus reminded them about the five thousand and the four thousand who were fed by Him, and He continued, sadly, saying to them, "How is it you do not understand?"

The Miracles continued when Jesus reached Bethsaida. There he was approached by some, bringing Him a blind Man that He might heal him. Jesus took the man out of town and restored his sight, telling him, "Neither go into the town, nor tell anyone in the town.

Jesus traveled again with His disciples. Along the way He asked His followers "Who do men say that I am? They told Him that some men called

GOSPEL II: THE GOOD NEWS ACCORDING TO ME, MARK

Him Elijah, while others said that He was John the Baptist. Some merely said He was a prophet.

Then Jesus looked at them and questioned them. "But, who do you say that I am."

Peter spoke up and told Jesus that He was The Christ, and He told them not to tell anyone who He was.

Jesus began telling them that the time would soon come when He would have to suffer, be rejected by the elders, chief priests, and the scribes, and die. He also told them that after three days He would rise again. Now, Peter took Jesus aside from the rest and told Him that he disapproved of the things Jesus was saying.

Jesus turned back to the others and quietly spoke, saying "Get behind me Satan, for you are not mindful of the things of God, but the things of men." I think, at this point, that Jesus wasn't talking directly to Peter himself, but He knew that Satan was using Peter's words and therefore needed rebuking.

Jesus then met a crowd and started talking to them. "Whoever desires to come after me, let him deny himself, and take up his cross, and follow me. For whoever desires to save his life, will lose it, but whoever loses his life for my sake and the Gospel's, will save it. For what will it profit a man if he gains the whole world, and loses his own soul? Or what will a man give in exchange for his soul? For whoever is ashamed of me and my words, in this adulterous and sinful generation, of him the Son of Man will also be ashamed when He comes in the glory of His Father, with the Holy Angels."

Part 16

TRANSFIGURED

AFTER SIX DAYS, THE Lord took John, Peter, and James up into the mountain. When they arrived Jesus was transfigured. That is, his appearance was changed completely, in a way that did not conform to nature. His clothes shone as white as new fallen snow– whiter than any modern detergent could get them. As this change was going on, Elijah and Moses appeared with Jesus.

Peter said that they should build three tabernacles in honor of what they saw happening. It was miraculous, but the disciples were afraid, too and fell on their faces. Who wouldn't be? Then a cloud came over all of them and the voice of God said, "This is my Son. Hear Him!"

Being afraid and amazed at the same time, the disciples looked up, but all that they had seen was gone, all except for the Son of God. At that point, Jesus told the three they were to say nothing of what they had seen, until after He had risen from the dead. Even though they question what Jesus meant by risen from the dead, they kept this secret to themselves.

The three did ask Jesus a question about what the scribes had been saying, to try and prove Jesus wasn't the Christ. Since they had seen Jesus with Moses and Elijah, they knew, without a doubt, that He was the Son of God. "Why do the scribes say that Elijah must come first?"

Jesus answered, "Indeed Elijah is coming first and restores all things. And how is it written concerning the Son of Man, that He must suffer many things and be treated with contempt. But I say to you that Elijah has also come, and they did to him whatever they wished as it is written of Him."

GOSPEL II: THE GOOD NEWS ACCORDING TO ME, MARK

Indeed, Elijah had already come, according to the scriptures. The scribes had believed that Elijah was going to come back from the dead, so Jesus couldn't be the Messiah. However, Jesus told them that John the Baptist was Elijah. He was not reincarnated in John, but John was the power and spirit of Elijah. Remember, it was an Angel who had told this to Zacharias, and Elizabeth—that their son would be filled with the holy Spirit in his mother's womb. Jesus had explained how the people had killed John as the scriptures had said, and that He, too, must be sacrificed.

Part 17

WHY CAN'T WE DO IT?

WHEN THE FOUR MEN returned to the rest of the twelve, there was a crowd that had already gathered. One man came to Jesus and explained how he had asked the disciples to help his child, But they could not do it.

Jesus being dismayed answered, "O faithless generation, how long shall I be with you. How long shall I bear with you? Bring him to me."

They brought the possessed man to Jesus and he began to convulse when he came near to the Messiah. He fell to the ground, foaming at the mouth. Jesus asked the father how long the child had been this way. The father told him it had been since birth, and more than once he had tried to kill himself by fire or by drowning. The man then asked that Jesus to have compassion on them and heal him if he could. Jesus stated that he could, "If you can believe all things are possible to him who believes."

And the father said, "Lord, I believe, help my unbelief." Jesus commanded the deaf and dumb demon to come out of this man's son. The spirit cried out, left, and the boy fell down as if he were dead. Jesus walked up to him, and took his hand. The boy rose up, healed.

When they were alone again, the disciples asked Jesus why they had been unable to cast out this demon. Jesus explained to them that this kind of demon will not come out unless it is preceded by prayer and fasting. And in that was the lesson. He Who Isn't Against Us, Is For Us.

Jesus then taught His disciples about the future, as they walked toward Capernaum. He told them that He was soon to be betrayed, afterwards He would be killed, and then He would rise from the dead. They, of course at this time, did not understand Him, but were afraid to ask.

GOSPEL II: THE GOOD NEWS ACCORDING TO ME, MARK

When they reached Capernaum, Jesus asked them what they were concerned about while they were on the road. They kept silent, not wanting to tell Jesus they were discussing who among them would be the greatest. It didn't matter that they did not answer, for Jesus knew.

Jesus called them into a friend's house and told them to sit and listen. "If anyone desires to be first, he shall be last of all and servant to all." Taking a child who had been sitting in the house, Jesus continued. "Whoever receives one of these little children in my name, receives me. Whoever receives me, receives not me, but Him who sent me"

John spoke up and told Jesus of a time they had seen someone, other than the twelve of them, casting out a demon. He said that they told him not to because he didn't follow them. Jesus explained that they should not do that because the man was, indeed, doing it in the name of Jesus. He stated this, "For he who is not against us, is on our side."

Jesus furthered His lesson by indicating that even a man would give them a cup of water in His name, would be rewarded. If, however anyone caused one of these little ones to stumble, it would be better for him to die at sea with a weight around his neck. He told them that if a hand made them sin, they should cut it off. It would be better for them to have only one rather than spend eternity in Hell fire. He referred to their hands and eyes, too, suggesting they would fare much better without these things. The alternative Hell, for Heaven's sake, was much worse. No pun intended.

Part 18

MARRIAGE AND CHILDREN

JESUS WENT, NEXT, TO Judea. A crowd gathered and among them were the Pharisees, who were still trying to trick Jesus into making a mistake they could capitalize on. They asked, "Teacher, is it lawful for a man to divorce his wife."

Knowing what they were up to, Jesus asked them a question. "What did Moses command you?"

They quoted the scriptures stating that Moses had given permission for them to give a certificate of divorce. Jesus specified that Moses had done that because of the hardness of their hearts.

He continued, "But, from the beginning of creation, God made them male and female. For that reason, a man shall leave his mother and father and be joined to his wife. And the two shall become one flesh. Therefore, what God has joined together, let no man separate."

The people then brought children to Jesus so that He might bless them. The disciples told them Jesus was busy and the children should, well, be seen and not heard. Jesus was displeased at this.

He commanded, "Let the little children come to me, and do not forbid them; for of such is the Kingdom of God. Assuredly I say to you, whoever does not receive the Kingdom of God as a little child, will by no means enter it." And He, taking them into His arms, blessed them.

Part 19

HOW TO GET TO HEAVEN

JESUS AND HIS FOLLOWERS traveled the roads of Judea. A rich man saw them and, calling Jesus a good man, asked Him how he could get into Heaven. Jesus stated that one should follow the commandments. They should not commit adultery, or murder, or steal, or bear false witness (that is to be deceitful or untruthful). Of course, the man told Jesus he had kept the Ten Commandments all of his life, since childhood. Jesus looked at him and said that this man did lack one thing that would keep him away from Heaven.

"Go your way," Jesus answered, "sell all whatever you have and give to the poor, and you will have treasures in heaven; and come take up the cross and follow me. "

Because this man had many possessions and was exceedingly rich, he left Jesus and the others, being sad and miserable. Jesus referred to this man as one of many who were wealthy and depended on riches, rather than trusting in the Kingdom of Heaven. At this point Jesus compared this man's actions to a camel trying to go through the eye of a needle. The people then asked how any of them would be able to enter the Kingdom, to which He answered, ". . . with God, all things are possible."

Peter reminded Jesus that the twelve of them had left all they had and followed Him. I can guess that Peter was pleased when Jesus expressed how those who gave up things for His sake, would be paid back a hundred-fold in eternal life. "But many who are first will be last, and the last first." With that, Jesus went to Jerusalem.

Part 20

THE SON OF MAN WILL SUFFER

He called to Himself His disciples, wanting them to know what was about happen to Him. He outlined what would be coming, saying that the Son of Man was about to be betrayed to the chief priests and scribes, found guilty of sins He had not committed, turned over to the gentiles, and crucified. He described how they would mock Him, scourge Him, spit on Him, and then kill Him. The good news, and, really, the reason that I write this in the first place, is that the Messiah would rise again, after three days.

Then, the sons of Zebedee, James and John asked Jesus if they could sit on His right side and left side, after He came to His glory. Jesus revealed that this request was not even up to Him, for it was His Father's decision.

The other disciples were a bit upset at James's and John's request, but Jesus called them all together and said, "Whoever of you desire to be first, shall be slave of all; for even the Son of Man did not come to be served, but to serve. And to give His life as a ransom for many."

As they were traveling from Jericho, a blind man cried out for Him to have mercy. The crowd tried to quiet him, be he only shouted louder, asking the Son of David to have mercy on him. Jesus heard him and called out to him, asking what he wanted. The blind man called him Rabboni, (or teacher) and asked Jesus to restore his sight. This Jesus did, and the man followed the Master as they journeyed to Jerusalem.

Outside of Jerusalem, at the Mount of Olives, Jesus directed two disciples to go into the city and after finding a colt of the donkey, that had never been sat upon, they should untie it and bring it to Him. If anyone tried to stop them, they were merely to state that the Lord was in need of it

GOSPEL II: THE GOOD NEWS ACCORDING TO ME, MARK

and whoever it was would give it to them. This was exactly what happened, and they brought the young colt to the Christ.

Jesus sat on it and went into the city As He did, those along the way put their garments and palm branches on the ground in front of Jesus. They shouted, as the Lord passed, "Hosanna! Blessed is He who comes in the name of the Lord. Blessed is the Kingdom of our father, David, that comes in the name of the Lord. Hosanna in the highest!"

To define the meaning of what was happening, let me tell you that Jews would usually consider Abraham their father. They used the term Kingdom Of David, because Jesus was a descendant of David and it would be respectful while honoring Jesus as the triumphant King of the Jews. At this point the crowd was basically admitting that Jesus was the Messiah, Their savior.

Part 21

THE FIG TREE AND THE MONEY CHANGERS

Jesus, as a victorious King, would not be long lived., but He was still all powerful. As He and His disciples went into Jerusalem, Jesus was hungry. Seeing a fig tree, He went to it to gather some figs, The tree had none, so Jesus proclaimed that no one would ever be able to eat from this tree again.

He, then, went to the Temple in Jerusalem and observed the money changers selling animals as sacrifice. In that day, sacrifice was of utmost importance. It was done for the atonement of sins. It was special and a way for man and God to have a relationship. Now the money changers, as well as the Temple rulers were making a profit from this practice, and that would have angered the Son of God. So, when Jesus saw this, He overturned the tables of money, set the animals free, including the doves, and, making a whip from some rope, drove out the money changers. He shouted, "It is written, My house shall be called a house of prayer, but you have made it a den of thieves."

The Scribes and the priests, when they heard what had happened, wanted to destroy Jesus. He had left, though, but returned the next morning. On His way to the city, Peter saw the fig tree that Jesus had cursed. It had withered and died and he called it to the attention of his Master.

Jesus replied, "Have faith in God. For assuredly I say to you whoever says to this mountain be removed and be cast into the sea, and does not doubt in his heart, but believes that those things he says will be done, he will have whatever he says. There I say to you whatever you ask when you pray, believe that you receive then and you will have them."

Part 22

THE CHIEF PRIESTS, SCRIBES, AND PHARISEES

Jesus arrived at the Temple and the chief priests, scribes, and elders came to Him and asked Him, "By what authority do you do these things. And who gave you the authority to do these things."

Jesus answered with a question of His own. He told them if they answered His question, He would answer theirs. "The Baptism of John," Jesus questioned, "was it from Heaven or from man? Answer me."

The elders were afraid to answer. If they said Heaven, then Jesus would ask them why they didn't believe John. If they answered man, they were afraid the crowds would rebel against them, for the people believed John to be a prophet. They remained silent. And Jesus replied to them, "Neither will I tell you by what authority I do these things."

This, of course, made the chief priests, the scribes, and the elders more angry. They had been silenced by the Lord and they must have looked pretty confused about what to do next. Jesus decided it was time for them to hear a parable.

He told them about a vineyard owner who leased out his land to vine dressers, those who cultivated grape vines. The owner left and went on a long journey. Later, when he came home, he sent three servants to pick up the fruit from the vine dressers. They saw the three coming and beat up one servant. Then they killed the second, and stoned the third servant. The owner sent more servants and they, too, were killed. Finally, He sent beloved son, thinking he would have more respect from the vine dressers.

THE CHIEF PRIESTS, SCRIBES, AND PHARISEES

The vine dressers decided they should kill him, also, saying that his inheritance would be theirs.

Jesus asked them, "When the owner of the vineyard comes, what will he do to those vine dressers? He will come and destroy the vine dressers and give the vineyard to others."

Jesus rebuked them saying, "Have you not even read this scripture? The stone which the builders rejected, has become the chief corner stone. This was the Lord's doing and it is marvelous in our eyes" (Psalm 118).

The Chief priests, being angrier than ever and knowing Jesus was talking about them, wanted to arrest Him, but they were afraid of the crowd. Therefore, they left and sent to Jesus the Pharisees and the Herodians (political religious leaders). They would try to trick him into saying something they might use against Him.

They told Jesus they understood that He was an honest man, teaching the ways of God as truth and that He didn't regard the person of man (or Caesar for that matter). They were, of course, saying Jesus did not judge men by their outside but by their inner soul and that was the important thing. They asked the Lord if they should be required to pay taxes to Caesar.

Jesus knew their sin of hypocrisy and asked, "Why do you test me? Bring me a Danarius that I may see it." He continued after taking the coin, "Whose image and inscription is this?

They answered "Caesar's."

Jesus stated, "Render to Caesar the things that are Caesar's, and to God the things that are God's."

You could probably imagine them standing there in awe, with their jaws dropping. But, the Sadducees, the upper class rung of Jewish society and the ones who didn't believe there was any resurrection, were there and had come to question Jesus. They explained how Moses had told them that if a man's brother dies and leaves a wife with no offspring, The brother should take her as his wife. Even if there are seven brothers and they all die with no offspring, They would have all married her. "Now if she dies, who would be her husband after the resurrection? After all, they all were married to her?"

Jesus answered. "Are you therefore not mistaken, because you do not know the scripture. For when they rise from the dead they do not marry or are not given in marriage, but are like Angels in Heaven."

GOSPEL II: THE GOOD NEWS ACCORDING TO ME, MARK

Jesus further explained that God was not the God of the dead, but the God of the living, and the scriptures had told them that. He therefore rebuked them by asserting that the Sadducees were wrong.

It seems that the scribes also took a turn trying to prove Jesus wasn't who he claimed to be. They asked, "What is the greatest Commandment?"

"The first of all the commandments is:" Jesus began, "Hear, O Israel, The Lord our God, The lord is one, and you shall love the Lord your God with all your heart, with all your soul, with all your mind, and with all your strength. This is the first Commandment. And the second, like it, is this: You shall love your neighbor as yourself. There is no other greater commandment greater than these."

After the scribes listened to this, they had to agree, but they didn't like it. Jesus continued teaching, and the average person heard Him and listened to His words willingly. He warned them to beware of the scribes who desired to walk around in their long robes, greeting people in the marketplace. They were the ones who wanted the best seats in the synagogue and at the feasts. They devoured widows houses, for they, under the pretense of knowing the law, manage their estates and embezzle money from them. Then they leave them homeless. It is these scribes who will be condemned. As He was teaching, he watched as people gave to the synagogue. The rich gave much and were proud. Then, a woman came to the treasury and put two mites (now about half a cent) into the collection.

Jesus called to His disciples and expressed His joy toward her. "Assuredly, I say to you, that this poor widow has put in more than all who have given to the treasury; for they all put in out of their abundance, but she, out of her poverty, gave all she had." After this lesson, they left the Temple.

Part 23

THE END TIMES

His followers pointed out all the buildings of the Temple. Jesus declared that not one of the stones there would be left on top of another. The entire Temple would be destroyed! The twelve went with Jesus to the Mount of Olives and, there, John, James, Peter, and Andrew asked Him to explain to them when all of this was going to happen. What were the signs before His words would be fulfilled?

Jesus warned them to be aware so that no one would deceive them. He testified that many would come in His name, claiming to be the Messiah, The Christ. He said there would be wars and rumors of wars, and that one nation would rise up against another, and one Kingdom would be against another. He indicated that there would be earthquakes and famine and many worldwide troubles. He discussed with them how they would be persecuted for His sake and even killed, but the Holy Spirit would be with them always, giving them the power they needed to get through it all. He asserted that brother would be against brother and son against his father causing them to be put to death. Christians will be hated for the Lord's sake, but if they resisted the evil and endured, they would be saved. Jesus emphasized the fact that there was going to be a great tribulation such as the universe itself had not seen or would ever see. The sun, He told them, would be dark and the moon would give no light. The stars would fall from the sky and the heavens, themselves, would shake.

It was then that mankind would see the Son of Man coming in the clouds with great power and glory. He would send His Angels to the four corners of the world, gathering His chosen ones to Himself. Just like the

GOSPEL II: THE GOOD NEWS ACCORDING TO ME, MARK

fig tree, whose branches become tender, foretell that summer is coming, so will all these things happen, and they will know it is time. When these things occur, He expressed, that generation currently on earth would not pass away. He stressed that Heaven and earth would end, but His words would never end. Finally, he said that they needed to watch and pray so that His coming would not be missed. Finally, He pointed out to them that what He was telling them, He was telling all people.

Part 24

PASSOVER, THE LAST SUPPER, THE GARDEN

THE PHARISEES AND SCRIBES were busy plotting how they could arrest Jesus and kill Him, But they knew they could do nothing until after the Passover Feast, At that time, Jesus was in Bethany at the house of one of His followers, Simon the Leper. As He sat at the table a woman came to Him and, using expensive alabaster, anointed the head of Jesus. Some of the disciples were upset at this because the money that had been spent on the oil, could have been used to feed those who were hungry.

"Let her alone. Why do you trouble her. She has done a good work for me." Jesus explained, "For you have the poor with you always, and whenever you wish you may do them good; but me you do not have always. She had done what she could. She has come beforehand to anoint my body for burial." Jesus then explained that what this woman would be honored and memorialized for what she had done.

As the Christ was talking, Judas Iscariot went to the Chief Priests in order to betray Jesus. They all promised to give Judas money if he would sell out his Master. He made plans with them and they were excited about being able to arrest Jesus.

Now, to explain, I don't think Judas knew exactly what he was about to put in motion. He, like most of the other people in his time thought the Messiah would overthrow the Romans and become King. Maybe Judas thought that he could force Jesus's hand and He would then start the revolution. It would then be possible for him to benefit from his friendship with

GOSPEL II: THE GOOD NEWS ACCORDING TO ME, MARK

the new King in the new Kingdom. Maybe, too, when Jesus had told all of His disciples that He was about to die, Judas assumed that Jesus could not be the Messiah they were expecting. Whatever the reason, Judas planned to betray His Master.

On the day of Unleavened Bread, or the first day of Passover, the disciples asked Jesus where they were to celebrate the supper. Jesus sent out two of His disciples and said, "Go into the city and man will meet you carrying a pitcher of water; follow him." He also told them to go into the house and see the upper room, and it will have already been prepared for the twelve and Jesus.

I knew this part well, because I was the man, at the time, John Mark, carrying the water and I took the two to the upper room. Small world, huh? Anyway, Jesus and His disciples came that evening to eat supper. As they sat and ate, Jesus told them, "Assuredly, I say to you, one of you who eats with me will betray me." Sadly, one by one, they asked, "Is it I, Lord?"

Jesus answered by saying that it would be ". . . one of the twelve who dips with me in the dish. The Son of Man indeed goes just as it is written of Him, but woe to the man by whom the Son of Man is betrayed. It would have been good for that man if he had never been born."

Now while they ate, Jesus took the bread, blessed it, and broke it saying, "Take, eat; this is my body."

Then He took the cup. After He gave thanks to His Father, He gave it to the disciples and said, "This is my blood of the new covenant; which I shed for you. Assuredly, I say to you, I will no longer drink of the fruit of the vine until that day when I drink it new in the Kingdom of God." They all sang a hymn and then departed for the Mount of Olives.

Jesus explained to His disciples how they would all face fear and stumble this very night. Again noting scripture, He stated the verse that had been written, "I will strike the shepherd and the sheep will be scattered."

Peter spoke up quickly and cried, "Even if all are made to stumble, yet I will not be. "Jesus looked at Peter and told him that before the rooster crows, in the morning, he would deny His Master three times. Peter strongly stated that He would die for his Lord, and all the rest agreed.

When they had come to Gethsemane Jesus asked the disciples to stop, pray, and wait for Him. He took Peter, James, and John with Him, a little farther into the garden. He spoke to them, "My soul is exceedingly sorrowful, even to death; stay here and watch."

PASSOVER, THE LAST SUPPER, THE GARDEN

He went a little farther and then fell on the ground. He prayed that the hour might pass. He spoke again to God, "Abba, Father, all things are possible for you. Take this cup away from me, nevertheless, not what I will, but what You will."

He returned and found His disciples sleeping. He asked them again to wake and pray and watch. He even said, "The Spirit is indeed willing, but the flesh is weak." Jesus went to pray again, and once again, His men fell asleep. He came back a third time and woke the disciples saying. "The hour has come. Behold the Son of Man is being betrayed into the hands of sinners. Rise, let us go. See my betrayer is at hand."

It was then that Judas walked up to Jesus, called Him Master, and betrayed Him with a kiss. A large mob grabbed Jesus and took Him. The disciples became so afraid that they all scattered, just as scripture had foretold. I heard about the arrest, and sleeping at the time, I grabbed my linens and ran toward the mob. I saw them taking away Jesus and followed a little behind the crowd. A man grabbed me. I thought I was being arrested also, so I had to slip out of my linens and I ran naked and in great fear, away from the persecutors. Ask scholars today, they will tell you.

Part 25

FALSE ACCUSATIONS AND DEATH

THE MOB TOOK JESUS to the High Priest. There with him were the chief priests, the elders and the scribes. Many people came forward bearing false witness against the Christ. It was sad, but their false testimonies didn't even match. It didn't matter, for they sought to kill Jesus for He was a threat to them.

The Chief Priest asked Jesus, "Are you the Christ, the Son of the Blessed?"

Jesus answered, "I am. And you will see the Son of Man sitting at the right hand of the Power and coming with the clouds of Heaven."

The Chief Priest tore his clothes as he shouted that Jesus had spoken Blasphemy. No other testimony was necessary. Then some spit on Jesus, blindfolded Him, and mocked Him, asking Him to speak prophesy and identify the person who had hit Him. They then condemned Him to death.

Meanwhile, Peter was out in the courtyard and had been asked if he knew this Jesus. He stated he didn't know Him. A second person asked him, and again he said he was not a follower. A third asked him, and he cursed denying that he even knew this Jesus. At that exact second, the rooster crowed. Peter crying in sorrow ran, remembering the words his Master had told him, "Before the rooster crows twice, you will deny me three times."

The next morning, the priests, elders, and scribes took Jesus to Pilate. They explained all the things Jesus was charged with, and stated Pilate should know Jesus said He was the King of the Jews. Pontius Pilate asked, "Are you the King of the Jews?"

Jesus simply stated, "It is as you say."

FALSE ACCUSATIONS AND DEATH

Question followed question, but Jesus remained silent, even when Pilate had stated, "Do you answer nothing? See how many things they testify against you?" Jesus was still silent.

Since it was the time of the Jewish feast, Pilate reminded the crowd that he could release a prisoner on their Holiday. After asking who they wanted to release, The chief priests stirred up the mob and the Jews shouted loudly to release Barabbas, not Jesus. Pilate, didn't want to fight a crowd, but instead, please it, released Barabbas and delivered Jesus to be crucified.

The soldiers took Jesus and clothed Him in a purple robe. They struck Him on the head with a stick and then made Him hold it like a King's scepter. They fashioned a crown from sharp thorns and jammed it on His head. They mocked Him and struck Him and spat on Him. They went to their knees and pretended to worship Him. Then they put on Him his own clothes and led Him to be crucified.

On the way to Golgotha, the soldiers compelled Simon, a Cyrenian, to carry the cross of Jesus. When they arrived, the soldiers tried to give Jesus wine mixed with myrrh, but He refused it. They nailed Him to the cross and then cast lots for His clothes. They hung a sign above Him which said, King of the Jews.

Part 26

"THE KING OF THE JEWS"

Jesus was crucified along with two thieves, one on His right and one on His left. This fulfilled scripture, for it had been written that He would be numbered with the transgressors. I have to tell you it was in Isaiah 53:12 that the prophecy concerning the Messiah was found. Now, as I understand, when I say "numbered with His transgressors, I mean that Jesus was crucified with sinners. He, Himself, was without sin and blameless.

The chief priests mocked Jesus as He hung there telling Him to come down from the cross, if He was so powerful. They constantly made fun of Him, until the ninth hour, when Jesus cried out, "Eli, Eli lama Sabachthani." which translates to: "My God, My God, why have you forsaken me?"

Some stated that He was calling for Elijah and another ran and got a sponge filled with sour wine and offered it to the Christ. Jesus then took his last breath and in that second, the Temple curtains were torn in two from top to bottom. Standing there was a Centurion who believed and said, "Truly, this man was the Son of God."

When Jesus was taken down, He was carried to the tomb owned by Joseph of Arimathea. He had gone to Pilate and requested the body and was given permission. When He was buried, a stone was rolled over the entrance.

On the day after the Sabbath, Mary Magdalene, Mary, the mother of James, and another woman named Salome came to the tomb to anoint the body with oil. They questioned each other asking who they could get to roll away the stone covering the tomb. When they arrived, the stone was already removed. When they entered, they saw a young man dressed in white and they were afraid.

He spoke to them saying, "Do not be alarmed. You seek Jesus of Nazareth who was crucified. He is Risen He is not here. Go, tell His disciples, and Peter, that He is going before you to Galilee; there you will see Him, as He said to you."

Mary saw Jesus first, but the disciples did not believe her. Then two disciples saw Him on the road, but still others did not believe. Now when the eleven were together, Jesus appeared to them and rebuked their disbelief.

He spoke to them saying, "Go into all the world and preach the Gospel to every creature. He who believes and is baptized, will be saved, but he who does not believe will be condemned. And these signs will follow those who believe. In my name they will cast out demons; they will speak in new tongues; they will take up serpents; and if they drink anything deadly, it will by no means hurt them; they will lay hands on the sick, and they will recover."

After the Lord had spoken to them, He was taken up to Heaven where He sat on the right hand of God. And they went out and preached everywhere and they did what Jesus had asked. Amen!

I had to write about the good news of Jesus, the Son Of God. I hope I have used many details that will help you understand what happened back then. Jesus was indeed here and He came to serve and to save mankind, if they only accept it. He sacrificed His own life so that we (and you) could be with Him forever.

Gospel III

THE GOSPEL ACCORDING TO LUKE

Part 1

. . . BECAUSE I CARE

CALL ME DOCTOR LUKE, for I am a Physician, a family doctor, if you will. Because I am used to keeping accurate documents, I will convey my message to you and be as faithfully correct as I can. I will write and outline, with precision, the facts that occurred, starting in the time of Herod. I have a purpose and a direction for my gospel, which you will soon discover. Everything I write has a direction, for my Lord had a direction. What I describe, starts a journey . . . a journey toward Jerusalem.[1]

Everything that was done was leading to this city. The Christ was always heading toward Jerusalem for it was there that all would be complete. From that point, the direction goes out into the rest of the world. It was, after all, Jerusalem that ended all and then started all. Please read on and you will see what I mean. I have used the New King James Version, just as my brothers Matthew and Mark, to quote and record what was said.

I must tell you from the start, that I was not with Jesus personally, but I was a Christian and a companion of the Apostle Paul of Tarsus. In Gotquestions.org, the author writes, "Little is known about Luke, the author of the books of Luke and Acts in the Bible. We do know he was a physician and the only Gentile to write any part of the New Testament. Paul's letter to the Colossians draws a distinction between Luke and other colleagues "of the

---

1. Ministry Voice, "Why Did Luke Write His Gospel: Understanding the Purpose and Meaning Behind Luke's Message," https://www.ministryvoice.com/why-did-luke-write-his-gospel/.

GOSPEL III: THE GOSPEL ACCORDING TO LUKE

circumcision," meaning the Jews (Colossians 4:11). Luke is the only New Testament writer clearly identifiable as a non-Jew.[2]

True, I am not Jewish, but as a physician I recommend that it would serve you well for you to listen carefully and, now, I will begin.

---

[2]. Got Questions, "Who Was Luke in the Bible?," https://www.gotquestions.org/Luke-in-the-Bible.html.

Part 2

MARY AND ELIZABETH

In the days of Herod, there lived a certain priest named Zacharias and his wife Elizabeth. They both followed the Commandments of God faithfully, but they were without a child. Elizabeth was barren (she could not have a child) and both of them were getting up there in years. One day, while Zacharias was burning incense, for that was his allotted job in the Temple, an Angel came to him and told him not to be afraid. The Angel explained how God was going bless him with a son and he was to name him John.

The Angel said to Zacharias, "You will have joy and gladness and many will rejoice at his birth. For he will be great in the sight of the Lord and shall drink neither wine or strong drink. He will also be filled with the Holy Spirit, even in his mother's womb. And he will turn many children of Israel to the Lord their God. He will also go before Him (the Messiah) in the spirit and Power of Elijah to turn the hearts of the fathers to the children and the disobedient to the wisdom of the just to make ready a people prepared for the Lord."

Now Zacharias was taken aback. He stated that his wife could not have a son, because they were both old and she was barren. The angel explained that he was Gabriel, the one who stood in the presence of God, and it was God who had sent him to tell the news.

Since Zacharias had not believed him, his speech would be taken from him until his son was born. When he came out of the Temple the people assumed he had a vision, but he could not speak and tell them. Zacharias left and went home and no one could believe it, but Elizabeth did get pregnant.

GOSPEL III: THE GOSPEL ACCORDING TO LUKE

Six months after she had conceived, Gabriel was sent by God to Galilee to inform Mary, who was betrothed to Joseph, that she, too, was going to have a son. She was afraid and worried, because she was not yet married. Gabriel told her not to be afraid, for she had found favor with God.

She was to have a son and call him Jesus. The Angel added that her son would be great and called the Son of the Highest. He would also be given the seat of His father David, and reign over the house of Jacob forever. His Kingdom would have no ending. Furthermore, ". . . the Holy Spirit will come upon you, and the power of the Highest will overshadow you; therefore, also, that Holy One who is to be born will be called the Son of God."

Before Gabriel left, he revealed to Mary that her relative Elizabeth, even though she was old, was also to have a son. Mary told the Angel that since she was a maidservant to the Lord, she would gladly let happen as the Angel had announced.

Later, Mary went to visit Elizabeth. And when Elizabeth greeted her, the baby in her womb leaped for joy, and Elizabeth was filled with the Holy spirit. Mary praised the Lord and expressed how God was her Savior for having given her this Almighty gift. Now Mary stayed with Elizabeth and Zacharias for three months, before returning home.

When Elizabeth gave birth the neighbors and relatives were also filled with joy and celebrated his birth. When it was time to name him, the family wanted him to be called Zacharias, after his father. Elizabeth answered them, telling then he would be called John. Now they were confused, for no one else in her family had that name. They made signs to Zacharias, for he still had not spoken, and he wrote down on paper that his son would be named John.

Immediately his speech returned and he gave praises to God. He proclaimed how God was going to save Israel from their enemies and how his child was going to be a prophet of the Highest. His son would be used by God to give light to those in darkness, and lead God's people to peace. Zacharias' son grew and became spiritually strong and went to the desert to live until it was time for him to do the work God had sent him to do.

Part 3

THE BIRTH OF THE KING

CAESAR AUGUSTUS SENT OUT a decree to all of his world that everyone needed to go to the city of their birth to complete a census. Joseph, being from the house of David, needed to go to Bethlehem, in Judea. He would have to register himself, Mary, and maybe their child, who would soon be born. Mary was ready to give birth, but there was nowhere for the two of them to stay. An Inn keeper told Joseph that hie could use their stable because there was nowhere else. Mary gave birth, wrapped her new son in swaddling clothes, and laid him in a manger.

It happened, too, that there were shepherds in the fields working, when an angel of the lord came to them and said, "Do not be afraid, for behold, I bring you good tidings of great joy which will be to all people. For there is born to you this day, in the city of David a savior, who is Christ the Lord. And this will be a sign to you: you will find the babe wrapped in swaddling clothes and lying in a manger." And then they heard a multitude of Angels singing, "Glory to God in the highest, and on earth, peace, goodwill toward men. "The shepherds came to the city, found Jesus, and told everyone what had occurred.

On the eighth day the child was named Jesus, as the Angel had said, before he had been conceived in his mother's womb. They brought Him to the Temple and made a sacrifice according to the law. While they were there, they saw a man named Simeon, who had been promised by God that he would not die until he had laid eyes on the Messiah, the Son of God. Simeon held up Jesus and said that God was allowing him to die in peace, for he had been permitted to see God's salvation in the flesh.

GOSPEL III: THE GOSPEL ACCORDING TO LUKE

He continued by saying that this child would also bring revelation to the gentiles and glory to Israel. Now, at the same Temple was a prophetess named Anna. She was very old and never left the Temple, fasting and praying day and night. She saw Jesus and she, too, thanked God for sending a savior to Israel.

And Jesus started to grow up. He grew in spirit, and started gaining great wisdom; and the Grace of God was with Him. When Jesus turned twelve, Joseph and Mary took Him to Jerusalem to celebrate the Passover. When they were finished at the festival, they started back home. Jesus, however, lagged behind. Mary and Joseph assumed their son was with a crowd of relatives, but soon realized Jesus was not with them.

They returned to the city to find Him. When they did, He was in the temple listening to the teachers, and asking questions. All of the people in the temple were amazed at His questions and the answers He had for them. His mother and father were upset, to say the least.

They asked him why he had not gone with them. They explained how worried He had made them. He answered, "Why do you seek me? Do you not know that I must be about my Father's business?"

They did not understand the things He was saying, but Jesus went with them and did as they asked, following the fifth Commandment. From that point He honored His father and mother. Mary, not fully understanding the things that had gone on, kept things close to her heart. Maybe someday She would.

Part 4

JOHN THE BAPTIST

It was in the fifteenth year of the reign of Tiberius Caesar, and Pontius Pilate was the Governor of Judea. Herod was the Tetrarch of Galilee. In other words, he was the ruler of one fourth of the province. Caiaphas was the High Priest of the Jewish people.

Now God's word came to the son of Zacharias, John, and he came from the wilderness to preach that his Jewish brothers and sisters needed to repent. He called it the baptism of repentance for the forgiveness of sins, and he baptized those needing forgiveness in the river Jordan.

Isaiah had told the people long ago that there would be someone coming from the wilderness to prepare the way of the Lord. This man would precede the Christ—the Messiah. And John was doing just that. When he baptized, he told the people to bear fruit worthy of repentance. It was no longer enough to simply say that you were a descendant of Abraham. He described the sinners as a tree that didn't bear fruit, for it would be cut down, and thrown into a fire.

The people asked what they should do and John told them this. If you have two shirts, give one away to someone who has none. He who has food, should share. The tax collector, who was baptized, should take no more than was owed. The soldier who had sought forgiveness should not accuse someone based on falseness and should be satisfied with what he earned.

Now the people were beginning to ask each other if John was actually the Christ. He, in no uncertain terms, told them no he was not. He told them he baptized with water, but there was one coming who baptize them with the Holy Spirit and fire. He would be like one who gathers the wheat and burns the chaff.

Now Herod, being married to his brother's wife, was also called out by the Baptist for the years of sins he had committed. John told Herod that he was sinning by marring Herodias and it was time for him, too, to repent for all the evil he had done. Herod (but, mainly Herodias) was angry and sought to put John in prison.

On one occasion, John was baptizing and a man came and stood in front of him. When He was baptized, the Heavens opened and John heard the voice of God saying, "This is my beloved Son in whom I am well pleased."

When He was about thirty years old, and after the baptism, Jesus began His ministry. Now I traced the lineage of the Christ from Joseph back to David and then back to Abraham. Then I went farther back to show he was a descendant of Seth, the son of Adam, but most importantly, He was the Son of God.

Part 5

JESUS IN THE WILDERNESS

Jesus, being led by the Holy Spirit, went into the wilderness to fast. For forty days He ate nothing. As a physician I would not recommend humans do this, but we all know Jesus was more than human. Now, after the forty days, Jesus was hungry. Satan appeared to Him and said that if He really was the Son of God, He could demand that a stone become a loaf of bread, and He could then eat.

The Son of God answered saying, "It is written, Man shall not live by bread alone, but by every word of God."

Then, the devil took Jesus to the top of the highest mountain, telling Him that everything Jesus could see would be His if He would fall down and worship him, the evil one.

Jesus replied quickly. "Get behind me Satan! For it is written, you shall worship the Lord your God and Him only you shall serve.

A third time, the Devil tempted Jesus. He took Him to the very top of the Temple and said to the Christ, If you are the Son of God, throw yourself down from here, For it is written—He shall give His Angels charge over you to keep you and, in their hands, they will bear you up, lest you dash your foot against a stone."

Then, Jesus answered, "It has been said that you shall not tempt the Lord your God." The devil then had to leave, and Jesus returned to Galilee filled with the power of the Spirit. He taught in the Temple and was actually glorified by the many.

Part 6

NOT ACCEPTED BY HIS OWN

He did return to Nazareth to preach and teach. On the Sabbath He went to the Synagogue, near the place He had been brought up. He wanted to read, and someone handed Him the Book of Isaiah. Jesus read, "The spirit of the Lord is upon me, because He has anointed me to preach the gospel to the poor. He has sent me to heal the brokenhearted, to proclaim liberty to the captives, and recovery of sight to the blind, to set at liberty those who are oppressed, to proclaim the acceptable year of the Lord."

To explain, I must tell of the importance of this scripture, found in Isaiah. When Jesus said that the Spirit of the Lord was upon Him and God had anointed Him, He, in no uncertain terms, was proclaiming that He was the Messiah. He has been sent to heal His people and set them free. Now He wasn't going to set His people free from Roman rule, He undoubtedly was expressing that His people would be free from their sins. This was the gospel, or good news! The acceptable year of the Lord, then, would be the Jubilee Year for the Jewish People.

When He had closed the book, and given it back to the scribe, all of the eyes in the synagogue were upon him. He emphasized to them, "Today the scripture is fulfilled in your hearing." In other words, with your own ears, you have heard the Messiah.

They looked at Jesus and then each other, thinking how marvelous the words were. To them, however, he was merely the son of Joseph. How could He claim these things? He was the son of a carpenter, and they had watched Him grow up in their midst. They were ready to throw Him out of

NOT ACCEPTED BY HIS OWN

Nazareth, take Him to the highest hill, and throw Him off of the cliff. Jesus said, "Assuredly, I say to you, no prophet is accepted in his own land."

Part 7

MIRACLES AND CHOOSING HIS DISCIPLES

Passing through them, He went to the town of Capernaum, in Galilee, to preach. The people there were in awe and filled with wonderment because of His words. He spoke with such authority.

Now, while He was in the Synagogue, a man possessed by an unclean spirit came up to Him shouting, "Let us alone! What have you to do with us Jesus of Nazareth, Did you come to destroy us? We know who you are—the Holy One of God."

Jesus simply said, "Be quiet and come out of Him." To the astonishment of the people, the demon came out and could no longer hurt the man.

Because the people knew that this Jesus spoke with authority and had the power over demons, the word of his preaching and miracles spread quickly. Jesus left the synagogue and went to the house of His friend, Simon. Now Simon's wife's mother was sick with a very high fever and could not get out of bed. Those in the house requested that Jesus help her. He stood over her and rebuffed the fever. Immediately the woman was well and she rose up and served them.

When the sun set, many people, who had come to seek the Lord, were healed of their afflictions and were freed from their demons, who shouted as they were cast out "You are the Son of God. You are the Christ."

In the morning, Jesus tried to go and find a deserted place. Crowds, nevertheless, followed Him. He told them that He must go and preach to other people in other cities, too. That was the reason He was sent to this

MIRACLES AND CHOOSING HIS DISCIPLES

world. He traveled to many synagogues in Galilee and preached the good news of forgiveness of sins to His people.

Jesus knew that He would need to choose men, who would be willing to learn from Him and then carry on His good news when His work on this earth was finished. He got onto a boat, that had come in from an unsuccessful night of fishing, and from a little distance out in the water, He continued teaching.

When He was finished, Jesus told the fisherman on board to cast their nets on the side of the boat, in deeper water. The explained to Him that they had been fishing all night and there were no fish to be caught during this trip. He told them to listen, so they reluctantly did as He said.

They threw their nets into the water, then began pulling them in. The boat nearly tipped over, because they had caught so many fish the nets nearly tore. One Fisherman, named Simon, knelt before Jesus and asked Him to leave, because He was a sinning man, and not worthy to have Jesus with him. Jesus said to Simon and his brothers James and John, "Do not be afraid. From now on you will catch men. "They, at that very moment, gave up everything they possessed and followed the Master.

In the first city they visited, the new disciples saw a leper come to Jesus. He fell at the Master's feet and said, "Lord, if you are willing, you can make me clean."

Jesus put out his hand and laid them on the man and quietly said, "I am willing. Be cleansed." At that very second, the leprosy left the man and Jesus asked the man not to say anything to anyone, but commanded him to go to the priests, and make an offering for his cleansing. ". . . As a testimony, just as Moses had commanded."

Humans will be humans, and words have a way of traveling quickly. Everyone heard what the Christ had done and masses came to listen and see Jesus and many sick came to be healed. Because of the throngs, Jesus would leave, go to a deserted place, and pray.

One day, while Jesus was teaching, from the house of a friend, the Pharisees and the teachers of the law happened to be close by watching and listening. Some people' brought to Jesus' a paralyzed man lying on his bed. They could not get close to house because of the size of the crowd. Instead, they took the paralytic to the roof, cut a hole, and lowered the man down in front of Jesus. When the Messiah saw their faith, He said to them, "Man, your sins are forgiven you."

GOSPEL III: THE GOSPEL ACCORDING TO LUKE

The scribes and the Pharisees started to mumble to each other that Jesus was a blasphemer. After all, only God could forgive sins. Jesus knew what they were thinking and asked them why they thought that way. He then asked them, "Which is easier to say, your sins are forgiven you, or rise up and walk?" He told them that if they wanted to know that the Son of Man had the power, He would show them both. "I say to you, take up your bed and go to your house." Instantly, and glorifying God, he rose and went to his house. All of the people present, were amazed and they, too, glorified God, even though they were a bit fearful.

Part 8

WHY BE WITH THE SINNERS?

THE NEXT TIME JESUS went out, He saw a tax collector, sitting at his tax office, and He said to this man named Levi, "Follow Me."

It may have been a bit shocking, because this man had always sinned, cheated people out of money, but Levi got up, left everything, and followed Jesus. Levi invited Jesus to his house, and presented Him with a great feast. Along with Jesus and His new disciples, were more tax collectors and other sinners. The Pharisees saw what Jesus was doing, and went to His Disciples asking why they would eat with tax collectors and sinners. It was just not done.

Jesus knew what they were asking, and called to them, "Those who are well, have no need of a physician, but those who are sick (do). I have not come to call the righteous, but the sinners to repentance."

The Pharisees asked Jesus why the disciples, then, didn't fast, like they did. Jesus answered them with the story of the bride groom and his friends. He described how friends do not fast while they are with the bridegroom. There would be time to fast after he was gone.

Jesus spoke another parable so that the Pharisees might understand. The Lord asserting that no intelligent person would sew new cloth to an old article of clothing because it would tear further and, of course, it wouldn't match. The same was true of an old wine skin. New wine put in a worn-out wine skin would only cause the loss of the new wine. It wouldn't make sense to do that. New wine must be put into new wine skins and that way both are protected. I think Jesus was saying, in a way, that His disciples were full of a Pentecostal gift or, if you will, the new wine.

Part 9

THE LORD OF THE SABBATH

It happened during one Sabbath, when Jesus and His disciples were going through a grain field. They were hungry and picked some stalks of grain, rubbed them through their hands, and ate. Well, the Pharisees saw this and immediately asked why the disciples of Jesus were breaking the Law given them by Moses. Jesus looked at them and said, "Have you not even read this, what David did when he was hungry and those who were with him: How he went into the house of God and ate the show-bread, and also gave some to those with him, which is not lawful for any, but the priests, to eat?" Jesus continued. "The Son of man is also Lord of the Sabbath."

On another Sabbath, Jesus went into the Synagogue and preached. There was a man present who suffered because of a right hand which was withered. The Pharisees were watching Jesus closely, so they might catch Him breaking their Laws. Jesus knew what they were doing. He knew everything, and reached out to the man and asked him to stand near Him. Then Jesus asked the Pharisees if it was lawful to do good or save a life on the Sabbath. He looked around and then told the man, "stretch out your hand." Jesus healed him. Now, the Pharisees were filled with rage. They started to plot ways to get rid of this Jesus.

Jesus went out to the mountain one night to pray to god. He spent the entire night in prayer, and when the morning came, He called all of His followers to Himself. He then picked twelve who would become His Apostles. There was Simon, who He named Peter, and Andrew, his brother. There, too, were James and John, Philip and Bartholomew, as well as Matthew and Thomas and James, the son of Alpheus, and Simon the Zealot along with

Judas the son of James. Finally, there was Judas Iscariot, who would become a traitor.

Jesus then came down from the mountain with His twelve and there was a multitude waiting to hear Him and see Him. There were many who wanted to be healed and released of demons. Jesus healed them and began teaching.

He lifted His eyes toward the twelve and began to speak, "Blessed are the poor, for yours is the Kingdom of God. Blessed are you who are hungry, now, for you shall be filled. Blessed are you who weep now, for you shall laugh. Blessed are you when men hate you and when they exclude you and revile you and cast out your name as evil, for the Son of Man's sake. Rejoice in that day and leap for joy! For indeed your reward is great in Heaven, for in like manner they did to the prophets."

Jesus continued to explain. "But woe to you who are rich, for you have received your consolation. Woe to you who are full, for you shall hunger. Woe to you who laugh now, for you shall morn and weep. Woe to you who all men speak well of, for so did their fathers to the false prophets." I think the most important part of the teaching was about to come.

Jesus then exclaimed, "But I say to you who hear: Love your enemies. Do good to those who hate you. Bless those who curse you, and pray for those who spitefully use you. To him who strikes you on one cheek, offer him the other. And from him who takes away your cloak, do not withhold your tunic. Give to anyone who asks of you and from him who takes away your goods, do not ask them back. And just as you want men to do to you, you also do to them, likewise."

Jesus furthered His speech by explaining that loving someone who loves you is easy. Even sinners do that. He argued that there is really no sense in just doing for those who do you good. Sinners are capable of that, too. Do for others, not expecting anything in return. Jesus told them to also be merciful and not to be judgmental of condemning. He insisted that they be forgiving as well as constantly giving. They were to be like this because what they give will be given to them in measure. Jesus emphasized that they not see the speck in their brothers eye when they have a log in theirs. They were not to be hypocrites. He insisted they bear good fruit, as it were and most important judge not least they be judged by God. They should build their life and works on a firm foundation like building on rock, because if a foundation is like sand, what they build will be destroyed.

Part 10

THE CENTURION'S SERVANT AND THE DEAD YOUNG MAN

After Jesus was finished teaching, He went to Capernaum. On the way a group of Jewish elders came to Him. They told Him they had been sent by a centurion who had a servant who was sick and ready to die. This Gentile Centurion loved God's people and had heard about the miracles Jesus had been doing. Jesus decided to go to the Centurion. When he was close, The centurion sent servants out to meet Jesus and tell Him not to come to his house. He had said that he was not worthy to have the Christ enter his home. He didn't even think he was worthy enough to come to Jesus. He did however, send a message. He told another servant to say, "Lord . . . say the word and my servant will be healed. For I also am a man placed under authority, having soldiers under me. And I say to one, go and he goes; and to another, come, and he comes; and to my servant do this, and he does it."

Jesus was astounded by this man and turned to the people following. "I say to you, I have not found such great faith, not even in Israel."

Right there and right then Jesus healed the servant from a distance because of the respect he had for this Centurion.

The next day, Jesus came near the City named Nain. As He was about to enter, a group came out with a widowed mother, carrying the body of her only son. When the Christ saw her, He was filled with compassion. He went to her and told her not to weep. Then He went up to the open coffin and touched the young son. He said, "Young man, I say to you, Rise."

THE CENTURION'S SERVANT AND THE DEAD YOUNG MAN

Those carrying the coffin could not move as they watched the young man sit up and speak. Jesus took him to his mother and all glorified God saying that a great prophet had been given to the people of Israel.

After this, John the Baptist sent his disciples to Jesus to ask if Jesus was the Messiah, or if they should wait for another. The disciples of John watched as Jesus performed miracles, and Jesus told them to go and tell John the things they had seen and heard. He had cured the lepers, and made the lame walk and the blind see and the deaf hear. He had raised the dead, and was teaching to bring hope to the poor. The messengers of John departed. Jesus turned to the crowd and said to them that He was, indeed, the one that had been written about by the prophets. He also told them that there was no greater prophet then John and when the people heard this, they justified God, having been baptized by John, but the Pharisees and the lawyers had rejected the will of God by not being baptized. The Pharisees, scribes, and law givers of this generation, were like children playing their music. They got mad at John because he would not dance to their song, and they were out to get Jesus because he would not weep for their song, as it were.

Part 11

THE WOMAN WHO WASHED THE FEET OF JESUS

One of the Pharisees invited Jesus to supper. When The Lord arrived, He sat down to eat. There was this certain woman who heard where Jesus was, and went into the house of the Pharisee. She knelt at the feet of Jesus weeping because she was indeed a sinner. She used her own tears to wash His feet and dried them with her hair. She then anointed His feet with oil and kissed them.

The Pharisee thought that if Jesus were a real prophet, He would know what kind of woman this really was and would not allow her to touch Him. Now Jesus knew his thoughts and spoke. "Simon, I have something to say to you." After Simon acknowledge Jesus, the Lord continued. "There was a certain creditor who had two debtors. One owed five hundred denarii (a roman silver coin) and another fifty. When the two had nothing with which to repay, he freely forgave them both. Tell me. Which one of them will love him more?" Simon said that it was probably the one whom he forgave more. And Jesus told him he had rightly judged.

Jesus turned to the weeping woman and said to Simon, "Do you see this woman? I entered your house and you gave me no water for my feet, but she has washed my feet with her tears and wiped them with the hair of her head. You gave me no kiss (a greeting kiss), but this woman has not ceased to kiss my feet since the time I came in. You did not anoint my head with oil, but this woman anointed my feet with fragrant oil. Therefore, I say to you, her sins, which are many, are forgiven, for she loved much. But to whom

THE WOMAN WHO WASHED THE FEET OF JESUS

little is forgiven, the same loves little." Jesus turned to the woman and told her that her sins had been forgiven and she should go in peace. Those who observed this wondered who this Jesus was, for He even forgave sins.

Part 12

THE PARABLE OF THE SEEDS

THE MESSIAH WENT TO all villages and cities, teaching and conducting miracles for men and women. He healed the sick and drove out demons. On woman, Mary Magdalene had seven demons and Jesus saved her. Others like Joanna the wife of Chuza, who was Herod's steward, and Susanna, along with many others were healed of their infirmities.

When many people followed Him to hear His message, Jesus spoke in parables. One of them dealt with a Sower who was planting. As he threw the seeds, some fell by the wayside. Others fell on rocks, some more fell in the thorns. There were some, however, that fell on fertile soil. Now the ones that fell by the wayside, were eaten by the birds. The ones on the rocks sprouted, but dried up because of the hot sun. Those that fell among the thorns grew, but were choked out. The seeds that fell on fertile soil sprang up and provided a large yield.

When Jesus was finished speaking these things, He said, "He who has ears to hear, let him hear."

The disciples, finally being alone with Jesus, asked Him the meaning of the parable. He told the twelve, to them the mysteries of the Kingdom of God had been given and they could understand what these people did not. Therefore, He had to teach the people using parables. Jesus explained the parable like this: The seed was the word of God. The seed that fell by the wayside are people who hear the word, but the devil comes and takes it away from their hearts. The ones that fell on the rocks, are people who hear the word and are filled with joy. Soon, though, temptation dries up their belief. The seeds in the thorns are people who hear, but go out into the

THE PARABLE OF THE SEEDS

world and are choked off by the riches, cares, and pleasures of life. These bear no fruit. The ones that fall on fertile soil hear God's word, keep His word, and with patience, bear fruit.

"No one who has a lit lamp," Jesus began, "covers it with a vessel or puts it under a bed, but sets it on the light-stand that those who enter may see the light." Jesus completed teaching His disciples by telling them heed this lesson so that they would receive more and more of His word.

Now, the mother and brothers of Jesus showed up and asked to see Jesus, Jesus said that his mother and brothers where the people who heard the word of God and kept the word.

Part 13

THE DEMON LEGION AND THE SWINE

One day, Jesus and His disciples got into a boat to cross the sea. As they were traveling, Jesus fell asleep and a great windstorm came up. The boat was tossed and was filling with water, and the twelve were afraid of drowning. They woke up Jesus and told Him they were afraid. Jesus said, "Where is your faith?"

He then rebuked the wind and the sea became calm. The disciples said, "Who can this be. For He commands the winds and the waters, and they obey." Then they arrived in the land of the Gadarenes.

When they came to the shore, a man ran up to them who had been possessed by demons for many years. He didn't wear clothes and he didn't live in a house, but chose to live among the tombs. He came up to Jesus and fell at his feet. He began shouting, "What have I to do with you Jesus, the Son of the most high God? I beg you do not torment me."

Jesus commanded the demon to tell Him his Name and he answered that He was Legion, for there were many demons who had possessed this man. They then begged Jesus not to cast them out into the abyss. So, Jesus, seeing a herd of swine cast Legion into them. They ran down a hill, into the sea, and drowned.

The herders, who keep the swine fed, saw this and ran through the countryside and to the city telling the people what had happened. They all came to the site and found the man they had known sitting in front of Jesus, fully clothed and in his right mind. The people of Gadarene were so afraid, they asked Jesus to leave and take His disciples with Him; they wanted nothing to do with Jesus. The man, who had been possessed wanted

THE DEMON LEGION AND THE SWINE

to follow Jesus, but he was told to go home and tell anyone who would listen what God had done for him.

Part 14

JAIRUS AND HIS DAUGHTER

When the group had arrived back across the sea, a multitude was waiting for Jesus and the twelve. One of the rulers of the Synagogue, named Jairus, was there and he fell at the feet of Jesus. He begged the Lord to come to his home, because his daughter was very sick. Jesus walked with him, and as He did, a woman who had had a bleeding problem for twelve years touched the hem of his cloak. She had spent every dime she had on physicians and no one had been able to help. I have to say though, if I may interject, in my day medical attention was not an exact science.

Anyway, Jesus felt power leave him when she touched Him, and He asked His disciples, "Who touched me? Somebody touched me for I perceived power going out of me."

They tried to point out that He was in a large crowd and they would not be able to tell. Jesus looked around and saw the woman. She came to him with a bit of fear and explained to Jesus what she had done and why.

And Jesus said, "Daughter, be of good cheer; your faith has made you well. Go in peace." and then Jesus continued to the house of Jairus. As they walked, a servant of the house came to them and told them the girl had died. There was no longer a need to bother the Teacher.

When Jesus heard this, He turned to Jairus and asserted that his daughter wasn't dead. He said, "Do not be afraid; only believe and she will be made well."

When they come to the house, Jesus let none of the crowd go into the girl. He took Peter and James, John and Jairus, and the girl's mother only. The servants and other family members who were kept outside, were

JAIRUS AND HIS DAUGHTER

weeping. Jesus exclaimed to them that the girl was merely sleeping, and they all scoffed at Him, knowing the girl was no longer alive.

Jesus went to the daughter of Jairus and spoke with authority, "Little girl, arise."

Immediately the spirit reentered the girl and she sat up. Jesus told them to feed her and told the parents not to say anything about what had happened.

To clarify a bit, Jesus understood that the word would get around, After all, He had touched a dead girl and now she was alive. Even so, Jesus told the parents not to say anything. The Messiah knew His work was not yet ready to be fully revealed. He did not want to face the anger and jealousy of the Pharisees and scribes at this time, for His work had not been completed. Besides, everyone knows Jesus did nothing for applause and acceptance. He knew the people and He could not allow them to make Him King in this world: who would simply be commanding the disciples, feeding the multitude, and telling them He was who they thought He was.

Jesus then called the twelve disciples to Himself. He gave them the power to heal and to cast out demons. He outlined for them what they were to do and how they were to do it. He told them they were to take nothing with them, not bread, nor money nor a staff—not even a change of clothes. He added that they were to go into a house, where they were invited, and stay there while they taught the Word of God to the people. If they, for example, found themselves in a place where they were not wanted, they were to leave and shake the dust from that place off of their feet as a declaration against them. He, then, sent them two by two into the towns where they preached the Gospel and healed the sick.

Well, Herod had heard about this Jesus and all of the things He had said and done. Some had declared that Jesus was really John the Baptist. Some claimed He was Elijah, while others simply stated Jesus was another old prophet risen from the grave. Herod, however, knew it was not John the Baptist, because he had beheaded the Prophet. He was perplexed and questioned who this man of miracles was, as I am sure many did.

When the disciples returned from their journey, they reported all that they had accomplished. Jesus met with them, near the city of Bethsaida, where they could speak without crowds being around.

This, however didn't last long, for a multitude heard where Jesus and the twelve were and came to hear Him. He described the Kingdom of Heaven to them and healed the sick among them. It was getting late and the

GOSPEL III: THE GOSPEL ACCORDING TO LUKE

disciples told Jesus there was no food to feed the thousands that had come. Jesus told them to give the people food. But they explained they only had five loaves and two fish; it was hardly enough for five thousand. The Christ explained to them how the people were to be put in groups of fifty. He took the bread and fish, and looking toward Heaven, He blessed the food. He handed it to the disciples and they, in turn, handed it to the people. The five thousand were fed and there were twelve baskets left over when they were through.

After sending the people away Jesus met with the twelve. He asked them, "Who do the crowds say that I am?"

They answered Him saying that the people thought He was John the Baptist or Elijah. Others proclaimed that Jesus was a prophet of old, risen again.

The Master spoke to them and asked, "But, who do you say that I am?"

Peter answered quickly, "You are the Christ of God!" Now I know it is popular to call God's son—Jesus Christ. Christ, however is not His last name. It actually comes from the Greek word christos which translates to The anointed one of God. So, Jesus really is The Christ, The Messiah, The one and only anointed Son of God.

Jesus told His disciples not to tell this to anyone, until the proper time. He said, "The Son of Man must suffer many things and be rejected and be killed. On the third day, though, He would rise from the dead." Jesus added, "If anyone desires to come after me, let him deny himself and take up his cross and follow me. For whoever desires to save his life will lose it. And, whoever loses his life for my sake, will save it. For what does it profit a man if he gains the whole world, but loses his soul."

Part 15

THE TRANSFIGURATION, THE DEMON, AND THE CHILD

Jesus then took Peter, James, and John to the mountain. There they saw Jesus transform. The appearance of his face changed, and His garment was pure white and Shining. The three disciples saw The Christ talking with two others, In fact, It was Moses and Elijah. They were speaking about what Jesus was about to go through and the glory that was His. Peter shouted that the disciples should build three tabernacles in honor of what they had witnessed: one for Moses, one for Elijah, and one for Jesus.

After he said this, a cloud came over them and they heard the voice of God say, "This is my beloved Son. Hear Him!"

When the voice ceased, Jesus was once again alone with the three disciples. They descended the mountain and found the others surrounded by yet another crowd. A man came to Jesus and implored Him to heal his only son who had been possessed by an evil spirit. He was constantly convulsing and foaming at the mouth. He had also, on many occasions, tried to end his own life.

Jesus gently rebuked his disciples for not being able to heal this man. He knew that this demon was so strong that it required constant prayer and fasting to remove it. Jesus walked toward the man and as He did the possessed son fell to the ground convulsing again. Jesus cast out the evil spirit, healed the son, an gave him back to his father.

The crowd was amazed at the power of Jesus, but He turned to the disciples to remind them that He was about to be betrayed into the hands

GOSPEL III: THE GOSPEL ACCORDING TO LUKE

of man. They, however, did not understand His words at that time. and were afraid to ask.

When they arrived at the home of a friend, the twelve started arguing over who would be the greatest among them. Jesus sitting at a table, picked up a child who was there, and put the child on his lap. The Master warned His disciples, saying, "Whoever receives this little child in my name, receives me and whoever receives me receives Him who sent me. For he who is least among you will be great."

Part 16

THE MANY FOLLOWERS AND MY NEIGHBOR

JOHN THEN INFORMED JESUS that while they were out preaching, they had seen a man cast out demons in the name of the Christ. John added that they banned this man from doing that because he was not one who followed Jesus every day.

The Messiah looked at them and said, "Do not forbid him, for he who is not against us is on our side."

Jesus knew it was getting to the time He would have to go and fulfill all the things which He had come to the world to do. He continued in the direction of Jerusalem, allowing nothing to sidetrack Him. His disciples knew their Master had said He was about to die, so the asked Jesus why He did not command fire from Heaven to destroy those who were going to kill Him, like Elijah did.

Jesus responded. "You do not know what manner of spirit you are of. For the Son of Man did not come to destroy men's lives, but to save them."

Many more than the twelve disciples were following Jesus. As a matter of fact, there were seventy. He appointed them to go into every city and town ahead of Him sending them two by two, just as He had the twelve.

As He did, He commented, "The harvest truly is great, but the laborers are few; therefore pray the Lord of the harvest to send out laborers into the harvest. Go your way; behold I sent you out as lambs among wolves."

He explained how they were to travel, just as He had to the twelve before. He told them to heal the sick there, and spread the word that the

GOSPEL III: THE GOSPEL ACCORDING TO LUKE

Kingdom of God was at hand. He informed them, too, on what to do if they were accepted or if they were rejected. The seventy did as Jesus commanded and He prayed and waited until they came back to Him.

When the seventy returned, they told Jesus how even demons had been cast out in His name. He rejoiced with them saying, "Behold I give you the authority to trample on serpents and scorpions, and over all the power of the enemy, and nothing by any means will hurt you. Nevertheless, do not rejoice in this, that the spirits are subject to you, but rather rejoice because your names are written in Heaven."

Jesus prayed to His father thanking Him for all He had done so far. He praised His father saying how all things had been delivered to Him by His father. Jesus turned to His disciples and expressed how blessed they had been to see what was happening; even the prophets would have wanted to see and hear what they had seen and heard.

When The Lord had finished talking to His disciples, a certain lawyer questioned Jesus, testing Him. He asked, "Teacher, what shall I do to inherit eternal life?"

Jesus answered by asked a question, "What is Written in the Law? What is your reading of it."

The lawyer answered, "You shall love the lord your God with all your heart, with all your soul, with all your strength, and with all your mind, and your neighbor as yourself."

Jesus, in turn said, "You have answered rightly; Do this and you shall live."

The lawyer, who wanted to absolve himself, asked The Christ, "Teacher, who do you say is my neighbor"

Jesus began the story of the Good Samaritan. He explained how a man was traveling from Jerusalem to Jericho He was attacked by thieves who had taken his clothes, beaten him, and left him for dead. A priest passed him first, and did not help, not wanting to get involved. A Levite (a Jew from the tribe of Levi) also passed. Then a Samaritan, one of the most hated people on earth at the time, walked by and saw the injured man. He felt compassion and bandaged his wounds, brought him to an inn to help him, and paid for his room and board. Jesus asked the lawyer which one of the three was really the neighbor? When the Lawyer answered saying it was the one who showed mercy, Jesus told him to go and do likewise.

Part 17

THE MEANING OF PRAYER

JESUS WAS PRAYING ON a certain day, and one of the disciple of our Lord asked Him to teach them to Pray as John the Baptist had taught His disciples.

Jesus said to them, "Our Father in Heaven hallowed be your name. Your Kingdom come. Your will be done, on earth as it is in Heaven. Give us this day Your daily bread, and forgive us our sins, for we also forgive everyone who is indebted to us. And lead us not into temptation, but deliver us from the evil one."

Now I hear some have added "For thine is the Kingdom and the Power and the Glory forever, Amen." This is fine, as far as I am concerned, because even though some manuscripts (especially some Greek and Latin texts) have not said this, it was used by the Jewish people and many Christians. Also almost the same words are used in 1 Chronicles 29:11, so go ahead and use it.

Now Jesus didn't stop with just telling them words they could speak. As He often did, He added a lesson. He continued saying that if one of them would go to a friend late at night and asks for some food, because unexpected visitors came and there wasn't enough, he might say go away. It's so late and everyone is asleep. If you continue asking and are persistent, he will eventually give you what you need.

Jesus then said, "So I say to you, ask and it will be given to you; seek and you will find; knock and it will be opened to you. For everyone who asks receives, and he who seeks finds, and to him who knocks it will be opened. If a son asks for bread from any father among you, will he give him a stone? Or if he asks him for a fish, will he give him a serpent instead of a fish? Or if he asks for an egg, will he offer him a scorpion? If you, then, being evil, know how to give good gifts to your children, how much more will your Heavenly Father give the Holy Spirit to those who ask Him!"

Part 18

SOME REJECT, SOME WANT PROOF, AND SOME BELIEVE

Jesus was casting out a demon from a mute. As soon as it was out of him, the mute spoke. Now the Jewish Leaders began saying that this was the work of Beelzebub. And others, trying to trip Him up, asked for more signs from Heaven.

Knowing what they were up to, Jesus answered saying, "Every Kingdom divided against itself is brought to desolation, and a house divided against a house falls. If Satan is divided against himself, how will his kingdom stand . . . If I cast out demons by Beelzebub, by whom do your sons cast them out? Therefore, they will be your judges. But if I cast out demons with the finger of God, the Kingdom of God has come upon you."

I wrote about this demon in one short verse, and then turned to what the people wanted to believe. Other friends of mine wrote many verses about what happened before, during, and after Jesus cast out this demon. First, I was interested in the reaction of different people, because, just as it is today it was back then. There were some people who rejected Jesus, some who wanted proof, and then others who by faith accepted.

Second, Jesus asked the Pharisees and scribes how their sons were able to cast out demons. What power did they use? Maybe, Jesus was saying that what He did was the same as what the Jewish exorcists did. If they were saying Jesus was casting out demons by Satan's power, then they, too, were to blame for using the power of Satan. Or, maybe, Jesus was talking about his own disciples (your sons) who also cast out demons. Jesus was the one

GOSPEL III: THE GOSPEL ACCORDING TO LUKE

who had given them power in the first place, and they would also be judging those non-believers who had not accepted the Christ. Jesus finally said that He wasn't alone in His work and He had proved that it was because of the power of God, not Satan. It was He who would bring salvation by taking the sins of man onto Himself. His blood would be the sacrifice. Jesus was in fact saying that He had the power and authority that was promised by God to save His people.

Jesus wasn't finished. He told the people that this was an evil generation. Naturally, he was standing up to the scribes and Pharisees. The battle between Jesus and the Jewish Leaders who rejected Him as the Messiah, had begun. He further explained that these people were seeking signs. None would be given to them except the sign of Jonah, the profit. It was Jonah that was the sign for the people of Nineveh.

This to me is obvious. Jonah symbolized a man who was dead for three days. Those who lived in Nineveh saw Jonah come to shore alive, even though he had been in the belly of a great fish for three day and nights. The Ninevites repented their sins because of Jonah. Jesus, too would be dead for three days and He, too, would come back to life. This was the only sign for the Jewish Leaders, and they did not believe or repent, even though the Messiah was right in front of them.

Part 19

DINING WITH THE PHARISEE

ONE OF THE PHARISEES asked Jesus to come to his house for dinner. Jesus went and sat down to eat. The Pharisee was shocked that did not wash His hands before the supper.

Jesus told him, "Now you Pharisees make the outside of your cup and dish clean, but your inner part is full of greed and wickedness. Foolish ones, did not He who made the outside make the inside, also?"

Jesus continued with condemnation for the Pharisees. If they were to repentant, than they would be clean, but the Pharisees were a group who had forgotten to practice justice and to love God. They preferred the best seats at the feasts and wonderful greetings at the marketplace. Jesus called the scribes and the Pharisees all hypocrites. He followed this by condemning the Lawyers, too, because they burdened people and never helped them.

They built the tombs for the profits and gave them praise, but it was their ancestors who killed the profits. It was the lawyers who had taken away the key of knowledge and tried to keep others from that knowledge. Jesus left the house and all of the Pharisees began to cross examine Him. They lashed out at Him trying to find something, anything, that they could use to condemn Him.

Jesus found Himself once again in the midst of a great crowd. Before He spoke to them, He said to His disciples, "Beware the leaven of the Pharisees which is hypocrisy." He was, indeed, conveying to them the importance of not getting caught up in all this attention Jesus was receiving. He tried to express that being popular can make one want more popularity.

GOSPEL III: THE GOSPEL ACCORDING TO LUKE

This would lead to self-importance and not putting God first. This was the way the Pharisees had become.

Jesus continued to define how the disciples and God's children should act. First of all, they should be truthful. No one was to cover up anything, for it would end up coming to the light. As Shakespeare once wrote: The truth will out. Whatever is said in darkness will eventually reach the light. God will always know!

The second thought has to do with people who hurt others. Jesus told them not to fear the one who could hurt them and kill them. There was nothing more that could be done to them after their time in this world was complete. He informed them that they must, however, fear the one that had the power to cast them into Hell. Because of the importance of this, Jesus stressed again that people should surely fear this one.

The Master also told them that God would not forget them. After all, even the sparrow was not forgotten by God. Jesus added that every hair on the believer's head was counted and mankind was more important to God than any sparrow. Therefore, The Christ said to His twelve they should not even worry what must be said by them, even if they were being questioned by any worldly authority. For the Holy Spirit would teach them what to say at that very time. There was one man listening, in the crowd, who asked Jesus this, "Teacher, tell my brother to divide the inheritance with me."

Jesus decided a parable should be used at this point. He eluded to the rich man who had a successful year and an extremely large crop. His barn was not big enough to hold it all, and He wondered what He was to do. He decided to tear down the old and build a bigger barn in which to put his crop and everything else he owned. He was storing up everything he had and cared for no one but Himself. He felt no obligation for his fellow man. He was merely concerned with the treasures of this world and, according to the Messiah, He was dead wrong.

The Lord told His disciples not to be concerned with the things of this world. They didn't need to worry about clothes, or food, or what they put in their body. Eternal Life was more important than all of these things.

Jesus commented to them on what was important. He said, "Consider the ravens, for they neither sow or reap . . . and God feeds them. Of how much more value are you than the birds? And which of you by worrying, add one cubit to your stature? . . . Consider the lilies, how they grow. They neither toil nor spin, and yet I say to you, even Solomon in all his glory was not arrayed like one of these."

DINING WITH THE PHARISEE

Jesus then expressed how God would clothe them and feed them and they need not worry. What they should be doing was seeking the Kingdom of God, and all of these other things would be given to them. Jesus explained how the twelve, as well as all followers of the Messiah, should be observing and should constantly be aware, waiting for the return of the master in the last days. Jesus would die, be buried, and rise again, soon to return to His Father in Heaven. He would, however, return one day like a thief in the night and call all of His children to Him.

The Master continued teaching, healing those with infirmities, and delivering others from the evil spirits all while heading, eventually, toward Jerusalem. The scribes and Pharisees would argue and denounce Him. They followed Him to find something which they could use to get rid of Him permanently.

On one Sabbath, Jesus healed a woman who had been suffering for eighteen years. The Pharisees were indignant and full of rage. They condemned Jesus for healing on the Sabbath, because God told man there were only six days in which to work, but the Sabbath was to be kept Holy.

Jesus answered, "Hypocrite! Does not each one of you on the Sabbath loose his ox or donkey from the stall and lead it away to water it. So ought not this woman, being the daughter of Abraham, whom Satan had bound—think of it—for eighteen years be loosed from this bond on the Sabbath?"

When He had finished, the Pharisees had been put to shame and the crowd rejoiced. Jesus continued teaching the multitude. He showed them that many people would try to get to heaven by saying they knew the Lord and ate and drank with Him, listening to Him teach. Then they would be told by the Savior, they were unknown to Him because they were filled with sin and had not repented, asking the Christ to save them. Jesus warned them that there would be, in that time, "a weeping and gnashing of teeth."

On a certain day, some of the Pharisees told Jesus that He should leave, and never come back, because Herod wanted Him dead. Jesus, called Herod a fox. This may have been because he was cunning in the way he lived. He was evil and sinful, just as the Pharisees were. I am sure Jesus knew the Pharisees had made up this crafty story to get rid of Him. So Jesus said they should tell Herod He was not going anywhere, for it wasn't right for a profit to die outside of Jerusalem.

Then Jesus cried out, "O Jerusalem, Jerusalem, which kills the prophets, and stones those who are sent to her; how often I wanted to gather your children together, as a hen gathers her brood under her wings, but you were not willing!"

Part 20

ANOTHER SUPPER WITH PHARISEES

JESUS WENT, ON ANOTHER occasion, to have supper with one of the leaders of the Pharisees. The Rulers of the Synagogue were watching every move Jesus made. While He was there, a man came to Jesus who was suffering from dropsy. Now it is called edema: a painful illness that causes severe swelling.

Jesus asked the Pharisees and the Lawyers if it would be lawful to heal this man on the Sabbath. They, consequently, would not answer, so Jesus healed the man. He then said to them, "Which of you, having a donkey or an ox that has fallen into a pit, will not immediately pull him out on the Sabbath?"

The Leaders could not answer, so Jesus told the following parable. He asserted a man would not go to a wedding and sit in one of the best seats at the table. Someone more noble or worthy may have been invited and should have those seats. Instead, he should pick a lowly seat, and if the host sees him and invites him to sit nearer the him, he will receive glory from all the guests. In other words, pride may bring a fall, but humbleness is what really brings honor. Jesus suggested that a person inviting friends to supper, have invited those who can pay him back. Instead, have a supper for those who cannot pay him back. Invite the poor, those who can't see, and those who can't walk and, Jesus added, "You will be rewarded at the resurrection of the just."

The Master then began another parable. It was about a man who had invited many guests to his supper. At the time of the supper, one by one, the invited made excuses as to why they could not come. The host then told his servants to go into the streets and invite anyone thy saw, whether they were

ANOTHER SUPPER WITH PHARISEES

known or not. If there was still room find more people in the countryside. But, be assured, no one originally invited, who had rejected, would ever have supper with him again.

What did Jesus mean? Well, God sent His Only Son to save His people, the Jews. Many were rejecting the Christ, so Jesus said He would invite the gentiles. Heaven was now available to anyone, rich or poor sick or well, Jewish or non-Jewish—anyone who accepted the invitation from the Messiah.

Jesus told all of us to "count the cost" of accepting Him as the Lord and Savior and becoming a disciple. A disciple must truly deny himself and give up the old sinful ways and follow Christ. It will not be an easy task, but must be done to be the salt of the earth, as it were, to season everyone with the flavor of Christ Jesus.

Part 21

TAX COLLECTORS, SINNERS, AND THE PRODIGAL

JESUS ATE SUPPER WITH tax collectors and sinners, and the Pharisees criticized Him and denounced Him. Again, Jesus used a parable to teach these men who hated Him. He began, "What man of you, having a hundred sheep, if he loses one of them, does not leave the ninety-nine in the wilderness, and go after the one which is lost until he finds it? And when he has found it, he lays it on his shoulders, rejoicing. And when he comes home, he calls together his friends and neighbors, saying to them, Rejoice with me, for I have found my sheep which was lost! I say to you that likewise there will be more joy in heaven over one sinner who repents than over ninety-nine just persons who need no repentance."

The Teacher then described a woman who had ten coins and lost one. She practically tore the house apart, looking under everything and in every corner. When she found it, she was full of joy. Jesus ended this one with, "Likewise, I say to you, there is joy in the presence of the angels of God over one sinner who repents."

Finally. Jesus told them about a certain man who had two sons. The one son went to his father and demanded his share of the inheritance. He took his share and left for a far place. There he spent his inheritance with prodigal living. Now, anyone who behaved in a prodigal way would spend all of his or her money irresponsibly without thinking about what would happen when he or she had no more money. Soon this son's money was gone, and a famine came to the country. He had to get a job, but the only

TAX COLLECTORS, SINNERS, AND THE PRODIGAL

one he could find was feeding pigs. He was always hungry, but no one would give him food, so he was forced to eat what the pigs had.

He finally came to his senses and decided to go and ask his father to forgive him. He told his father that he had sinner against him and heaven, itself. He admitted he no longer was worthy of being called son, but he pleaded to at least be allowed to work with the other servants.

Now the father greeted his son, told the servants to bring him the best robe available and put it on him. He put a ring on His son's hand and sandals on his feet. He told one servant to kill the fatted calf, for they were going to celebrate the return of his son by having a feast.

Now the son who had stayed with his father, obeying him faithfully, was angry at all the fuss being made over his brother. He told his father how he felt and complained that he had never gotten as much as a goat to use for a feast. The oldest son's father said that he loved him and, because of his loyalty, everything that the father had was his. He further explained to the oldest why he was rejoicing, "for your brother was dead and is now alive again. He was lost, but now was found."

Part 22

THE UNJUST STEWARD

Jesus went to his disciples, telling them the parable of the unjust steward. The Teacher explained to them that what they had actually belonged to God. They were mere stewards of what had been given them. Now a Steward, in my time, was a man who was in control of his masters goods and dealings.

The teacher began to explain that once, years ago, there was a rich man who had a steward. Now, this steward was accused of mishandling his masters goods and the master call him on it. The steward feared that he was about to be fired and knew he could not get another job. Not wanting to have to become a beggar, this man called on the debtors of his masters, in hopes they might gain acceptance from them.

He asked one how much he had owed his Master. The debtor said that he owed one hundred measures of oil. The steward asserted that the debtor should write down that he only owed fifty measures. To another who owed one hundred measures of wheat, the steward told him to change it to eighty. The master, when he heard what he steward had done, commended him on his shrewdness.

The Lord was not telling his disciples the steward was honest and good, but that he was more shrewd than the master had been. He was not justifying his dishonesty, but merely stating he was good at being cunning and calculating just as unbelievers of this world were. Jesus clarified this by stating the true believer must lay up there treasure in heaven, and expect their portion from there. They must not expect to gain all the treasures of the world in whatever manner they can and gain treasures in heaven, too.

THE UNJUST STEWARD

The Messiah then indicated, "No servant can serve two masters. For either he will hate the one and love the other, or else he will be loyal to the one and despise the other. You Cannot serve both God and Mammon."

Part 23

THE FULFILLED LAW

The Pharisees, who loved money, had been listening and began to criticize and mock the Christ. Jesus answered them, "You are those who justify yourselves before men, but God knows your heart." He then revealed that what is good for earthly non-believers and men who do not live for God and His Son, is an abomination to the Father in Heaven.

Until the time of John the Baptist, the only law given to the Jewish nation was the law of Moses and the prophets. The scribes and Pharisees believed they were in charge and they were the leaders of the Law and the Jews. It didn't hurt that they also profited by being in their positions.

However, since Jesus was now among them, the gospel of the Kingdom was being preached. The Christ now had the authority and not the Pharisees. Jesus was persuading many that the Kingdom of Heaven was through Him and no longer through the leaders and priests of the Synagogue. The Christ, the Messiah, had come and the law had indeed been fulfilled.

To fully explain to the Pharisees what the problem was, Jesus told them the parable of the Rich man, and the beggar, Lazarus. For there was a rich man who had everything. He ate well and was clothed in royal attire. At his gate, however, was a beggar named Lazarus. He was covered in sores and ate the crumbs thrown out by the rich man. While he waited for a crumb now and then, the dogs would lick his sores.

The two eventually died and Lazarus went to Heaven and the rich man went to Hades. He was in so much torment, that he begged God to send Lazarus to cool him a little with some water. God told him there was no passage between the two places. He then asked the Heavenly Father to send

THE FULFILLED LAW

Lazarus to his five brothers warning them to repent, so they would not suffer his fate. God answered that they had the Law of Moses and the prophets, to which the rich man replied, Yes, but they would more likely believe someone who had come back from the dead. God then told him that truly if they didn't believe the Laws of Moses, they wouldn't believe in one who had risen from the dead. Once again Jesus was telling the Pharisees they were gathering their treasures on earth and not in Heaven and they were refusing to believe that Jesus was the Son of God.

Part 24

FORGIVENESS, FAITHFULNESS, HUMBLENESS

WHILE WAITING FOR THE return of God's Kingdom Jesus began teaching His disciples about forgiveness. He told them that if their brother sinned against them, they should rebuke him. If he repents, they should forgive him. If he sins against you even seven times a day, but asks for forgiveness, then do so.

The Lords followers then asked Jesus to increase their faith. He explained by saying, "If you have faith of a mustard seed, you can say to this mulberry tree be pulled up by the roots and be planted in the sea, and it will obey you."

Jesus also taught them to be humble. He indicated that the working man must still follow the commandment of His master, even if he thinks he has done enough. He must humble himself to the master so that he can say at the end, "We have done what was our duty to do."

Jesus and the twelve then went toward Jerusalem. They passed through the area between Samaria and Galilee and there they met ten lepers who asked Jesus to have mercy on them. He healed them and told them to go and show themselves to the priests. After they did as they were commanded, only one returned. He happened to be the only Samaritan, and when he did return, he glorified and praised God, thanking Jesus for what He had done.

Jesus asked where the other nine were, but He knew the only one to return with praise, was this foreigner from Samaria. The Master said to him, "Arise, go your way. Your faith has made you well."

FORGIVENESS, FAITHFULNESS, HUMBLENESS

The event showed His disciples that ten men had been cleansed on the outside, but only one was cleansed inside and out. He was the one who had humbled himself before the Lord. Jesus, through His actions, underlined the meaning to His disciples of the fruits of being humble.

The Pharisees came to Jesus and asked Him when the Kingdom of God would come. The Christ told them, "The Kingdom of God does not come with observation: nor will they say, see here or see there! For indeed the Kingdom of God is within you."

I think what He meant here was that the Kingdom of God was a spiritual Kingdom and not a worldly one. It's not a Kingdom found here or there, but one that will be everywhere at one time. His Kingdom's return will be for everyone, Jews and Gentiles, just as a lightning strike shines where it is as well as all the other part of the sky.

Jesus then communicated this fearful fact to His disciples: First, though, this Son of Man ". . . must suffer many things and be rejected by this generation." He had to go through pain and suffering and even death before the days of the return of God's Kingdom.

He did illustrate to them that in the day of His coming back, the world would be as it was in the days of Noah and the days of Lot. Sin would be rampant. Evilness will reign. When Jesus returned along with the Kingdom of God, the rapture would occur. When He does return, there will be no time to gather anything. Two men would be together and the one who believed in Jesus and had accepted Him into his heart, would disappear. Two women may be making bread together and one would be taken up because she was a Christian, while the other remained. Judgment will have come and will have come swiftly.

Part 25

PRAYER FAITH AND ETERNAL LIFE

JESUS SPOKE ANOTHER PARABLE to them stating that men should pray and not lose heart. He alluded to a certain Judge, who didn't fear God and had no respect for man. On one occasion, a woman came before him and wanted justice for she had an opponent who had wronged her. He did not give her justice, but the woman continued to come before him. Finally, he said that he was tired of seeing her all the time, so, because of her persistence he gave her what she had asked.

Then Jesus expressed how God wanted His children to continue to ask Him for what they needed. They were to pray without ceasing. They should never stop, for God would give them justice.

Another story Jesus used was designed for those who thought they were better than anyone else. Obviously, He was speaking of the Pharisees and those like them. He recalled the story of one Pharisee and a tax collector who went to the Temple to pray. The Pharisee thanked God that he was not as bad as other sinners and certainly not as bad as the tax collector. He reminded God that he fasted and that he gave to the synagogue. The tax collector merely asked God to forgive him, because he was a sinner and wished to repent. Jesus testified that the tax collector went back home forgiven, ". . . For everyone who exalts himself shall be humbled, and he who humbles himself, will be exalted."

Now while he was teaching, people brought children to him so that He might touch and bless them. The disciples told the crowd not to, but Jesus called to them and asked them to come. He expressed, "Let the little children come to Me, and do not forbid them; for of such is the kingdom of

PRAYER FAITH AND ETERNAL LIFE

God, Assuredly, I say to you, whoever does not receive the kingdom of God as a little child will, by no means, enter it."

Now of course, and I am sure you understand, that means that adults should be childlike, not childish. We can never get into the Kingdom of God through works, or by figuring out some great problem. We get in by accepting, as a child would, without question. It is something we receive by grace and with faith.

It was then that a ruler came and asked the Messiah how to receive eternal life. Jesus told him that he must follow the Commandments. The man assured the Master that he had, even when he was young. Jesus told him that he still lacked one thing. He must sell everything he owns, give the money to those who have none, and then follow Him. The man went away full of sorrow, because he was very rich, and didn't want to lose that. Jesus told everyone that it was easier for a camel to go through the eye of a needle than for a rich man to enter God's Kingdom. He turned to His disciples and expressed to them that they who had given all they had would see eternal life.

The Messiah explained to His twelve followers that it was time for them to go to Jerusalem. Everything that had been written and spoken by the prophets of old was about to come true. He discussed with them that the Son of Man would be delivered to the gentiles, He would be insulted and mocked. They would spit on Him and beat Him and kill Him. BUT, in three days, He was rise from the dead. The disciples didn't understand, at that time, what Jesus was saying.

On the way, Jesus came across a man who was blind. The man shouted in the direction of the Savior, asking that Jesus have mercy on him. Jesus ask him what he wanted and the blind man asked the Christ to help him see. Jesus once again said, "Receive your sight. Your faith has made you well." The man was cured and started glorifying God, as did those who saw what had happened.

Part 26

TRAVELING TOWARD JERUSALEM

Jesus was passing through Jericho toward Jerusalem, the place where He was to sacrifice His life for the sins of the world. As usual, as he was passing, a large crowd followed. Among them was the chief tax collector, Zacchaeus. Now, Zacchaeus was a rich man, but short in stature. He could not see over the crowd, so he climbed a sycamore tree, to get a glimpse of this teacher.

As the Master walked by, He noticed the tax collector sitting in the tree and instructed him, by saying, "Zacchaeus, make haste and come down, for today I must stay at your house."

When the Pharisees and scribes saw and heard this they complained, for this teacher was about to consort with sinners. They could not believe their eyes, because they would never associate with sinners. They were better than that!

Zacchaeus spoke to Jesus and explained how he had always given half of what he had to the poor. He also added that if he ever did take more than he was owed, he paid it back four-fold.

Jesus said to him, "Today salvation has come to this house, because he is also a son of Abraham. For the Son of Man has come to seek and save that which was lost."

Jesus began another parable as he was traveling to Jerusalem. The people had the impression that when Jesus arrived, the Kingdom would immediately appear, and the Master knew their thoughts. He told the story of the nobleman of one city, who had to go to another country to receive a new kingdom. He called his servants and gave them money to use so they could conduct business while he was gone. Since some of the citizens of the

TRAVELING TOWARD JERUSALEM

city hated the nobleman, they did not want him to reign over them. They tried to stop this nobleman who was ready to bring forth a new kingdom as their new king. They, however, failed!

The Nobleman returned after receiving the Kingdom and called his servants to him. The first, who had been given ten coins and had doubled his amount. Because the servant had obeyed, his master put him in charge of ten cities of the new kingdom. The second had been given ten coins and had earned an additional five coins. He was given five cities of the new kingdom to oversee. Now the third servant, fearing the master, hid away the coins he had been given. He returned what he had, and there was nothing else to show for his work. The coins were taken from him and were given to the first servant. The third hadn't used what he had been given to further the good of the new kingdom, so he was due nothing.

There are three types of people participating in this story. One is the Nobleman, the second are the servants, and the third are the city people. I, Luke, must interject here and explain. Jesus was the Nobleman going to get his kingdom. The servants represented those who served Jesus. The third group were the people of Israel, who said they followed the Laws of the Kingdom of God. These people, like the Pharisees, scribes, and priests would not accept the Christ, because they said He was questioning their authority and condemning what they did. Those who hater this new king of the new kingdom, and had tried to stop him, were eliminated from the new kingdom because they did not repent.

Jesus continued on His journey to Jerusalem. When he had arrived near Bethany, at the Mount of Olives, He sent two of His disciples to the City and told them they would find a donkey tied there, on which no one had ever sat. He stated that if anyone asked them why they were doing this, they were to say that it was for the Lord, and they would let it go.

The disciples returned to the Master, with the colt, and Jesus got on and rode it into the city. The people went before Him praising God because they had seen the mighty works of this man. As Jesus rode, they lay palm branches before him and shouted, "Blessed is the King who comes in the name of the Lord. Peace in Heaven and Glory in the highest."

They Pharisees saw and heard this and told Jesus he needed to silence the people, But Jesus replied, "I tell you that if these should keep silent, the stones would immediately cry out."

Jesus, Drawing near to Jerusalem, knew that this city would be destroyed in the future, because The people of Israel would not accept His

GOSPEL III: THE GOSPEL ACCORDING TO LUKE

coming. He longed to save all of His children, but they would not let Him. Jesus wept.

Part 27

THE AUTHORITY QUESTIONED— THE SAVIOR HATED

A FEW DAYS LATER, Jesus was teaching in the Temple at Jerusalem, and the Pharisees and elders of the Synagogue came to Him demanding that He affirm His authority. Actually, they wanted to destroy Him, so they asked, "By what authority do you do these things? Or who is He who gave you this authority."

Jesus answered by providing a question to them. "I also will ask you one thing, and answer me: The baptism of John, was if from Heaven, or man?"

The leaders were afraid to answer knowing that if they said Heaven, Jesus would ask why they didn't believe John then. If, however, they said man, the people would rise up against them because they believed John to be a Prophet. They stated they didn't know.

Jesus then said, "Neither will I tell you by what authority I do these things." making the Pharisees and Temple Leaders more angry.

Then, The Christ told the people another parable. It seems that a vineyard owner hired workers to tend his vines. When harvest time arrived, he sent one of his servants to collect the grapes so he could produce wine. The workers, or vine dressers as they were called, beat the man, sending him away empty handed. The owner sent another, and they beat him, too. Finally, the owner sent his only son, for they would surely respect him. The workers, when they saw him coming, said they would kill this son and take away his inheritance for themselves. They killed the son and the owner destroyed them and gave the vineyard to others.

GOSPEL III: THE GOSPEL ACCORDING TO LUKE

Knowing now what happened back then, I can tell you the meaning of this parable. Jesus was telling the people all about the Pharisees and other leaders that supposedly worked for God. They would kill the son, who was really Jesus, and reject His teaching. Jesus was then saying that His Kingdom would be taken from them and be inherited by believers, even gentiles, who would begin the Christian faith and way of life.

The chief priests and scribes would have arrested Jesus at that very moment, had they not feared the multitude of people following His teachings. They did, nonetheless, kept watching, looking for their chance to arrest Him and have Him crucified. On one occasion they asked Jesus if they should pay taxes. He answered telling them to render unto Caesar what was Caesar's, but they should render unto God what was His.

At another time they asked Him about the resurrection and those who were married here on earth. Suppose one woman, because of the death of her husband, married another man? Who would she be married to when they all ended up in Heaven. Which man would be considered a sinner and adulterer? Jesus explained that there was no marriage given after the resurrection, nor was there any more death, because those in Heaven would be like angels and sons and daughters of God.

Again, Jesus warned the people, "Beware of the scribes who desire to go around in long robes, love greetings in the marketplaces, the best seats in the Synagogue, and the best places at the feast who devour widows' houses, and for a pretense make long prayers. These will receive condemnation."

Part 28

THE END AND THE RETURN

When Jesus, during one trip to the Synagogue, left, He was shown all of the buildings of the Temple, He told His disciples that there would be a day where one stone would not be left upon another. So, they asked Him what signs there would be to signify the end times had come.

Jesus answered and said, "Take heed that you not be deceived. For many will come in My name, saying, I am He, and, The time has drawn near. Therefore, do not go after them. But when you hear of wars and commotions, do not be terrified; for these things must come to pass first, but the end will not come immediately."

Then He added, "Nation will rise against nation, and kingdom against kingdom. And there will be great earthquakes in various places, and famines and pestilences; and there will be fearful sights and great signs from heaven. But, before all these things, they will lay their hands on you and persecute you, delivering you up to the synagogues and prisons. You will be brought before kings and rulers for My name's sake."

Jesus also referred to that time as one that would find father against son, and brother against brother. Some of them would call for the death of the believers. The world would hate the followers of the Messiah. There will be signs in the heavens, in the sun, and in the moon. The heavens, themselves will quake and all will see the Son of God coming in the clouds with power and great glory. Jesus said when these things occur, look up for the redemption of His children is near.

He then made clearer his explanation by comparing this time to the fig tree. He told them when the tree was ready to bud, they knew summer was coming. Likewise, the believers in the end times, (the time of the fig tree budding) would know and that generation would not pass away, but would see His return. Watch and stay in constant prayer always, that you may be worthy to stand before the Son of God.

Part 29

PASSOVER AND THE LAST SUPPER

The feast of Unleavened Bread was at hand. The chief priest were busy, not preparing for the feast, but planning how to kill this Jesus. It so happened, at the same time, Satan entered Judas Iscariot.

Judas left the side of Jesus and the other eleven and went to speak to the chief priest and the captains. He agreed to betray Jesus for the sum of thirty pieces of silver. They decided to arrest Jesus when He did not have a great crowd around Him.

Jesus sent Peter and John to the city to prepare the Passover supper. He told them they would know where to go because they would see a man carrying a pitcher of water. The Master informed them they were to follow this man and go into the same house that He entered. Then Peter and John were to tell the master of the house they were there to prepare the supper in the upper room for the Lord and His disciples. Everything happened as Jesus had described.

Later, the twelve and Jesus went to the upper room and sat, ready to eat. The Messiah told them this was something he had wanted and desired for quite some time. He then expressed how He was about to suffer. I am sure they all looked at each other, wondering what He was talking about.

Jesus, taking the wine and giving thanks said, "Take this and divide it among yourselves; for I say to you I will not drink from the fruit of this vine until the Kingdom of God comes."

He then took the bread, also giving thanks, and divided it up among the twelve. He said, "This is my body which is given for you; do this in remembrance of me."

GOSPEL III: THE GOSPEL ACCORDING TO LUKE

He again took the cup and expressed, "This cup is the new covenant, in my blood, which is shed for you. But behold, the hand of My betrayer is with Me on the table. And truly the Son of Man goes as it has been determined, but woe to that man by whom He is betrayed!"

The disciples began to question who it was that was about to betray Jesus. They also began arguing about who among them was the greatest. Hearing them, Jesus described for them two types of Kingdoms: the world's kingdoms and God's Kingdom. In the world, kings exercise sovereignty over his subjects. It wasn't so with the Kingdom of God. For there, the one who governs is a servant to others. In other words The least among them would be the greatest. Jesus, Himself, said how He had come to serve, not to be served. Jesus then bestowed upon them the honor of being able to sit with Him at His table in God's Kingdom. He also gave them the authority to one day sit upon thrones, when they were in Heaven, to judge the twelve tribes of Israel.

The Lord turned to Peter and told Him that Satan would try to sift him as Wheat. In other words, Satan was going to try to work on Peter to shake his faith, as a worker would shake wheat to divide the grain from the chaff. Jesus continued, telling how He had prayed for Peter so that his faith would not fail. Peter assured the Christ that he would be willing to go with his Master, even if it meant death.

Jesus answered, "I tell you, Peter the rooster shall not crow this day before you will deny three times that you know Me."

All of the disciples remained silent, as Jesus then commissioned them to go into the whole world. It would not be the same as when He sent them out to preach in their own land. This time they would be among strangers, face trials, and confront danger. Therefore, it would be fitting, this time, to take provisions and money; for Jesus was about to die and they would carry His message to the ends of the earth.

Jesus then asserted that His life had to end in the way in which it would—to fulfill every single one of the prophecies and Laws found in the Old Testament. He had to be betrayed, suffer at the hands of both the Jews and the Gentiles, and die on the cross. For this is why He had come in the first place.

Now Jesus noticed that there were two swords among the eleven disciples left. Peter had one and the other owner was unknown. It was customary to carry a sword, for defense in a world filled with others who could harm them. Anyway, Jesus told them that two swords would be more

PASSOVER AND THE LAST SUPPER

than sufficient for all the disciples and what they were to accomplish. The followers of the Lord thought Jesus was speaking of real swords to use to defend themselves, but Jesus meant the swords they were to use were for spiritual warfare. They did not understand and Jesus did not continue the discussion.

Part 30

BETRAYED MOCKED AND KILLED

Coming out of the upper room, Jesus and His disciples went to the Mount of Olives. The Messiah asked His followers to pray that they would not enter into temptation. Jesus went a little ways off and knelt to pray, pleading, "Father, if it is Your will, take this cup away from me; nevertheless, not My will, but Yours be done."

At that moment, an Angel from Heaven came to Him, giving Him the strength to complete His mission. He was, indeed, filled with suffering. Even being in anguish, He prayed more resolutely and remained steadfast in the will of His Father. He was in such agony at this hour that His sweat actually became like drops of blood.

When He came back to His disciples, they were asleep. He looked at them and once again asked them to remain awake and pray that they would not be tempted. While He was speaking a gang of Captains and chief priests came upon them. Judas was with them and he walked up to Jesus and kissed Him.

Jesus said to Him, "Judas, are you betraying the Son of Man with a kiss?"

When they began to arrest the Lord, Peter drew his sword and cut off the ear of the High Priest's servant. Jesus told them to stop and let them do what they were about to do. He touched the ear of the servant and healed him.

Jesus then asked the chief priests, captains, and elders who had seized Him, "Have you come out, as against a robbers with swords and clubs? When I was with you in the Temple you did not try to seize me. But this is your hour and the power of darkness."

BETRAYED MOCKED AND KILLED

I have to tell you that the hour of darkness is how Jesus expressed His arrest. The power may have come from the prince of darkness, or from inside the mob, themselves (or both). Their conduct and deeds came from the fact that they were born and raised in darkness. They were ignorant of the light and it was, therefore, easy for them to follow evil . . . for the evil truly love darkness. This is why they chose the darkness of night to arrest the Savior. Now back to my Gospel.

The mob brought Jesus to the house of the High Priest. Peter followed in the shadows, so as not to be caught himself. The crowd had built a fire in the courtyard of the house, and Peter came and sat with them. A servant girl recognized him and told others that he had been with Jesus. The disciple told her he didn't know this man. After a while, another person asked Peter if he was one of them and he said that he was not. An hour later, another one of the crowd said that Peter was one of them, for he looked like a Galilean. Peter shouted that he did not know what this man was saying. Immediately the rooster crowed and Peter remembered the words of his Master. Peter left and wept heavily.

Now the men who held Jesus mocked Him and beat Him. They blindfolded Him, struck Him, and then asked that He prophesy about who had hit Him. Many testified falsely about the things Jesus had done.

The next morning, they brought the Christ before the counsel. They said, "If you are the Christ, tell us."

Jesus answered in this manner. "If I tell you, you will by no means believe. And if I also ask you, (enter into a debate with you) you will in no means answer me and let me go. Hereafter, The Son of Man will sit on the right hand of the power of God."

One asked Him if he was the Son of God, and He stated, "You rightly say that I am."The Pharisees, scribes and elders then declared they needed no more proof. Jesus was guilty. The entire group took the Messiah to Pilate. They told him that they had found this Galilean, Jesus, perverting the nation, refusing to pay taxes to Caesar, and claiming to be Christ, the King.

Pilate asked Jesus if He was the King of the Jews and He told Pilate that it was as he had said. Pilate turned to the crowd and said that he found not fault in this man, but since He was from Galilee, it was Herod's problem. While in the presence of Herod, Jesus remained silent. Herod and his men treated Jesus with contempt. They mocked Him, and clothed Him in a rich robe, sending Him back to Pilate.

GOSPEL III: THE GOSPEL ACCORDING TO LUKE

Pilate told the chief priests and the elders that Jesus was not a guilty man, so he would chastise Him and release Him, for it was the custom at Passover to release one prisoner for the Jews.

The mob of Jewish people began shouting that they wanted Pilate to release Barabbas, a convicted murderer, and to crucify Jesus. Three times, Pilate told the crowd that this man Jesus had not committed a crime worthy of a death sentence. The mob, however continued to shout that He should be crucified. Pilate gave in, released Barabbas, and sent Jesus to be killed on the cross. The Roman soldiers began to lead Jesus to the Place of the Skull and, on the way, they commanded Simon of Cyrenian to bear the cross of the Christ.

A multitude gathered and watched while women there began to morn and cry. Jesus said to these woman of Jerusalem that they should not weep for Him, but should weep for their children. In the future, woman without children will be better off for they will not have to watch their sons and daughters go through the evils that are to come. If men are willing to put to death the innocent Son of God, what will they be willing to do when He is gone.

Along with Jesus, that day, two others were crucified. These men were indeed guilty of crimes and had been fairly judged. One was crucified on the right side of Jesus and the other on the left.

And Jesus spoke, "Father forgive them, for they know not what they do" as the Romans cast lots for His clothes.

Many people watching, mocked and questioned The Christ as He hung there, saying He had saved others, why couldn't save Himself? The soldiers also mocked Him and tried to give Him sour wine and Pilate had ordered that a sign be made to be placed on the top of the cross where Jesus was dying. It read, in Greek, Latin, and Hebrew: THIS IS THE KING OF THE JEWS.

Now, one of the criminals hanging there asked Jesus to save Himself and them also. The other rebuked him and asked why he did not fear God. He told the other they were there because they were actually guilty. Jesus was innocent. He then turned to the Savior and asked if Jesus would remember Him when He came into His Kingdom.

Jesus told that sinner, "Assuredly I say to you, today you will be with me in Paradise."

During the sixth hour, the sky grew dark and remained that way until the ninth hour. Then the sun became dark and the Temple veil was torn

BETRAYED MOCKED AND KILLED

in two. Jesus cried out in a loud voice, "Father into your hands I commit My Spirit." and as He took His last breath, the Centurion seeing all of this glorified God and said, "certainly this was a righteous man."

The crowd ran away because of the darkness of the skies and the earthquake. They were full of fear thinking they may be facing certain judgment for what they had done. The only people remaining were some of the followers of Christ like Mary His mother, John the beloved disciple, Mary Magdalene, and another woman named Solome, the mother of the children of Zebedee. They wept and stood at a distance watching everything that was happening. When He was taken from the cross, a man named Joseph of Arimathea, who had asked permission to bury the Christ, came for the body.

Part 31

THE RESURRECTION

Because the Sabbath was approaching, Joseph could not fully prepare the body of Christ. He wrapped it in a linen and also a face cloth, planning for the woman to fully prepare Him for burial after the Sabbath.

Now, on the first of the week, three day after His death, the women came to prepare the body of their Lord with spices and fragrant oils. When they arrived, they found the stone rolled away and the tomb was empty. The women went in and were met by two angels who asked them, "Why do you seek the living among the dead.? He is not here, but is risen." They told the women to remember what Jesus had told them before. He was going to die and, in three days, rise again.

They ran to the eleven disciples and other believers and told them about what had occurred. The men did not believe them, but Peter arose and ran to the tomb. He saw the linens there, without a body, and he was in awe of the situation, and wondered to himself what had really happened.

Later, on the same day, two followers of the Lord were walking to Emmaus. As they traveled, a stranger walked with them and asked what they were discussing and why they were sad. The follower, named Cleopas, asked if this stranger was new in the area, because He must be the only person who did not know about the crucifixion of the One who they thought may be the Messiah, the redeemer of all of Israel.

The two explained how they had been with the eleven after the crucifixion. The women who had gone to the tomb came to them claiming the Christ had risen, for they had seen angels at the tomb instead of the body.

THE RESURRECTION

Some of the disciples went to the tomb to see this sight for themselves, and found that the woman had been truthful.

The stranger began telling these two about this Christ, calling them "slow of heart to believe." He quoted scripture and described how The Messiah had fulfilled all the prophecies found there. These two followers, though, still did not recognize Jesus.

When they had come to the city, the followers asked the stranger to have supper with them. As they began to eat, this stranger broke bread, gave thanks for it, and gave it to them to eat. At that second their eyes were opened and they recognized their Savior, but He vanished from their sight.

These two returned to the twelve explaining how they had seen Jesus and that he had truly risen. They revealed how He broke bread with them and, at that very moment, they knew Him.

As they were talking, Jesus appeared the all of them and said, "Peace be with you." but the followers and disciples thought they were seeing a ghost and were afraid.

Jesus called to them saying, "Why are you troubled? And why do doubts arise in your hearts. Behold my hands and my feet. Handle me and see, for a spirit does not have flesh and bones as you see I have."

When He said this, he showed them the holes in His wrist and feet. They were all filled with joy and marveled at what had happened. He asked them if they had any food and they gave Him fish and honey.

He ate it in their presence and said, "These are the words I spoke to you when I was still with you, that all things must be fulfilled which were written in the Law of Moses and the Prophets and the psalms."

It was then that they all understood the scriptures. They understood why Jesus had come to suffer and rise from the dead. He was the one whose blood was shed for the remission (pardon) of sins.

Jesus told them to remain in Jerusalem until they had received the power of the Holy Spirit. It would be then, they would go to all parts of the world teaching the good news and describing all they had seen and heard. They would bring the message of redemption to Jews and Gentiles alike so that these people could also have eternal life through belief in Jesus the Christ.

Jesus led them to Bethany and lifted His hands to bless them. After He had blessed them, He was carried up into Heaven. They worshiped Him and continually praised and blessed God Almighty. Amen.

Part 32

CONCLUSION

As I have stated, at the beginning, I am a doctor. I am a native of Syrian Antioch and I was one of the seventy apostles, accepting my charge from Jesus, Himself. I, too, was with Cleopas on the road to Emmaus, where Jesus appeared to us after He had risen. I first met the Apostle Paul in Troas, the major city on the Aegean Sea in Asia Minor where Paul was on his second missionary journey. I was still Paul's companion when the Romans imprisoned him and I saw to him medically.[1] As a matter of fact, you could call me a medical missionary.

I have made my statements precise and to the point. Each section of my text here has been dissected to show what I have learned and what I wish to pass on to you. I guess the message I leave with you, is that I knew Jesus. I knew His message of redemption and salvation was one I had to preach to the world. I actually saw Him on the road Emmaus and that convinced me that what I write to you is truth, the quotes are truth, and the message that Jesus gave us all is truth. My medical advice is the accept this truth and be saved.

---

1. Orthodox Times, "Memory of Apostle and Evangelist Luke," Oct. 18, 2024, https://orthodoxtimes.com/memory-of-apostle-and-evangelist-luke-18-october/.

Gospel IV

THE BELOVED DISCIPLE
I'm John, and I'm All about the Love

Part 1

THE WORDS OF THE FIRST FOUR

THE STORY OF THE Good News of Jesus was told by four of His disciples and, contrary to popular belief, were written within the first century AD.[1] The gospels were originally written in Greek because that was the language which was the most common to the Eastern Mediterranean Area. There are some reports that suggest that some of the gospel was written in Hebrew or Aramaic, but the consensus among scholars is that Greek was the chosen method.[2] The Koine Greek, or common Greek dialect used at the time, was the texts used to translate the Bible we read today.[3]

The Gospels of Matthew, Mark, Luke, and John all start at different beginnings. Matthew and Luke wrote their books around 85—90 AD. Mark's book was 66—70 AD. John, however penned his words somewhere around 90 AD although there have been Dead Sea Scrolls found that show this could have happened in 50—70 AD. This is consistent with the biblical timeline because The Christ was crucified, traditionally, around 33 AD. The date is determined by looking at the ministry of John the Baptist, which began in 29 AD under the reign of Tiberius. This would have been very close to the start of the ministry of Jesus.[4]

---

1. Cholee Clay, "Comparing the Gospels: Matthew, Mark, Luke, and John," Owlocation, Jun 19, 2024, https://owlcation.com/humanities/Comparing-the-Gospels-Matthew-Mark-Luke-and-John.

2. The Christian Bible Reference Site, "Introduction—the Gospels," https://www.christianbiblereference.org/jintro.htm.

3. Wikipedia, "Koin," https://en.wikipedia.org/wiki/Koine_Greek.

4. Wikipedia, "Marcan Priority," https://en.wikipedia.org/wiki/Marcan_priority.

GOSPEL IV: I'M JOHN, AND I'M ALL ABOUT THE LOVE

Matthew and Luke began their Gospels describing the birth of the Messiah. They do, however differ in that Matthew explains the visit of the Magi and Luke describes the shepherds tending the flocks by night. Matthew explains the ancestry of Jesus beginning with Abraham and ending with the birth of the Messiah. Luke begins with Jesus and goes back to the very beginning: Adam. Matthew is more focused on the fact that Joseph and Mary had to take Jesus to Egypt to escape Herod, while Luke explains the humble beginnings showing a baby born in Bethlehem.

Some skeptics look at the differences and see this as a controversy because of the details contained in each stories. If we look at current books written about the same subject, but composed by two different authors, we often find controversial differences. The biographies written by Colin Duriez and A. N. Wilson both concentrate on C. S. Lewis, but are written from two different perspectives.

In 2013 the author Colin Duriez wrote: "C.S. Lewis: A Biography of Friendship' . He said, The bio ". . . is a fascinating and insightful plunge into the life of a literary legend through the friends he keeps closest. Through collecting previously un published research, interviews and insider knowledge, Colin Duriez has compiled a sparkling biography of C.S. Lewis by studying his closest friends, family and the famous literary society, the Inklings."[5] Arend Smilde stated this about A.N. Wilson and his bio of Lewis: . . . the book was condemned by most of those who were, or who at least seemed to be, familiar with the subject."[6] How great an example of two authors writing about the same person! Everyone writes his or her story with biases and prejudices and they could all be correct.

Two of the disciples, Matthew and Luke, were no different than any other writer in history. These disciples, along with Mark and John, wrote from totally different perspectives. Although all four were inspired by God and Jesus to write their gospels, it was not dictated to them by the Holy spirit or God as the Prophets in the Old Testaments were.

Matthew for example was an outcast. He was hated by his fellow Israelites because he was a tax collector for Rome. He was also considered a traitor to his own people. He did, however think with the mind of one who deals with exact facts. He became the disciple who could recall facts and bring them to the forefront. He would remember an Old Testament

---

5. Colin Duriez, *C. S. Lewis: A Biography of Friendship*, Lion Books, 2013.

6. Arend Smilde, "Sweetly Poisonous in a Welcome Way: Reflections on a Definitive Biography, A. N. Wilson, *C. S. Lewis: A Biography* (1990)," 2009, https://lewisiana.nl/definitivebiography/.

THE WORDS OF THE FIRST FOUR

prophecy concerning the messiah and knew how it was fulfilled by Jesus. Matthew used proof and the ability to use facts from the prophets to come to the conclusion of who Jesus was. His writing was a precise narrative, clear and insightful, and used exact facts just as would be expected from a man who dealt in numbers.

Luke, on the other hand was a doctor. He was a man, well-educated and compassionate. His writing was well organized and shows how this man wanted truth and he wanted to write something he could verify. He was dedicated to every detail and wanted to write nothing but the truth. Many say that Luke was a gentile.[7] Others consider him a Hellenistic Jew, a Jew raised within the Greek culture and not following the kosher lifestyle. Either way, he knew he was an outsider accepted by Jesus through grace and mercy and not a true follower of Abraham and the religion of Judaism. His writing showed the exactness and details needed by a doctor, and yet the thankfulness of a man in need of Salvation given by the Jewish Messiah.

The disciple Mark was a youth when he met Jesus. He was a bit educated because he spoke Greek and possibly interpreted it for Peter. He was usually writing from the perspective of the disciple Peter, who many considered the leader of the twelve. Mark did write about the miracles that Jesus performed and he was considered the scribe of the disciples. When Jesus spoke, healed, and performed miracles, Mark recorded it, and he was very detailed in his descriptions. He wrote of the life of Christ, possibly using the Aramaic words Jesus spoke, Latin words and phrases used at the time, and often explained of Jewish customs that would be unknown to gentiles. Mark expressed that Jesus was the Messiah because of what did, what He taught, and what He had to go through during His death. He concluded by describing the resurrection and the command that the disciples should spread the Gospel to all the world.

The fourth Gospel was written by me, John, the beloved disciple. Again, I will write in the third person, because I don't like the attention. So, John highlighted the importance of the spiritual life of Jesus. He stressed that Jesus was divine as well as human, and He was the source of all salvation. John met Jesus while he and his brother James were fishing from their boats on the Sea of Galilee. The brothers had experienced an unsuccessful fishing trip. Jesus came up to them and told them to lower their nets one more time. Even though they thought that this would be fruitless, the did as

---

7. Cameron Joyner, "Was Luke Really a Gentile?," Friends of Israel Gospel Ministry, Sept. 16, 2022, https://www.foi.org/2022/09/16/was-luke-really-a-gentile.

GOSPEL IV: I'M JOHN, AND I'M ALL ABOUT THE LOVE

Jesus asked. When they pulled up the nets this time, they had caught more fish than could fit in the nets. This was the first miracle that John witnessed and when Jesus asked them to follow Him, they dropped their catch and nets and did just that, never to return to fishing. We find it hard, sometimes, to understand why John was called the beloved disciple. Their close relationship was seen throughout the gospel and even at the crucifixion, where Jesus told John to take care of His mother.

John considered himself the beloved disciple because of his relationship with the Master. He was the one follower who know that Jesus was not only the Messiah, the Son of God, but He was also God in the flesh. Not everyone follows this train of thought, but it is my belief that John knew Jesus as God, Master, and The Messiah. At the end of the life of Jesus, John was the only disciple who did not desert the Christ. The gospel of John was written as a testament of the love Jesus had for all of mankind. It is almost poetic in the way different kinds of love were expressed. It is written in such a personal way, culminating into the realization that, as John wrote, "For God so loved the world, that He gave his only Begotten son, that whoever believes in Him shall not perish but have eternal life." (John 3:16)

The love that Jesus expressed and the love of His best friend, John, showed in the disciple's writings as he explained that mankind needed to love as God loves. It was the only love that could be explained as a sacrifice to others. The word John used most was actually the Greek word, ἠγάπα. The Greek word ἠγάπα is a form of the verb agapao [17],[8] which means to love unconditionally and sacrificially, just as Jesus did.

It is no wonder that The Gospel of John is the message used most to express the meaning of Gods sacrifice by sending His only Begotten to earth so that none would perish. Although the other three Gospel writers have the same mission of describing the Son of God to understand the reason for his coming, it is John who merely uses love as the defining message of Jesus. All four of these men had life changing events that showed how a sin filled world should be saved. Each wrote with their own different experiences and each fulfilled a mission to express the good news of redemption.

It is not my intention to show one disciple as "better" than another. That is simply not true. It is merely my mission to show the world what God did for all of us. He offered His son to die for our sins, and it is through the writings of John and His use of love that one can best understand and accept this sacrifice performed by God and the Son of God.

8. Bill Mounce, ἀγαπάω, Free Online Greek Dictionary, https://www.billmounce.com/greek-dictionary/agapao.

Part 2

I'M DIFFERENT FROM THE OTHERS

John's Gospel is a love story. It isn't one you might find on the Halmark Chanel. It isn't one you would read between the pages of a book of fiction authored by a famous writer. But it is all about love; a love stronger than has ever been experienced before.

John 20:30–31 discussed the reason why he wrote the way he did. "Jesus performed many other signs in the presence of his disciples, which are not recorded in this book. But these are written that you may believe that Jesus is the Messiah, the Son of God, and that by believing you may have life in his name." John wanted both Christians and unbelievers alike to know of the Love that God has for all. He wanted to bring faith to those who were hearing the good news for the first time, and he wanted to strengthen the faith of the believers.

It is not that Matthew, Mark, and Luke were not writing for believers and non-believers, But the style of the first three disciples were different than John's. The first three are given the name Synoptic Gospels and are very similar in the stories they tell and the way they write about the events which they witnessed. The word "synoptic" comes from the Greek "synoptikos", which means able to be "viewed together."[1] Their works used discretional facts and concise wording to express what happened. Their stories were also written in the third person. These three recorded what they observed and what was being said at the time they heard and saw it.

---

1. Etymology World Online, "Synoptic Etymology," https://etymologyworld.com/item/synoptic.

GOSPEL IV: I'M JOHN, AND I'M ALL ABOUT THE LOVE

John, who also wrote in the third person point of view, was much more thoughtful in his words and explanations. His insightful word choice was, more than likely, written long after the events he witnessed. He seems to be looking back and reflecting, giving reasons for the things Jesus did and spoke. John wanted us to experience what he did and understand why Jesus did what He did. He wanted us to be able to see the love Jesus taught and the truth Jesus spoke. He needed us to almost feel the pain and suffering the Son of God faced and that He was doing this for us.

John deliberately omitted his own name, instead choosing to call the viewer of the events "the beloved disciple". The reader, however, understands that it is John who is the witness to the acts demonstrated by the Messiah. I don't think "John" was written to record what Jesus did while he was there. He was remembering what had happened and reflecting on what had taken place. Most important was that John wanted us to realize that Jesus indeed was born as God in the flesh, lived and taught as the Son of man and the Son of God, and died as the Messiah of the Jewish people even though he is rejected. To him, Jesus was resurrected to show Jew and non-Jew alike that salvation was for everyone who accepted it. Jesus may not be with us in physical form, but He is with us because He is indeed God.

Part 3

RELATIONSHIP WITH JESUS

JOHN WAS LOVED BY Jesus just as all the disciples were loved. The difference was that John was closer to Jesus and responded to Him, so that Jesus didn't have to correct him or rebuke him. Their relationship was based on the fact that John's belief and actions, for the most part, were aligned with the thoughts and words Jesus expressed. John was faithful and committed to Jesus. Their closeness was evidenced by the fact that John loved Jesus. It wasn't because of his strengths, although he possessed many, it was because of the strength of the love Jesus showed to him.

Because of the love, John was committed to Jesus. He truly believed that Jesus was the Messiah. As a disciple of John the Baptist, he heard about Jesus, saw Jesus, and left the Baptist to become a follower of the Christ. He was willing to go where Jesus went and he didn't complain. John was one, as was Peter and James, chosen to be a part of the inner circle that were present during special moments in Jesus's mission. He saw the miracles, witnessed the raising of Lazarus, was at the transfiguration, where Jesus was seen with Moses and Elijah, and was asked to be close at the Garden of Gethsemane. He stood by his Savior as The Lord was being questioned and as He was being crucified. He didn't flee as the other disciples did.

If John was ever afraid, which he probably was, he never showed it. He had no problem going with Jesus into towns where people rejected The Son of Man. He once wanted to call down fire from Heaven because Samaritan villagers didn't believe in the Messiah. Because of this, Jesus gave him and his brother James the nick name of "sons of thunder". He was probably afraid, as he stood at the cross and witnessed the death of his Master, be

GOSPEL IV: I'M JOHN, AND I'M ALL ABOUT THE LOVE

he remained steadfast. He even became a loving son to Mary, the mother of Jesus. He took her with him and provided for her for the rest of her life. John, therefore, was the beloved disciple all through the life of Jesus and he dedicated the rest of his life to bringing others to salvation. His love for the Son of God grew even more evident as he taught, preached and became one of the leaders of the early church. John spent his entire life dedicated to Jesus and showed others the Love of God.

Part 4

RELATIONSHIP WITH PETER

I AM SURE THAT John loved the other disciples, especially Peter who he traveled with as a companion and preached the Gospel. John regarded Peter as the "Rock" He understood the Church that was to come would be led by Peter because Jesus had given him that charge. After the resurrection and ascension of the Master, Peter took that position. John respected that. It wasn't always like that. John's love for Jesus was based on the love Jesus had for him. Peter relationship with the Messiah, at first, was dependent on his own thought process. Peter was a hot head, as it were. He was impulsive and was led by the emotion he happened to be feeling at any particular time. His love for the Christ was not always based on his faith. That would sometimes waiver, as evidenced by his fear when He denied Jesus. John was not the same. He never denied his Master and was with him until the end.

John was different than Peter, too, when it came to believing that Jesus had risen from the grave. John and Peter both went to the tomb. John, arriving first, stood at the entrance as Peter simply barged into the opening. John may have stayed outside, because he was educated in the law. He knew that entering a tomb made a person unclean and unable to worship in the Temple. Peter, being more hot headed, just ran in without thinking. After leaving, though, Peter was unsure of what was taking place. John, on the other hand, instantly believed that Jesus was alive.

Peter and John differed, too, in that their life expectancy was different. Although John was never promised a long life, many think that he was. In the Gospel of John, Jesus was explaining to Peter that his life would be hard and people would, "be taking him where he doesn't want to go." He

GOSPEL IV: I'M JOHN, AND I'M ALL ABOUT THE LOVE

was expressing to Peter a look into the future, where he would have to face persecution and death. When Peter heard this, He look and pointed to John and asked, "what about him?" In John 21:23, Jesus said, "If I want him to remain alive until I return, what is that to you?" History showed us that Peter died a martyr's death while John had a long life. As a matter of fact, John was the only disciple not killed for his beliefs. Throughout each of their lives, though, both men had an important mission in starting, building up, and guiding the new church of believers—called Christians.

All the differences John showed and wrote, though, require a closer look into the man and the reason for His Gospel. John had to tell the world what he had experienced and because of the love he had for his Master and for the rest of the world, He knew he must spread the good news. What he wrote changed many lives throughout the years and brought the souls of many to salvation through acceptance, and his words still change lives to this day.

Part 5

THE WORD BECAME FLESH

Yohanan Ben Zavdai was born in Bethsaida, a small town in northern Israel, around the year 6 AD. He is better known as John, the son of Zebedee.[1] His mother was Salome, and was said to be the sister of Mary, the mother of Jesus.[2] John, then, would have been the cousin of Jesus. However, there is no word for cousin in the Aramaic language, the native tongue of the Lord. Often cousins would be referred to as "brother" instead, and this would not have needed any correction.

John, along with his older brother, James, helped their father in the family business: fishing. The family was rather successful and Zebedee was a wealthy man with many connections in high places. John spent much of his time, when not fishing, going with his father to what was called the "House of Life", or Necropolis of Beit Shearim. This was a small room attached to the Synagogue. It would have been here that he was educated in the Torah and many of the psalms of David. He would have learned how to read and write, as well as probably becoming familiar with the Koine Greek language because of the non-Judaic people there.

John and his brother James had heard the stories of a man who was preaching in the wilderness. He was telling the people to prepare for the coming of the Messiah. John 1:36 records what James and young John heard the Baptist say. ". . . As Jesus walked by, John looked at him and

---

1. Josh Weidmann, "The Apostle John: Beloved By God to Love Others," https://joshweidmann.com/meet-john-son-of-zebedee-the-disciple-jesus-loved.

2. Joanne Holstein, "Salome the Mother of James and John Zebedee," Guided Bible Study for Hungry Christians, Feb. 3, 2015, https://guidedbiblestudies.com/?p=2191.

GOSPEL IV: I'M JOHN, AND I'M ALL ABOUT THE LOVE

declared, "Look! There is the Lamb of God!" I believe this is where John started to understand that Jesus was the true Messiah. It is where the love for the Master began. John, the Baptist, and John, the beloved disciple, had something in common. Neither one of them would be apt to take credit for things. Their goal seemed to be to testify of the love of Jesus and the fact that He had come to show a love never seen before.

John understood love and he did so because of the man he followed. When Jesus found him, he and his brother James were fishing, He asked them to drop everything and follow Him. John and James never gave it another thought. They dropped what they were doing and followed. Matthew 4:18–12, explains the meeting. "One day as Jesus was walking along the shore of the Sea of Galilee, he saw two brothers-Simon, also called Peter, and Andrew-throwing a net into the water, for they fished for a living. Jesus called out to them, "Come, follow me, and I will show you how to fish for people!" And they left their nets at once and followed him. A little farther up the shore he saw two other brothers, James and John, sitting in a boat with their father, Zebedee, repairing their nets. And he called them to come, too. They immediately followed him, leaving the boat and their father behind."

To show the love of the man He was following, John had to describe who He was. To John, Jesus was more than the son of God. He was God and John wanted to bring this news to everyone. He began by expressing the very nature of Jesus. John 1:1 starts out at the very beginning and before. "In the beginning was the Word, and the Word was with God, and the Word was God. In Greek the verse is written Ἐν ἀρχῇ ἦν ὁ Λόγος, καὶ ὁ Λόγος ἦν πρὸς τὸν Θεόν, καὶ Θεὸς ἦν ὁ Λόγος.[3]

The purpose here is not to learn Greek, but to understand the message John was telling. The rest of the verse continues, "He was with God in the beginning. Through him all things were made; without him nothing was made that has been made. In him was life, and that life was the light of all mankind. The light shines in the darkness, and the darkness has not overcome it." To understand what John meant it Is necessary to understand the meanings of the Greek language that John knew.

The language contains many words for the same idea. Nouns, verbs, and adjectives possess different meanings and could change the context of the words we read. Words found in English, for example, are not adequate or descriptive enough. Greek contains many words that, in English,

---

3. Bible Hub, "John 1:1 Text Analysis, https://biblehub.com/text/john/1-1.htm.

are merely one word. Love, for example in English, is simply "love". In the Greek, however, love can be one of many words.

Philia (φιλία) is the Greek word that describes "affectionate regard" or "friendship". This is also often described as brotherly love, as in the American city Philadelphia. Again, it can be found in words such as Philosophy, which is the love of wisdom. Love can also be named Eros in the Greek. Eros (ἔρως) means "love" or "desire". Looking at the word erotic we understand this is a sensual or passionate love. Philautia (φιλαυτία) means "self-love". This can be described in the word hubris or great self-esteem. Storge (στοργή) is "love, affection", especially between parents and children while Xenia (ξενία) is an ancient Greek word that means "hospitality" or "guest-friendship". The greatest love, found in the Greek language, though, is Agape. Agape (ἀγάπη) is the Greek word that means "love," especially unconditional love, charity, or the love between God and humans.

It is Agape, then, that led John to see Jesus for who he truly was. John, in the first verse of his Gospel explained three things. First God was in the beginning. In Greek verbs, the verb itself explains the action the word describes. The verb John used, "was" actually means—In the Beginning was the WORD (logos) and the WORD was at the beginning and before the beginning. So, God existed before creation. Second, John stated "The word was with God". God is tripartite meaning three parts in one. We define the Trinity as God the Father, God the Son, and God the Holy Spirit. John wrote that "logos", the word, was also with God before creation.

You and I could be in the same room at the same time and for the same reason. John said something similar, but related it to the WORD. God and the WORD were in the same place at the same time before creation. Many well-respected educators and scholars believe this verse compares the nature of Jesus to the nature of God.

By looking at the other writings of John, in his Gospel, this explanation can be realized. Using the words of Jesus, John wrote, "Your father Abraham rejoiced as he looked forward to my coming. He saw it and was glad. The people said, "You aren't even fifty years old. How can you say you have seen Abraham? Jesus answered, "I tell you the truth, before Abraham was even born, I am! (John 8: 56–58). John 8:23 expresses the divinity of Jesus. John 8:23 told us what Jesus said to the Pharisees "You are from below; I am from above. You are of this world; I am not of this world". I told you that you would die in your sins; if you do not believe that I, am he you will indeed die in your sins." Later John explained what Jesus said to

GOSPEL IV: I'M JOHN, AND I'M ALL ABOUT THE LOVE

His disciples, "My sheep listen to my voice; I know them, and they follow me. I give them eternal life, and they shall never perish; no one will snatch them out of my hand. My Father, who has given them to me, is greater than all; no one can snatch them out of my Father's hand. I and the Father are one." (John 10:27–30). Since John knew Jesus as a part of God's nature, yet separate, he understood the love of God through His only begotten Son.

John then, wrote his book using the basic theme of love. He told us Jesus's only command to the disciples were to love one another. He said, "My command is this: Love each other as I have loved you." (John 15:12). John actually used the term "love" fifty-six times in his Gospel. He talked about the love between the Father, the Son, and the Holy Spirit. He expressed the love God has for humanity, He explained the love He had to be willing to be the sacrificial Lamb. Jesus spoke of the love He and the Father had for His chosen people, and He gave an example of how we should love one another.

Through this knowledge and experience John gained by being the beloved disciple, it is understandable how John knew about sacrifice through love. He lived it, he loved it and he wrote about it. Before examining the Gospel of John, the types of love explained by him need to be defined.

Part 6

FIVE TYPES OF LOVE

1 AGAPE

THE FIRST LOVE DESCRIBED by John's Gospel deals with Agape love. The original Greek word, ἀγάπη (Agape) was first described in the time of Plato and Socrates. The word to Plato was sometimes interchangeable with Eros (personal love) and has gone through some definition changes since then. In Greece, the "highest good" was virtue. Plato argued that love was egocentric, or self-centered, because it satisfies the self. Socrates expressed that desiring something meant that someone lacked something. Through time, the defining of Agape changed to satisfy a deeper meaning of love. After all, If God loved it couldn't be a self-centered love. Otherwise, God would also be imperfect because He was lacking something. Since God is far above humankind, He lacks nothing.

The definition of Agape changed a bit during the writing of the Gospels. God, being eternal, showed a love beyond the self. The authors of these books expressed a Godly love far above human capacity. It became the highest form of love incorporating unconditional sacrificial love and evolving into a selfless love for one another. John wrote about God's unequaled love in his Gospel. In John 3:16 he said, "For God So loved The World That He Gave His Only Begotten Son, that whoever believes in him shall not perish but have eternal life."

The "world" that God loves in Greek is Kosmos. Therefore, this includes all humans from the beginning who have fallen short because of sin. God is perfect and we, as humans, do not understand perfection. The

GOSPEL IV: I'M JOHN, AND I'M ALL ABOUT THE LOVE

love God showed was the sacrifice of his only Begotten and "unique" Son who died to satisfy the need for punishment of sin. If anyone accepts God's sacrifice and repents for their sins, they will receive everlasting life.

God is all powerful, everywhere at the same time, and is the epitome of goodness. We often question why God doesn't just forgive sin with a wave of His hand. We forget the fact that God is more than love. He is just, He is fair, and He is perfect. Perfection requires justice and punishment. Even we, who are so imperfect believe in justice for things done to us and against us. God, being just and good, cannot excuse us for our failure because, if He did, He would not be just or fair. He must punish any and all sin.

This is the true meaning of Godly love or Agape. Sin is not the end. God gives us good news and John reports it. Because of His love He allowed His Son to die, as a human, and take our place. We are all forgiven, if we just believe, because Jesus took our sin upon Himself. He was sinless, yet He loved. Instead of us having to face eternal death, we have a choice to accept God's sacrifice.

John continued describing Agape love through his book. In John 3:19 He wrote, "And this is the verdict, that the light came into the world, but people preferred darkness to light, because their works were evil." The comparison here, showing love as Darkness and light, is defining the difference between Agape love and Eros, or self-love. God, being love, is the light of the world. That love shines in everything He does and the things His followers try to do. The world's love is selfish and would prefer darkness to cover its sin. The author furthers this comparison in John 12: 42–50 where he showed the Eros, or self-love of the Pharisees and counters that with the Agape love shown by the light of God.

> "Yet at the same time many even among the leaders believed in him. But because of the Pharisees they would not openly acknowledge their faith for fear they would be put out of the synagogue; for they loved human praise more than praise from God. Then Jesus cried out, "Whoever believes in me does not believe in me only, but in the one who sent me. The one who looks at me is seeing the one who sent me. I have come into the world as a light, so that no one who believes in me should stay in darkness. "If anyone hears my words but does not keep them, I do not judge that person. For I did not come to judge the world, but to save the world. There is a judge for the one who rejects me and does not accept my words; the very words I have spoken will condemn them at the last day. For I did not speak on my own, but the Father who sent

me commanded me to say all that I have spoken. I know that his command leads to eternal life. So, whatever I say is just what the Father has told me to say."

God's love is the light of the world and that light is shown through His Son, the Messiah and Savior. Jesus said "I am the light of the world. Whoever follows me will not walk in darkness, but will have the light of life" (John 8:12). This light and God's love is so strong nothing could ever put it out. John told us how Jesus explained this love. Jesus said, "I am the light of the world. Whoever follows me will never walk in darkness, but will have the light of life" (John 8:12). This quote ties Jesus with His Father in heaven and explained the reason for His birth. John Piper, in his sermon about "The Person of Christ" explained that "Jesus speaks from God and for God and as God." As God, Jesus is love.

Chapter 8, verse 12 of John's Gospel said, "I am the light of the world" His love is our light, the source of our spiritual truth, and our understanding of Godly love. It was because of this love that He came so that we would not die in our sin. Throughout His ministry Jesus wanted us to also show others the light that Jesus brought. In verse 24, Jesus explained who He really was. "Unless you believe that I am he (or, "I am") you will die in your sins." By accepting that love and forwarding that same type of love, we find forgiveness. After all, according to John in John 13:34, Jesus said, "A new commandment I give to you, that you love one another: just as I have loved you, you also are to love one another". That love is the supreme, unselfish, sacrificial love given by God Almighty.

2 EROS

Eros (eh·rows) is a love best defined in Greek myths. Eros was mischievous and sometimes evil. He taught self-love and a love that was satisfying to one person only. Self-gratification and self-desires often leads to destruction or eventually sadness and loveliness. It is a love that cares for no one else. On the other hand, God taught that we need to love one another, but he also understood that man loves himself. Survival depends on this, but loving oneself is not what we should be focused on. Eros is good as long as we remember what has been taught to us. The commandment, Jesus left with us, was to love our neighbor as we love ourselves. It has never suggested that we need to love ourselves before we can love others. We must discern the difference here with the words *as* and *before*. Many psychologists say

GOSPEL IV: I'M JOHN, AND I'M ALL ABOUT THE LOVE

you need to love yourself. This is true, especially because we should accept ourselves as who we are. We need to strive for success and we need to learn to forgive our own shortcomings. However, Jesus said Love your neighbor *as yourself* (ὡς σεαυτόν). The phrase actually is reflexive. For example, the person performing the act of loving is also affected by the act. If we love ourselves, we love others. If we love ourselves more than we care about others we are not following the words expressed by John. This Pharisees showed Eros love in John 12:43 "For they loved the praise of men more than the praise of God" This is the total opposite of the meaning of Jesus's words. It is not reflective in that the Pharisees thought only of themselves.

John showed us Eros love found in those who opposed Jesus, but it is well defined throughout the bible. In Genesis, "The Lord God said, "It is not good for the man to be alone. I will make a helper suitable for him." This is the first description of a good example of Eros. It was God's intention that a man and a woman be together, in a state of marriage. When the love becomes self-centered or outside the realm of marriage, then it can become destructive.

3 STORGE

John, so far has shown and contrasted two types of Love: Agape, or Godly, unselfish love, and Eros, a sometimes-unhealthy self-love or a good physical love between a husband and wife. There is though, a third type of love and that is presented, although implied and not specifically defined in John. Storge, (stor-gay) is the love found within family or blood ties. God indeed loves his followers, who are found all over the world, and considers them children. John, in his other writings, told us that Jesus considered us children. In 1 John 3:1 he wrote "Behold what manner of love the Father has bestowed on us, that we should be called children of God." Jesus loves us as a father loves his children.

There are many examples of Storge in the Bible. John's other writings describe this type of love throughout his letters. John did write, "We love because he first loved us. If anyone says, "I love God," and hates his brother (including family), he is a liar; for he who does not love his brother whom he has seen cannot love God whom he has not seen. And this commandment we have from him: whoever loves God must also love his brother" (1 John 4:19–21).

FIVE TYPES OF LOVE

Not to be confused with brotherly love (which we discuss later), Storge is a bit different. It is used to show family love, but also includes the love of a parent for a child and a child for a parent. If a child loves a parent, that child will more than likely grow to be like that parent in many ways. In John 5:19–20 Jesus has just finished healing a man, and the Pharisees were indigent. Jesus explained to them that He was doing what He did because of love. This quote concerns itself with Storge love although is very close to other types. "Very truly I tell you, the Son can do nothing by himself; he can do only what he sees his Father doing, because whatever the Father does the Son also does. For the Father loves the Son and shows him all he does."

Jesus is talking about His Father in Heaven, but this could be applied to our lives also. In the New Testament, Peter, Paul, Timothy, as well as John also talked about this love. A mother's and father's love is also implied in John's words, "Greater love has no one than this: to lay down one's life for one's friends" (John 15:13). We know that Jesus put his life on the line for His disciples, but we also know that a parent's love would want that parent to protect their children, even if it meant death. Storge is a complex love. Through this love we guide children to reach goals and meet dreams. Yes, it comes, sometimes, with much discipline but it is needed as we lead children with love toward their ultimate goals.

4 PHILIA

Agape, Eros, and Storge are only three loves of the five we will discuss. The fourth type of love is Philia (FILL-ee-uh). Now this is brotherly love and encompasses warm affection or intimate friendship. It is seen in a caring, heartfelt consideration of others and it is similar to a kinship. Many disciples of the Christ explained Philia love when they wrote. In Romans 12:10, the word told us "Be kindly affectionate to one another with brotherly love, in honor giving preference to one another" John talked of Philia When Lazarus had died, John wrote of the love Jesus had for His friend. He expresses the sorrow the Lord showed toward all the family of Lazarus. Showing his human side,

"Jesus wept. Then said the Jews, Behold how he loved him! And some of them said, Could not this man, which opened the eyes of the blind, have caused that even this man should not have died? Jesus therefore, again groaning in himself cometh to the grave" (John 11:36–38). Because of brotherly love Jesus raised Lazarus from the dead.

GOSPEL IV: I'M JOHN, AND I'M ALL ABOUT THE LOVE

John was one who spoke of love, wrote of love, and also loved others. His writing showed this especially when describing different types of love in the same verses. For example, John showed Agape love along with Philia when summarizing the talk between Jesus and Peter while they were eating. This mixture of brotherly love and Godly sacrificial love is better understood by inserting the types of Greek love into their conversation. John wrote, "When they had finished eating, Jesus said to Simon Peter, "Simon son of John, do you love (agape) me more than these?"

"Yes, Lord," he said, "you know that I love (phileo) you." Jesus said, "Feed my lambs." Again, Jesus said, "Simon son of John, do you love (agape) me?" He answered, "Yes, Lord, you know that I love (phileo) you." Jesus said, "Take care of my sheep." The third time he said to him, "Simon son of John, do you love (phileo) me?" Peter was hurt because Jesus asked him the third time . . . He said, "Lord, you know all things; you know that I love (phileo) you." Jesus said, "Feed my sheep".

Jesus uses the term "phileo" (Philia) instead of "agape" when he questioned Peter the third time. John was very specific whenever he wrote because, as an educated man, words had meaning to him. In his Greek text of his Gospel if different words were used meanings would be better understood.

Before going into the differences written about, (Agape and Philia) we must look at the question Jesus is actually asking Peter. Jesus said, "Do you love me more than *"These"* Who or what are "these" referring to? Many knowledgeable pastors divided the answer into three statements. The word these could have meant that Peter loved Jesus more than the other disciples loved Jesus. It could have meant that this disciple loved Jesus more than Peter's job as a fisherman, or it could have been did the love Peter had for Jesus was more than his love for the other disciples.

It is Jesus who is actually asking Peter if he would be willing to sacrifice. Will he love the Lord more than anything? Would Peter be willing to put Jesus before anything else in the world, even death? In the book John by Andreas Köstenberger, he explained that Peter "was called to love Jesus more than these other men do and to be willing to render extraordinary sacrifice on behalf of his master. (Köstenberger, 597) Jesus is asking Peter if he is really committed to more . . . and this is the definition Jesus expects and John shows in his Gospel.

Now the words Philia and Agape are used during this questioning because Jesus wants Peter to be willing to put Him first. By the time the third question arises, Jesus concedes, knowing that Peter is not ready for the ultimate sacrifice yet, so he uses brotherly love instead of sacrificial love. Being the all-knowing God, though, Jesus understands what will eventually happen.

5 INTRA-TRINITARIAN LOVE

John mentioned a lesser-known fifth type of love not usually represented in books. God loved the world and His people, people love themselves, people get married, family loves family, but God also loves himself, because He is the definition of love. This type of love is called intra-Trinitarian love. This described the love that God has for Jesus, Jesus has for God, and the love shared between both of them with the Holy Spirit. We have been taught since we were little children that God is Love—and He is. God is defined in the trinity as three in one. He is the father, the Son, and the Holy Spirit. John 3:35. explains, "The Father loves the Son and has given all things into his hand". We can infer here the Holy Spirit, even though it is not written.

Many are quick to say that God loves you, and this is truth. However, God is more than that John wrote, in his first letter, "Anyone who does not love does not know God, because God is love" (1 John 4:8). God is Love! So, let's define love. Dictionary.com defines love as "a strong feeling of warm personal attachment or deep affection, such as for a parent, child, friend, or pet. Oxford Languages defines it as, "an intense feeling of deep affection." Love, though, is actually God. Love is a relationship. If god were not three in one (trinity) before time, how could we describe the love found at the beginning of creation?

The relationship of God is tripartite, God loves God. God loves His creation, and God loves us. His love is shown before time in the words of Moses who wrote Genesis. The Bible says, "And God said, Let us make man in our image, after our likeness: and let them have dominion over the fish of the sea, and over the birds of the heavens, and over the cattle, and over all the earth, and over every creeping thing that creepeth upon the earth." (Genesis 1:26). He loves us even when we sin, but because of sin we were to face a final death. However, He loves us so much that He sent Himself, in human form to pay for our sins, and to die as a sacrifice For all believers. He also left Himself, in the form of the Holy Spirit and as a helper in times of need, when He returned to His Heavenly Throne.

Many find it hard to understand the tripartite of God. We must understand that if God were not three in one, He couldn't be love because Love

GOSPEL IV: I'M JOHN, AND I'M ALL ABOUT THE LOVE

requires an object. Therefore, before creation, before time itself, there was God the Father, God the Son, and God the Holy Spirit. How else could John have claimed that "In the beginning was the Word and the Word was God and the Word was with God."

Part 7

UNDERSTANDING TRIPARTITE

IF WE LOOK AT our world and ourselves, it may become a bit easier to understand the trinity of God. He is not the only thing that is divided three times in one nature. All we need do is to look at our universe, our world, and our own selves to understand three in one. The results are a bit surprising, but with God all things are possible and all things are ordered.

To begin, let us look at the Universe. Defined as simply as possible, the universe is everything. It is all energy, all matter, and all of space. It includes time, past, present' and future. It contains our world along with billions of others, and it contains us. The universe is everything above us, below us, and within us.

Science is slowly making strides in understanding the universe, but has a long way to go. Every hypothesis science creates and proves has a way of leading to a new hypothesis and a new understanding. The only thing that science proves, in all of our research and acquired knowledge, is that we are at the very beginning of full understanding.

The universe is actually made of three parts. Today's understanding is that it takes normal matter (also called visible matter), dark matter, and dark energy to fill our universe. First, we can see matter. Although man has a way of naming that matter, stars, galaxies, planets, moons, comets, meteorites and meteors, all matter, itself, seems to follow and obey the natural laws of science.

The universe is also made up of things we cannot see. Scientist call this matter—dark matter. The scientific world is constantly trying to understand dark matter and although they believe the universe will not work without

GOSPEL IV: I'M JOHN, AND I'M ALL ABOUT THE LOVE

it; they still do not understand what cannot be observed. It is, however, realized because of the action it performs and gravitational effects that can be observed.

Finally, the universe is made up of dark energy. Scientists do not fully understand this part of the universe, but they know that it exists. As a matter of fact, they estimate that almost 70% of the universe is dark energy. Because, in the 1900's, science began to notice that the universe was beginning to speed up, they theorized that this was caused by an unseen force they named Dark Energy.[1] I cannot claim to understand all of this, but it is interesting that the universe is, indeed, tripartite.

Looking out into the abyss of space we, too, can witness things divided into three different parts. Suppose I describe a fact I observed in the stars when I was a child. Then we look up and see another celestial event happening at this very minute. Talking a bit more, we discuss another event in the future we decide to observe together. We know we are actually talking about time. Time, for us, is divided into three parts, but it is still—time.

Albert Einstein is best known for his theory of relativity. In his theory, he explained that time is relative to the observer's point of reference. We all see time, as it passes, through our own eyes, so we assume that it is linear . Physicist Brian Greene clarified Einstein's theory but showed that there is no well-defined answer between past, present, and future. Today's scientists believe that past, present, and future all exist in what they call space-time; a mathematical concept that places space and time into a single idea called a continuum. Since time doesn't flow for everyone exactly the same, because of perspective, time could be an illusion.[2] However, we are once again left with three being one.

We looked at time and space, giving us a big picture. We can look at this idea of tripartite just as well by looking at very tiny things. What about the atom? The speck science used to call "the smallest thing in the universe, soon was explained as having three parts. The Atom is made up of protons, neutrons, and electrons. They are three in one. For years, when I was growing up, I was taught these were the smallest things known to mankind. However, science has now realized that atoms, especially protons and

---

1. Nasa, "The Universe's Building Blocks," https://science.nasa.gov/universe/overview/building-blocks/#:~:text=Everything%20scientists.

2. Brian Greene, "AskScience AMA Series: I'm Brian Greene, theoretical physicist, mathematician, and string theorist, and co-founder of the World Science Festival. AMA!," Reddit, 2020, https://www.reddit.com/r/askscience/comments/gquwbq/askscience_ama_series_im_brian_green .

UNDERSTANDING TRIPARTITE

neutrons, can be divided into even smaller parts. These are called quarks and, you guessed it, are divided into six pair of three "flavors", Up quarks, Down quarks, and Strange Quarks. These now are thought to be building blocks of ordinary matter.[3]

We have looked at the vastness found above and we have looked at the smallest things known. How about the place we call home? Could that be tripartite? We live on Earth and earth is made of three areas: the geosphere, hydrosphere, and cryosphere. The geosphere is made up of rocks/minerals, water, and air yet it is still earth. The hydrosphere deals with all the water on earth. It is found in three places: under the earth, on top of the earth and in the air. Finally, the cryosphere contains sea ice, glaciers/ice sheets, and permafrost.[4] Even the Earth's elements are divided into solid, liquid, and gas.

Humans are no different than the rest of the universe. We, too, are divided into three parts. 1 Thes. 5:23 explains this "…and I pray God your whole spirit, and soul and body be preserved blameless unto the coming of our Lord Jesus Christ". Man is a tripartite being. We possess a body, and within that body, we have a soul and a spirit. These are separate entities. The body is not eternal. The soul and the spirit are (where they spend eternity is really up to each individual). The soul and the spirit, however, cannot be separated.

First, the role of the body is to gather information about the world around us. It is the vessel used to communicate what our senses observe. The human body allows us to complete any responsibilities we feel must be accomplished. Through its structure, we are able to live, breath, walk, talk, and think. With a brain we are able to communicate thoughts and express our understanding of the physical world in which we live.

The body, however, has a much more important role. It is our outer shell which encompasses the soul and the spirit. The soul, although not separable from the spirit, has three parts. It contains the intellect, the will, and the emotions. The intellect gives us cognitive and spiritual power. It allows us to think and reason. Proverbs 24:14 says "wisdom is "sweet to your soul; if you find it, there is a future hope for you, and your hope will not be cut off."

Our soul not only deals with intellect, it contains our will. We were created in the image of God. God, though, gave us free will. We can plan

---

3. Patrick J. Kiger, "Quarks Are the Building Blocks of All Matter," Jun 9, 2023, https://science.howstuffworks.com/quarks.htm.

4. Sheri Amsel, "Earth's Systems—Geosphere, Hydrosphere, Atmosphere, and Biosphere," Exploring Nature, Dec. 23, 2024, https://www.exploringnature.org/db/view/Earths-Systems-Geosphere-Hydrosphere-Atmosphere-and-Biosphere.

GOSPEL IV: I'M JOHN, AND I'M ALL ABOUT THE LOVE

with intent. We are given information by the intellect and we act upon that because of our will. Job 7:15 states that, "The soul chooses, which is a decision made by the will." The choice we make can be the choice between right and wrong.

Right and wrong are controlled by the third part of the soul: emotion or our feelings. Our emotions sometimes lead us to a wrong decision, but we try to justify our reasons because of our feelings. We know what is good and we know what is not. We could explain emotions as the voice of the soul, linking us with inner knowledge.

That inner knowledge leads us to defining the spirit. When we are created, God breathes into us life. This breathe of God is what gives life, and brings us our spirit. This spirit, too, contains three parts. It is our conscience, it is our need to fellowship, and it contains our intuition. Our conscience guides us. We are human, but we already possess the understanding of right and wrong. Genesis 2:7 explains: "Then the LORD God formed a man from the dust of the ground and breathed into his nostrils the breath of life, and the man became a living being". It was the spirit of God giving a living spirit to man.

The spirit given to mankind connects men and women to God and to the unseen heavenly realm. This sheds light onto the soul and provides it with spiritual knowledge. Romans 2:15 defines this when it is written, "They show that the requirements of the law are written on their hearts, their consciences also bearing witness, and their thoughts sometimes accusing them and at other times even defending them."

It is our God, then, that has put into our spirits the ability to know right from wrong no matter what life we are living. We have an inner need to fellowship with others and with God. Even if someone refuses to believe in God, there is a spark inside everyone that makes us question. That search requires us to share the understanding we have gained. Because we possess intuition, (direct knowledge in our spirit that allows us to comprehend truth) we can reach conclusions. This is a gift from God, but because He gave mankind free will but we do not always follow what we know to be good and right.

We now understand how our universe is tripartite, our world is Tripartite, the very matter that makes up all of that is also three in one. We humans are also a trinity. We possess three parts, body, soul, and spirit. We can understand we have one nature but it is divided. With that knowledge it seems easier, now, to understand the three parts of God.

UNDERSTANDING TRIPARTITE

    The disciple, John, knew that God was Father, Son, and Holy spirit. Because of his good news, we too now knew the nature of God. John explicitly taught this concept and told us that Jesus explained how He and the father were one. John wrote, "There are three who bear witness in heaven, the Father, the Word, and the Spirit; and these three are one"(1 John 5:7). With that understanding it is time to further explore the Gospel according to John.

Part 8

THE "I AM THAT I AM" AND THE "I AM"

John had showed us that Jesus was love and Jesus was with God from the very beginning and before. He actually told us that Jesus was God and equal in every way. So far, John had explained God the Father and God the Son, two of the three separate but equal parts of the Trinity. John was a believer. The disciple wanted to express that Jesus used the phrase "I am" seven times as recorded in his Gospel.

I AM

The first time John knew he believed, was when he described Jesus using the words "I am". It happened when the Pharisees were questioning Jesus. The Lord had stated that God deserved all the Glory and that He was not there seeking glory. In John 8:50–59, the disciple tells the following: Jesus told them (the Pharisees), "Truly, truly, I say to you, if anyone keeps my word, he will never see death."

The Pharisees said to Jesus, "Abraham died, as did the prophets, yet you say, 'If anyone keeps my word, he will never taste death.' Are you greater than our father Abraham, who died? And the prophets who died! Who do you make yourself out to be?"

Jesus answered, "If I glorify myself, my glory is nothing. It is my Father who glorifies me, he of whom you say, "He is our God, though you do not know him. But I know him; if I would say that I do not know him, I would

THE "I AM THAT I AM" AND THE "I AM"

be a liar like you. But I do know him and I keep his word. Your ancestor Abraham rejoiced that he would see my day; he saw it and was glad."

Then the Jews said to him, "You are not yet fifty years old, and have you seen Abraham?"

Jesus said to them, "Very truly, I tell you, before Abraham was, I am."

This outraged the pharisees So they picked up stones to throw at him, but Jesus hid himself and went out of the temple. It was not the time yet for Him to be sacrificed. John compares this use of the words "I am" to show the correlation between John's gospel and the statement made by God in Exodus 3:14. God said to Moses, "I AM WHO I AM." And he said, "Say this to the people of Israel: 'I AM has sent me to you." John furthered the examples of Jesus as the I Am by expressing to us the seven times Jesus used the words.

Poet, William Price, in "OUR CREATOR'S WORK: Poems and Thoughts Of a Christian Poet" (who happens to be this book's author) wrote the following to show the seven times Jesus used I Am.

HIS SEVEN I AM'S

Jesus said and used the words
"I Am the Bread of Life."
Explaining He ends the hunger we have
And eliminates all of our strife.
"I am the light of the world" Christ said,
And the Pharisees challenged him.
They asked Him who He thought He was.
His answer to them was, "I Am."

"I AM the Door of the Sheep." He said.
The only one you will see—
That lets the sheep be safe from harm.
And "No one comes in, but by me."

"I AM the Good Shepherd" He said in John.
A promise He'd surely keep.
As any Shepard would do for his flock;
He'd give His life for His sheep.

"I AM the Resurrection," He cried,
Followed by, "and the Life."
He was explaining that He was the source
To continue to live when we die.

GOSPEL IV: I'M JOHN, AND I'M ALL ABOUT THE LOVE

"I AM the Way, the Truth and the Life."
He said He was more than God's son.
"You've seen your Father if you have seen me,
For I and the Father are one."

When Jesus expressed, "I AM the True Vine."
And disciples would all bear good fruit,
He explained how all the branches would live
Because He was their nurturing root.

Jesus declared "I AM" seven times,
Like the God of Abraham
Said to Moses, who asked Him for His name
And He answered, "I Am That I Am."

Jesus said, I am the bread of life, the light of the world, the door, the good shepherd, the resurrection and the life, the way the truth and the life, and the true vine. Each of the seven examples explained the divinity and love of Jesus as God in human form.

I AM THE BREAD OF LIFE

All throughout the history of mankind people have experienced times of famine. They, one time or another, have known what it is like to be hungry. When the 5,000 gathered to listen to Jesus speak, they spent the whole day. During that time, Jesus knew they would get hungry. He asked His disciples what they had to eat and all they had was five loves and two fish. The miracle occurred when Jesus took all the disciples had and created enough for the people to eat, with 12 baskets of food left over. Jesus had power over the natural world and brought forth food for the hungry. Jesus said to His followers, "I am the bread of life. Whoever comes to me will never be hungry, and whoever believes in me will never be thirsty" (John 6:35). This, however, was more than a physical manifestation of food. Jesus was telling them He was essential for life, not just physical hunger, but spiritual life and fulfillment. He is claiming that He is the food necessary for eternal life.

THE LIGHT OF THE WORLD

We live in a dark sinful world and we are often in need of a guiding light. When a ship is struggling with rough waves and crashing seas, the captain and crew are very dependent on the lighthouses which may guide them to safety. We, too, need light and Jesus knew that. He called Himself, Ph[set macron over o]s tou-kósmou in Greek or "light of the world" in English. Our Lord is the one who will guide us through this dark world and help us find the light of truth. He will direct us and lead us to the ultimate light which is eternal salvation, far from the darkness of the Devil and sin. It is this light of life that we all need to strive toward. We need to find our safety in that eternal light.

THE DOOR

John, in His chapter 10, verse 9 wrote, I am the door; whoever enters through me will be saved. They will come in and go out, and find pasture. If you have ever seen a sheep farm. You will see a gate where the sheep go from the pen to the pasture. The pen is safety and the pasture sustains the sheep. There is only one gate, or door that is used in the quote used by Jesus. As the sheep do, we must do. Jesus told us that He is the gate, or the door. He is the only way to safety and salvation. There is only one door that leads to eternal life, and that door is the Son of God. We enter eternal life with Jesus, but accomplish this through Him only.

THE GOOD SHEPHERD

During the time of Jesus, people understood what it meant to be a good shepherd. The shepherd was relied upon to protect the sheep. If any danger would arise, the man would use his very life to protect the sheep. When the shepherd would speak and begin to walk, the sheep would hear his voice, recognize it, and follow their protector. Jesus used this metaphor to explain who He was. Jesus was the one willing to give up His life for His believers. Our Messiah is actually the one who loves us and was willing to be the sacrifice to save us from eternal death. Through the Good Shepherd, we can find salvation and eternal life.

THE RESSURECTION

I am the Resurrection has become the main principle of Christianity. If Jesus had not chosen to lay down His life and die on the cross then there

GOSPEL IV: I'M JOHN, AND I'M ALL ABOUT THE LOVE

would be no hope for mankind. He died for our sins, but that wasn't the end. On the third day, he was resurrected and showed to us that there was life after death. It also gave us all a glimpse of the power possessed by Jesus.

In John 11:25, Jesus said, "I am the resurrection and the life. The one who believes in me will live, even though they die; and whoever lives by believing in me will never die." Our Lord showed us that He is the one with the power to give us eternal life with Him, if we only believe and trust Him. Because of God, we no longer are faced with eternal misery, grief, and despair.

THE WAY, THE TRUTH, AND THE LIFE

Try going to your local store by driving in the wrong direction. Unless you turn around, you will never make it. The statement "I am the way" is our roadmap to truth and life. Jesus is the only way to reach eternal life. The choice is up to each individual. The route you choose will take you whereever you are going. Wrong route—wrong destination! Jesus is the way, the truth, and the life. He is the mediator between this life and eternal life with Him. Again, Jesus said "No one comes to the Father except through me." There is only one road and that is our faith in the Christ.

THE TRUE VINE

It is the job of a Christian to witness to others about the Lord and Savior, Jesus—the Christ. Every believer does this in his or her own way. Some talk about Jesus. Others show the love by the way they live their lives. Still others may be chosen to write down the things that lead to a life in Jesus. It is our job to bear fruit and to bring others to Jesus. In the first century A.D. the purpose of the vine was to make wine. Grapes that had a strong root system produced a better fruit that would improve the taste of the wine being created. This has always been a symbol of the power of God. The True Vine was Jesus and we are to be rooted in Him. We must be steadfast in the word and we must bear fruit for God. If we do not, we will not help others and we will not be in harmony with our Savior and our God.

Part 9

THE FIVE PARTS OF MY GOSPEL

#1 — THE DEITY

JOHN'S GOSPEL CAN BE described as a book divided into five parts. First was the description of Jesus as God in the flesh. The second part of John's book talked about Jesus as the worker of miracles. Third, was the last night the disciples spent with Jesus as a group. After that John wrote about the Passion of the Christ: the arrest, trial, crucifixion, and resurrection. Finally, The beloved Disciple explained what was called the Commission of Peter. Jesus knew, as we have read and heard, that Peter had denied Him three times during His trial. Before Jesus left His disciples, He personally asked Peter three times If he loved Him. Peter answered three times that he did. The commission that Jesus left Peter and the others was, "Feed my Sheep". Peter understood that he was to lead the church of these new Christians and future followers of the Messiah.

For Christians, especially new Christians, the first section of the Gospel of John helps with understanding because the verses expressed the deity or divinity of the Lord, Jesus. In Chapter one, John called Jesus the Word (Logos). Calling Him that described the fact that Jesus came into this world to introduce God to humanity. The disciple also alluded to Genesis where the first four words in the Bible are "In the beginning, God . . ." In other words, there was nothing except God before anything was created. Then God created the Heavens and the earth. "And God said, 'Let there be light'; and there was light" It was the word of God that brought everything into

GOSPEL IV: I'M JOHN, AND I'M ALL ABOUT THE LOVE

existence. "and He said It was good." With each word God spoke, creation happened.

We have discussed the tripartite nature of God and we know that God was the Father, the Son, and the Holy Spirit. So, it was natural for John to state that "In the beginning was the word, and the Word was with God, and the Word was God" John, here, was more than implying. His statement declared that Jesus was with God before creation and He also—was God. Jesus was the word that spoke everything into existence. Because John described Jesus in this way, it is easier to understand God when He created mankind. God said, in Genesis 1:26, "Let us make man in *our* image, after *our* likeness . . ." This made it clear for us since we, too, are body, spirit, and soul. John let us know that Jesus was in the beginning with God, but furthered that when he wrote, "All things were made through Him, and without Him nothing was made that was made."

Next, John declared that Jesus was the light of man. "In him was life, and the life was the light of men. The light shines in the darkness, and the darkness has not overcome it" (John1:4–5). Mankind has separated himself and herself from God because of sin. Sin lead all of us away from God. When Jesus came, He came as light to show us the way out of our darkness. When a light is on, we can see more clearly. Try walking in a totally dark room that is unknown to you. Tripping over the unseen leads to a fall. The world was dark, as it were, when Jesus came. Those living in the world, living in sin, could not understand the light until they accepted the light. Satan always attempts to blind people from God. That blindness will not let in the light.

Because of the Darkness in this world, John continued next writing about another that was born to make way for this light. In John 1: 6–8 he wrote, "There was a man sent from God, whose name was John. He came as a witness, to bear witness about the light, that all might believe through him. He was not the light, but came to bear witness about the light. John the Baptist was sent to tell others that the Messiah was coming. Some accepted this and repented, Others were blind and did not accept the words of the Baptist when he said in verses 9–14,

> "The one who is the true light, who gives light to everyone, was coming into the world. He came into the very world he created, but the world didn't recognize him. He came to his own people, and even they rejected him. But to all who believed him and accepted him, he gave the right to become children of God. They are reborn—not with a physical birth resulting from human passion or plan, but a

THE FIVE PARTS OF MY GOSPEL

birth that comes from God. So, the Word became flesh and made his home among us. He was full of unfailing love and faithfulness. And we have seen his glory, the glory of the Father's one and only Son."

God became man so that man could see, understand, and return to God. Our Heavenly Father wanted us to be his children which meant that we needed to believe and follow Jesus. This is the foundation of the Christian faith.

When we know something, we proclaim it! John, next, showed us a man who knew immediately who Jesus was. The beloved disciple, John, and his brother James were followers of John the Baptist. The Baptist told everyone who would listen that the Messiah was coming. Soon people were asking if he was the Messiah. John, in no uncertain terms let the people know he was not. John the Baptist would shout, "I am a voice shouting in the wilderness, Clear the way for the Lord's coming!" (John 1:24).

The Pharisees, or religious leaders, asked John why he thought he had the right to baptize people if he were not the Messiah. The Baptist replied that he was baptizing with water. He said, "but right here in the crowd is someone you do not recognize. Though his ministry follows mine, I'm not even worthy to be his slave and untie the straps of his sandal." John, later, saw Jesus He explained to the crowd how he knew that this was the Messiah in John 1:29–34.

> *The next day John saw Jesus coming toward him and said, "Look! The Lamb of God who takes away the sin of the world! He is the one I was talking about when I said, A man is coming after me who is far greater than I am, for he existed long before me. I did not recognize him as the Messiah, but I have been baptizing with water so that he might be revealed to Israel. "Then John testified, "I saw the Holy Spirit descending like a dove from heaven and resting upon him. I didn't know he was the one, but when God sent me to baptize with water, he told me, 'The one on whom you see the Spirit descend and rest is the one who will baptize with the Holy Spirit.' I saw this happen to Jesus, so I testify that he is the Chosen One of God."*

After Jesus was baptized by John, He began to gather those who would be His disciples so that He could teach them.

Little by little people began to listen to Jesus as he talked to crowds about His mission. The first was Simon, who was given the name Peter. Next, Jesus choose Peter's brother, Andrew. Two disciples of the Baptist were next. They had seen Jesus when John the Baptist claimed, ""Behold the

GOSPEL IV: I'M JOHN, AND I'M ALL ABOUT THE LOVE

Lamb of God who takes away the sins of the world" (John 1:29). James and John, then, followed Jesus. Later Jesus chose Phillip, Nathanael (also known as Bartholomew though this is sometimes debated), Matthew, Thomas, James son of Alphaeus, Thaddeus (also known as Judas or Lebbeus), Simon the Zealot, and then Judas Iscariot.

As Jesus was choosing the twelve, these new disciples gave Him different titles. They called Him The Word, The Light of the world, Son of God, The Christ, lamb of God, King of Israel, and the Son of Man. Names were rather important in the time of Jesus because they were often used for identification. The name would also describe the character of the person and give meaning to his name.

John defined Jesus, in his Gospel, as Logos (word) which showed power and divinity. Jesus was considered the voice or spokesman of God. John also uses the word light seven times to describe the Messiah. It is a light that is pure, makes anyone secure, and leads one away from darkness or sin. John wrote about Nathaniel (Bartholomew) who called Jesus the Son of God claiming He was more than a man. Andrew told Peter that they had found the Messiah, the Christ. Here Christ is a title meaning "the chosen one". The Baptist exclaimed that Jesus was the Lamb. This would have shown that John recognized Jesus as the sacrifice for the sins of the world. Nathaniel called the Lord, King of Israel. At the time he would have considered Jesus as a king just like David was. Later it became known that Jesus was the King of Kings and Lord of Lords. Jesus called himself the Son of Man over 80 times. He knew He was God's son, but he often considered Himself human in that he was hungry, thirsty, and felt pain just as a human would. He wanted people to understand that He was God (I Am) but that He was also a human being.

Seven titles were given to one man. The number seven would have been of great importance in the first century Jews and Christians. This number symbolized completion. It is actually found in the Bible more than 800 times beginning in Genesis with Creation, which was seven days. Then the week was established with seven days ending on the Sabbath. John, himself, uses seven in his Gospel. It is interesting that he wrote 21 chapters (seven three times).

His Gospel explains the entire life of our Savior and told the seven times that Jesus used the words I Am. John wrote the words Jesus claimed: I am the Bread of Life, the light of the World, the Gate for the Sheep, the Good Shepherd, The Resurrection and the Life, the Way the Truth and the

Life, and the True Vine. Each one of these statements shows the divine nature of the Christ. He is the source of truth and he is everyone's salvation.

#2 — MIRACLES OF JESUS

The defining moments in the second section in John's Gospel show the divinity of Jesus.

Chapter two through chapter twelve show Jesus performing Miracles everywhere from weddings to funerals. John needed to show Jews and new Christians, alike, that Jesus was the one who had fulfilled all of the law and all of the prophecies from old. These seven supernatural miracles, done by the Lord, These signs of divine power give proof to the claims made by the Beloved Disciple.

The first miraculous event occurred when Jesus decided to go to the wedding which was held in Cana, Galilee. The bride and the groom are not mentioned by name, but because Mary, the mother of Jesus, was present, and it is assumed that it could have been one of her relatives. The best way to observe the first miracle performed by Jesus is to let John's story explain.

The Wedding

Nothing is more honored, in ancient times and even in today's era, than a wedding. The joining of two people in holy matrimony was not only honored, but also sacred. I think Jesus, who was invited to a wedding, went to give his blessing to this act of love.

It was on the third day, following this man Jesus, that Andrew, Peter, Philip and Nathanael found out that they, too, were going to a wedding in Cana of Galilee. Mary, the mother of Jesus was there also. They were enjoying the festivities when Mary told Jesus the host had run out of wine. Mary explained to the servants to do exactly what Jesus asked of them. Sitting there at the wedding were six water pots containing twenty to thirty gallons apiece. Jesus told the servants to fill the pots with water.

He then commanded them to draw some out and take it to the master of the feast. They took it and the master drank. Imagine the shock, when this man commended the bridegroom on saving the best wine for the end of the feast. He had no idea where this excellent wine had come from, but the servants and disciples did. Jesus had turned the water into wine. I know

GOSPEL IV: I'M JOHN, AND I'M ALL ABOUT THE LOVE

that unbelief must have quickly turned to belief when the disciples saw this *sign* Jesus showed them.

There are several reasons Jesus did this. First, it showed the almighty power possessed by Him. He had the ability the change one substance into another. It was also showing how Jesus could change material things as well as any person who wanted to change, which allowed for Him to be glorified. In John 2:11the disciple said, "This, the first of His signs, Jesus did at Cana in Galilee and manifested His glory."

It didn't only show the Messiah's glory, it possessed several symbols, too. The wine was a symbol of the blood that Jesus was about to sacrifice. It also showed the joy and majesty possessed by Jesus. Weddings signified unity and harmony because it explained the covenant God had with His people. Jesus was, in a way, showing a new covenant defining the Messiah and His new Kingdom.

The Nobleman's Son

Later, Jesus returned to Cana. While He was there people began believing in Him. John in chapter 4, verses 46–54 recalled the story.

> *There was a certain royal official whose son lay sick at Capernaum. When this man heard that Jesus had arrived in Galilee from Judea, he went to him and begged him to come and heal his son, who was close to death. "Unless you people see signs and wonders," Jesus told him, "you will never believe."*
> *The royal official said, "Sir, come down before my child dies."*
> *"Go," Jesus replied, "your son will live."*
> *The man took Jesus at his word and departed. While he was still on the way, his servants met him with the news that his boy was living. When he inquired as to the time when his son got better, they said to him, "Yesterday, at one in the afternoon, the fever left him." Then the father realized that this was the exact time at which Jesus had said to him, "Your son will live." So he and his whole household believed. This was the second sign Jesus performed after coming from Judea to Galilee.*

This second sign was of such significance because Jesus had the power to give life due to someone's faith. It didn't matter who the person was, it only mattered that he believed in the power that Jesus showed. Jesus was not contained to any specific time or space either. His power was not controlled by that, it was beyond that. At the same hour Jesus said that the nobleman's son was healed, he was healed. Jesus showed that He was in charge of life, itself.

Paralysis Is no Challenge

Jesus was doing the work that God had sent Him to do. In John, chapter 5, Jesus went to Jerusalem. And went in by the Sheep Gate where there was a famous pool, named Bethesda. This pool was used by the sick, because it was believed to be visited by an Angel of God. When the angel entered the pool, the waters stirred, and the person who entered at that time was healed.

Jesus met a man there who had an infirmity for thirty-eight years. When Jesus saw him, he asked, "Do you want to be made well? "The sick man said that he had tried, but every time he saw the water stir someone else always beat him into the pool, because he had never gotten help. Jesus looked at him and said, "Rise, take up your bed, and walk." Instantly the man was able to walk and he left.

The Jews saw him carrying his bed and yelled at him. "It is the Sabbath. It is not lawful for you to carry your bed." He told them that a man had healed him and said that he must do it. The Jews asked him who the man was, but he didn't know.

It wasn't until later that Jesus saw the man and told him to sin no more, or a worse thing could happen to him. That man then left and told the Jews it was Jesus who had healed him. Because it was the Sabbath, the Jews wanted to hunt down Jesus, persecute Him, and kill Him.

When they found Him, He told them, "My father has been working until now, and I have been working." The Jews became even more livid. This man had not only broken the Law of the Sabbath, but he dared say that God was his father. The pious Jews would often attack the law breakers, because it made them believe they were better than anyone else. They acted as though they were shocked by the words Jesus spoke.

Jesus made the claim that He was the Son of God. This miracle showed the authority that He possessed. It also exhibited His power over the Human body. He could not only heal the sick, but he could cure any physical disabilities. Jesus was not confined to the laws of man.

GOSPEL IV: I'M JOHN, AND I'M ALL ABOUT THE LOVE

The Fish, Loaves, And The Sea

Chapter 6 of the Gospel of John described the fourth miracle Jesus displayed. The following retells what john wrote. The quotes are from Jesus and some of His disciples excerpted from the Holy Bible. The power of God, through Jesus, continued.

It was at the sea of Galilee that Jesus went up into the hills with His disciples. Jesus looked up and saw the multitude of people who had followed them to hear His words. Already knowing what He was going to do, He leaned to Philip and asked, "Where shall we buy bread that these may eat?" I think Jesus was testing His disciples a little.

Philip answered that they did not have enough to feed such a crowd. Andrew came to Jesus and said that there was a boy who had five barley loaves and two fish, but that wouldn't begin to feed the people.

Jesus told us, "Make the people sit down." there were about five thousand there and they sat so they could hear. Jesus took the five loaves and the two fish and, after giving thanks to God, he gave them to us who in turn gave them to the crowd. We, with shocked looks on our faces, handed out the bread and fish and every one of the five thousand ate, with enough left over to fill twelve baskets. The multitude had witnessed another miracle and claimed that Jesus was the Prophet sent by God to the world. Jesus, however departed alone, because He knew that if He had stayed the crowd would have tried to make him King.

When the evening came, we, the disciples went to the sea, got into a boat, and started out for Capernaum. We had gone about three or four miles when the sea became rough. The waves rose and the wind began to blow. Some men look out at the sea and saw Jesus walking on the water. We immediately became afraid.

Jesus said to us. "It is I; do not be afraid." After He had said this, we received Him onto the boat and found that we immediately had reached our destination.

When the crowd had realized that Jesus had left, they too went to Capernaum to find Him. When they arrived, they saw Jesus and asked Him, "Rabbi, when did you come here?"

Jesus answered, "Most assuredly, I say to you, you seek me, not because you saw the signs, but because you ate of the loaves and were filled. Do not labor for the food which perishes, but for the food which endures to everlasting life which the Son of Man will give you."

The people then asked what they needed to do to see the works of God. He answered, saying, "This is the work of God, that you believe in Him who He sent."

The crowd began wondering what signs Jesus would do so they would believe in Him. After all, Moses had given them Manna from Heaven while they were in the desert. He knew what they were asking, so he told them that Moses had not given them the bread from Heaven. It had been His father. And now His father was giving the world the true bread of life.

Jesus told them, "I am the bread of life. He who comes to me shall never hunger and he who believes in me shall never thirst." He then emphasized that He had come not to do His own will, but the will of His father who had sent Him. The people began to grumble and argue among themselves. Jesus had told them that the bread he was to give was His flesh and they did not comprehend this. He had said that they must eat His flesh and drink His blood. Many of the men who had followed Him did not believe after he had spoken. They did not understand He was speaking the words of Spirit and not of the flesh.

Out of five loaves of bread and two fish, Jesus feed over five thousand people. This miracle, Actually, told of His power over nature. It explained that Jesus sustains us, not just physically but spiritually. He is the bread of life

Walk on Water—Calm the Seas

Jesus always was willing to show His disciples love and provide them with comfort when they were fearful. No matter the situation, Jesus was in control. His power showed His followers of the love He possessed. Another power was shown when the disciples of the Christ were alone in a boat. Jesus had left them for a while and had gone up into the mountains. The disciples went down to the lake and started to cross over to the city of Capernaum.

It was beginning to get dark, the wind became extremely strong, and the seas became rough. When the men had gone about three or four miles, they were afraid. Next, to their surprise, they saw Jesus approaching the boat. He was walking on top of the water. They were filled with fear. Jesus told them not to be afraid. He had comforted them and they took Him into the boat. At that moment, the shore, where they had been heading appeared.

There is no place on earth that could block Jesus from going. His power was beyond any barrier that could stop mankind. The power of Jesus had control over nature itself and could intervene in any situation to be a

GOSPEL IV: I'M JOHN, AND I'M ALL ABOUT THE LOVE

help in time of need. He expressed to his disciples He was salvation, even in times of extreme distress. No matter what man's struggles may be, it is Jesus that will appear and calm our situation no matter what it is. Jesus, being God, had that power

The Blind Man

Imagine for a moment that your world was completely dark. From birth, you have never been able to see. Others may try to explain what things are and you could always touch something that was unseen to you. This could help a bit, but the lack of sight would completely change your perspective.

Now, suppose someone came up to you, touched you, and you could see. What joy would fill your heart. This happened to a man who had been blind from birth. John wrote about this occurrence when Jesus had left the Temple and had run into a man blind from birth. Again, the quotes you read are spoken by Jesus and the blind man.

After Jesus passed from the Scribes and Pharisees in the Temple, He saw a blind man by the way. This man had been blind from birth. When we the disciples saw him, we asked Jesus what sin this man's parents committed that would have caused this affliction. According to the law of Moses, many sicknesses would affect the child because of the sins of the parents, so it was proper for the disciples to question this. Jesus told us that it wasn't a sin, committed by the man or his parents, that caused his blindness He explained that he was blind so that the works of God could be revealed to him. Jesus said that He must work the work of His Father who had sent Him.

Describing how He was the light of the world, Jesus knelt down and spat on the ground, making mud, which he placed over the eyes of the blind man. He then spoke saying "Go. Wash in the pool of Siloam" (which actually means sent).

The man went, washed, and came back with full sight. The neighbors saw the man and were astonished, asking how he got his sight. He explained what had happened, stating a man called Jesus had performed this miracle. When the people asked where this Jesus was, the newly sighted man answered that he did not know, They, therefore, took the man to the Pharisees.

The Pharisees, seeing that Jesus had performed this act on the Sabbath, told the crowd that this Jesus was not from God, because He didn't keep the Sabbath. They turned to the former blind man and asked him what he had to say now, about this Jesus. He looked at them and merely said, "He is a Prophet!"

The Pharisees where so determined to dispute this man's word, they summoned his parents asking them if this were really their son. They admitted he was and that he had been blind from birth. They stated they didn't know how he had gotten his sight and told the leaders to question him. After all, he was of age and could speak for himself. I know that they answered in this y because they were afraid of these Jewish leaders.

They called the son back and questioned him again. They told him they knew Jesus was a sinner and while he may want to become a disciple of Jesus, they were disciples of Moses. They knew God spoke to Moses, but they didn't know where this healer had come from.

The man said, "While you do not now where He is from, He opened my eyes . . . If this man were not from God, He could do nothing." Angry, yet again, the Pharisees cast the man out of the Synagogue telling everyone that he was completely born in sin.

Jesus heard that they had cast him out, so He found him and asked, "Do you believe in the Son of God?"

He answered, "Who is he, Lord, that I may believe in Him."

Jesus said, "You have seen Him and it is He who is talking to you."

After that the man who had been blind, but could now see clearly stated that he believed and he worshiped Jesus. The Pharisees, however, were the ones who were blind, because they did not believe.

This event discussed the power possessed by Jesus. It also explains why we are to be obedient to His requests. Jesus, (Logos) always had the power of light and darkness. It was He who divided the two in the first place. Even though the disciples questioned why the man had been born blind, the Lord told them that this revealed God's glory.

This miracle was so much more, though, than helping a blind man see. The significance of this allowed us to know that Jesus brings spiritual truth and brings to light the Insite needed to understand true life: eternal light in Christ. It is for those who accept the word of God and listen to Him.

Lazarus, Come Forth

The seventh miracle, discussed by John, was one that completely showing the Love of God. It also showed both the deity and the humanity of Jesus. The power of God would show His Glory and would also show that Jesus,

GOSPEL IV: I'M JOHN, AND I'M ALL ABOUT THE LOVE

too, possessed that same Glory. His power was God's power because they were one. To better explain John's story, I have taken the words for his Gospel and used the quotes from Jesus directly from the Gospel of John.

It was in the town of Bethany, that Martha, Mary, and Her brother Lazarus lived. They were friends of Jesus and He loved them. Lazarus became sick, so the sisters sent for Jesus to come and heal him. I think the disciples were all a bit surprised, as anyone would be, when Jesus told all of them that this sickness would not lead to death, but for the glory of God. He also told them that He would be glorified, too, through whatever was going to happen. None of the twelve understood, however, why Jesus waited two days until He decided to go to Lazarus.

Finally, Jesus told them that they were going to see Lazarus. He said, "Our friend Lazarus sleeps, but I go that I may wake him up."

The followers told Jesus that maybe if he were sleeping, he would get well, because they didn't understand that Jesus was actually telling them Lazarus was dead.

It was then that he told John and the others plainly, "Lazarus is dead. I am glad for your sake that I was not there, that you may believe. Nevertheless, let us go to him."

All of the disciples were a bit confused, especially when they arrived to find that Lazarus had been dead four days. While there, a crowd had gathered, including a group from Jerusalem, which was only a few miles away. They had come to comfort Mary and Martha.

As Jesus was coming, Martha came out to meet Him while Mary was at the house. Martha told Jesus that she didn't understand why He hadn't come to heal Lazarus. She added, "But even now I know that whatever you ask of God, God will give you."

Jesus looked at Martha and said, "Your brother will rise again." He continued, "I am the resurrection and the life. He who believes in me, though he may die, he shall live. And he who lives and believes in me, shall never die. Do you believe me?"

Martha told him that she did and that she knew He was the Christ, the Son of God. After talking with Him, Martha went to Mary. When she heard that Jesus was there, she left the house quickly. All of the comforters saw he leave and followed. They went up to Jesus. Mary fell at His feet and told him that if He had come sooner, her brother would not have died. When Jesus saw them all weeping, his spirit was troubled.

THE FIVE PARTS OF MY GOSPEL

"Where have you laid him?" Jesus asked, and they took him to the tomb where Lazarus had been buried. At that very moment, we couldn't believe our eyes. Jesus wept.

The others spoke among each other expressing how much Jesus must have loved Lazarus. Some complained that if He had come earlier, he could have saved Lazarus.

Jesus came to the tomb and told them to move away the stone. Martha reminded Jesus that it had been four days and there would be a terrible smell.

Jesus said to her, "Did I not say to you, that if you believed, you would see the glory of God?"

Jesus stood there as the men rolled away the stone. He lifter his eyes upward and prayed, "Father I thank you that you have heard me. And, I know that you always hear me, but because of the people standing by I said this that they may believe that you sent me." He then cried with a loud voice, "Lazarus, come forth."

There was silence. As you would say today, you could have heard a pin drop and as you can probably guess, Lazarus came out. They unbound him and took away the grave cloth and the face cloth. He was alive and the people there believed in Jesus. They all observed this miracle and believed.

Some of them went and told the Pharisees what had happened The Rulers of the Jews gathered for a meeting, and from that moment on, they plotted to put Jesus to death. They commanded that the people should report to them if they saw Jesus, so they could seize Him.

If we believe, as the followers of Jesus did, God's glory will be shown to each and every one of us. This is probably the greatest recollection John wrote, because it shows the power of the Savior. First, when Jesus wept, His heart was indeed broken and his humanness was brought into the light. Beyond that, though, His power over death itself, was proof of his divinity. When He told Lazarus to come forth and he came forth, Glory was His. Because of the action of Jesus, all humans who accept Him as their Lord and Savior will be raised again after their own death.

#3—THE LAST NIGHT WITH THE TWELVE

The third section of John's Gospel, chapters 13-17, showed Jesus as the servant and the sacrifice. He had come to Jerusalem, as many Jews had, to celebrate Passover. A week before the Feast, Jesus entered the city riding

GOSPEL IV: I'M JOHN, AND I'M ALL ABOUT THE LOVE

on the colt of a donkey. As He entered, people gathered and waved palm branches and laid them in front of Jesus as he rode by. They shouted out, "Hosanna! Blessed is He that comes in the name of the Lord! The King of Israel! Fear not, daughter of Zion, behold your King is coming on a donkey's colt" (John 12:13–16). At that time, John recalled the words of the Prophet, found in Zechariah 9:9 "Exult greatly, O daughter Zion! Shout for joy, O daughter Jerusalem! Behold: your king is coming to you, a just savior is he, Humble, and riding on a donkey, on a colt, the foal of a donkey." Everyone was excited. The Jewish people was accepting . . . for now.

It took less than a week for the entire scene to change. Those who had been shouting and claiming that Jesus was the King of the Jews soon forgot all the praise they had given. They started disbelieving. Soon they turned skeptical and that led to hate. John was well educated in the words of the prophets and knew that Isaiah had said that God hardened the hearts of His people and had blinded them to the truth because they had rejected their God.

If John were retelling the story now, he would more than likely tell us the following while using the words of Jesus from the Bible. This would help in the understanding of John's Gospel. So, let's imagine John was here and we had an opportunity to listen.

John would say today, "Now Jesus knew and I am telling you that this was done just as the old testament prophecy had foretold. Jesus began to explain why it was that the hour had come and He would be glorified. We did not understand at this point, but Jesus explained again how He was the Messiah."

Jesus used these words, "Most assuredly, I say to you, unless a grain of wheat falls into the ground and dies, it remains alone. But if it dies, it produces much grain. He who loves his life will lose it and he who hates his life in this world will keep it for eternal life. If anyone serves me, let him follow me, and where I am, there my servant will be also. If anyone serves me, him my father will honor." John would continue telling us what Jesus felt. He was troubled and, yet, that was the reason He had come to the world, so He would not ask His Father to save Him from this hour. Jesus said, "I, if I am lifter up from the earth, I will draw all people to Myself."

He was actually telling us how he would die, but we didn't understand. As a matter of fact, many believed in Him, but would not confess that because they were afraid of the Pharisees. They loved praise of man more than praise of God. And they were looking for any reason to get rid of our Lord.

THE FIVE PARTS OF MY GOSPEL

The same was happening as Jesus and the twelve were preparing for the Passover. During the Last Supper that The Lord would have with His followers, Jesus began by performing an ancient ritual of washing the feet of His disciples. The washing of feet was well documented in the Old Testament as well as the new. To show hospitality, even to strangers, the feet were washed by the host, the host's wife, or by a servant. In the Jewish culture, a rabbi would never have washed the feet of his disciples. They would have been the ones showing servitude toward their teacher.

This, however, was the meaning when Jesus washed the feet of His disciples. He had come as a servant to all of humanity, and this was the symbolism written about by John. When Peter told Jesus he was not worthy to have the Messiah wash his feet Jesus said, "Unless I wash you, you have no part with me" (John 13:8). Jesus washed Peter's feet.

After Jesus completed this task and showing his love, He explained to them how they, in the future, should wash each other's feet. He said that they must do what he showed them by example. In John 13:16 he recorded the words of the savior. "Truly, truly, I say to you, a servant is not greater than his master, nor is a messenger greater than the one who sent him."

Jesus continued by telling His disciples that one of them would betray Him. They looked at one another and were confused. One disciple, who John hardly ever named, was resting his head on Jesus. He was the beloved disciple. He asked Jesus who the betrayer was and Jesus answered, "I am not referring to all of you; I know those I have chosen. But this is to fulfill this passage of Scripture: He who shared my bread has turned against me. I am telling you now before it happens, so that when it does happen you will believe that I am who I am. Very truly I tell you, whoever accepts anyone I send accepts me; and whoever accepts me accepts the one who sent me" (John 13: 16–20).

The Messiah then told them that He was going away. He explains how this must happen to fulfill the reason His Father sent Him. He did explain to them how He would leave with them an "Advocate" who would always be with them. This promise of the Holy Spirit would give them the power to follow in Jesus' footsteps. Jesus said, "You must love (agape) one another as I have loved you." He ended by reminding them that He came from the Father and now He must return to the Father.

We all remember the Last supper recorded by Matthew, Mark, and Luke. John, however, does not include the bread representing the Body of Christ or the wine representing the blood shed for the sins of the world.

GOSPEL IV: I'M JOHN, AND I'M ALL ABOUT THE LOVE

John's Gospel, instead, concentrates on the love that Jesus had for all. Jesus was a comfort to them, and was willing to illustrate the love He would leave them with. In fact, John always preferred to express the spiritual love of Jesus, rather than the physical actions He took. John did, however, tell of the love, care, and concern Jesus had for them. He wrote the following:

> I will not leave you as orphans; I will come to you. Before long, the world will not see me anymore, but you will see me. Because I live, you also will live. On that day you will realize that I am in my Father, and you are in me, and I am in you. Whoever has my commands and keeps them is the one who loves me. The one who loves me will be loved by my Father, and I too will love them and show myself to them." Then Judas (not Judas Iscariot) said, "But, Lord, why do you intend to show yourself to us and not to the world?" Jesus replied, "Anyone who loves me will obey my teaching. My Father will love them, and we will come to them and make our home with them. Anyone who does not love me will not obey my teaching. These words you hear are not my own; they belong to the Father who sent me. All this I have spoken while still with you. But the Advocate, the Holy Spirit, whom the Father will send in my name, will teach you all things and will remind you of everything I have said to you. Peace, I leave with you; my Peace, I give you. I do not give to you as the world gives. Do not let your hearts be troubled and do not be afraid (John 14: 18–27).

It was John who helped us to understand the divinity of our Lord. He wrote of the special relationship between God the Father and Jesus, who was God the Son. He imparted to us that Jesus was one who would never desert those He loved and those who loved Him. There would always be a part of Him to guide them and give them the power they would need to share the Gospel to the world. Jesus was the vine, and the disciples were the branches. It was God's love and sacrifice that would transform the world and the disciples would bring that message to the people no matter the dangers or the outcome. Persecution would come, but the love would conquer all.

John was all about love. He taught about it; he shared it and he lived it. He was the disciple, although one of the most modest, who trusted and loved Jesus. That is the reason that John was the beloved disciple. He loved Jesus, so Jesus loved him. As stated, The Messiah didn't love John more than he loved others, it was just because He was close to John and John was close to Him. John never sought fame and was willing to be obedient to the words Jesus spoke. God does love everyone, but He is more passionate to those who have a burning desire to follow Him and do what He teaches, and John was the most passionate of the twelve.

John was also one of the twelve who was accepted into the inner circle of disciples that spent the most time with the Lord. Peter, James, and John were the inner circle, but John, however, had a notably closer relationship. I believe there was a spiritual connection. He was like a best friend as well as an obedient servant. His brother, James, wrote the words of Jesus. "Very truly I tell you, whoever accepts anyone I send accepts me; and whoever accepts me accepts the one who sent me." John accepted Jesus unconditionally and always drew near Him where ever they were. It was this that led John to a closeness that stirred within him an understanding of the heart. Jesus appreciated this and when another disciple complained Jesus simply told them to nourish their own relationship with Him and not to compare themself to anyone else. Jesus loved them all but we will find that the beloved disciple stayed with Jesus when all the others ran in fear because of what happened next.

#4—ARREST, TRIAL, CRUCIFIXION, AND RESURRECTION

John 18-20 elaborates on the Beloved Disciple's closeness to the Lord and Savior. After the Last Supper, Jesus led His followers to the Garden of Gethsemane (Hebrew for "olive press"). John simple called it a garden beyond the Brook Kidron. Jesus had gone there with the disciples before, but this time was different. Matthew, Mark, and Luke wrote about this in their gospels, but John presented a distinguishable contrast concerning what he saw and understood. During the arrest, trial, and crucifixion of the Christ, John seemed to see a Jesus that was in charge of His own fate. Earlier, John recalled that Jesus had said, "The reason my Father loves me is that I lay down my life—only to take it up again. No one takes it from me, but I lay it down of my own accord. I have authority to lay it down and authority to take it up again. This command I received from my Father" (John 10:17-18).

The Arrest

While in the Garden, "... Judas, who betrayed him, knew the place, because Jesus had often met here with his disciples. So, Judas came to the grove, guiding a detachment of soldiers and some officials from the chief priests

GOSPEL IV: I'M JOHN, AND I'M ALL ABOUT THE LOVE

and Pharisees. They were carrying torches, lanterns and weapons" (John 18:2–3). Unlike the other Gospels, John reported that there were Roman soldiers among the crowd. This was done to prevent a riot that might occur during the arrest.

In John's account, Jesus appeared to know what was about to happen. In Chapter 18: 4–12, he responded differently to this event—than the other gospel writers. The following, in the words of Jesus, explain. As the soldiers approached, with Judas, "Jesus, knowing all that was going to happen to him, went out and asked them, "Who is it you want?"

They answered "Jesus of Nazareth,"

"I am he, Jesus said. And Judas who betrayed Him was standing there with them. When Jesus said, "I am He," they (those who came to arrest Him) drew back and fell to the ground. The power possessed by Jesus was too much for them.

They may not have understood, but the divine the Son of God, or God in Human form, caused the men to fall on the ground in awe of His power and in fear of this deity. Without knowing it, this act actually showed them the power of God.

"I Am" are the words used by God when He was speaking to Moses on the mountain. When Jesus said I am (egō eimi) He was referring to that quote found in Exodus. There was no doubt of His claim as a part of the Godhead.

Again, He asked them, "Who is it you want?"

"Jesus of Nazareth," they said.

Jesus answered, "I told you that I am he. If you are looking for me, then let these men go." Jesus was referring to His disciples. The Greek word for "Let them go" is (aphiēmi" and means "to pardon" or "to forgive". His words were much more than leave them alone and take me.

At this point Jesus had fulfilled His own prophecy found in John 6: 39. Talking to His Father in Heaven, He had said, "I have not lost one of those you gave me." He had protected them knowing what they would soon come to realize after this was all over.

Peter, then grabbed a sword and cut off the ear of Malchus, one of the servant of the Jewish High Priest Caiaphas. He may have done this to protect Jesus, or to avenge the treatment that the High priest had shown toward them all, or, because Judas was near, He may have tried to Kill Judas and missed. Whatever the reason, Jesus rebuked him. The Messiah commanded Peter to put his sword away saying, "Shall I not drink the cup the

Father has given me?" Then the detachment of soldiers with its commander and the Jewish officials arrested Jesus, and bound him.

When Jesus had said, "Shall I not drink the cup the Father has given me?" He was telling Peter that He had been born for this reason. He had to accept His fate and face the anguish, suffering, and death to fulfill the undertaking God had given Him to do. It was this, and only this, that would take away the sins of those who accepted Jesus so that they could see eternal life.

Trial

To record the trial that Jesus had to face, we rely on the disciples and what they wrote. There are, however, some non-Christian accounts of this event. Two of the surviving non-Christian accounts had been written during the first century. One was by the Roman historian, Tacitus, and another by a Jewish historian, Josephus. These sources both confirm a trial and Pilate's order to execute Jesus. Even though Jewish Christians writers would never copy Roman sources or non-Christian records of the account, both groups showed similar information. Actually, there have been found around 14 writings from 7 different authors who authenticate the stories written by John and the other disciples.

For our purpose, we will refer to John's account He wrote that Peter and "another disciple" followed their arrested savior. The other disciple, that John doesn't name, knew the High Priest and he went with the crowd into the courtyard of the High Priest. Understanding that John's father, Zebedee, often visited he friend the High Priest and that his son often accompanied him, it is clear that John was talking about the Beloved disciple; It was himself.

After the troops arrested Jesus and took Him away. Peter followed and stood at the door of the courtyard, while John went inside. Soon John realized that Peter had left and went to the door motioning for his friend to come in. He saw a servant girl, that he probably had seen before and ask her to let Peter in. Again, Peter stayed outside most likely filled with fear. The servant girl saw Peter and asked him if he was one of the disciples. He said that he was not. Peter then stood near a fire just outside of where they were questioning Jesus. A group warming themselves there saw Peter and asked him if he was one of them. He said he was not.

The following is a synopsis of John's chapters 18 and 19 with the words that Jesus spoke: John reported, in his Gospel that Jesus ended up in front

GOSPEL IV: I'M JOHN, AND I'M ALL ABOUT THE LOVE

of the high priest, Annas. Annas asked Jesus about His disciples and His teachings.

Jesus answered him, "I have spoken openly to the world. I have always taught in synagogues and in the temple, where all Jews come together. I have said nothing in secret. Why do you ask me? Ask those who have heard me what I said to them; they know what I said."

After speaking, an officers standing near Jesus struck Him with his hand. "Is that how you answer the high priest?"

Jesus answered him, "If what I said is wrong, bear witness about the wrong; but if what I said is right, why do you strike me?"

It was then that Annas sent Jesus to Caiaphas the high priest. While Caiaphas was questioning Jesus, a relative of the man who Peter had cut in the garden, saw him and stated that he was sure Peter was in the garden with Jesus. It was then that Peter basically shouted, "I do not know this man." Just then, the rooster began to crow. Peter had denied Jesus three times, just as the Lord had said. When Peter looked up, Jesus was being led to Pilate.

Pilate came out them and asked what they had accused this man of, saying, "Why don't you punish Him?" The Jews explained that they were not allowed to put any man to death. So, they had brought Him there.

Pilate turned to Jesus and asked, "Are you the King of the Jews?"

Jesus said, "Are you speaking for yourself about this, or did others tell you this concerning me?" Jesus continued by explaining that His kingdom was not of this world, so Pilate asked if he was a king, then.

Jesus stated, "You say rightly that I am a King. For this cause I was born and for this cause I have come into the world. That I should bear witness to the truth. Everyone who is of the truth, hears my voice."

It was then that Pilate asked Jesus what truth was. He turned to the Jews and said that he had found no fault in Jesus at all. He did however, remind the Jews of the custom that stated they could choose a prisoner to be released at the time of Passover. The Jewish people shouted that they wanted Pilate to release a robber named Barabbas, and they wanted Jesus crucified.

Pilate took Jesus and had him whipped. The soldiers twisted a crown made from thorns and forced it on His head. They put a purple robe on Him, saying "Hail, King of the Jews", and they beat Him. Pilate once again told the Jews that he found no fault in Him. He brought Jesus in front of them and said, "Behold, the man."

The Pharisees and Chief Priests shouted that He should be crucified because He had claimed He was the Son of God. Pilate, being afraid of what might happen. He spoke again to Jesus, but this time Jesus remained silent. Pilate yelled at Him and told Him that he had the power to Kill Jesus.

Jesus answered, "You could have no power at all against me unless it had been given you from above."

Pilate still wanted to release Jesus, but the Jews kept shouting that they wanted Barabbas released and Jesus crucified. When Pilate asked if they wanted him to crucify their King, they said, "We have no King but Caesar." Pilate then delivered Jesus to be crucified.

The Crucifixion

The Old Testament prophet, Isaiah, was told by God to proclaim exactly how the Messiah would be punished. He stated, "But he was pierced for our transgressions. He was crushed for our iniquities. The punishment that brought our peace was on him; and by his wounds we are healed" (Isaiah 53:5). Jesus would be crushed, punished beyond recognition, and His body would be pierced—all of this would be done to Him to take upon Himself all of our sins and transgressions of mankind and to bring us peace. This prophecy was told around 700 years before the act of crucifixion was even invented.

Although this horrific act was first used by the Assyrians and Babylonians, around the 6th century B.C., The Romans perfected this brutal act around the 3rd century before the Christ. They would execute the crucifixion after the torture of the accused. This torture was usually in the form of scourging, or beating, the guilty person. The equipment used was called a "flagrum" or "flagellum". To scourge a prisoner, the romans whipped him with this device. It had three or four leather straps attached to a handle. Tied to the end of each strap were sharp pieces of bone, hooks, or sharp metal fragments. This would tear the flesh every time it hit a body. The Jewish Temple guards also used this method of punishment, but their law demanded they stop at 39 strikes because 40 could kill a person. The Romans, however, had no such law. To understand the severity of this punishment, look at the word we derived from "flagrum". We get our English word "fillet" from this tool which means strips of flesh or meat.

Jesus, King of the Jews, having been sentenced to be crucified was first scourged. To further the humiliation, the Romans pulled His beard out,

GOSPEL IV: I'M JOHN, AND I'M ALL ABOUT THE LOVE

crushed a crown of thorns on His head, spit on Him, and mocked Him. He was beaten so badly that Jesus was basically unrecognizable. Isaiah had written about this saying the Messiah would be "So marred from the form of man was His aspect, that His appearance was not as that of a son of a man" (Isaiah 53:1–3).

The next step was to make Jesus carry His own cross through the city streets and to a mound called Golgotha, or the Place of the Skull. They crucified Him along with two others. Pilate wrote a sign and had it placed at the top of the cross. JESUS OF NAZARETH, THE KING OF THE JEWS. Even though this angered the leaders and Pharisees, Pilate told them it was to remain as he had written it.

It was then that they nailed the hands and feet of Jesus to the cross. Psalm 22:16 prophesied this when David wrote, "the assembly of the wicked have enclosed me: they pierced my hands and my feet." The nails used at the crucifixion were actually placed in the wrists directly above the hand and into the feet near the ankle. This method would not have broken the bones of the accused.

The Soldiers took the garments belonging to Jesus, and cast lots for it. The winner of the dice game would get to keep the clothes. This, too was a fulfillment of the scripture, for it was written in Psalms 22:18: "They divide my garments among them, and for my clothing they cast lots."

As Jesus hung there and in front of the cross, were the mother of Jesus, Mary Magdalene, and the beloved disciple, John. Showing the love He had for this disciple, Jesus looked down at his mother and said, "Woman behold your son." Looking at His disciple, Jesus also said, "John, Behold your mother." From that hour on, Mary was taken care of. John, being the closest to Jesus at that hour and the only Disciple who had not run away in fear, considered Mary his mother and took care of her for the rest of her life.

Later, knowing that the scripture must be fulfilled, Jesus said, "I Thirst." which had been foretold in Psalm 69: 21: ". . . for my thirst they gave me sour wine to drink." When He had said this, a guard put Vinegar on a sponge, and put it to his mouth. When Jesus received the sour wine, He said, "It is finished," and He bowed His head in death.

There are many scriptures fulfilled by this crucifixion. Jesus never had his bones broken, even though the soldiers were known to take a hammer and broke the legs of others to quicken their death. This was also a fulfillment of Psalm 34:20. David wrote, "For the Lord protects the bones of the righteous; not one of them is broken!" The soldiers did not take a hammer to the feet of Jesus because the Centurion proved He was dead by piercing His side with a spear, just as Isaiah had prophesied.

Finally, Joseph of Arimathea, a friend of the family of Jesus, was given permission to take the body and bury it. The family and friends wrapped the body and placed it in the tomb. They could not completely prepare the body, because the Sabbath was near. Afraid that some of the disciples would steal the body and claim Jesus had risen, the Priests and Pharisees asked Pilate to send soldiers to place a stone over the entrance and there they should stand guard.

The Resurrection

The act of raising someone from the dead defines resurrection. In John's Gospel this happened because of the Love God had for humanity. Because Jesus was resurrected, true believers will also never have to see eternal death. The very act showed that Jesus conquered death itself and by doing so, gave true believers the power over sin and Satan. John, the beloved disciple also believed that his Master had risen from the dead, even though he did not understand it at the time. He believed this because he, along with Peter saw the empty tomb. Although he did not mention his name as the disciple who beat Peter to the site of the grave, he had the faith that Peter did not have at the time. The reason he won the race to the tomb would be obvious, because John was the youngest and probably a lot quicker than the older man, Peter!

John had yet to connect the Old testament prophecies with this amazing occurrence he was witnessing. When he finally wrote his Gospel, he didn't treat it as an article written by a reporter. Instead, he expressed the need for faith and love and the need to believe without sight. Showing that faith, John described the action which I now give an account of by using the quotes of Jesus found in the John's Gospel and by imagining what John might say if he were here today.

On the third day (actually the first day of the week), Mary Magdalene went to the tomb and found that the stone had been rolled away. She came to Peter and this beloved disciple and told them what she had seen. We all ran to the tomb and Peter went in, finding the facecloth folded and the linen lying by itself. We then believed. The scriptures had been correct. Jesus had risen from the dead. The disciples left and Mary was crying as she knelt by the tomb. When she looked in, she saw two Angels; one sitting

GOSPEL IV: I'M JOHN, AND I'M ALL ABOUT THE LOVE

at the head and one at the feet, where Jesus had been. They said to Mary, "woman, why are you weeping?" She answered them, stating that she was afraid someone had taken her Lord's body. She turned to see a man who she thought was the gardener.

The Man said to her, "Woman, why are you weeping? Whom are you seeking?"

She answered, "Sir, if you have carried Him away, tell me where you have laid Him, and I will take Him away"

Jesus quietly said, "Mary" and she immediately recognized Him. She called Him teacher and reached for Him, but He told her not to touch Him, for He had not yet ascended to His Father. He told her to go and tell the disciples that He was going to ascend to "... My Father and your Father, and to my God and Your God." Mary did as Jesus asked.

If this had been the end of the story, I would Have said that it was sufficient. But, Jesus didn't stay away. He appeared to us, and others many times after He had risen. The same day He saw Mary, Jesus appeared to us and said "Peace be with you.

I was greatly shocked at first, but then there was the realization of what had occurred. Jesus continued. "Peace to you! As the Father has sent me, I also send you."

Now Thomas was not with us then and when we had told him what had happened, He doubted. "Unless I see the print of the nails in His hands and I place my hand in His side, I will not believe." It was eight days later, when appeared to his us again. This time Thomas was there, too.

Jesus came to Thomas and said, "Reach your fingers here, and look at my hands. And reach your hand here and put it in my side. Do not be unbelieving, but be believing."

Thomas didn't need to touch Jesus. He simply answered, "My Lord and my God."

I, John, don't have time to write about all the things that Jesus did after that. I can tell you, however, that Jesus appeared many times and to many people.

#5—PETER'S COMMISSION—JOHN'S LOVE

Chapter 21 of the Gospel of John completes the five parts of his work in this book. John has been telling us of the Love Jesus possessed. He also conveyed the message that all of us need to rid ourselves of trying to control everything, and trust Jesus. John knew well the verses in the Old Testament and could just as well have retold the following to us. Proverbs 3: 5–6 stated. "Trust in the Lord with all your heart and lean not on your own understanding. In all your ways submit to him, and he will make your paths straight."

John reminded us that Jesus, God in the flesh, gives us all second chances. It may be that we have sinned, repented, and sinned again. We once again come to Jesus and ask Him to pardon us . . . and He does. It could also be that someone has never accepted Jesus as the Messiah even though they have hear the message. Jesus will give us chance after chance all the way up to the time we leave this life.

Why would he do this? It's simple, really, Love is the answer. God loves His creation and has a plan for each of us who believe. He never wants us to die without accepting that love, but because we have free will, it is really up to us.

Chapter 21 also explains what happened to Peter who had denied that he ever knew Jesus. The forgiveness and second chances that He gives each of us was also afforded to Peter. Jesus reinstated Peter and commissioned him to go out and save other souls as well as establish the Christian Church. This last part of the Gospel of John also explains what Jesus asked of Peter. John ends his book by letting us all know that what he wrote was all true. He knew it because he witnessed it first-hand.

John's chapter 21 begins after the resurrection. Jesus was seen at the Sea of Tiberius, where Peter, Thomas, and Nathaniel were fishing and not catching anything. The risen Master told them to cast the nets on the other side of the boat, and the nets nearly tore when they pulled it up, because there were so many fish. When Peter realized that it was actually Jesus speaking to them from the shore, he jumped into the sea and swam to Jesus shouting, "It is the Lord." This was the third time that Jesus had showed himself to His disciples. He asked them if they had anything to eat, and went with then to share breakfast.

When they all had finished eating, Jesus said to Simon Peter, "Simon, do you love me?" and Simon Peter answered that he did. And Jesus continued, "Feed my lambs." Jesus asked a second time, "Simon, son of Jonah, do you love me?" and again Peter assured Jesus that he did. Jesus said, "Tend my Sheep."

Then Jesus asked a third and fourth time, "Simon, do you love me? Do you love me?"

GOSPEL IV: I'M JOHN, AND I'M ALL ABOUT THE LOVE

Simon Peter answered, "Lord you know all things and you know that I love you."

Jesus said to him, "Feed my sheep." He went on to explain that Peter, when he was young, went wherever he wished. Jesus said that there would come a day when Peter would be girded and led where he did not wish. He seemed to be telling that Peter would also be persecuted for the Lord's sake, to glorify God. When Jesus told him, "You must Follow Me." I think that Jesus was explaining to Peter that he had an immense job to do. After all, as my friend had said before, and some think now, Peter was to be the Rock. He was going to be the foundation of a new group of believers, called Christians.

It is now that I must testify that what I have written is true. I know it because I was a witness. There are many other things that Jesus did but there aren't enough scrolls for me to write everything that I observed. If it were all to be written down, I suppose that there wouldn't be enough space in the world that could contain all of those books. At this time, All I can say is Amen.

Part 10

MY LETTER TO YOU WITH LOVE

DEAR YOUNG DISCIPLE OF the 21st Century,

I hope you take to heart what I have written because it is the absolute truth and I tell it to you with love. As usual for me, I have tried not to use my name as the author of this Gospel. I never did seek attention, and I tried to follow my usual way of communicating.

Anyway, I, along with my brother James and my friend Peter, were called by Jesus to leave the life of fishing and fish for the souls of men instead. As a part of the three fortunate disciples (and I say that because we were blessed enough to be close to Jesus) I saw seven miracles that Jesus did. I saw Him change water into wine—not just any wine, but the best wine ever given to guests at any wedding. I was able to see Jesus raise a young girl from the dead. I saw Him heal the sick and have the blind see and the lame walk. I saw Him raise Lazarus from the dead.

I actually saw Jesus speaking to Moses and Elijah. The Messiah looked like a heavenly King. His face was as bright as the shining sun. He garments became white as snow. He was there with Elijah who, I think, represented the prophecies soon fulfilled by our Lord. Moses, too, was there and represented the Law that God gave His children. The three of them together showed me that Jesus was the fulfillment of the Law and the Prophets.

I was at the Last Supper sitting next to our Savior. I even leaned against Him as He explained what was about to happen. I may not have understood at the time, but I would remain at His side not matter what. You see, I loved the Lord and He loved me. That kind of love we shared is hard to come by. It is a Godly love filled with trust and joy. It is a love that surpasses any

GOSPEL IV: I'M JOHN, AND I'M ALL ABOUT THE LOVE

understanding that mankind can have, but it is a love that anyone can accept. I was soon to understand that love more than I could imagine and, I believe, it got me through the next stage of our journey.

Most import, and the saddest hours of my life, I saw The Messiah die on the cross. I listened as He told me to take care of His mother and I obeyed. I watched as He took His last breath. There is no Him after that when he appeared to so many people.

I was blessed so much when He left us, but because of His ambassador, The Holy Spirit, I received the power to face anything this life would throw at me. I knew what I had to do and because of Him I faced that without fear.

You see, He had taken our sin onto Himself, so we, too, could have eternal life. Because I was blessed enough to go through all of this, I was an elder of the first Christian Church. I helped to spread the good news of Christ being the Lamb of God, who took away all of our sins. I told so many that all they need do was ask Jesus and He would change their life. I end in asking that you accept Jesus as your Lord and Savior and He will change you. God Bless you.

One last thing I will leave you with. Do not be afraid. Everything that Jesus promised, He will keep. I know this because I faced so many hardships. I wasn't martyred like I brothers in Christ, but I was arrested many times. I was even stranded on an island called Patmos. While there, God gave me a vision of the final days of earth, and a peek at heaven. In the vision I saw the Holy City, Jerusalem, coming down from heaven to the new earth, for the old earth had been destroyed. However, that is another book that I wrote and I will explain that at another time.

Thank you for reading. All my love in Christ, I leave you.
John, the beloved disciple

Part 11

FINAL
WHAT DO I DO NEXT?

Romans 3:10–12: explains what we actually are compared to God. It states, "There is none righteous, not even one; there is none who understands, there is none who seeks for God; all have turned aside, together they have become useless; there is none who does good, there is not even one." It is impossible for human beings to be "good".

We may do something that is commendable from time to time, but we are not worthy to be with God or receive eternal life because we all fail and sin. Just go through the Ten Commandments and honestly ask yourself if you have always followed each and every one. I haven't, and being honest to yourself, you haven't either. Remember what Jesus said about sin. Matthew 15: 9 Explains: "For out of the heart come evil thoughts—murder, adultery, sexual immorality, theft, false testimony, slander." If we do something against God's law, we sin. If we think about doing something, we sin, and we know that sin is what keeps us from forever being from God.

How do we get to heaven, then? The best answer, I think, is found in the words of the Savior. While Jesus was teaching, He was approached by a wealthy man, who asked how he would be able to get into heaven. The best thing to do is read the story:

Now behold, one came and said to Him, "Good Teacher, what good thing shall I do that I may have eternal life?"

So, He said to him, "Why do you call Me good? No one is good but One, that is, God. But if you want to enter into life, keep the commandments."

GOSPEL IV: I'M JOHN, AND I'M ALL ABOUT THE LOVE

He said to Him, "Which ones?"

Jesus said, "'You shall not murder,' 'You shall not commit adultery,' 'You shall not steal,' 'You shall not bear false witness,' 'Honor your father and your mother,' and, 'You shall love your neighbor as yourself.'"

The young man said to Him, "All these things I have kept from my youth. What do I still lack?"

Jesus said to him, "If you want to be perfect, go, sell what you have and give to the poor, and you will have treasure in heaven; and come, follow Me." But when the young man heard that saying, he went away sorrowful, for he had great possessions.

Then Jesus said to His disciples, "Assuredly, I say to you that it is hard for a rich man to enter the kingdom of heaven. And again, I say to you, it is easier for a camel to go through the eye of a needle than for a rich man to enter the kingdom of God."

When His disciples heard it, they were greatly astonished, saying, "Who then can be saved?"

But Jesus looked at them and said to them, "With men this is impossible, but with God all things are possible."

Not one of us is good enough to make it. However, all of us can follow Jesus and accept Him as Lord and Savior. All it takes is faith. We need to admit to God that we are not worthy. We need to admit to ourselves we are not worthy. When we come to grips with this, we can be saved. To be saved we must ask. We must admit we are sinners. We must accept Jesus as the way. Jesus is God and we need to understand that, ask forgiveness, and follow Him.

Appendix

FOR YOUR CONSIDERATION

John 3:16
"For God so loved the world, that he gave his only Son, that whoever believes in him should not perish but have eternal life".

Romans 6:23
"For the wages of sin is death, but the gift of God is eternal life in Christ Jesus our Lord"

John 14:6
"I am the way and the truth and the life. No one comes to the Father except through me.

Philippians 4:6–7
"Don't worry about anything; instead, pray about everything. Tell God what you need, and thank him for all he has done"

James 4:8
"Draw near to God, and he will draw near to you"

Hebrews 11:6
"And without faith it is impossible to please him, for whoever would draw near to God must believe that he exists and that he rewards those who seek him."

APPENDIX

I Chronicles 16:10–11
"Glory in his holy name; let the hearts of those who seek the Lord rejoice! Seek the Lord and his strength; seek his presence continually!"

Philippians 3:10
"I want to know Christ and the power that raised him from the dead."

SINNER'S PRAYER

Dear Jesus,

I know that I have sinned. No one is worthy of eternal life, unless they follow you. Please forgive me for my sins and come into my heart. I know that I will never be perfect, but I also know that you will keep your promise. You said, "Ask, and it shall be given you; seek, and you shall find; knock, and it shall be opened unto you: For every one that asks receives; and he or she that seeks finds; and to him or her that knocks it shall be opened." Jesus thank you for saving me and help me to better follow you.

BIBLIOGRAPHY

Bible Hub. John 1:1 Greek Text Analysis'" https://biblehub.com/text/john/1-1.htm John 1:1 Greek Text Analysis—Bible Hub.

Carousel Front Page, Spirituality. "Memory of Apostle and Evangelist Luke". 18 October, 2024 orthodoxtimes.com. https://orthodoxtimes.com/memory-of-apostle-and-evangelist-luke.

Christian Bible Reference Site. "Introduction—The Gospels" The Christian Bible Reference Site. N.d. https://www.christianbiblereference.org/jintro.htm. orthodoxtimes.com.

Clay, Cholee. "Comparing-the-Gospels-Matthew-Mark-Luke-and-John". owlcation.com. Updated Jun 19, 2024. https://owlcation.com/humanities/Comparing-the-Gospels-Matthew-Mark-Luke-and-John

Culp, Doug. "Matthew: From tax collector to apostle." FAITH Catholic, September 20, 2022 https://dioceseofraleigh.org/news/matthew-tax-collector-apostle.

Dr. Pat's Orthodox Super Sunday School Curriculum Egypt: "Egypt: St. Mark of Alexandria." Dr. Pat's Orthodox Super Sunday School.org.2020.https://orthodoxsundayschool.org/church-history/10-12-years-old/egypt-st-mark-alexandria.

Duriez, Colin: C. S, Lewis: A biography of friendship: Amazon.com. April 19, 2013. Books C. S. Lewis: A biography of friendship Paperback. https://www.amazon.com/C-S-Lewis-Biography-Friendship/dp/0745955878

Got Questions. "Who was Luke in the Bible?" gotquestions.org Jan 4, 2022. http://www.gotquestions.org/Luke-in-the-Bible.html

Greene, Brian. "Ask Science". Reddit, N.d. https://www.reddit.com/r/askscience/comments/green AskScience AMA Series: I'm Brian Greene, theoretical physicist, mathematician, and string theorist, and co-founder of the World Science Festival. AMA!

Holstein, Joanne. "Salome the Mother of James and John Zebedee" Guided Bible Studies for Hungry Christians.com. February 3, 2015. https://guidedbiblestudies.com/?p=2191 Salome the Mother of James and John Zebedee joanneholstein.

Joyner, Cameron. "Was Luke Really a Gentile?" The Friends of Israel Gospel Ministry. September 16, 2022. https://www.foi.org/2022/09/16/was-luke-really-a-gentile/.

Kiger, Patrick J. "Quarks Are the Building Blocks of All Matter'" How Stuff Works. Jun 9, 2023. https://science.howstuffworks.com/quarks.htm Quarks Are the Building Blocks of All Matter'

BIBLIOGRAPHY

Marcam, Vita: Life of Mark. N.d. e-clavis-christian-apocrypha. https://www.nasscal.com/e-clavis-christian-apocrypha/life-of-mark/.

Ministry Voice. "Why Did Luke Write His Gospel: Understanding the Purpose and Meaning Behind Luke's Message". Ministry Voice.com. N.d. https://www.ministryvoice.com/why-did-luke-write-his-gospel/.

Mounce, Bill. "Free Online Greek Dictionary" W. Monce blog. N.d. https://www.billmounce.com/greek-dictionary/agapao Bill Mounce ἀγαπάω | Free Online Greek Dictionary | billmounce.co

Nelson, Ryan: Who Was John Mark? The Beginner's Guide. Overview Bible.com. Apr 17, 2019. https://overviewbible.com/john-mark/ who was john mark? the beginner's guide.

Nickens, Mark: Mark's House: Early Gathering Place for Christians Plus: It was probably the site of the Last Supper. studythechurch.com, 2010. . http://studythechurch.com/articles/early-church/marks-house Mark's Ho use: Early Gathering Place for Christians

Science Mission Directorate. "Building Blocks—NASA Science'" https://science.nasa.gov/universe/overview/building-blocks/#:~:text=Everything%20scientists

Scott, Hilda: What Was Mark's Occupation In The Bible. NASSCAL. February 12, 2024. e-clavis-christian-apocrypha, https://www.theholyscript.com/what-was-marks-occupation-in-the-bible.

Smilde, Arend. "SWEETLY POISONOUS IN A WELCOME WAY". lewisiana.nl, 1990. https://lewisiana.nl/definitivebiography/ SWEETLY POISONOUS IN A WELCOME WAY Reflections on a Definitive.

Weidmann, Josh. "The Apostle John: Beloved By God to Love Others". Josh Weidmann (blog) N.d. https://joshweidmann.com/meet-john-son-of-zebedee-the-disciple-jesus-loved The Apostle John: Beloved By God to Love.

Wikipedia The Free Encyclopedia: "Koin Greek". https://en.wikipedia.org/wiki/.

Wikipedia, the Free Encyclopedia "Marcan priority". https://en.wikipedia.org/wiki/Marcan priority.

Christology to be preoccupied with ontological debates. This volume also includes a creative attempt to appreciate the longer ending of Mark, using it as an example of how Christological imagination changes under shifting historical pressures. Whether or not Vena's model will succeed in "bridging the gap" between *Christus Victor* and traditional "Suffering Servant" atonement Christologies remains to be seen. But this book will surely help seminary and sanctuary return to the roots of the gospel tradition by re-centering the call to discipleship—Jesus' and ours.

Mark wrote to help imperial subjects (in the first century and today) learn the hard truth about our world and our selves. This story of Jesus does not pretend to represent the Word of God dispassionately or impartially; it was written by, about, and for those engaged in God's work of justice, compassion, and liberation in the world. To the otherworldly religious, Mark's Jesus offers no "signs from heaven" (Mark 8:11–12). To scholars who refuse to commit themselves concerning the life and death issues of the day, Jesus declines engagement (11:30–33). But to those willing to risk the wrath of empire, Jesus offers the Way of discipleship (8:34ff.)—which Way he not only proclaims, but embodies, thus empowering us to follow. This is the *old* story, Vena argues, and its time has come again.

References

Bonhoeffer, Dietrich. *The Cost of Discipleship*. New York: Macmillan, 1966.
Gill, Athol. *Life on the Road*. Dandenong, Australia: UNOH Publishing, 2009.
Myers, Ched. *Who Will Roll Away the Stone: Discipleship Queries for First World Christians*. Maryknoll: Orbis, 1994.
Neville, David, ed. *Prophecy and Passion: Essays in Honour of Athol Gill*. Adelaide: Australian Theological Forum, 2002.
Schweizer, Eduard. *Lordship and Discipleship*. Studies in Biblical Theology 28. London: SCM, 1960.
Segovia, Fernando, ed. *Discipleship in the New Testament*. Philadelphia: Fortress, 1985.

Preface

JESUS WAS NOT A celebrity, but his contemporaries, and those who came after them, made him into one. His town's people were the first to capitalize on the notoriety of the prophet from Galilee. His disciples and followers did the same. After the resurrection, the early Jesus movement needed to counteract Jesus' negative celebrity status, earned by his execution on a Roman cross, and so believers took to the task of writing apologetic works, including the gospels, pointing at the empty tomb and the resurrection appearances as proof that God had vindicated Jesus' life and ministry. This, in turn, laid the foundation for what was to come, namely, the elevating of Jesus of Nazareth to the position of Lord of the universe, *Christus Victor*, Savior of the world, and Eschatological Judge.

For millennia, the official church has expropriated and misinterpreted Jesus' true vocation and message in order to build itself into an institution that, to this very day, has controlled the way Jesus is understood by the majority of Christians. The church has dictated the content of Christology in order to achieve the church's broad and long-lasting goals of self-preservation and theological hegemony. Some of the social ramifications of this Christology, just to mention a few, are: the subordination of women and their exclusion from positions of leadership in the church; the glorification of redemptive suffering, which justifies violence perpetrated against women and sexual and racial minorities; the glorification of redemptive violence, which justifies war, colonization, and genocide in the name of a supposedly sacred mission to Christianize the world. The list can continue endlessly, but these are sufficient to prove my point, which is that the content of Christology has lasting ethical implications. Or to put it in other words: Christology and social practice are intricately related.

In this book, I try to take a critical view of the church's Christology and suggest an alternative way of looking at Jesus from the perspective of a community, Mark's, which could be considered pre-church and pre-institution, even though the signs of institutionalization are beginning to

Preface

surface. It is a way to envision and imagine a different kind of church and, therefore, a different kind of Christianity, not unlike the one envisioned by the Gnostics of the second century or the Jewish Christians of the first. It represents a bold deviation from the norm and a desire to make Jesus' words and ministry consistent with and relevant to the community's context, both ancient and modern.

I am grateful to all those people—colleagues, church members, friends, and family members—who have been conversation partners through all the years during which this idea was conceived and brought to fruition. They have been instrumental in the idea's coherence and validity, which the reader will have to evaluate on his or her own terms. I am especially indebted to Garrett-Evangelical Theological Seminary for granting me a leave of absence to complete this work. I am also grateful to my research assistant, Kerri Allen, and my teaching assistant, Melanie Baffes—both doctoral students at Garrett—for their invaluable work of editing and formatting the final manuscript.

Finally, I offer this book to all those who have felt uncomfortable with the church's view of Jesus of Nazareth, and I thereby suggest a new way of looking at him—as the disciple par excellence of the kingdom of God, a model for our daily, contemporary journey as God's people.

Osvaldo D. Vena
March 2013

Abbreviations

BDAG	*Greek-English Lexicon of the New Testament and Other Early Christian Literature*
Bib	*Biblica*
BR	*Biblical Research*
BTB	*Biblical Theology Bulletin*
CBQ	*Catholic Biblical Quarterly*
HCSB	*The HarperCollins Study Bible*
JSNTSup	*Journal for the Study of the New Testament: Supplement Series*
JBL	*Journal of Biblical Literature*
PSB	*Princeton Seminary Bulletin*
RevistB	*Revista Bíblica*
SNTSMS	Society for New Testament Studies Monograph Series
TDNT	*Theological Dictionary of the New Testament*

Introduction

I BEGIN THIS WORK WITH the assumption that Christologies[1] are not given revelations or spontaneous historical manifestations but rather community-constructed models, that is, ways of talking about Jesus that are born out of a community's theological identity. There are some good reasons that a given community ascribed to Jesus different titles and roles. For example, it is very interesting to note the way Paul talks about Jesus and the way Mark does; or the way the authors of Ephesians and Colossians talk about Christ as compared to the way Paul describes him. Each Christological description is different because the make-up and situations of the communities are different. This cannot be overstated. Christology is always driven and fed by the praxis of the community.[2] It is not a given. It has to be constructed. It is never deductive, but inductive. It is never from above, a revelation implanted in people's minds and heart *by* God, but always from below, from the human sphere where people struggle to remain faithful *to* God. Christology then is not an abstract, value-free reflection[3] about who

1. By Christology, I simply mean a discourse about Christ that is based on the historical recollections of the community informed by its current situation. In that sense, any talk about Jesus that tries to make his person and message relevant for a given community is a Christology. Christology is born then in the crucible of memory and praxis, or remembrance and practice. Its purpose is to guide the community in times of struggle by giving them a sense of identity and by encouraging them to remain faithful to the God of Israel. For a similar understanding and treatment of Christology, see Tilley, *Disciples' Jesus*, 1–15.

2. To quote Jon Sobrino: "The diverse Christologies of the New Testament were elaborated from two poles. Jesus of Nazareth was one pole. The other was the concrete situation of each community. Each had its own cultural backdrop and its own set of problems both within the church and vis-à-vis the outside world. The resurrection of Christ made their faith possible, but in the elaboration of a Christology they had to deal with the concrete features of Jesus' life. They would have to select and choose between those elements, rejecting some and accepting others. In today's situation the various churches are confronted with the same task." Sobrino, *Christology at the Crossroads*, 13.

3. Sobrino, *Christology at the Crossroads*, xvi, criticizes the tendency in traditional and dogmatic Christologies to reduce Christ to a sublime abstraction that introduces a

Jesus, Disciple of the Kingdom

Jesus is but a practical response of the faithful done from the perspective of interested discipleship. Here I agree with Terrence W. Tilley, who proposes that Christology "must begin where we are. . . . Christology always arises in disciples' imagination. We start with Jesus as he is perceived and imagined on this earth. We start telling the story *here* even if the story we tell begins in heaven."[4] This starting point of Christology is made even more poignant by Jon Sobrino:

> [We] will give preference to the praxis of Jesus over his own teaching and over the teaching that the New Testament theologians elaborated concerning his praxis. Thus the New Testament will be viewed primarily as history and only secondarily as doctrine concerning the real nature of that history.[5]

Starting the Christological task deeply embedded in the praxis of the community is something advanced by Liberation Theology and nicely summarized in Gustavo Gutierrez's famous dictum concerning the relationship between theology and praxis: "Theology follows," he says, "it is the second step."[6] I treat Christology as a subset of theology,[7] namely, the discourse[8] about Jesus as Christ, so the dictum still applies. This "second-step" characteristic of any theology explains very well the process by which the New Testament books were written, as well as any contemporary reflection on these texts. What comes first is an experience with God channeled through and rooted in a historical event, namely, the ministry of Jesus of Nazareth. The second step is the discourse we construct, from the practice of discipleship,[9] about who this Jesus was/is and therefore who we are as

---

separation between the total or whole Christ on the one hand and the concrete history of Jesus on the other. This quite often leads to an alienating understanding of Christ, as seen in spiritualizing practices that invoke vaguely the Spirit but do not look for the concrete spirit of Jesus as the driving force behind his ministry.

4. Tilley, *Disciples' Jesus*, 37.
5. Sobrino, *Christology at the Crossroads*, xxii.
6. Gutiérrez, *Theology of Liberation*, xxix.
7. Greene, *Christology in Cultural Perspective*, 1.
8. My understanding of "discourse" is informed by Elisabeth Schüssler Fiorenza's discussion of the subject in *Jesus and the Politics of Interpretation*, 14–20, as she applies this concept to historical-Jesus research. I also tend to view discourse as ideological construction.
9. I borrow this expression from Terrence W. Tilley, because it corresponds somehow to Gutierrez's understanding of "praxis." Tilley says that practice is a term of art where the key is the learning aspect of the practice: "One learns *how* to engage in a practice;

Introduction

God's people on earth. Since there are a variety of practices of discipleship due to the fact that we are all immersed in different contexts and social locations, there will always be a variety of Christological affirmations that need to be seen not so much as competitive but as complementary. They need to be brought into dialogue so that each one of our communities may contribute to the other a new insight that can be used in the practice of discipleship. The goal here is not orthodoxy, an agreement on the right doctrines, but orthopraxis, a strategy for knowing what the right practice is in a given context.

As the New Testament clearly shows, this process of Christology-building started in the early years of the movement, even before followers were called "Christians."[10] One of the first, and perhaps most influential "Christologists,"[11] was indeed the Apostle Paul. Furthermore, this process can also be found in the Markan community, as its members struggled to find their place as followers of Jesus of Nazareth in a conflicting and changing world. But I would argue that in Mark's community, the Christology that developed was less exalted, and certainly less apocalyptic, than the one manifested in and by the Pauline communities.

The essence of my argument is that of trying to find support for a Christology that sees in Jesus the disciple par excellence (chapters 3 and 4). This is not going to be an easy task, for Jesus is usually seen as the teacher, the Messiah, the Son of God, etc., rather than as a disciple. I would contend that this might be precisely one of the reasons the church has often failed in its work of proclamation of the good news, namely a mistaken understanding of Jesus' identity and mission, which in turn impacted the way the church has understood itself and its own mission. If we can get back to a

---

only then can one know *what* the practice is and what participation in the practice produces—including among the products of practice those dispositions we call 'beliefs' and formulate in sentences.... The practices are primary; the doctrines are derivative." Tilley, *Disciples' Jesus*, 13, 14.

10. "The various theologies present in them [the texts of the NT], accordingly, fail to be interpreted, in part at least, as the symbolical provinces of meaning erected by the authors of the various texts, or by the traditions before them, to legitimate the early gatherings of Christians, not yet even bearing that name. In the light of the model, New Testament theologies become sacred canopies for those fragile social worlds seeking to find a place for themselves and their faith, in the teeth of opposition from without and dissention and ennui within." Esler, *First Christians*, 11.

11. This made-up expression is borrowed from a conversation with my colleague, Ken Vaux.

pre-Christian, or pre-canonical understanding of Jesus ministry,[12] as preserved by one community, Mark's, then perhaps we can find a way of being the church that is more in tune with God's redemptive mission in the world.

Since this is more a socio-rhetorical[13] than a historical-critical investigation my search for a discipleship model is done at the level of the text.[14] This means that historical insights into the possibility of seeing Jesus as a disciple of the kingdom are limited to a general background. Rather, the text is explored, looking for clues that may help us build the proposed model. But insights from the historical-critical methods, especially those of redaction and source criticism, are brought into the discussion in order to clarify and interpret the world of the NT writers in general and Mark in particular.

THE NEED FOR A NEW MODEL

According to Philip F. Esler,[15] a model is "a heuristic tool, allowing comparisons to be made with the texts for the purpose of posing new questions to them. The texts must supply the answers, not the model. . . . For this reason, it is inappropriate to debate whether a model is 'true' or 'false,' or 'valid' or 'invalid.' What matters is whether it is useful or not." Therefore, Christologies are more relevant for their consequences, their social repercussions, than for their content. For example, Mark's Christology may have seemed flawed to some (especially Matthew and Luke, who added to it!) but it was

---

12. William R. Herzog II has alerted us of the problematic nature of the word "ministry" when applied to Jesus. He writes: "The use of ministry to describe Jesus' activities implies that the model for understanding Jesus is Christian ministry. While this model might be useful in a number of theological or ecclesiastical contexts, it assumes too much and is anachronistic when applied to the historical Jesus." *Prophet and Teacher*, 1. Nevertheless, for our purpose in this work, the word ministry is still relevant because Mark is writing for a Christian community involved in ministry. The historical Jesus is not the object of our study, but rather Mark's Christological construction of Jesus as the disciple of the kingdom.

13. For this idea, see Robbins, *Tapestry*, 1–17.

14. Here it is important to remember what Robbins says about the nature of texts, namely, that they are "performances of language, and language is part of the inner fabric of society, culture, ideology, and religion." Robbins, *Tapestry*, 1. Therefore, Mark's use of language cannot be separated from the society and culture that produced it. Both aspects will be considered as we delve deeply into the inner workings of Mark's text.

15. Esler, *First Christians*, 13.

useful to the community that produced it. The same could be said about Paul's Christology and ours.

The traditional, and I would say orthodox,[16] descriptions (or models) of Jesus as Messiah, Son of God, and Savior tend to confine him to ethnical, religious and metaphysical descriptions that alienate those who want to find in him an example for Christian living and praxis.[17] Something similar happens with the roles of prophet and servant. The first one could be interpreted too narrowly in terms of gender (most of Israel's prophets were men), and the second may send the wrong message to those people in society who already have a secondary position, such as women and ethnic minorities. For people whose lives are defined by continuous and ill-rewarded service, the description of Jesus as the ideal servant is not very comforting.[18]

We need a more inclusive and liberating model, one that can speak to people who have always felt that the Jesus proclaimed by the *kerygma* is too divine, too out of touch with reality. Often this Jesus seems to be playing a game called "Now I'm human, now I'm not." For just when one begins to identify with a down-to-earth Jesus, the one who eats with sinners and publicans, who is thirsty and asks water from a woman in Samaria, who cries in front of the tomb of his friend Lazarus, the game changes. Now Jesus is divine, the Son of God, the agent of God's final kingdom, an almost unreachable character who predicts his death to the last detail, forewarns his followers of the impending coming of the last days, and ascends to heaven in a cloud, as two heavenly figures tell the perplexed disciples that one day he will return in the same way as he now ascends. The game of biblical chess ends in a tie when the Orthodox Church, meeting at Chalcedon in 451 CE proclaims that Jesus was "fully human and fully divine." That may have worked in the fifth century. but not so well in the twenty-first century. Thus, Jesus of Nazareth is made into this impossible entity who can only inhabit the world of theological and abstract thought, but never

---

16. I use "orthodox" in a broad sense. What I mean is any view of the Bible or of the Christian tradition that claims to be the "right one," and therefore, the only valid interpretation. Even though, for the most part, I have in mind conservative approaches to biblical scholarship, the term can also be used to describe any view that takes on the mantle of normativity.

17. It needs to be said, from the outset, that in emphasizing "orthopraxis" over "orthodoxy," I will be proposing an alternative view to the traditional one of Jesus as Lord and Savior.

18. Schüssler Fiorenza, *But She Said*, 72–73.

(or seldom) the real world of contemporary women and men, who have a difficult time identifying with someone who is not completely one of them.[19]

The Jesus who has been proclaimed by the various historical-Jesus researchers has also alienated people both in the church and in society at large, for this Jesus seems to be the product of liberal Christianity (Jesus the charismatic genius and great hero), or of scientific, and thus positivist, investigation that sees in Jesus a healer, preacher of renewal, cynic, and so on, who is at odds with the Judaism of his time. The problematic images of Jesus coming from these different quests have been addressed in depth by Elisabeth Schüssler Fiorenza in her book, *Jesus and the Politics of Interpretation*. She advocates for an ethics of interpretation that recognizes that any presentation of Jesus, whether religious or scientific, is really a reconstruction done with the tools available to the researcher that condition the results of the investigation. She says:

> [An] ethics of interpretation seeks to analyze the nexus between reconstructions of the Historical-Jesus and those theoretical, historical, cultural, and political conceptual frameworks that determine Jesus research. Hence biblical scholarship . . . must learn to understand itself as a critical rhetorical practice which carefully explores and assesses its own impregnation with hegemonic knowledge and discursive frameworks that made "sense" of the world and produce what counts as "reality" or as "common sense."[20]

Yes, we need a new model, and I would like to suggest that this model is one that sees in Jesus the ideal disciple of the kingdom.[21] What would it mean to see Jesus, in the Gospel of Mark primarily, but also in the other gospels, as the supreme example of discipleship? Among other things, it requires a rereading of the titles and roles traditionally associated with

---

19. James H. Cone has said that "without the historical Jesus—and by that he means the human Jesus—theology is left with a docetic Christ who is said to be human, but is actually nothing but an idea-principle in a theological system." Cone, *God of the Oppressed*, 118.

20. Schüssler Fiorenza, *Jesus and the Politics of Interpretation*, 59.

21. I already anticipated this, ever so intuitively, in a previous publication in which I say: "In the gospel of Mark Jesus is the one who embodies authentic discipleship." And also, "The gospel of Mark is then more about discipleship than it is about Christology, it is more about who is a true disciple than it is about who is the real Messiah." But at that point, I had not yet made the connection between discipleship and Christology that I am making in this book. At the time, I still thought of Christology in exalted terms, not in practical, praxiological ones, as I do now. Vena, "Rhetorical and Theological Center of Mark's Gospel," 343–45.

Introduction

him—Son of man, Son of God, Son of David, Messiah, prophet, etc.—from the perspective of Jesus' own sense of discipleship as interpreted by Mark. What would be the implications of such a reading for Christology, theology, ecclesiology and, especially, for Christian praxis? How would the Jesus that comes out of such a reading be regarded by the institutionalized church, by the guild of Biblical Studies, by everyday, real flesh-and-blood Christians,[22] and by those outside of the church? In the present work, I concentrate mainly on exploring the possibility[23] of constructing such a model given the textual data of the Gospel of Mark and I hint briefly at the ramifications of such a proposal in the life of the church.

The need to see Jesus as the example of true discipleship grows directly out of my own journey[24] in the Christian faith. I reached a point where theories of atonement and heavenly rewards became totally irrelevant for my life, and Jesus' question in Mark, "Who do you say that I am," now personalized as "What does Osvaldo think that I am?" [25] was asked anew.

22. In a first trial run of this idea in front of a Latin American audience, the comment was made that if it was already difficult for a believer to measure up to the disciples of Jesus, how much more difficult would it be, now that Jesus is made into the model of discipleship, to live up to these standards. I recognize that this is a problem, especially if one sees the difference between Jesus and the disciples as ontological. I will contend, though, that the difference is not ontological but relational. In this work, I will propose a different view of Jesus' relationship to both God and humans.

23. Schüssler Fiorenza criticizes the criterion of plausibility that judges materials on the basis of whether or not they can be made to fit into the culture and times of Jesus. This criterion tends to ignore the fact that that which is considered plausible, or common sense, depends on an hegemonic understanding of how the world works, and that this understanding is derived from a certain type of scholarship marked by the presupposition that women were not active participants in the Jesus movement. *Jesus and the Politics of Interpretation*, 51–55. Applying the same criticism to the criterion of plausibility, I would like to suggest that Jesus as disciple of the kingdom is not only plausible, since he started his career as a disciple of John the Baptist, but also possible, especially when one considers that the Markan community may represent a theological stand that is in some ways pre-Orthodox. Those who deny the possibility of a Christology where Jesus is presented as a model of discipleship, and that perhaps this was the main or prevalent way of understanding Jesus given the rhetorical shape and the theological flavor of the gospel, will have to prove that such possibility did not exist at the time of Mark.

24. I am very interested in the subject at hand. This means that my investigation is "interested." I come to the text with a pre-understanding. I do not consider this to be a hindrance or a drawback to the exegetical endeavor, but rather a healthy motivation. In the words of Daniel Patte, "Coming to the text with a vested interest, and thus a question or an expectation, does not in itself engender a misreading. In sum, preunderstandings motivate our readings, including our critical readings." Patte, *Ethics of Biblical Interpretation*, 56.

25. I owe this insight to my colleague, David Hogue.

It is *the* Christological question. And the only answer that made sense to me[26] was that Jesus is the supreme example for a life of discipleship that is understood as the construction of a new order,[27] a new society. And I found ample justification for this new understanding in the Markan story of Jesus. The metaphor that I like to use is that of Jacob wrestling with the man at Peniel in Genesis 32:26. When the man (angel?) wanted to leave, Jacob said: "I will not let you go, unless you bless me." My hermeneutical struggle with the text has resulted, in the end, in blessing. But like Jacob after the encounter with God disguised as an angel, I am not the person I used to be. My theological walk has changed. Now I am limping, forever affected by the encounter, and people, especially traditional Bible scholars, notice it. My walking is irregular because it acknowledges the paradoxes of life and the way they affect the interpretation of the text. Now my social location precedes me as I delve into the text in search for answers.[28]

Such an endeavor is a reconstruction, or better yet, a construction.[29] It is not offered so it will replace other constructions, but in the hope that it

26. Here it is important to notice how social location affects theology. What for me became irrelevant, for other people was crucial to their religious experience. For example, the slaves knew that their situation of oppression and exploitation was going to be changed the day they died, when they arrived to the other shore of the Jordan; so they sang: "Sooner-a-will be done with the trouble of this world, going home to live with God." Because of their predicament, they were not interested in the Christological affirmations of the Fathers of the Church, such as Athanasius, who said that the Son is of one substance with the Father, the question of *homoousia*. That is not a black question, says James Cone. Blacks ask "whether Jesus is walking with them, whether they can call him in the 'telephone of prayer' and tell him all about their troubles." Cone, *God of the Oppressed*, 14. In my case, my oppression was not social, but intellectual and psychological; therefore, the need to escape from it was not impeded by any social structure, but by my own self-imposed religious consciousness triggered and fed by the conservative missionary preaching I was subjected to during my youth.

27. For this idea, I am deeply indebted to Ched Myers and his seminal work, *Binding the Strong Man*.

28. Schüssler Fiorenza states: "A critical interpretation for liberation does not begin with the text; it does not place the bible at the center of its attention. Rather, it begins with a reflection on one's experience and socio-political religious location."*Wisdom Ways*. 90.

29. Tilley, *Disciples' Jesus*, 7–11, makes three affirmations worth quoting: (1) Theology is construction. (2) Theological construction is undertaken on a particular social location. (3) The traditions in which we work provide a "building code" that each construction has to follow. For Christology, he proposes that one such code could be "do not deny either the true humanity or the true divinity of Jesus Christ." I am not sure that I am willing to follow the Nicene-Chalcedonian creed as my guiding light or my building code as I unpack the meaning of Jesus as disciple in Mark. Rather than seeing these ancient creeds as the building blocks for my Christology, I prefer to use Mark's text, which

will contribute to a host of other images and views of Jesus that have been proposed throughout history. My only ethical exigency is that the model I propose will result in liberation, giving of life instead of taking it away from people. This general goal is unpacked by Schüssler Fiorenza when she says that any historical-Jesus research should be mindful of not reinscribing, in and through its scholarly discourse, the anti-Judaism inscribed in the gospels; that it should consider how much it has contributed to the liberation or oppression of women and other minorities around the world; that it should criticize the ideologies of colonization and domination that often use the biblical text as justification for their colonial agenda; and that it should assess whether or not it promotes a politics of exclusivity, inferiority, prejudice, and dehumanization when it comes to cultural or religious identity formation.[30] Furthermore, my model has to prove that it can coexist peacefully with these four areas of concern. At the end of the book, I evaluate whether or not this has been the case.

CHALLENGES TO THE PRESENT WORK

To speak of Jesus as disciple presents us with many challenges. First and foremost, there is the text of the New Testament: in no place does Jesus speak of himself—nor is spoken of by others—as a disciple of anybody.[31] Jesus is either the teacher, the Lord, the Logos, one with the Father and so on. Therefore, searching for this model will prove to involve a bit of detective work. We have to look at passages[32] where Jesus is "functioning" as a disciple or is speaking of himself in discipleship categories, or using terms such as "servant"[33] or "slave" that present him in a less exalted manner. These representations will have to be seen as synonymous or similar to discipleship, if not historically at least theologically and literarily. In that sense, Lone Fatum has said:

> A Gospel text may seem descriptive or narrative; in effect, however, it is prescriptive, as we know, and its purpose is to demonstrate

represents a pre-Chalcedonian Christology, as my building code.

30. Schüssler Fiorenza, *Jesus and the Politics of Interpretation*, 59–60.
31. But he speaks of himself as one who serves (Mark 4:45).
32. One of those passages is the account of Jesus' baptism. To many scholars, the likelihood that Jesus was indeed a disciple of John the Baptist is very high. This is the only way they can interpret his baptism by John. I should come back to this later.
33. I have explored this concept in "Gospel Images of Jesus as Deacon," 1–16.

to its Christian audience what it means to believe in Christ and to live the social lives of committed Christians. This implies that Jesus does not appear in the various texts as a human being or as a historical person of individual quality, but rather as the Christ of a particular congregation. Jesus as well as the people around him are actors in the reality of the text, and we know them only as such. We meet them playing their parts in the adaptation of Christian meaning that is the deliberate purpose of the text. In other words, in a particular Gospel text both Jesus and the people around him are bearers of just those symbolic values on which the universe of Christian plausibility is structured and meant to be sustained in a particular congregation. But, to be sure, an author is responsible for the literary construction as well as the deliberate staging of the actors as narrative agents, and so the author is present in the text as the structuring consciousness, as is the historical audience the author implies within the construction.[34]

A number of observations are in order here. First, the prescriptive nature of the narrative: Mark is not trying to describe the way Jesus was, but rather, to convince his congregation of how he should be understood. Second, this version is one geared toward a particular congregation. His Christ is the Christ of the Markan community, a group of believers that were undergoing a challenging time, as we will see. In that sense, they were different from the Matthean, Lukan, or the Johannine congregations. Third, Jesus and the people around him are actors in the reality of the text, bearers of the symbolic values that made possible the Christian universe. In this universe, discipleship is a prominent category. And fourth, the author is responsible for the construction, and therefore, present in the text as the structuring consciousness. One of the many ways in which this is implemented is through the rhetorical devices utilized by the evangelist, the most important of which may be the chiastic structure that I propose in chapter 2.

Seeing the text as prescriptive and as a construction will help me in my own endeavor, for I am not trying to discover the meaning already present in the text, but to construct one that I hope convinces the reader of the plausibility of such an interpretation, namely, that Jesus can be seen in the Gospel of Mark as the example par excellence of discipleship. Mark's narrative utilizes oral and written traditions about Jesus and fixes them in a text that is constructed to convey his understanding of who Jesus was, what he did, and how his life, death, and resurrection affected the life of his

---

34. Fatum, "Gender Hermeneutics," 160.

community. Mark's endeavor is not historicist, but theological and pastoral. Therefore, he embarks in the writing of a story where Jesus is present as a literary character more than as a historical personage. But Mark still has at his disposal vivid and lively traditions about the historical Jesus, memories of his words and deeds that were still very much alive among the believers. He is not constructing the character of Jesus out of thin air, but is basing it on the historical memory of the community. I don't have that. I have Mark's text, the only way to get to the historical Jesus via a (re)construction by the evangelist, whereby oral traditions, written texts, and plain memories come together under the theological supervision of the author to render a portrayal of Jesus that serves the needs of his community. But I also have, which Mark did not, a history of interpretation of the text, the way in which the church has ascribed meaning to the life of Jesus during two millennia and which conditions the way I read the text. And I also have my own reaction to that history of interpretation, which makes me privilege certain readings over others, in a similar fashion as the evangelist privileged certain traditions over others.[35]

Whereas the first challenge, the witness of the text of the New Testament in general and Mark in particular, is literary and rhetorical, the second, conceptualizing Jesus as a disciple of the kingdom, is theological. It requires admitting that there was an element of learning and obedience in the way Jesus approached his ministry. And this is something very difficult for orthodox scholars to accept, even when faced with the fact that a cursory reading of the gospels seems to suggest the possibility that John the Baptist may have been Jesus' teacher. Not only that, but Jesus' subjection to God, something again made plain by the gospel writers, is often missed in some Christologies, although not by the author of Hebrews, who declares in 5:8 that "Although he was a Son, he learned obedience through what he suffered." This seems to suggest that an element of learning, characteristic of every disciple, accompanied him throughout his life, since this passage refers to Jesus' final moments in Gethsemane. It follows then, that during his public work, when he was clearly being regarded as a teacher, he was still learning. He was a disciple of John the Baptist, yes, but primarily of God, a disciple of the kingdom. Together with other disciples, Jesus learned what it meant to proclaim God's coming rule, at a time when Rome was

---

35. It still puzzles scholars that Mark, if he had access to Q, did not include such important materials as the Sermon on the Mount, or some version of the birth narratives, etc. Obviously, he was making an editorial, and therefore theological, choice.

the unchecked world power. He was part of a movement of disciples who resisted Rome's imperial rule, for they had their eyes fixed on another reality, the kingdom (*basilea*) of God.[36]

Of course, the main obstacle to seeing Jesus as disciple of the kingdom is the Gospels' description of Jesus as teacher.[37] If he is a teacher—in fact, "the teacher" according to John 13:13—then how can he be a disciple? But in antiquity, every teacher or philosopher traced his teaching to a source, to a teacher. So, every teacher was a former disciple or student of someone. My contention is that humanly speaking, Jesus' teacher was John the Baptist, but that ultimately God was his Teacher. In that sense, disciples and prophets had their ultimate source of authority in the God of Israel who was regarded by all as a teacher (cf. John 6:45; Isa 54:13; Jer 32:33; Hos 11:13; Pss 71:17, 119:102, 143:8, 10).

To speak of Jesus as a disciple of the kingdom, then, implies that Jesus' ministry needs to be seen as paradigmatic, instrumental, temporary, and not necessarily absolute and final, qualities of God's reign to which Jesus seems to have always subordinated himself. The Gospel of John alludes to this when it says: "The one who believes in me will also do the works that I do and, in fact, will do greater works than these, because I am going to the Father" (John 14:12). Luke also shares this opinion by writing an entire book, Acts, devoted to the work of the apostles and their followers, thus making it clear that Jesus' earthly ministry was unfinished and was now being continued by the Spirit through the work of the community (cf. John 14:16, 26; 16:4–15; Acts 1:8).

In the Gospels, Jesus cannot be depicted as a disciple of the kingdom, because by the time they were written, the Christian church had already become uprooted from its Palestinian context.[38] Jesus had become the message, not the messenger of the kingdom. Nonetheless, there is a residue of tradition that is still perceptible in the highly theologized and constructed

---

36. "In speaking of the Jesus movement rather than of the person of Jesus himself, we are stressing the fact that it is the social fact, of which the person is to be sure a part, that has historical importance. It is a bourgeois admiration for heroic personalities that focused much of New-Testament research on the person of Jesus." Pixley, *God's Kingdom*, 111.

37. This is particularly evident in the Gospel of Matthew, where Jesus delivers five sermons that resemble the five books of the Law and teaches the disciples on far more occasions than in the other gospels. Of all the gospels, it is Mark that gives less importance to Jesus as a teacher.

38. Pixley, *God's Kingdom*, 65.

narrative of the Gospels, which reflects a time when Jesus was regarded and, I would contend, regarded himself as a messenger of God's kingdom alongside other figures such as John the Baptist. It is precisely this residue, this memory that we are interested in. Therefore, I explore the text of the Gospel of Mark looking for clues and vestiges hidden in the rhetorical tapestry of the text that may help us build the proposed model. Inter-textual connections with the Hebrew Scriptures are made, particularly when trying to imagine what would have been the possible traditions behind a certain model of discipleship.[39]

Historical and Sociological Approaches to Jesus

What was the historical Jesus, the real flesh-and-blood Jesus, like? This is what a historical approach to Jesus would try to find out, and many answers have been proposed, most of which have been treated ad nauseam by scholars from the nineteenth century to our own days and whose record appear, among a myriad of academic and popular works, in Craig S. Keener's monumental volume entitled *The Historical Jesus of the Gospels*. In his book, Keener traces the history of Jesus scholarship in detail, providing an invaluable resource for those interested in this kind of endeavor. Since mine is less historical than rhetorical, as previously noted, I refer the reader to Keener's book. Nevertheless, I would like to consider briefly some of these images, for they provide the background to my own investigation.

---

39. In attempting to portray Jesus as the disciple of the kingdom par excellence, I am not denying other portrayals. I am only making my assumptions known from the very beginning. At the same time, I also am acknowledging that there have been—and there are—many conscious as well as unconscious presuppositions scholars bring to their study of Jesus. I want to make mine clear, and I want to use them as hermeneutical lenses into the text. I have some historical basis for my affirmations, but the bulk of my argument will be literary; that is, it will be based on the text of the gospels, particularly Mark, with an eye toward finding support for my hypothesis. The end product will be, I hope, a theological construction dictated by my own theological journey.

Jesus, Disciple of the Kingdom

Jesus as a Wandering Charismatic

Nowadays, and thanks to the work of the Jesus Seminar and other historical and sociological reconstructions of Jesus' life,[40] we are familiar with the notion of a "Jesus' movement," which is seen as a precursor to what later became the early church as represented in the writings of the NT. This was, according to Gerd Theissen, a movement of wandering charismatics[41] composed of traveling apostles, prophets, and disciples that relied on a group of sympathizers that took care of their everyday needs.[42] During this time, it was the kingdom of God, rather than the death of Jesus, which held salvific value. The kingdom was seen as the message and Jesus as the messenger. To this time belongs some of the earliest stratum of the Q tradition. Even Paul testifies to this early stage (Paul's authentic letters and Q's earliest traditions come roughly from the same time period, 50–66 CE). We have Paul advising believers to have the "faith of Jesus" and telling them that God justifies the one who has this faith (Rom 3:26). Jesus also exhorts disciples to have faith in God, and he obviously sees himself as one who has such faith.[43] All of this would agree with the idea that Jesus was the messenger of the kingdom, someone like John the Baptist, and not the message.

But while messenger is a more passive concept, disciple has a more active connotation.[44] A disciple is someone who has been formed by a teacher who embodies a worldview, an ideology, and sees himself as a follower of that teacher or a subscriber of their ideology. But disciples are hardly ever solitary individuals. They belong to groups and/or movements that hope to make an impact in the society of their time. Jesus was part of such a movement. He was not just a heroic person who appeared out of the blue,

---

40. See especially Theissen, *Sociology of Early Palestinian Christianity*.

41. Pixley affirms the importance of Theissen's approach of focusing on the Jesus movement, but recognizes that this is somehow different from his own and that of other Liberation Theology scholars. While Theissen sees the narrative as a source for the reconstruction of the Jesus movement, Pixley and others, such as Fernando Belo, to whom I would add also Ched Myers, see it as an ideological construction of the author. The words of Jesus lose their significance when taken out of the narrative. Pixley, *God's Kingdom*, 112.

42. Theissen, *Sociology*, 8.

43. "Unshakable faith and trust in God, the biblical *emunah*, was the hallmark, the ideal of Jesus which he preached and practiced. It was the spiritual engine of his whole life's work." Vermes, *Changing Faces of Jesus*, 220.

44. I owe this insight to Jerry Moyar, a member of the Koinonia class at the First United Methodist Church in Downers Grove, Illinois, USA.

and, yet, see the abrupt way in which Mark describes Jesus' beginning of his ministry in 1:9! Rather Jesus is an individual deeply formed by the social group to which he belonged.[45]

Jesus as the Broker of God

The social-science model of patron, client, and broker also has been used to explain Jesus' relation to God and the kingdom. From this perspective, Jesus can be seen as a broker of God, the heavenly Patron. In his work, Jesus made accessible to people the benevolence of God dispensed as grace, forgiveness, and mercy. This model allows us to see Jesus always in a relationship of dependence and subordination to God, even when as a teacher he was also a sort of patron to the disciples, who in turn acted as his brokers. Nevertheless, realizing how connected Jesus was with God, it is better to see both him and the disciples as brokers of the heavenly Patron, co-disciples in the service of the kingdom.[46]

Jesus as a Mystic

First-century Jewish mysticism adds another layer to this picture. According to this model, Jesus was taught by John to meditate on the vision of God depicted in the first chapter of Ezekiel, the Chariot, the moving throne of God. Bruce Chilton describes the Chariot as the "source of God's energy and intelligence, the origin of his power to create and destroy. By meditating on the Chariot, John and his disciples aspired to become one with God's Throne."[47] Jesus, as one of John's disciples, learned the secrets of this meditation and in turn taught it to his disciples. This heavenly vision became the source of Jesus' power and authority. Therefore, it is possible to affirm that Jesus remained a disciple of that vision, a servant, if you will, of a higher source of authority: God's throne, God's heavenly realm. His experience was similar to that of Isaiah, Ezekiel and, later, the Apostle Paul (cf. Isaiah 6; Ezekiel 1; 2 Cor 12:1–4).

---

45. For the importance of group formation in the early Jesus movement, see Malina, *Social World of Jesus and the Gospels*, 60–67.

46. Malina, *Social World of Jesus and the Gospels*, 149–57.

47. Chilton, *Rabbi Jesus*, 50.

Jesus, Disciple of the Kingdom

Other Possible Models

Besides the models of itinerant charismatic, broker, and mystic, there are many other historical and/or sociological possibilities for a Jesus who, in the eyes of some early Christian communities, behaved as a disciple of the kingdom. Some would like to see him as a cynic or a sage—an idea advanced by the Jesus Seminar[48]—or as a prophet like Moses and/or Elijah, a favorite theme in Liberationist Christologies.[49] All of these models reflect the perspectives of those proposing them, and are all contextual interpretations, and as such valid, inasmuch as they remain aware of their contextual nature. My own investigation in the present work seeks to be a contribution to an on-going dialogue between Christologies, with the hope that it may help to clarify for some readers their own participation as disciples in the work and ministry of the church.

LITERARY APPROACHES TO MARK

By literary approaches, I refer to those methods that concentrate mainly on the text of the gospel without any concern for the way that text came to exist. They are basically *synchronic* rather than *diachronic*, for they assume the autonomy of the text to convey meaning without the control imposed on it by the author or the social location that gave it birth. Among these methods, we find narrative criticism, rhetorical criticism, structuralism, semiotics—as well as various post-modern approaches such as reader-response and, especially, deconstruction. For the sake of this work, I limit myself to a brief examination of narrative and rhetorical criticism.

According to Elizabeth Struthers Malbon, the term "narrative Christology" was introduced by Robert Tannehill in his article, "The Gospel of Mark as Narrative Christology."[50] She quotes Tannehill as saying that "we learn who Jesus is through what he says and does in the context of the action of others."[51] She goes on to affirm that the main question of narrative studies on the gospels is: *How* does the story mean?[52] She acknowledges the

---

48. John Dominic Crossan qualifies this idea by stating that Jesus was a peasant Jewish Cynic who embodied the values of the lower Galilee culture. *Historical Jesus*, 421–22.

49. See here specially Segundo's ground breaking work, *Christology at the Crossroads*.

50. Tannehill, "Gospel of Mark as Narrative Christology," 57–95.

51. Malbon, *Mark's Jesus*, 4.

52. Ibid., 6–14.

Introduction

importance of the historical context in which the gospel was produced and its religious significance for Christian faith (*What* does the story mean?), but her own research is strictly literary. It concerns itself with the narrative aspects of the gospel, which include settings, characters, plot, and rhetoric, all of which are conscious devices utilized by an implied author to try to communicate with an implied audience.[53]

My own approach in this book is slightly different. I take seriously the social context of the author and the way in which he is trying to address some problems arising from his context by means of a literary production. Therefore, I concentrate on one of the aspects of Malbon's method, namely, the rhetoric of the gospel, the way in which the evangelist has placed the traditions available to him, as well as its own redaction of them in order to convey an understanding of who Jesus was that would answer some of the questions the community had. In that sense, this work could be described as an example of socio-rhetorical[54] Christology more than narrative Christology. I will be more interested in the *what* than in the *how* of Mark's portrayal of Jesus, although how the evangelist puts together his resources will play an important role in my argument. This is illustrated mainly by my work in chapter 2, where I discuss the rhetorical center of the gospel and its theological implications. I conclude there by saying that the whole gospel betrays an intentional form used by the evangelist to drive home his main theological point.

Also important in this rhetorical analysis of Mark is how the evangelist has incorporated into the narrative some key religious and philosophical concepts of the Jewish and Greco-Roman culture, which Robbins calls "intertexture," the relationship of data in the text to various kinds of phenomena outside the text, including oral-scribal, historical, social, and cultural intertexture.[55] In chapter 1, I analyze two expressions that are examples of intertexture: "disciple" and "Son of Man." Disciple represents a case of what Robbins calls *echo*, meaning by that a word or phrase that evokes a cultural tradition,[56] both in the Jewish and Greco-Roman world. I examine then the traditions behind the idea of disciple/discipleship present in the first-century Mediterranean world. The other expression, "Son of Man," is an example of *re-contextualization*, an aspect of the oral-scribal

53. Ibid., 6.
54. I borrow this concept from Robbins, *Tapestry*, 1–17.
55. Ibid., 96.
56. Ibid., 110.

intertexture that utilizes words from biblical texts without necessarily stating that the words are written anywhere else.[57] In Mark 13:26, the reference is to Daniel 7:13–14, but the evangelist does not mention, as he does in 1:2–3, the Hebrew Scripture text he is using. In this book, unless explicitly stated, all occurrences of intertexture are referred to as *rereadings*, which is the preferred expression for theological reappropriation used by Liberation Theology exegetes.

Conclusion

Recovering an early Christology that sees Jesus as the ideal disciple of the kingdom of God is a constructive and creative task that moves us from the comfort zone in which orthodoxy has placed us into the realm of possibility and imagination. This task makes us all Christologists, builders of new understandings of who Jesus was and therefore is for certain communities. It assumes that Christologies have always been, and therefore are, community-constructed models, that is, ways of talking about Jesus that are born out of a community's theological identity. They all bear the marks of contextuality and contingency and, therefore, are not universal and objective but particular and subjective. They are born not in busy minds detached from the real problems of the world, but in busy hands engaged in a praxis that tries to change the world. My hope is that this book will demonstrate precisely that.

---

57. Ibid., 107.

1

Christology and Discipleship
Paul and Mark

IT HAS BEEN MY CONTENTION in the introduction to this work that Mark's Christology is born out of his community's situation. It is a communal construction that has as its starting point that community's self-understanding. Crucial to that self-understanding is the stress and anxiety produced by the Jewish-Roman war of 66–70 CE, which produced a crisis of faithfulness as the members of the community were pulled between allegiance to the Zealot movement or to the teachings of Jesus. This was particularly heightened by the fact that God's eschatological kingdom, as announced by the historical Jesus in Mark 1:15, had not manifested itself, thus creating a sense of disillusion, not to mention frustration and plain fear (cf. Mark 16:8). Therefore, the idea of faithful discipleship is conveyed through the example of Jesus, the ideal disciple of the kingdom, whom the believers are encouraged to imitate. Also, the eschatological Son of Man, a symbol/character extracted from the book of Daniel and the intertestamental Jewish literature, is deployed by the evangelist and placed to the service of his exhortation to faithful discipleship. In Mark's mind, faithful discipleship leads to an appropriate stance at the time when God brings God's kingdom. Therefore, these two ideas, discipleship and eschatology, are interconnected in Mark's Christology. My purpose in this book is to unravel such connection and flesh out Mark's theological perspective.

But in order to understand how Mark connects these two ideas, it is necessary to start with an historical-literary investigation of the two terms that seem to convey the ideas proposed above, namely, "disciple" and "Son of Man." Now, this investigation has to start with a chronology of the usage of these expressions. That is, what are the occurrences of these two expressions in the NT and who is the first writer to use them? When the question of chronology is asked, the obvious answer is that the Pauline letters take precedence over any other document. They represent the earliest examples of canonical writing, followed very closely by Mark, probably the first narrative gospel ever to be written. If Paul's literary production stopped with the letter to the Romans, which is believed to have been written by the middle of the first century (55–58 CE), and Mark was perhaps writing during or slightly after the Jewish War of 66–70 CE, then an investigation of the expressions "disciple" and "Son of Man" in these two authors is in order. Being as they were so close to each other in time, one is tempted to speculate as to the relationship between both of them. To what extent was Mark trying to correct, appropriate, or develop some of Paul's theological affirmations?[1] In other words, was Mark being remedial, trying to do damage control for his community? That will have to be assessed once we conclude our investigation.

The Occurrences of the Term "Disciple" in the NT

The word "disciple," μαθητής, appears nowhere else in the NT but in the Synoptic Gospels, John, and Acts. Paul does not use it; neither do any of the other writers of the NT, including the author of Revelation. If Paul, who wrote between 49–58 CE, does not use the term "disciple," and Mark, who probably wrote between 66–70 CE does, then that means that unless we

---

1. These issues, related also to the other gospels, are addressed in a recently published collection of essays. In this book, two of the contributors take seemingly divergent positions. One, James G. Crossley, advocates for a lack of direct influence of one author over the other, although this is certainly possible not only of Mark being influenced by Paul but of Paul being influenced by Mark, which requires an uncomfortable early date for the gospel. In his view, the overlaps between Paul and Mark are due to the "swirling mix of ideas" present in early Christianity, something proposed by Martin Werner almost one hundred years ago. The other contributor, Michael F. Bird, taking the traditional position that John Mark was the author of the second gospel, which contains a synthesis of Petrine tradition and Pauline theological perspective, concludes that even acknowledging this relationship does not deny the fact that Mark is an independent thinker who uses other traditions even when these traditions may potentially go against Paul's own perspective. Bird and Willitts, *Paul and the Gospels*, 2–3.

can find another document prior to Mark[2] where the word is being used, then Mark is the first NT writer to use the expression.[3] Now, he does not expand theologically on what it means to be a disciple; but Matthew and Luke, using Q, do. See, for example, Matthew 10:24, 25 / Luke 6:40; 14:26, 27, 33, where Jesus addresses the issue of the cost of discipleship utilizing the technical term "disciple." In Mark, it is only the narrator who uses the term, never Jesus. In the Gospel of John, "disciple" is used profusely. It is placed on the lips of Jesus (8:31, 13:35, 15:8), the Pharisees (9:27, 28) and the narrator (2:2, 11; 3:32; etc.). In the book of Acts, "disciple" refers to believers in general (6:1, 7; 9:10, 36; 13:52; 14:20ff; 16:1; 21:4, 16), while "apostles" refers to the twelve original disciples of Jesus (1:26).

What does this all mean in terms of chronology? Matthew and Luke, using Q, represent a later tradition. By this time, the concept of discipleship had been reappropriated to refer to a follower of Jesus. The same thing happens in John. The interesting thing, though, is that Paul never uses the concept of discipleship in his letters, nor does he develop the idea of the believers as disciples of Jesus Christ. To describe himself in relationship to Christ, Paul uses δοῦλος and ἀπόστολος. To refer to the believers in general, he uses mainly ἅγιοι and ἀδελφοί.

An analysis of the chronological data produces the following chart:

Paul (49–58 CE)	no Disciple Terminology (DT)
Synoptic Gospels (66/70–85 CE)	*abundance of DT*
John (90–95 CE)	*abundance of DT*
Acts (80–85 CE)	*abundance of DT*
Pseudo-Pauline Epistles (80–120 CE)	no DT
Catholic Epistles (90–120 CE)	no DT
Revelation (90–95 CE)	no DT

How can this data be explained?

2. The word appears throughout the Gospel of Thomas (Logia 12, 13, 19, 20, 21, etc.), but the dating of this gospel is still highly contested. Probably some of its traditions are early but the core of Thomas comes from after the canonical gospels were written. One interesting occurrence of the word "disciple" is in saying #61, where Salome tells Jesus "I am your disciple."

3. I assume for this work the Markan priority which proposes that Mark was the first gospel and that Matthew and Luke used it as well as the Q source and their own materials (M and L). This is known as the Two-Source Hypothesis. For a different take on this issue, see Farmer, *Gospel of Jesus*.

Jesus, Disciple of the Kingdom

1. There is no discipleship language in Paul.

Since Paul does not emphasize Jesus' earthly ministry, he has no place for disciples as characters in the story of Jesus. No story, no disciples. The risen Lord, who appeared to him, does not need disciples but apostles (1 Cor 15:8–10) and believers. But an earthly Jesus needs disciples, followers, not believers, since he never made himself the object of people's beliefs. God was always the object of his and people's beliefs. Faith was placed on God's power to execute liberation through miracles, healings, and exorcisms, both his and the disciples'.

Disciples and discipleship suggest a mission to be carried out and, even though Paul saw himself as a missionary and an apostle to the Gentiles, he did not envision a long mission because according to him the world was soon going to be transformed at the Parousia. His mission[4] was to be short-lived. Necessary, yes, but soon it was going to be rendered irrelevant by the appearance of Jesus Christ from heaven (cf. 1 Thess 2:19; 3:13; 4:15; 5:23; 1 Cor 15:23; Rom 13:11–14, etc.). Paul does not live to see the destruction of Jerusalem in 70 CE. According to tradition, he dies in Rome around the year 66 CE.[5] Therefore, he does not witness the beginning of the rabbinic movement started by the post-war Pharisees, who did have disciples (see Mark 2:18; Matt 23:15; Luke 5:33). So, to what extent is the discipleship terminology part of the Gospels' rhetoric[6] rather than a reality in Jesus' ministry or, for that matter, Paul's? Paul, who lived closer to the time of Jesus, does not use the expression "disciple," not even once. Now, that in itself is a huge piece of data that raises all kinds of questions: why didn't he see himself as a disciple but rather as an apostle of Jesus Christ? Are the terms synonymous? For if they are, then Paul may have meant "disciple of Jesus Christ" when he writes "apostle of Jesus Christ." But the terms are not synonymous. In the Gospels it is only the Twelve who are called apostles (Matt 10:1–2; Mark 6:20; Luke 6:13; 9:10; 22:14; 24:10). And in Mark and Matthew, they are the only ones who are "sent" with a specific mission. The rest of the disciples are not given specific instructions, except

---

4. Did Paul envision a mission for the believers also? Does he talk about the believers having to preach the gospel? Or is it always he and his associates who engage in this activity? For the most part, it is a task reserved for apostles and their companions, but sometimes the congregations are included in the task of proclamation. See, e.g., Phil 1:14.

5. Ignatius of Antioch, *Letter to the Ephesians*, chapter 12.

6. Schüssler Fiorenza alerts us to the issue of confusing the author's rhetoric with the reality his rhetoric is addressing. See her book *Power of the Word*, 55.

that they are to follow Jesus and be willing to give their lives for the gospel (Mark 8:34-38). Things change in Luke, though, where besides the Twelve, seventy others are sent by Jesus to proclaim the kingdom of God (10:1-24). This is found only in Luke and may point to his understanding of Jesus' mission as including also the Gentiles. Conversely, it may betray a Mosaic theme by which Jesus is turned into a new Moses who chooses leaders from the people in order to "share the burden" of the proclamation (cf. Num 11:17).[7]

In the book of Acts, this identification of the apostles with the Twelve is especially clear when the group has to find a replacement for Judas. Luke writes:

> Then they prayed and said, "Lord, you know everyone's heart. Show us which one of these two you have chosen to take the place in this ministry and apostleship from which Judas turned aside to go to his own place." And they cast lots for them, and the lot fell on Matthias; and he was added to the eleven apostles. (Acts 1:24-26)

This sets up the chain of authority in the nascent church. Authority is going to come from God, through the Holy Spirit, directly into the hands of the apostles. In fact, the distinction between the apostles and the Holy Spirit is at times blurred, as is the case in Acts 5:3, where lying to the apostles is equated with lying to the Holy Spirit. The twelve apostles are the ones who, together with the elders (15:2, 4, 6, 22, 23; 16:4) and the Holy Spirit, make the big decisions (15:28). The difference between the disciples and the apostles is clear in passages such as Acts 6:1-7, where a number of deacons are chosen by the apostles from amongst the disciples to serve the growing needs of the community.

Another feature of the book of Acts is that it refers to the early movement as "the Way" (9:2; 18:25; 19:9, 23; 22:4; 24:14, 22). This talks about the movement as a people in motion, on their way, following as disciples the teachings of the apostles, those who had witnessed the ministry and the resurrection of Jesus from the dead (cf. Acts 1:22). Unlike them, Paul's claim to apostleship depended on his having had a vision of the risen Christ. He knew nothing about Jesus' earthly ministry. He did not witness it, and because of that, his authority was questioned many times; he had to defend himself by saying that he had received his apostleship directly from the Lord, as a revelation, not from any human leader such as Peter or

---

7. The number 70 may refer to the seventy nations of Genesis 10 or to the seventy elders chosen by Moses in Exodus 24:1, 9; Num 11:16, 24.

James (cf. Galatians 2). He distinguished himself clearly from the apostles in Jerusalem, and yet he spoke of himself as an apostle, called by God to preach the gospel to the Gentiles. Using the term "disciple" would have amounted to recognizing a link to the earthly followers of Jesus or to the beginning stages of the church, where believers were called by that name. Paul would not have any of that. His preaching had to do with the power of God manifested in Christ's resurrection. He emphasizes the lordship of Christ, not his teachings. Rather than following the teachings of an earthly Messiah, the believers were to experience the power of the Holy Spirit as it is manifested in the *ekklesia*. For Paul, Christ was the Son of God, not the Son of Man of the Gospels; he was the Lord of the universe, not the prophet from Galilee. As the Lord, Jesus required unconditional allegiance and obedience, not simply adherence to his teachings. No, Paul could not use the word "disciple" to talk about those who believe in Jesus as the Christ. He used the word "believers," for that is what they were. Coming as they did from a Gentile background, they lacked the knowledge of the Jewish traditions, which would have qualified them as followers of a Jewish rabbi. They were more accustomed to experiencing the power of the Greco-Roman deities in the liturgical context of the Greek temples. They did not have a doctrine that they could follow, or books with the teachings of the founder that they could read. They came to the temples and engaged in liturgical practices (prayers, sacrifices, etc.) that assured them that the gods' blessings on their lives would result in good fortune. Paul switched the pagan gods with the Lord Jesus Christ and assured them of much more comprehensive benefits, such as life after death in God's presence, or being taken up while still living at the Parousia of Jesus Christ from heaven, which would put an end to their suffering. Good fortune was not in Paul's mind but rather eternal life. What Paul preached was not a way of life, but a way out of a life of enslavement into which humans have been brought by two cosmic powers: death and sin. By sharing in Christ's death and resurrection through baptism, people were sanctified, becoming members of the body of Christ, empowered by the Holy Spirit with gifts to nurture the body while they waited for the coming of the Lord from heaven. In Paul's mind, there is no time for forming disciples, only time to snatch people from the fires of hell preparing them for God's glorious reality which was about to be revealed.

If we take a sample of Paul's terminology from Romans 16, we see that he refers to people using a variety of terms, but he avoids the word "disciple." He uses terms of endearment to express how he felt about certain people who were emotionally very close to him: "beloved" (vv. 5, 9, 12), "beloved in the Lord" (v. 8), and "eminent in the Lord" (v. 13). He uses technical terms to refer to some people's specific function in the church, for example, "deaconess" (v. 1) and "apostles" (v. 7). He uses descriptive terms to talk about people's relationship to him, whether as an individual: "mother to me" (v. 13), "benefactor/helper" (v. 2) or as an apostle: "fellow workers" (vv. 3, 21), "compatriot" (vv. 7, 11, 21), "fellow prisoners" (v. 7), "fellow worker in Christ" (v. 9), "approved in Christ" (v. 10), and "workers in the Lord" (v. 12). Finally, he uses terminology that refers to people in the *ekklesia* in a more general way, namely, "sister" (vv. 1, 15), "brethren" (vv. 14, 17, 23), "saints" (v. 2, 15), and "convert" (v. 5).

Perhaps the closest Paul gets to using discipleship language is when he refers to believers as those who are "called to be saints" (1 Cor 1:2; Rom 1:7) or "those who are the called" (1 Cor 1:24). Obviously, God is the one who calls (1 Cor 1:1; Rom 1:1; 8:30), but whereas God called him to be an apostle, God called the believers to be saints or to be part of "the fellowship of his Son, Jesus Christ, our Lord" (1 Cor 1:9). There is here a hierarchical difference not present in the Gospels, except perhaps in the distinction between the Twelve and the other disciples or the crowd. Inasmuch as he has been given a special revelation that made him an apostle to the Gentiles, Paul distances himself from the rest of the believers. It is clear that, even though there are other apostles (cf. Rom 16:7; 1 Cor 4:9; 9:5; 12:28; 15:7, 9; Gal 1:17, 19), there is only one apostle to the Gentiles, Paul himself.

The expression "apostle" may of itself have a hierarchical connotation not conveyed by the term "disciple." Paul may have wanted to use it precisely because of that. In other words, Paul may have been intentionally hierarchical, reproducing in his letters a system of dominance and obedience that replaced the Roman *kyrios* with Jesus the *kyrios*.[8] In the *Greek-English Lexicon of the New Testament*, W. Bauer says that "apostle" was used in classical Greek and later writings for a naval expedition and its commander, or for a ship ready for departure, and that in isolated cases, it meant ambassador, delegate, and messenger.[9] This last meaning is the primary usage of the term in the NT, where it is applied primarily to "a group of highly honored believers, who had a special function."[10] Paul, as a ship ready to depart in

---

8. For a criticism of Paul's inscription of imperial language in his letters, see Schüssler Fiorenza, *Power of the Word*, 82–109.

9. *BDAG*, 99.

10. Ibid.

search of new regions to colonize, or new cities in which to sell merchandise, understood himself as the apostle to the Gentiles, God's messenger of good news—the gospel, but not any gospel, rather Paul's version of the gospel (cf. Rom 2:16; 16:25)—to the world. Yes, "apostle" is the term he needed to use, not "disciple," which conveys the idea of pupil and apprentice.[11] Even though, according to Luke, Paul the Pharisee was a disciple of Gamaliel (Acts 22:3), Paul the missionary to the Gentiles received the gospel from no one. He received it from God, through a direct revelation. He did not have to consult with any human being; he did not go to Jerusalem to receive it from James and the other apostles. And when Paul finally went to Jerusalem, he said that "those who were supposed to be acknowledged leaders . . . contributed nothing to me" (Gal 2:6).

We conclude then by saying that the discipleship terminology is missing in Paul's letters, because it did not fit his understanding of both the *kairos* he thought he and his communities were living in and the *kyrios* he was proclaiming. He did not see much time left for the world, for this was the moment when God's final word, spoken in the death and resurrection of Jesus Christ, was about to be fully realized at the Parousia (cf. Rom 13:11–12). Disciples were not what the world needed, but apostles and believers. Apostles were sent by God. They did not follow any earthly teacher. Since in his view, Jesus had become the Lord (*kyrios*) of the universe, one much more powerful than the one of the present day, Caesar, he did not necessitate disciples to propagate any of his teachings. In fact, his teaching were not the focus of Paul's gospel but, as he himself states it, his death and resurrection as the power of God for salvation for everyone who enters in a trusting relationship with God through Christ (Rom 1:16–17). And Paul saw himself as a vital instrument in that economy. His role in the divine plan of salvation was eschatological, for it was taking place at the end times, but also because in many ways, Paul came to fulfill the role of the eschatological Elijah of Malachi 4:5–6.[12]

---

11. Ibid., 485.

12. Vena, "Paul's Understanding of the Eschatological Prophet of Malachi 4:5–6," 35–54.

2. There are numerous references to disciples in the Synoptic Gospels and John.

From a literary and theological perspective, one might say that the higher the Christology of a given document, the lesser the need for discipleship terminology. Is this true? Well, Paul's Christology is higher than that of the Synoptic Gospels. Therefore, he does not use discipleship terminology. Paul uses "apostle," which is "sent" terminology. Sent by whom? By God, obviously.

On the other hand, disciples are sent by their human teachers. So, in a sense, disciple terminology could be a matter of Christological awareness. But, not always. For example, the Gospel of John has a very high Christology, and yet it uses discipleship terminology throughout, even more than the Synoptic Gospels. But since John probably is not using the Synoptics as sources, it is possible that he is utilizing the term "disciple" in a different manner.

Historically and chronologically speaking, the Synoptic Gospels belong to the time after the destruction of Jerusalem. After some time, the eschatological expectations connected with this event started to wane and so the post-war communities had to prepare for life on earth. Therefore, discipleship became the way by which these communities started to build themselves up as they adjusted to the disappointment that accompanied the unrealized Parousia. Out of a growing number of oral traditions, they wrote the story of Jesus, describing him as appointing disciples. Now, whether or not the historical Jesus did that is irrelevant for our purpose here, although there is a good chance that Jesus did precisely that, especially if we take seriously the possibility that he himself had been a disciple of John the Baptist. Given this scenario, it is not unlikely that Jesus would have modeled the *modus operandi* of his teacher of having disciples and may have even implemented similar practices, such as style of proclamation (Mark 1:15) and piety (Luke 11:1).

Presenting Jesus as appointing disciples in order to help him in his ministry of proclamation, healing, and exorcisms (Mark 6:12) legitimized and encouraged later communities such as Mark's to engage in the work of proclaiming the gospel to all nations (Mark 13:10), which then became their primary preoccupation. This task necessitated a structure, the church, which was made up of disciples (Matthew 28).

3. There are no references to disciple or discipleship in the Pseudo-Pauline Epistles, the Catholic Epistles, or Revelation.

But not all the communities that emerged after 70 CE utilized discipleship terminology in their writings. The Pseudo-Pauline Epistles, 1 and 2 Peter, 1, 2, and 3 John, James, Judas, and Revelation do not use this terminology either. Why? If Paul was super-eschatological and the Synoptic Gospels and John were less so, does it necessarily follow that the higher the eschatological expectation, the lower the occurrence of disciple terminology? And, conversely, that the lower the eschatological expectation, the higher the use of disciple terminology? Let us consider the evidence more closely:

Document	Level of Eschatology	Degree of Discipleship Terminology
Pauline letters	*High*	*None*
Synoptic Gospels	Moderate	High
Gospel of John	Low	High
Acts	Low	Moderate
Ephesians	None	None
Colossians	None	None
2 Thessalonians	*High*	*None*
Pastoral Epistles	Low	None
1 & 2 Peter	Low	None
James	Low	None
Revelation	*High*	*None*
Jude	None	None
1, 2 & 3 John	None	None

Our assumption cannot be fully corroborated, for there are documents that show a low eschatological expectation and, at the same time, show no DT (discipleship terminology). But at least in the case of Paul's authentic letters, and in 2 Thessalonians and Revelation, the presence of eschatological language coincides with the absence of discipleship language. And in the case of the Synoptic Gospels, John and Acts, occurrences of less, or at least qualified, eschatological language appears to coincide with the presence of a robust DT. This is a considerable amount of material that at least preliminarily and partially justifies our hypothesis. Nevertheless, the presence of this technical terminology has to be explained differently.

One way of solving the problem is to say that the documents that demonstrate a low eschatological expectation, and which according to the general assumption enunciated above should have contained discipleship language, have replaced it with something akin and comparable to disciple terminology. K. H. Rengstorf provides some clarity on this issue when he notices that the book of Acts applies the term "disciple" to all believers, to Christians in general (cf. Acts 9:1; 13:52; 14:20; 16:1; 21:4, 16), but identifies that this is not the only term used by Luke to describe Christians. He also uses "believers," "saints," "brethren," etc. Rengstorf suggests that the reason the Greek communities stopped using the term μαθητής to speak about believers was probably because "it tends to suggest that Christianity is simply a philosophical movement rather than personal fellowship with Christ as Lord."[13] Therefore, he argues for a sociological, and not necessarily theological, reason behind the absence of discipleship language.

THE MEANING OF THE TERM "DISCIPLE" IN THE NT

The equivalent term for μαθητής in the Hebrew Scripture is *talmid*, which occurs only once, in 1 Chronicles 25:8. In the LXX, it does not even appear.[14] According to Rengstorf, the reason for this absence is that the Hebrew Bible does not want to differentiate between a special group and the rest of the people, for God has chosen the whole people to learn God's will, not a select group. Therefore, one cannot speak of a teacher-disciple relationship. The prophets of the Hebrew Bible were seemingly organized in guilds ("the sons of the prophets" in 2 Kgs 2:5, 7, 15, etc.), sharing the same charismatic endowment rather than devotion to a leader. Rengstorf notes that, for example, Joshua is the servant of Moses, but when Moses is gone Joshua enjoys full authority on his own, authority given by God (see Num 27:15–17; Josh 1:2–5). He is appointed as leader of the people by God, not by Moses. In the same manner, Elisha is commissioned by God, and receives authority directly from God, not from Elijah (2 Kgs 2:9–12; 3:11–12). Elisha's relationship to Elijah is more that of a servant, an assistant or even a son, for he calls Elijah "father" (2 Kgs 2:12). Elisha, in turn, is called "father" by Joash, the king of Israel (2 Kgs 13:14). This same kind of relationship seems to be that of Baruch and Jeremiah's (Jer 36:4–8). In

---

13. Rengstorf, "Manthano, Mathetes" 562.
14. In this section, I will rely heavily on Rengstorf's article.

other words, the teacher-disciple relationship, so prevalent in the Gospels, is non-existent in the Hebrew Scriptures.

The other problem that Rengstorf points out is that of an absence of the so-called "principle" of tradition. By this, he means the desire to fulfill the master's intention and to preserve his sayings. This, which is a characteristic feature of the Greek philosophical world, is also missing in the Hebrew Scriptures, where Moses is not venerated as a liberator or founder of a religion, but more as the one on whose shoulders everyone who succeeds him stands.[15] The reason for these distinctions, Rengstorf suggests, is that the religion of Israel is a religion of revelation. God reveals God's will to the people through inspired stewards. Moses is one of them. He is presented as God's minister (Exod 4:10–12), who acts on God's behalf, not his own. His legislation comes from God, who is the Master or Teacher on whose name he, and the other stewards, speaks.[16]

But Rengstorf's argument can be challenged on more than one count. First, even though the members of the prophetic guild enjoyed the same charismatic endowment, leadership was still recognized. Elisha calls Elijah "father" (2 Kgs 2:12) and the company of the prophets staying at Jericho refer to Elijah as Elisha's "master" (2 Kgs 2:5). In the notes to the *Harper Collins Study Bible*, Robert Wilson states that "father" is a traditional title used for the head of a prophetic guild and also often used by a disciple speaking to a master.[17] Secondly, one could say that Elisha's petition to receive a double share of Elijah's spirit points to Elisha's special status as his successor, one who in many ways outshines his master. So even though the Spirit is equally distributed among all of the prophets, some have access to a privileged status by virtue of their relationship to the head of the guild. The other members of the prophetic guild recognize this when they say: "The spirit of Elijah rests on Elisha" (2 Kgs 2:15). Their recognition of Elisha's leadership role follows immediately, for they "bowed to the ground before him" (2 Kgs 2:15). Thirdly, Rengstorf's idea that the principle of tradition is absent in the Hebrew Bible may be true, but still Elisha starts his ministry invoking the power of Elijah. There is perhaps no desire to fulfill the master's intention and to preserve his sayings, but certainly Elisha starts his prophetic ministry invoking the God of Elijah (2 Kgs 2:14). If not

---

15. Rengstorf, "Manthano, Mathetes" 556–57.
16. Ibid., 558.
17. Wilson, "2 Kings," 521.

preservation of sayings, at least we could talk of continuation of ministries, as well as an acknowledgment of the same source of power.

When we consider Jesus' ministry, the parallelisms are striking. First, by coming to John to be baptized he acknowledges John's leadership. Second, by being recognized as the one who will baptize with the Holy Spirit, his independence and supremacy over John is established. This is confirmed by the miracles performed by Jesus, which clearly outshines John, who is never said to have performed miracles. Thirdly, by calling God "Father," Jesus acknowledges God as the Master and Teacher. He never calls John "father," but invites his disciples to do so with God, thus placing himself at the same level with his co-disciples in identifying the God of Israel as the ultimate source of power. This language betrays a master-discipleship relation between God and the group of followers, of whom he is but another member. Rengstorf recognizes that Jesus' call to discipleship represents a call to partnership in service, something that comes out in sayings (Matt 5:13–16; John 17:13–15), parables (Matt 25:14–30), and specific directions (Matt 10:5–15; Mark 6:6b–13).[18]

The term μαθητής is also missing in the LXX. This means that the only literary source for its usage in the gospels is the Greek environment, where it is used to denote the idea of pupil, one engaged in learning in relationship to a teacher. In a broader sense, we also find it used as pointing to an intellectual link between people who are not in direct physical relationship but rather distant in time as, for example, Socrates being a disciple of Homer.[19] But among philosophers, the term is highly nuanced. It is used to talk about a pupil, which simply refers to someone who gains knowledge or skill under expert direction. When understood in this way, μαθητής is used alongside other terms that ensure the independence and dignity of the student.[20] It is also used to denote a master-disciple relationship. This usage of the term is especially important for Socrates, Plato, and the Academy. The goal of these philosophers is not information for a fee, but more the idea of a fellowship where the teacher/master offers himself, rather than his knowledge. This is reinforced by the practice of common meals. In Plato's Academy, for example, this is a salient feature, and the director is regarded as the first among equals.[21]

18. Rengstorf, "Manthano, Mathetes" 561.
19. Ibid., 556.
20. Ibid.
21. Ibid.

The Mystery religions provide another context for the master-disciple relationship. Here, both the learning that takes place, as well as the master's personality, are secondary to the main purpose, which is that the initiate may enter into fellowship with the deity. Accordingly, the term μαθητής is not used.[22]

Perhaps the closest resemblance to the idea of discipleship in the NT is what happens with some of the philosophers of the Greek and Hellenistic world such as Pythagoras, Epicurus, and Apollonius. In each of these cases, the person of the philosopher acquires great relevance, sometimes even to the point of being considered a god or at least more than human, whereby their disciples develop a sense of being a religious and moral community committed to spreading the fame of the founder.[23] Many of these groups associated with great teachers continued even after the death of their leaders, forming religious unions with the responsibility of presenting the leader's ideas and concerns to the wider world. Rengstorf says that "loyalty to the teaching of the master finds expression in the principle of tradition, i.e., the desire to fulfill his intentions and preserve his sayings."[24] This is exemplified especially by the Epicureans and the Stoics who took special care in handling down their teachers' sayings, even though this was done without an explicit reference to παράδοσις as the actual process of transmission, which at this time was generally accepted in practice.[25]

The Rabbinic movement, which came after the birth of the gospel traditions, made use of the term *talmid* to refer to someone who is a student of Scripture and its interpretation. Though, ideally, every Israelite is to study the law under God as the supreme Teacher, it is only some who actually become experts in the law and constitute a sort of guild where people are admitted by ordination and who offer authoritative answers to disputed matters.[26] These are the ones referred to as *talmid*. The term designates a member of a school or tradition who is bound to obedience and submission to a teacher for whom the student performs even menial tasks. The school develops out of a specific teacher's interpretation of the law and these teachers may at times hold opposing views. An example of such is the schools of Hillel and Shammai. The teachers, *rabbis*, are thus engaged

22. Ibid.
23. Ibid.
24. Ibid.
25. Ibid., 557.
26. Ibid., 558.

in a rereading or reappropriation of the traditions, and this becomes the distinctive mark of that particular school. But no rabbi can go beyond what the law teaches, and especially beyond Moses, who is regarded as the absolute teacher. The law is the supreme authority and this limits the authority of individual teachers.[27] Even though Moses always remains a mediator of the divine will, the emphasis on his person is akin with how the philosophical schools treated their founders. Therefore, concludes Rengstorf, there are obvious Hellenistic influences in the rabbinic movement's conceptualization of the teacher-disciple relationship, an influence that can be seen even in the writings of Josephus who calls Joshua the μαθητής of Moses and Elisha the μαθητής of Elijah, and describes the four sects of the Judaism of his time as philosophical schools.[28]

The question for our enquiry is: which are the particular influences behind Mark's use of the word μαθητής, and what might he mean by that. A number of things need to be pointed out:

First, Mark writes for a Greek-speaking audience, which may have been familiar with the teacher-disciple relationship of the Hellenistic world. When they read about Jesus having disciples, they would immediately connect with this tradition. But then Mark goes on to tell a story in which this relationship is qualified and fleshed out.

Second, Mark engages the prophetic tradition of the Hebrew Scriptures by mentioning Elijah and utilizing parts of the books of Daniel and Isaiah. He refers to John the Baptist as the Elijah who was to come and makes Jesus initially subservient to John in a teacher-disciple relationship. Then Mark goes on to show Jesus' superiority to John, while still making Jesus subservient to a higher vision, that of God's kingdom, into which he calls people as disciples to help him construct this vision.

Third, Mark writes before the arrival of the rabbinic age, but during a time when the teachings of famous rabbis such as Paul of Tarsus, Hillel, and Shammai were widely known. He may have evaluated these great rabbis as teachers and his followers as disciples who were intent on preserving their teachings but when it came to Jesus, he wanted to modify this idea. Jesus is presented not so much as the teacher and master but as one who models true discipleship. He is a disciple of God, whose primary mission is to embody the values of God's kingdom to such an extent that suffering and even death will constitute the distinguishing mark of his discipleship.

---

27. Ibid., 558.
28. Ibid., 559.

Jesus' disciples are therefore not those who preserve his teachings only, but also those who are challenged to imitate him even to the point of sharing in his own destiny of suffering and death (Mark 10:38–39). This is hardly what was expected of the disciple of a philosopher. Therefore, Mark utilizes the cultural wrapping of the concept disciple, but reappropriates it by placing it at the service of a higher vision, the soon-to-arrive kingdom of God.

Fourth, Mark is a contemporary of Josephus who, as we said above, referred to the Jewish sects of his time, the Pharisees, Sadducees, Essenes, and Zealots, as philosophical schools. This way of referring to the followers of a given teacher may have become customary in Jewish-Hellenistic circles, for Mark also talks about the disciples of John the Baptist (2:18; 6:29) and the Pharisees (2:18). Therefore, Mark adopts this way of referring to the followers of a prominent leader/teacher, but when it comes to Jesus he modifies it, for Jesus' disciples are not to be compared to the disciples of other teachers. What they do is even shocking for their contemporaries' views of discipleship (Mark 2:18–22; 23–28).

Therefore, I propose that Mark is qualifying the Hellenistic idea of discipleship and master-disciple relationship by using Jesus as the supreme example. Unlike the disciples of the philosophers, Jesus' disciples are not to transmit their teacher's ideas but rather to commit themselves to the person of Jesus, as he is committed to the God of Israel. They are to obey Jesus to the point of leaving everything and following him, just as Jesus left his home in Galilee to follow the vision initially given him by John the Baptist. They are to suffer as a consequence of their witnessing, as John the Baptist did and as Jesus will. In that sense, discipleship becomes very similar to the work of the prophet, that of denouncing the powers that be in the name of the God of Israel, or, as in the case of the disciples, with the gospel message. In this, Jesus is an example too. The main task of the disciples is to witness to what God is doing in the world through Jesus' work. As they witness, they are invited to participate in Jesus' work as co-disciples, following the one who fulfills this role ideally. I believe Mark is intentionally constructing this model because his community was experiencing a time when such a model was either weakening or non-existent.

Christology and Discipleship

The Occurrences of the Term "Son of Man" in the NT

In chapter 4 of the present work, I explore in depth Mark's unique appropriation of the term "Son of Man." Nevertheless, I believe it is important at this point to attempt to explain its usage in the NT. Even so, our investigation will be brief, given the massive amount of work already done on the subject.[29] Scholars still continue to debate the meaning of the expression "Son of Man," but it is not my intention, nor is this the place, to discuss the intricacies of such debate. I will limit myself to mention the most common ways of explaining the term and opt for one of them as my working hypothesis.

The expression "Son of Man" (ὁ υἱὸς τοῦ ἀνθρώπου) occurs almost exclusively in the Synoptic Gospels and John,[30] and is practically missing in the rest of the NT. It occurs twice in Revelation (1:13; 14:14), once in Hebrews 2:6, and once in Acts 7:56. In each one of these last four instances, there is an inter-textual connection with either the Hebrew Bible or the Synoptic Gospels, which shows the secondary nature of its use. Revelation 1:13 and 14:14 allude to Daniel 7:13, Hebrews 2:6 is part of a quotation from Psalm 8, and Acts 7:56 refers back to Luke 22:69. Strangely enough, Paul never uses the expression "Son of Man," although he makes a reference to the παρουσία of Jesus Christ in 1 Thessalonians 4:17 in ways that point unmistakably to Daniel 7:13.[31]

In terms of chronology, we can be fairly certain that all of these non-Synoptic occurrences come from after 70 CE and, therefore, are later than Mark. I suggest that the chronological order would first be Mark, followed by Matthew, Luke, Acts, Hebrews, and Revelation. Of course, Mathew and Luke use the logia source Q and therefore some of their Son of Man sayings have to be traced back to that source rather than Mark.[32] But at least with

---

29. For a recent discussion on the Son of Man scholarship through the years, see Yarbro Collins and Collins, *King and Messiah*, 149–74, and Burkett, *Son of Man Debate*. See also Lindars, *Jesus, Son of Man*; Wink, *Human Being*; and Vena, *Parousia and Its Rereadings*, 176–77, footnotes 2 and 3.

30. Mark, 14 times; Matthew, 30 times; Luke, 25 times; John, 13 times. Schnelle, *Theology of the New Testament*, 148.

31. This idea will be fleshed out in chapter 4.

32. Given the fact that the Gospel of Thomas lacks any futuristic eschatology it is not surprising that it does not include too many references to the Son of man. There is only one clear instance, Saying 86, where it parallels Luke 9:57–62; Matt 8:18–22. The other

the evidence that we have in the NT, it is important to notice that Mark seems to be the first author who introduces the expression "Son of Man" and who puts it on Jesus' lips. He also introduces the word "disciple," as we said above, but unlike "Son of Man," this word is never found on Jesus' lips. These two expressions are innovative ways of talking about both Jesus and the believers, different at least from the way Paul refers to them. In and of itself, this makes Mark a very creative Christologist.

The fact that the Son of Man sayings appear in other independent sources such as Q, the Gospel of Thomas, and the Gospel of the Hebrews[33] seems to suggest that this tradition was pretty strong. We have three independent witnesses to the use of this expression in the Jesus tradition. Because of this evidence, many scholars agree that the historical Jesus probably used this expression himself. Now, which of the sayings ought to be traced back to Jesus, and which to the early church, is still a matter of contention. We will not attempt to solve this conundrum here, but rather, take all of the sayings as they appear in the Gospel of Mark and try to make sense out of them as part of the evangelist's story. That is to say that, in Mark's story world, Jesus *is* the Son of Man. Why was it necessary for Mark to stress this aspect of Jesus? Why wasn't Paul interested in it? Why is this tradition relegated almost exclusively to the Gospels? What does it tell us about the Christology of the evangelists as opposed to that of other NT writers such as Paul, for example? These are some of the questions this book seeks to address.

---

occurrence is Saying 44, paralleling Luke 12:10, where Man is dropped and only Son is included. Scholars generally agree that, in both instances, Thomas is relying on the Synoptics and not the other way around.

33. John Dominic Crossan disagrees. He affirms that: "[the] apocalyptic judge's title, the Son of Man, did not stem from Jesus himself or even from the common voice of all those early Christian communities. It is not present, despite the allusion to Daniel 7:13, in the apocalyptic expectations of Paul, in the source used by *Didache* 16, or in the apocalyptic visionaries opposed in the Gospel of Thomas. But it did arise very early in the tradition, as is clear from its independent presence in the Sayings gospel Q, the Gospel of the Hebrews, and Mark. The conclusion is that Jesus' return could be described as the scenario of Daniel 7:13 without anyone using a titular Son of Man. Why, then, did a titular Son of Man ever arise at all, even among those circles in which it did? How did Son of Man become so early, so easily, and even so emphatically a special title for Jesus in certain communities and traditions? My proposal is that those early traditions also held texts in which Jesus spoke of 'son of man' in the generic or indefinite sense and that it was the presence of such texts that facilitated the transition from Jesus as apocalyptic judge from Daniel 7:13 to Jesus as the Son of Man from Daniel 7:13." Crossan, *Historical Jesus*, 255.

Christology and Discipleship

The fact that the expression "Son of Man" is limited to the Gospels and their sources and to a few other instances in the NT (see above), but is completely missing in Paul's letters, bespeaks of the Christological diversity of the early church. By that I mean the different and creative ways by which the followers of Jesus of Nazareth tried to explain to themselves and to the world the impact this person had on their communities. In order to do so, they deploy a number of expressions, some of which became later "Christological titles," for example, Son of God, Son of Man, Lord, etc., whose function was originally descriptive. Relying on the traditions available to them but also on their ethnic and cultural background (Greek, Aramaic, Jewish), these communities appropriated the Jesus traditions so as to suit their need for identity and survival in a world of confusion, dislocation, and death.

But even among the gospel writers, there is Christological diversity. If we assume the Markan priority theory as one way of assessing this diversity, especially when it comes to a particular tradition such as the Son of Man tradition, we must list those passages that parallel Mark and notice any editorial changes made by Matthew and Luke. And we must do the same with those passages that do not parallel Mark, those that come from their common source Q or from their particular materials, and notice how they modify—or not—Mark's picture.

Uses of Son of Man in Mark and in Parallels

1. The earthly Son of Man.

Mark's depiction of the Son of Man as one who is to suffer, die, and rise finds an appropriate correlation in Matthew and Luke's account, which also refer this image to the historical Jesus. The pertinent passages are:

- Mark 8:31 (Luke 9:22)
- Mark 9:9 (Matt 17:9)
- Mark 9:12 (Matt 17:12)
- Mark 9:31 (Matt 17:22; Luke 9:44)
- Mark 10:33 (Matt 20:18; Luke 18:31)
- Mark 10:45 (Matt 20:28)
- Mark 14:21 (Matt 26:24; Luke 22:22)
- Mark 14:41 (Matt 26:45)

Jesus, Disciple of the Kingdom

In all of these instances, Matthew and Luke follow Mark not only when the context clearly points towards Jesus as the Son of Man, (for example, Mark 14:17–21/Matt 26:20–25; Luke 22:21–23), but also when the link between the Son of Man and the historical Jesus is not so clear (the rest of the examples above). And at least once, Matthew adds the personal pronoun "he" to Mark's account (Mark 8:31/Matt 16:21), thus equating the Son of Man with the Messiah and with the historical Jesus, a theological move that the other evangelists seem to imply but not offer explicitly.

> "Who do people say that the Son of Man is?" . . . Then he sternly ordered the disciples not to tell anyone that he was the Messiah. From that time on, Jesus began to show his disciples that he must go to Jerusalem. (Matt 16:13–21)

Mark's use of Son of Man meaning "human being" is found in 2:10 (/ Matt 9:6; Luke 5:24) and in 2:28 (/Matt 12:8; Luke 6:5). In the first instance, the Son of Man is said to have authority on earth to forgive sins. In the second the Son of Man is declared as being Lord of the Sabbath. In both examples, Jesus is the immediate textual referent to the Son of Man. He is the one who expropriates the scribes' right to interpret who mediates God's forgiveness—it is God who forgives, not Jesus, as the Greek passive verb ἀφίενται denotes—for even though the priests in the temple are agents of God's forgiveness, they do not forgive sins: God does.

But the evangelist seems to think differently. In verse 10, he affirms that the Son of Man *has* authority on earth to forgive sins.[34] He seems to be not solely an agent, but the generator of the forgiveness. But probably this is not the case, especially if Mark is recalling here the imagery of Daniel 7, where one like a son of man is given authority by the Ancient of Days (God) to rule earthly nations at the *eschaton*. So, as Joel Marcus reminds us, "[the] heavenly God remains the ultimate forgiver, but at the climax of history he has delegated his power of absolution to a 'Son of Man' who carries out his gracious will in the earthly sphere."[35] But the difference with the Danielic figure is that this Son of Man exercises his authority through

---

34 Ched Myers has alerted us that the language of forgiveness is taken from the debt code and that the scribes, as interpreters of the Torah and co-stewards of the symbolic order, controlled how indebtedness was determined. Whatever debt the paralytic had with society or God, shown by his sickness that was attributed to his own or inherited sin, he was released of by Jesus. The scribes' anger was justified. Jesus had taken away from them their right. *Binding the Strong Man*, 155.

35. Marcus, *Mark 1–8*, 222–23.

forgiveness of sins, not through the overcoming of his enemies, as is the case in Daniel 7. In that sense, this may represent a novelty on the part of the evangelist, who is bent on counteracting the messianic ideology of the Jewish revolutionaries.[36]

Now, if the Son of Man is a communal symbol representing God's people, as we will propose throughout this work, then the forgiveness of sins is enacted by the community he represents. Soteriology then is linked to a people, not to an individual savior (see chapter 6 of this work). We can see this idea surfacing in Mark 2:27–28, when Jesus says "The Sabbath was made for humankind (ὁ ἄνθρωπος) and not humankind for the Sabbath; so the Son of Man is lord even of the Sabbath." Interestingly enough, neither Matthew nor Luke includes this affirmation, thus making the lordship of the Son of Man more of an individual feat than a communal responsibility. But, if according to Mark, Jesus is the representative of the community, then what the evangelist is really saying is that it is the community that has the right to decide how to interpret the Torah in relation to Sabbath observance. This obviously puts them at odds with other Jewish Christian communities at the time. Both groups are represented in the text, one by the Scribes and Pharisees, the other by Jesus. We will come back to this in chapter 5.

2. The eschatological Son of Man.

Mark's depiction of the Son of Man as a heavenly figure, who is to come in the clouds of heaven, is followed very closely by Matthew and Luke. In Mark 8:38/Matt 16:27, and Luke 9:26, the Son of Man comes in his Father's glory; in Mark 13:26/Matt 24:30, and Luke 21:27, he is coming in clouds; in Mark 14:62/Matt 26:64, and Luke 22:69, he is sitting at the right hand of God. In each of these contexts, the Son of Man is depicted in Danielic fashion as possessing power and glory bestowed by God the Father. He is an agent of God's final eschatological retributive justice. Matthew and Luke do not add any particular theological insight to Mark. Even when Luke fails to mention in 22:69 that the sitting Son of Man will return to earth riding on the clouds, he nevertheless acknowledges this return in other parts of the narrative (9:26; 21:27; cf. Acts 1:9–11).

---

36. Ibid., 223.

Jesus, Disciple of the Kingdom

Use of Son of Man in Q

The most popular hypothesis about the Son of Man traditions in Q is that they were added later, when the messengers of Q met with opposition from their fellow Jews and reacted with a proclamation of judgment that was going to be brought about by Jesus as Son of Man.[37] This approach has created the perception that what we have at play in Q, at a Christological level, is a two-stage Son of Man Christology. In the first stage, the Son of Man is presented in ways that coincide with the experience of the community as marginal, lacking theological acceptability, and social status. In the second, he is presented as coming in victory to vindicate his suffering people.[38] I believe this is a possible way of explaining the nature of Q as a community-produced document.[39] The circumstances of the community influenced the way in which the oral traditions were appropriated. In other words, their praxis shaped their theology. Or to put it in Liberation Theology terms, theology became a second step after praxis.[40] What we have in Q then, is the testimony of a community struggling for self-identity couched in apologetically driven rhetoric that utilizes the image of the Son of Man as a catalyst for this conflict. Let us consider now the passages in Q that refer to the Son of Man. As in the Markan tradition, they fall into two categories: the earthly Son of Man and the eschatological Son of Man.

1. The earthly Son of Man.

Luke 6:22 (/Matt 5:11). The Lukan version of the Sermon on the Mount—the Sermon on the Plain—says that the disciples are blessed when they are

---

37. Schröter, "Son of Man as the Representative of God's Kingdom," 40. See also Mack, *Lost Gospel*, 36–39.

38. See Foster, "Pastoral Purpose of Q's Two-Stage Son of Man Christology." In *Bib* 89 (2008), 81–91.

39. I am not sure that I am as optimistic as some scholars who affirm that behind Q stands an early Christian community. Burton Mack is a typical example of this position. I am more inclined to believe, with Paul Meier, that Q is a hypothesis and that it should remain as such until more evidence is gathered. But I am willing to entertain the idea that when Matthew and Luke received this tradition, which came to them probably in both oral and written form, it already had a certain theological shape which was the product of an intentional move on the part of certain believers (a community?) who wanted to make sense of their present predicament marked, possibly, by misunderstanding and ostracism from both the main Greek culture and their Jewish contemporaries.

40. See note 6 of the introduction.

reviled "on account of the Son of Man." The parallel in Matthew reads "on account of me," thus clearly identifying the Son of Man with the historical Jesus. Even though Luke seems to be referring to a future coming figure (cf. also 3:16; 7:19; 13:35), the immediacy of the beatitude being addressed to the disciples in the second person plural "you" shows that, for Luke, allegiance to the Son of Man has immediate consequences: people hate, exclude, revile, and defame the disciples *now*! The emphasis is on a present-day experience, not something that will happen in the future. The suffering modeled by the Markan Son of Man, which Luke includes in his gospel (9:22, 44; 18:31; 22:22), has already begun in the life of the post-Easter community.

Luke 7:34 *(/Matt* 11:18*)*. In this passage, the reference to the Son of Man is clearly directed to Jesus, whose lifestyle is contrasted with that of John the Baptist. Both John and the Son of Man "have come" (ἐλήλυθεν). Their ministries are still fresh in the community's memory,[41] giving people food for thought. And they are still controversial figures for the religious authorities, each on their own terms, one for his asceticism and the other for his apparent excesses.

Luke 9:58 *(/Matt* 8:20*)*. The itinerant and uncertain lifestyle of Jesus is presented as a challenge to those who wanted to become his disciples. Again, even though Jesus seems to be talking about another person when referring to the Son of Man, he is obviously referring to himself, since the prospective disciples promise to follow him "wherever you go." The community that produced and/or received this tradition knows that a lifestyle of duress and deprivation is in store for them if they decide to become disciples.

Luke 11:30 *(/Matt* 12:40–41*)*. This passage can go both ways. It can refer to the historical ministry of Jesus of Nazareth, in which case the sign of Jonah has to be interpreted as Jesus' prophetic proclamation against the religious authorities. But while Jesus' proclamation will not engender a positive response, i.e., repentance, Jonah's did, as attested in verse 32. The irony resides in the fact that for Luke, Jesus is greater than Jonah! Or it can also be interpreted in a futuristic manner, as referring to an eschatological figure who was to come and to whom Jesus bore witness, advising people to prepare for. When the Son of Man comes, Jesus says, he might find faithlessness and hardness of heart, rather than willingness to repent (cf. Luke 18:8).

41. This sense is conveyed by the perfect tense ἐλήλυθεν, which suggests that an action that happened in the past has repercussions in the present.

Jesus, Disciple of the Kingdom

These are all the Q passages that point towards an earthly Son of Man and his ministry. Whether this refers to Jesus or to one coming in the near future is difficult to assess, given the fact that this tradition has been woven into the theological frame of the Gospels, where Jesus is unmistakably identified with the Son of Man. However, what is clear is that no eschatological grandeur and power is attached to this personage but rather, the opposite, namely: rejection, hatred, criticism, and social deprivation.

2. The eschatological Son of Man.

Luke 12:8 *(/Matt* 10:32*).* Here Jesus is warning his disciples—and also the crowd (12:1, 13)—about the dangers of denying him before others. If this happens, Jesus says, the Son of Man will deny them before the angels of God, a clear reference to the eschatological judgment, also referenced by Mark in 8:38 and 13:24–27. There is no textual indication in Luke, nor for that matter in Mark, that this Son of Man is equated with the historical Jesus. That connection is made by the Gospel narrative at large, but not necessarily by the Q tradition. That is why it is necessary for Matthew to clarify this point. The Matthean parallel reads: "Whoever denies me before others, *I* also will deny before my Father in heaven" (Matt 10:33). Matthew does something similar in 5:11, where he changes the Q tradition to read "on account of me" rather than "on account of the Son of Man," as Luke 6:22 has it.

Luke 12:10 *(/Matt* 12:32*).* This is the Q version of the Markan tradition about blaspheming the Holy Spirit (Mark 3:28–30). In Mark, this blasphemy is perpetuated when people, in this case the scribes, affirm that Jesus' power to heal comes from the devil. For Mark, questioning Jesus' source of power amounts to sinning against the Holy Spirit. Not so for Luke, who seems to make a distinction between speaking against the Son of Man, which is forgivable, and blaspheming the Holy Spirit, which is not. In this way, Luke seems to differentiate between the Son of Man and the historical Jesus.

Luke 12:40 *(/Matt* 24:44*).* The text speaks about the sudden and unexpected coming of the Son of Man to usher in the kingdom which, although promised to the disciples, has yet to be materialized in their lives (cf. 12:32). Readiness, alertness, and diligent work are required from them if they expect to be welcomed into the kingdom. Otherwise, their fate will be with the unfaithful (12:46). For Q, it is the Son of Man, an eschatological figure, who is the agent of God's kingdom. But this figure is never clearly identified with the historical Jesus, an accomplishment of the overall theological work of the evangelists for whom Jesus *is* the Son of Man.

Luke 17:22, 24, 26, 30 (/Matt 24:27, 37, 39). Here, Luke uses the Q tradition that talks about the "days of the Son of Man." This is a tradition unique to Q, not appearing in any of the other gospels or in the rest of the NT. Luke uses it to theologically qualify the apocalyptic tradition of the end times, which is used by Mark and other NT writers. Interestingly enough, Matthew has replaced the expression τῶν ἡμερῶν τοῦ υἱοῦ τοῦ ἀνθρώπου with the word παρουσία, betraying knowledge of the Pauline tradition on the same subject (cf. 1 Thess 2:19; 3:13; 4:15; 5:23; 1 Cor 15:23). An analysis of the section provides us with a good sense of how Luke supplements the tradition with his own editorial work. The passage in question is Luke 17:22-37:

Verse 22: Lukan redaction. We think this verse represents a Lukan introduction to the Q motif of the days of the Son of Man meant to address the issue of the delay of the end times. The fact that Matthew omits it shows that the verse is not in Q or, if it is, that he still expects the *eschaton* to occur soon and, therefore, does not include it.

Verse 23: Q's version of the tradition behind Mark 13:21. We assume here that Luke is quoting Q, rather than Mark, because Matthew also uses it—although he adds "do not believe it," which seems to betray knowledge of Mark 13:21. Matthew, unlike Luke, will use it again in 24:23, but this time quoting straight from Mark.

Verse 24: Q. The theme of the days of the Son of Man is restated.

Verse 25: Lukan redaction. He takes the reference to suffering and rejection from the Markan tradition about Jesus' prediction of his death (see above).

Verses 26-27: Q. The theme of the Son of Man in his day is compared with the days of Noah. The catastrophic end of the pre-flood world is made into a model, or a type, of what is going to happen in the day of the Son of Man.

Verses 28-29: Lukan redaction. The theme of the fate of Sodom as a warning and reminder of what is going to happen at the final judgment is from Q (Luke 10:12/Matt 10:15), but Luke is not quoting directly from that document. This is seen by the fact that Matthew omits it. It looks more like his own midrash on Genesis 19:24-26.

Jesus, Disciple of the Kingdom

Verse 30: Q. Once again, we have the theme of the Son of Man in his day. The threefold repetition of the theme is already found in Q. Therefore, Matthew includes it in his gospel also (cf. Matt 24:26-28).

Verse 31: Mark. Here, Luke seems to be using his Markan source independently from Q, since Matthew omits it.

Verse 32: Lukan redaction. This is part of the midrash we mentioned above.

Verse 33: Q. This seems to be Q's version of the tradition behind Mark 8:35.

Verses 34-35: Q. Notice how Matthew uses the image of two in the field rather than two in one bed, thus moving the action from the house, the domain of females, into the outside world, the domain of males.

Verse 36: Some MSS omit this verse. It reads: "Two will be in the field; one will be taken and the other left." We assume it is from Q, because Matthew uses it (24:40) and it is missing in Mark. The fact that Luke has replaced it with the image of two sleeping in the same bed is very interesting, since the gender of those mentioned is masculine! (ὁ εἷς and ὁ ἕτερος).

Verse 37: Q. This saying is obviously from Q, for Matthew uses it also.

Following Q, Luke affirms that the day of the Son of Man, who through his redactional work he equates with the historical Jesus, will be a day of judgment comparable to the days of Noah and Lot, when God's wrath poured relentlessly over the whole of humanity and over the city of Sodom. But this day will be also a day of vindication for the faithful, the chosen ones, who "cry to him day and night." This is made clear by the Lukan material that follows immediately in 18:1-8 and which seems to deal with anxiety on the part of the believers due to the delay of the end times. In this way, the section represented by 17:22—18:8 comes to a close as a self-contained piece. It also closes Luke's famous "Large insertion," 9:1—18:14.

It is clear then that for Q, and for Luke and Matthew, the Son of Man is more of an individual figure similar to the one described in 4 Ezra and 1 Enoch who will inaugurate God's judgment on his day, an event akin to that described in the Hebrew Scriptures (cf. Joel 1:15; 2:1-2; Amos 5:18-20; Isa 2:11-22, 13:6-19; Ezek 30:1-4; Zeph 1:2—2:13). The Markan understanding of this figure is more corporate than individualistic, as we demonstrate in chapter 4, and it is pretty much missing from Q and also from Luke and Matthew, except when they use Mark. But even when they do that, they

Christology and Discipleship

make sure to highlight the individual aspect of the Son of Man. I suggest that the reason for this is that the community behind Q had experienced so much rejection by their contemporaries and so much disappointment because of the delay of the end times that they were not invested in becoming conduits of salvation for the world. They were waiting anxiously to be rescued from their present situation, vindicated, and welcomed into the kingdom. Something similar may be said about the Lukan and Matthean communities. They were aware of being part of the Greco Roman world and of having a mission in it. Matthew ends his gospel with the Great Commission (Matt 28:16–20), and Luke writes a second volume in which he describes this mission as exemplified ideally by the early church. But he still maintains an eschatological expectation made clear by the ascension narrative (Luke 24:50–53; Acts 1:6–11), which promises the coming of the risen Christ from heaven at a certain point in the now extended future.

Nothing like this is to be found in Mark, as I explore in depth in chapter 4. The experience of the Markan community was different. They were invested in participating in the redemption of the world via self sacrifice for the gospel, and they envisioned a time when the Son of Man, the risen Christ, was going to reissue the mission from Galilee, only that this time the community was going to be empowered to carry it on, thus acting as agents in the establishment of God's kingdom on earth.

The Use of Son of Man in "M" and "L"

In chapters 13 and 25, Matthew uses the expression "Son of Man" again (13:37, 41; 25:31), but this time utilizing exclusive material that does not appear in either Mark or Q. There are recurrent themes in both passages: a) the kingdom of heaven is the prevailing metaphor, explicitly mentioned in 13:24 and 25:1. It is also referred to as the "kingdom of their Father" in 13:43. b) People are separated into two groups, the righteous and the unrighteous, exemplified by the weeds and the wheat and the sheep and the goats. c) The Son of Man is both the sower and the eschatological judge sending his angels to gather people for the final judgment. As he has done before, Matthew makes it clear that this Son of Man is the historical Jesus. He does so by supplementing the parable of the sower from Mark, where the sower is equated with Jesus (see my analysis in chapter 3), with the parable of the weeds, where the sower is identified with the Son of Man (13:37). He also makes the ethical responsibility of the righteous toward the

45

weak and marginal members of society to be the main qualifier or disqualifier for entering the kingdom. The idea here is that, in the absence of Jesus, the believers find him in the lives of the marginalized. d) Shining like the sun in 13:43 and eternal life in 25:46 are also similar images.

But perhaps someone may say that there is a hint at corporate identity in Matthew 25, when the Son of Man is identified with the poor and the needy. How should this be interpreted? The king affirms that doing something to a member of his family amounts to having done it to himself (25:40, 45). As the *pater familias*, he represents his group's honor. So if a member of his family is honored, he is honored too, and if a member of his family is shamed, he is shamed also. But that does not seem to be the logic here, because both the righteous and the unrighteous did not know that by helping their neighbors, or by ignoring their needs, they were actually doing it to the king himself! A better way to explain this parable is to say that the rules of honor and shame are being reversed. Doing the kinds of things the righteous did to the needy would have been regarded as shameful, for a person was to relate honorably only to those who could replicate in kind or, in other words, someone holding the same social status, usually a member of one's own kinship group.[42] In a sense, then, the unrighteous were following the social conventions of retributive honor by not relating in a positive way to those who occupied an inferior position in the social ladder. Surprisingly enough, the king announces that this attitude, although it may have been logical and expected, goes against the very nature of his kingdom. It will send people into eternal punishment, eternal shame, while the opposite will ensure their inheritance of the eternal kingdom, that is, eternal honor. So, a reversal of statuses, as well as fortunes in the other world, seems to be operating here through the prevailing Mediterranean value of honor and shame. Therefore, we are not really talking about corporate representation, a symbolic way of conveying identity, but more along the lines of kinship and fictive affiliation.

Luke's own "L" material on this subject is only found in 9:56, 14:10, 21:36, and 22:48. In 9:56, there is a variant to the Greek text, an addition present in some late MSS that reads: ". . . rebuked them, and said: 'You do not know what spirit you are of, for the Son of Man has not come to destroy the lives of human beings but to save them.'" In this present context, it

---

42. "For Mediterranean people, the one great goal in life is the maintenance and strengthening of the kinship group and its honor. . . . Actions that strengthen in-group cohesion are honorable; otherwise they are not." Malina, *Social World*, 109.

Christology and Discipleship

points unmistakably to Jesus, to his ministry set against the popular nationalistic expectations of a messianic figure that would destroy the enemies of Israel, in this case the Samaritans. It also speaks of Luke's understanding of salvation as being universal, not solely for Jews.

In Luke 19:10, and as a conclusion to the story of Zacchaeus, Luke affirms that the Son of Man came to seek out and to save the lost. In the present context, it is Jesus who "came" and "sought out" Zacchaeus and brought "salvation" to his house, so there is no doubt that, when Luke refers to the Son of Man, that he has in mind Jesus.

In Luke 21:36, we have Luke's own ending to Mark's eschatological discourse. He paints the picture of a courtroom where people appear before the judge, in this case the Son of Man. Nevertheless, because these people are able to escape the events of the end times, they are confident to stand before him at the Last Judgment.

Finally, in Luke 22:48, we have a surprising addition to the Markan account of Judas' betrayal: "Judas, is it with a kiss that you are betraying the Son of Man?" Here Luke clearly identifies Jesus with the Son of Man. Although the historical Jesus may have meant simply "human being," or "son of humanity," the gospel audience understood this to be a title for the risen Christ, the eschatological Son of Man of the previous chapter (21:27, 36). That is why Judas' betrayal is so astonishing. It is like the Lukan Jesus telling Judas: Do you realize what you are doing? And perhaps that is precisely Luke's point, namely, to show the paradoxical nature of the betrayal that would lead to the paradoxical events of the last week.

Luke's own treatment of the Son of Man tradition refers to both Jesus' ministry and his role as an eschatological judge coming to exercise God's judgment on both the righteous and unrighteous. This idea is reinforced at the story level by the ascension narrative, not present in any of the other gospels, which provides an adequate and logical framework for Jesus coming from heaven at the end time (cf. especially Acts 1:11).

The Absence of the Term "Son of Man" in Paul's Letters

In chapter 4 of the present work, I try to demonstrate that given the minimal use of the book of Daniel in Paul's writings, the idea of the Son of Man as an apocalyptic figure was not part of the apostle's eschatology. However, there is one passage that resembles the description of the Son of Man in Daniel 7:13–14. We are referring to 1 Thessalonians 4:16–17, where Paul speaks of the coming of Christ with the clouds of heaven. This coming (παρουσία) has as its purpose the ushering of the final resurrection of the dead ("the dead in Christ will rise first") and the transformation of those alive at that time ("we who are alive, who are left, will be caught up in the clouds with them to meet the Lord in the air"). It is not, as many have thought, a description of the "rapture" of the church![43] A number of things are important here. First, it is the Lord, Christ, who descends from heaven, not the Danielic Son of Man. The risen Christ (4:14) is made the instrument of the believers' resurrection. It is through him (4:14) that God will "bring with him those who have died." Second, this does not mean that the dead believers are already with God and are being brought back to earth, as if they would have experienced already a "first" resurrection. It simply means that they are brought back to life, as verse 16 seems to suggest: "The dead in Christ will rise first." Third, the Lord, after being met in the clouds by both the newly risen and the transformed believers, does not return to heaven but stays with them on what is supposedly going to be the reign of God on earth ("and so we will be with the Lord forever.")

One of the main differences with Daniel 7 is that the risen Lord comes *in* (ἐν) the clouds and not *with* (μετά) or *upon* (ἐπί) the clouds. In this sense, Paul follows his contemporaries' reappropriation of the Daniel passage, that is, *if* he has this particular passage in mind. Chances are he does not and he is using some other kind of tradition, perhaps even an unacknowledged Synoptic tradition such as, for example, the metaphor of the thief in the night (1 Thess 5:2, 4; Luke 12:39; Matt 24:43). The Synoptic passages come from Q, where the thief is equated with the Son of Man. Mark has a similar tradition, but instead of using thief he uses "master of the house" (Mark 13:35–36). By using thief instead of master of the house, Paul seems to be closer to the Q tradition. If this tradition developed in the mid 50s, then it overlaps Paul's time, and there is a good possibility that he either knew about it or that the metaphor was in common use, and both the Q people and Paul had access to it.

But what about Paul's description of Christ as the second Adam? Does it not resemble the Son of Man theology, if not the apocalyptic Son of Man at least the primordial human being of the Genesis creation narrative? For Paul, Adam is a (proto) type of Christ (Rom 5:14), and Christ is the (arche)

---

43. Rossing, *Rapture Exposed*, 174–77.

type of humanity, the perfect human being through whom justification for the entire human race came (Rom 5:18-19). The first Adam was a living being, from the earth, a man of dust (1 Cor 15:47a), the ancestor of our physical bodies. The second Adam, on the other hand, is a man from heaven (1 Cor 15:47b), a life-giving spirit, the ancestor of our spiritual bodies, whose image we shall all bear at the resurrection of the dead, which according to Paul would happen soon, at the παρουσία (1 Cor 15:23).[44] So there is a sense in which Christ is made into a representative of God's people. He stands for redeemed humanity, whereas Adam stands for condemned humanity (Rom 5:15-21). Adam's representation leads to death while Christ's leads to life. Christ is the first fruits of a harvest already in progress, which will be completed at the final resurrection, when all those who belong to him will likely be raised (1 Cor 15:23).

Therefore, we conclude that even though Paul does not use the term "Son of Man," he apparently replaced it with his own images of Christ as the Second Adam and the Man from Heaven, both of these images bearing a hint of corporate representation similar to what we advocate for Mark. Given Paul's apocalyptic and mystic bent, his view of Jesus Christ is more individualistic. For him, Jesus is the Lord, and he is convinced that his soon-to-arrive Parousia would bring this evil age to an end and usher in God's wrath and judgment. We find nothing of this sort in Mark where, according to Horsley, "Most of the 'son of man' sayings . . . have nothing to do with judgment or the gathering of the elect."[45] Rather, "as indicated in its open ending of the empty tomb scene with Jesus 'gone before them into Galilee,' Mark's story emphasized not the resurrected and exalted Lord who was coming again but the continuation of Jesus' mission of renewing the people of Israel."[46]

The other ways of referring to Jesus used by Paul, such as Messiah (Christ), Son of God, Lord, First fruits (ἀπαρχή), etc, are not relevant for our discussion here and have been covered by a multitude of scholars. Suffice it to say that Paul does not acknowledge a tradition going back to either Daniel or some of its Second Temple interpreters, such as 4 Ezra and 1 Enoch, which picture an angelic being, the Son of Man, as the agent of God's final kingdom. For Paul, Jesus is the agent, as clearly seen in 1

---

44. See my discussion of this issue in *Parousia and Its Rereadings*, 129-34.
45. Horsley, *Hearing the Whole Story*, 127.
46. Ibid., 128.

Corinthians 15 and 1 Thessalonians 4:16–17, but his description bears almost no resemblance to the Danielic Son of Man.

The Meaning of the Term "Son of Man" in the NT

As we have seen in our discussion above, there are three primary uses of the expression "Son of Man" in the gospels: as a heavenly figure who is to come, as one who is to suffer, die, and rise and as a reference to human beings. Starting with the last usage, G. N. Stanton suggests that "Son of Man," although "used so frequently in the gospels, in Greek it is an awkward phrase. Hence there is general agreement that it is a clumsy translation of an Aramaic phrase *bar enash(a)* ['man' or 'mankind']."[47] In Ezekiel, for example, the prophet is addressed as son of man 93 times, and the meaning is that of a mere mortal, a human being.[48] Therefore, one possibility is that Mark is using Son of Man in this sense. But the problem arises when the evangelist places the expression in cosmological contexts where human being alone does not fully explain the function of the term.

As one who is to suffer, die, and rise Son of Man is obviously a reference to the historical Jesus. In Mark, Jesus tells his disciples about his own fate in the third person singular:

> Then he began to teach them that the Son of Man must undergo great suffering, and be rejected by the elders, the chief priests, and the scribes, and be killed, and after three days rise again. (Mark 8:31; cf. 9:31; 10:33-34)

In the narrative this is a clear self-reference, but it is difficult—if not impossible—to surmise whether or not this tradition goes back to the historical Jesus. The scholarly consensus is that it does not, that this is the post-Eastern construction of the church, already present in the oral traditions, which is taken by the evangelist and woven into his story. And by so doing, he becomes the first NT writer giving this expression a literary form and a narrative sequence. Unlike Q and Thomas, whose use of Son of Man is constrained by the very sayings format, Mark molds the tradition into a

---

47. Stanton, *Gospels and Jesus*, 227–30.
48. Yarbro Collins and Collins, *King and Messiah*, 75.

coherent story where the Son of Man becomes a character worth of imitating. As we shall see, he is the paradigm of discipleship.

Son of Man as a heavenly figure who is to come is the third use of the expression. Here we have the most controversial opinions by many authors, ranging from those who believe that this refers to a widespread myth of a Primal Man of Iranian origin from which the Jewish concept originated,[49] to those who believe that the apocalyptic Son of Man is really a phantom,[50] or a secondary midrashic stage of development,[51] or just a modern myth.[52] As one can see, the possibilities are many, and we must choose between them in order to see which one is a better fit for our working hypothesis.

For the time being, the most we can say is that Mark seems to be using the term in each of the senses described above. For Mark, Jesus was a human being, a mortal earthling (cf. Psalm 2) whose authority was given by and depended on God. As such, Jesus did God's bidding and faced humiliation and death, knowing that there would be a divine vindication for his martyrdom (*a la* Righteous Sufferer of the Psalms, the Suffering Servant of Isaiah, and the Maccabean Martyrs). But Mark also plays with the idea of the Danielic son of man. As we shall see in chapter 4, the evangelist seems to have a corporate understanding of this image, thus going against the prevailing hermeneutics of his time. All of these senses coalesce in the story to display Mark's complex and paradoxical understanding of who Jesus is, which strikes me as the evangelist's main accomplishment as a Christology builder.

Conclusion: Disciple and Son of Man as Nova Theologica in the NT

Given the fact that neither the term "disciple" nor "Son of Man" appear in Paul and that their first reference is in the Gospel of Mark, we can say then that they constitute a new theological development in the writings of the NT. Assuming the Markan priority as our working hypothesis, we suggest that even those occurrences in the Q source, which may represent an earlier tradition and therefore prior to Mark, still have to be properly

---

49. Ibid., 75–76.
50. Ibid., 77.
51. Ibid.
52. Ibid.

placed chronologically. Consequently, until we are able to produce an actual "document" that can be shown to be the product of a supposed Q community, Mark still remains our first written record of the expression "Son of Man," as well as the idea of discipleship. That is why it is so important. As we can see, Mark has proven to be a creative and innovative Christologist, leaving us with two crucial concepts that have shaped Christian theology and praxis for the last 2,000 years: the idea of discipleship, which refers to the relationship between the believers and Jesus, and the Son of Man metaphor, which talks about the relationship between Jesus and the community of believers. In this work, I try to expand on the relationship between these two ideas and suggest ways in which discovering how the evangelist weaved them together would help us understand the community he was a part of and how they responded to the pressing needs of their time. In doing so, we will be able to figure out the way we should respond to the pressing needs of our time. It will help us be creative and innovative Christologists as well.

2

Discipleship as the Rhetorical and Theological Center of the Gospel of Mark[1]

IN ORDER TO BE ABLE to posit Jesus as the model of discipleship for the Markan community we have to establish first that discipleship was the main issue the author was addressing. Countless books and articles have been written on the subject, most of them analyzing the nature of discipleship and emphasizing the failure of the disciples to understand what Jesus expected of them while other characters in the story, such as marginal people and women, showed a much greater awareness of what this expectation really was. Whereas all these studies are merited, my take in this book will be a little different. As already stated in the introduction, I want to see Jesus, not anybody else, as the epitome or the prototype of discipleship. I assume that this also may have been the intention of the author. As I pointed out in chapter 1, Mark appears to be the first New Testament writer ever to use the word "disciple" to refer to one of Jesus' followers. If this is so, then it is possible that he constructed the entire piece around this motif.

I assume that the evangelist was an author in his own right. He put together a coherent story out of oral and perhaps even written traditions available to him. He worked with these materials in such a way as to convey

---

1. This chapter is a reworking of my article, "Rhetorical and Theological Center of Mark's Gospel," written for a book in honor of teacher, mentor, and friend J. Severino Croatto. Curiously enough, my article, which emphasizes cruciform discipleship, lies at the very physical center of the book and, one could argue, at its theological center, as well. I commented on this to Severino, who agreed on the providential nature of this fact. Hansen, *Los caminos inexhauribles de la palabra*, 327–45.

his message as powerfully as he could. Probably the gospel was read aloud in the house churches of the time or even performed, as many recent studies have suggested.[2] The rhetorical force of the gospel can be appreciated from many different perspectives: argument, plot, characterization, setting, literary structure, etc. I have chosen to analyze the text of the gospel in terms of its literary structure, that is, how the evangelist organized his materials. I contend that this organization was used above all as a means for conveying his Christology but also perhaps as a memory aid or simply as a pedagogical tool.

Many scholars have attempted to demonstrate—with varying degrees of success—the existence of an intentional literary structure in the Gospel of Mark.[3] In writing the gospel, they say, the evangelist had in mind a rhetorical structure that would be detected by whoever read it or heard it being read. This structure, then, would guide the reader/hearer to decipher the gospel's central message. Ched Myers, in his book *Binding the Strong Man*, reminds us of the two key assumptions of a literary approach to the text:

> One is that the relationship between form and content is fundamental to interpretation. The other is that every narrative detail has its purpose. Every element in the story is there for a reason, which we will discover only by combing back and forth through the text until it yields its own narrative coherency.[4]

Therefore, I want to attempt a literary "combing" of the Gospel of Mark that will propose a coherent structure for it. I want to suggest, as a preliminary hypothesis, that what seems to have prompted this structure was the evangelist's *Sitz im Leben*. In other words, the rhetorical outline of the gospel mirrors the community's historical situation and is used by Mark as a vehicle for conveying that which he believes is the most pressing message that his audience needs to hear at the time.

---

2. See especially Horsley, *Hearing the Whole Story*, chapter 3.

3. For a detailed analysis of authors and methodologies, see Cook, *Structure and Persuasive Power*, 1–86.

4. Myers, *Binding the Strong Man*, 109.

Discipleship as the Rhetorical and Theological Center of the Gospel of Mark

MARK'S USE OF A CHIASTIC STRUCTURE

The use of chiasmus in antiquity has long been recognized.[5] It was used in both oral and written communication as a memory aid and pedagogical device. The New Testament is full of examples, and Mark uses them throughout his gospel. They have different names. Some call them "bracketing analysis."[6] Others refer to these structures as "concentric symmetry"[7] or "concentric pattern."[8] I prefer *chiastic* structures, a word that comes from the Greek letter *chi* and points to the way in which the material is arranged in a descending pattern from A to, say D, only to return back to A. The technical way of noting this pattern is ABCDC'B'A'.

I would like to mention two authors who have found similar structures: M. Philip Scott and Jeffrey H. Krantz. Both of them propose a concentric structure as the general framework of Mark's gospel. But they differ as to where the center lies. M. Philip Scott finds it in the narrative of the transfiguration and specifically in 9:7 "This is my Son, the Beloved; listen to him."[9] Jeffrey H. Krantz finds it in the question that Jesus posits to his disciples in 8:30 concerning his identity and in his first prediction of the passion that follows immediately.[10]

Scott's article relies on an intricate word count to prove that the transfiguration pericope is placed at the exact center of the gospel,[11] and on a choice of only one aspect of the evangelist's material, namely, the questions about Jesus' identity. In his own words, "the chiasmus of questions is the key to the interpretation of Mark's gospel."[12] Besides, he tends to let his Christological concern dictate his understanding of the Markan rhetoric. He wants to demonstrate that at the center of Mark's gospel lays a fundamental affirmation of Jesus' divinity.

---

5. See especially Breck, *Shape of Biblical Language*, 7–58.
6. Malina and Rohrbaugh, *Gospel of John*, 295.
7. Lohr, "Oral Techniques in the Gospel of Matthew," 424.
8. See Talbert, *Reading John*, 126 and throughout the book.
9. "It was then that the Transfiguration stood out as the unmistakable center of the whole gospel, with 9:7, 'This is my Son: listen to him' as the pivot of the chiasmus." Scott, "Chiastic Structure," 18.
10. Krantz actually criticizes Scott when he says: "Had Scott read Mark just a little less optimistically, I believe that he would have seen that the center of Mark's gospel is not so much a single sentence from a heavenly voice, but the question, 'Who do people say that I am?'" Krantz, "Crucified Son of Man," para. 5.
11. Scott, "Chiastic Structure," 18–19.
12. Ibid., 21.

Mark's position is clear: Jesus claimed to be not simply the Christ, not simply the Son of God, but God.[13]

His chiastic structure, then, leaves large blocks of material unaccounted for,[14] giving the impression that his affirmation concerning the intentionality of Mark's overall framework is an apology for an otherwise arbitrary selection of texts.[15]

Krantz' proposal of a chiastic structure is somehow more appealing. Although he also leaves parts of the text untouched, he finds the center of the chiasmus in Jesus' first passion prediction, Mark 8:31–33. But he specifically highlights the question, "Who do people say that I am?" as the theological center of the whole gospel. In his words,

> The entire gospel turns on the axis of the question of Jesus' identity, and whether or not the reader/hearer will choose the triumphalist Messiah of John or the crucified Messiah, who is Jesus.[16]

I could certainly agree with Krantz that the theological center of the gospel deals with what kind of Messiah Jesus was, especially as it is contrasted with John's idea of a Messiah. The reader is then made to choose between these two options. But this understanding of the gospel's theology still centers on the "who is Jesus" question. I do believe this question to be extremely relevant for readers, for it relates to what I consider the center in a "causative" manner. Still, I am convinced that the center lies elsewhere.

The Rhetorical Center of the Gospel: An Alternative Chiastic Structure for the Gospel of Mark

I would like to propose a structure for the entire gospel that could be described as a chiasm inside a chiasm. The first chiasm is formed by the letters ABCB'A', the second by the lower case abc . . . ijxj'i' . . . c'b'a.' Thus, we have

---

13. Ibid., 22.

14. This is inevitable in any chiastic reconstruction of the text, but some chiastic structures are tighter than others. I am claiming here that mine seems to include more text than the ones proposed by Scott or Krantz.

15. "*Without question* and as a *simple matter of fact*, the foregoing *is* in Mark's gospel; but there can hardly be any reasonable doubt that the bulk of it is there by intention" (italics added). Scott, "Chiastic Structure," 19.

16. Krantz, "Crucified Son of Man," 7.

Discipleship as the Rhetorical and Theological Center of the Gospel of Mark

two centers—a general center, letter C, with a center of its own, x, which in turn becomes the center of both chiasms, and the center of the whole gospel, as we shall see.

A: Preparation for ministry (1:1–13)
    a. Jesus came *from* Galilee (1:9)
       b. Jesus' baptism: acknowledged as God's Son by a heavenly voice. Heavens torn apart (1:9–11)
          c. Jesus is tested in the wilderness by Satan. Angels serve him (1:12–13)
B: Galilean ministry (1:14–7:23)
            d. The gospel is proclaimed in view of the proximity of the kingdom of God (1:14–2:12)
              e. Issues concerning table fellowship and public piety (2:13–22)
                 f. Issues related to the law (2:23–3:6)
                    g. Jesus teaches through parables (3:20–27; 4:1–34)
                       h. Controversy with religious leaders (Pharisees) *from* Jerusalem (7:1–23)
    C: Ministry outside of Galilee (7:24–10:52)
                          i. A blind man is cured (8:22–26)
                             j. Peter's confession and misunderstanding concerning Jesus' ministry (8:27–33)
                               x. Jesus' call to a suffering discipleship (8:34–9:1)
                             j'. Disciples' misunderstanding concerning Jesus' ministry (9:2–10:45)
                         i'. A blind man is cured (10:46–52)
B': Jerusalem ministry (11:1–14:31)
                     h'. Controversy with religious leaders *in* Jerusalem (11:27–33)
                  g'. Jesus teaches through parables (12:1–12)
               f'. Issues related to the law (12:13–44)
            e'. Issues concerning table fellowship and public piety (14:1–9)
         d'. The gospel should be proclaimed before the coming of the kingdom of God (13:1–14:[1–9]–31)
A': Conclusion of ministry (14:32–16:8)
          c'. Jesus is tested in Gethsemane. [An angel served him: Luke 22:43] (14:32–42)
      b'. Jesus' death: acknowledged as God's son by centurion. Veil of Sanctuary is torn apart (15:33–39)
   a'. Risen Christ goes *to* Galilee (16:7)

I find this outline compelling for a variety of reasons. First, it follows the natural progression of Jesus' ministry in terms of geographical regions.[17]

---

17. I depart slightly from Norman Perrin's outline in Perrin and Duling, *New Testament*, 239.

Whether or not this was the intention of the author, it is still helpful for monitoring the unfolding narrative as Jesus moves from place to place. The geographical markers clearly show how Jesus' ministry is gradually oriented toward Jerusalem: "They were on the road, going up to Jerusalem, and Jesus was walking ahead of them; they were amazed, and those who followed were afraid (ἐφοβοῦντο)" (10:32).The suffering that Jesus mentions in 10:33–34 will be inflicted by the leaders of the Jerusalem temple in collusion with the Romans. It is then understandable that those who followed him were afraid. Yet, Jerusalem is the unavoidable place of confrontation, where true discipleship will be tested and found wanting. However, there will be another opportunity for those fearful followers: Galilee.

Second, the geographical markers seem to point to the circular nature of the narrative, from Galilee in 1:9 and back to Galilee in 16:7. This has already been noticed by Ched Myers. He suggests that 16:7, "he is going before you to Galilee; there you will see him, just as he told you," is not pointing outside of the narrative world, to some encounter with the risen Christ as preserved in the apostolic tradition. Rather, it is pointing to the same place where discipleship had started in the beginning. He writes,

> This "future" point of reference is the same as the "past" one: Galilee. And where is that? It is where "the disciples and Peter" were first called, named, sent on mission, and taught by Jesus. In other words, the disciple/reader is being told that that narrative, which appeared to have ended, is beginning again. The story is circular![18]

Third, this concentric structure gives a rhetorical framework to that which for a long time has been considered Mark's narrative hinge, namely, Peter's confession at Caesarea Philippi. By emphasizing the nature of true discipleship, Jesus corrects and redirects Peter's tentative and traditional confession. The reader, or hearer, becomes aware of his or her own need to rethink the nature of discipleship. The structure I propose, then, makes this new definition of discipleship the centerpiece of the chiasmus.

But, let us consider how the different letters of the structure relate to each other, for it is in the relationship of the different parts of the chiasmus that its rhetorical force resides.

---

18. Myers, *Binding the Strong Man*, 398–99.

Discipleship as the Rhetorical and Theological Center of the Gospel of Mark

Pair A/A': (1:1-13/14:32—16:8)

a/a': Jesus came *from* Galilee/Risen Christ goes *to* Galilee (1:9/16:7).

In 1:9, Jesus comes (ἔρχομαι) from Galilee to the Jordan River to be baptized by John, who has been identified as the Lord's messenger in 1:2. He has been sent (ἀποστέλλω) to prepare the way of the Lord. In 16:7, the young man (νεανίσκος) tells the women that the Risen Christ is going before the disciples, leading (προάγω) them into Galilee. On both occasions someone—John or the young man—announces the coming of Jesus or the Risen Christ from or to Galilee. Both are messengers sent to point at the one who is coming to enact God's salvation. However, the historical Jesus met his disciples by the Sea of Galilee, whereas the disciples go to Galilee to meet the Risen Christ there. The movement in these two sections is directly opposite: Jesus meets his disciples and the disciples go out to Galilee to meet the Risen Christ.

b/b': Jesus' baptism: acknowledged as God's Son by a heavenly voice. Heavens are torn apart /Jesus' death: acknowledged as God's Son by the centurion. Veil of Sanctuary is torn apart (1:9-11/15:33-39).

The thematic connection between these two sections is provided by the Markan understanding of Jesus' death as a sort of baptism. In 10:38, Jesus asks James and John if they are able to "drink the cup that I drink, or be baptized with the baptism that I am baptized?" Obviously, and specifically in connection with the mention of the cup in the Gethsemane account, Mark is equating drinking the cup and being baptized with the experience of death. Luke seems to make the same connection in 12:50, where he has Jesus saying: "I have a baptism with which to be baptized; and what stress I am under until it is completed!"

Many scholars have noticed the many corresponding motifs present in both sections.[19] One of the most significant agreements is perhaps the verb, σχίζω, appearing both at 1:10 and 15:38. The heavens are torn and so is the temple's curtain. David Ulansey has suggested that this probably refers to the outer curtain, on which, according to Josephus, was pictured an image of the entire heavens.[20] This would then constitute an *inclusio* that

---

19. See the list provided by Ulansey, "Heavenly Veil Torn," 123.
20. Ibid., 124-25.

"brackets the entire gospel, linking together the precise beginning and the precise end of the earthly career of Jesus."[21]

At Jesus' baptism, the Spirit descends like a dove signaling the end of God's silence. The prophetic voice is present again on earth through the message of John the Baptist and in the person of Jesus, God's beloved Son. The heavenly voice bears witness to this last fact, although only Jesus and the reader know Jesus' identity as God's Son. At the end, Jesus gives the Spirit back to God (ἐξέπνευσεν), the veil of the sanctuary is torn in two from top to bottom, and the centurion asserts Jesus' heavenly origin. Notice the downward/upward movement in both sections: while Jesus comes up from the water (ἀναβαίνω), the Spirit descends (καταβαίνω). Then, when Jesus breathes his last (gives the Spirit back to God), the temple's curtain is torn from top (ἄνωθεν) to bottom (κάτω).

It is possible that what Mark is trying to convey here is that the ministry of Jesus has rendered the temple obsolete. God has spoken again and, this time, contrary to the baptism scene, God's voice is "seen" by all. The symbolism of the tearing of the temple's veil suggests that Jesus' death replaces the temple.[22] Now the community of followers will embody God's presence. Now everyone, Jew and Gentile, will have free access to God through the spirit-empowered ministry of those who proclaim, in word and action, Jesus' death.

c/c': Jesus is tested in the wilderness by Satan. Angels serve him / Jesus is tested in Gethsemane (1:12–13/14:32–42).

Another interesting parallelism can be found in these two corresponding sections. In 1:12–13, Mark clearly affirms that Jesus is driven by the Spirit to the wilderness (ἔρημος) to be tempted (πειράζω) by the devil for forty days,

---

21. Ibid., 123.

22. If the gospel were written after the destruction of the temple in 70 CE, readers/hearers would have understood the tearing of the outer curtain as a metaphor for that event. In the eyes of this community of Jewish and Gentile believers, Jesus' death had replaced the temple's role as redemptive medium. It was a way of coping with the tragedy of having lost their visible connection with the God of Israel. This connection was now available through the death of Jesus and his spiritual presence amongst the community. The same could be said if the gospel were written in the years leading to the destruction, the time of the Jewish uprising of 66–70 CE. Knowing the way the Romans suppressed the revolts of their subject peoples, the destruction of the temple was perhaps being anticipated.

Discipleship as the Rhetorical and Theological Center of the Gospel of Mark

during which he lived with the wild beasts (θηρίων) while angels (ἄγγελοι) ministered to him. In 14:32–42, Jesus goes with his disciples to a place (χωρίον) called Gethsemane. While some of his disciples are told to sit and wait, others—his inner circle formed by Peter, James and John—are told to wait and keep awake, or watch (γρηγορέω). Then Jesus goes through a time of intense intimacy with God, as well as self-doubt. That this is experienced by Jesus as a sort of test, or temptation, is clear when one considers his admonition to the sleepy disciples in verse 38: "Keep awake and pray that you may not come into the time of trial (πειρασμός): the spirit (πνεῦμα) indeed is willing, but the flesh is weak." These words seem to suggest that Mark understands the experience in Gethsemane as a time of testing. Jesus is being faced with the possibility of avoiding death, and this is seen as a temptation that can only be overcome by watchful prayer, like the experience in the wilderness. The reader is then admonished, together with the disciples in the story, to do the same, and the example of Jesus' final triumph over doubt serves as an encouragement for the doubting community. They are faced with the choice of identifying with the disciples or with Jesus.

A number of motifs are present in both accounts. In both cases, Jesus goes to a place, as shown by the preposition εἰς (εἰς τὴν ἔρημον and εἰς χωρίον). But these places are completely different. One is the wilderness; the other, a field, a piece of land and, according to the Gospel of John, a garden (κῆπος). In both, there is a time element. In 1:13, we are told that Jesus stayed in the wilderness for forty days. In 14:37, Jesus asks his disciples: "Could you not keep awake one hour?" and then in 14:41, "The hour has come." In 1:13, it is said that the angels were serving him. In the Lukan parallel account, Luke 22:43, some manuscripts include a verse that states that "an angel from heaven appeared to him and gave him strength." Even though his friends were close by, their lack of support in prayer made his spiritual struggle a lonely one. Therefore, a heavenly presence is needed to strengthen him, just as in the wilderness scene. Later on, his friends will desert him and he will then be utterly alone.

Jesus, Disciple of the Kingdom

Pair B/B': (1:14—7:23/11:1—14:31)

d/d': The gospel is proclaimed in view of the proximity of the kingdom of God/The gospel should be proclaimed before the coming of the kingdom of God (1:14—2:12/13:1—14:[1-9]-31).

In section *d* (1:14—2:12), Jesus comes (ἔρχομαι) into Galilee preaching the gospel (κηρύσσων τὸ εὐαγγέλιον), announcing that the time is fulfilled and the kingdom is at hand (ἤγγικεν). People are summoned to repent and believe (πιστεύω) in Jesus' proclamation. Immediately after that, Jesus calls his first disciples, Simon (Peter), Andrew, James, and John, and he himself embarks on a campaign of preaching, teaching, casting out demons, and healing. Since the narrator has already identified Jesus as the Jewish Messiah to whom the Jewish Scriptures bear witness (1:1-3), his ministry carries great authority (2:10). Here we have the first mention of the Son of Man (ὁ υἱὸς τοῦ ἀνθρώπου). Mark seems to be painting a very bleak picture of the Jewish society prior to the coming of the Messiah. There is great need all around, and Jesus has come to address people's situation. He says in 1:38, "Let us go on to the neighboring towns, so that I may proclaim the message there also; for that is what I came out to do."

In section *d'* (13:1—14:[1-9]-31), Jesus comes out of the temple in Jerusalem and, prompted by a statement from one of his disciples, he predicts the destruction of the sanctuary. Later on, four of his disciples (again Peter, James, John, and Andrew) ask him privately about the timing of this event. But the disciples' question now includes the end-times. This is obviously a redactional addition. Mark takes advantage of Jesus' prediction in order to outline his own eschatological understanding in which the destruction of the temple and the coming of the Son of Man are intimately related.[23] The Markan Jesus, then, affirms that the end is at hand (ἐγγύς, 13:29), but that the gospel must first be preached to all nations (καὶ εἰς πάντα τὰ ἔθνη πρῶτον δεῖ κηρυχθῆναι τὸ εὐαγγέλιον, 13:10). The disciples are then warned not to believe (μὴ πιστεύετε) the false messiahs who are trying to lead astray, says Mark, even the elect (τοὺς ἐκλεκτούς). They should rather wait for the coming (ἔρχομαι) of the Son of Man from heaven. There is another mention of the preaching of the gospel in 14:9, another reference to the Son of Man (14:21), and again the kingdom is mentioned in 14:25.

---

23. Vena, "La Expectativa Escatológica en el Evangelio de Marcos," 87n8.

Discipleship as the Rhetorical and Theological Center of the Gospel of Mark

We can see then that many of the themes of *d* are repeated again in *d'*: preaching of the gospel, kingdom of God as being at hand, the inner circle of Jesus' disciples, the need to believe (or not to believe), the Son of Man coming to address people's needs. But, whereas in *d* the themes relate directly to the ministry of Jesus, in *d'* they represent the culmination of his ministry and the beginning of the disciples' work. The preaching of the gospel is now the task of Jesus' followers, and it is situated in an eschatological time that is rushing toward its completion. The Son of Man of 2:10 points unmistakably to Jesus but the Son of Man of 13:27 refers to a heavenly figure who may relate to Jesus of Nazareth in some ways but who cannot be equated with him (see treatment of this symbol in chapter 4). Likewise, the preaching of the gospel in *d* is geared toward the Jewish people, whereas in *d'* is intended to reach the nations.

It is difficult to escape the conclusion that the Markan placement of these two sections, as well as the rest of the structure, is intentional. If discipleship is the central theme of the gospel, then it is being described as that activity that takes place between now, the post-resurrection time, and the coming of the Son of Man, an activity initiated and modeled by Jesus, who is also a prototype of that Son of Man, as we shall see.

e/e': Issues concerning table fellowship and public piety (2:13–22/ 14:1–9).

These two sections are obviously equivalent, having in common issues (table fellowship, matters of public piety such as fasting and offerings), characters in the plot (the scribes) and even grammatical constructions ("as he sat at table"). In both sections, we find Jesus keeping company with the outcast and marginalized. In 2:13–22, he eats with tax collectors and sinners. In 14:1–9, he enters the house of Simon the leper and is approached by a woman. And in both sections, we have references to the gospel. In 2:17b, Jesus states the purpose of his ministry: "I have come to call not the righteous but sinners." This truly is the gospel in a nutshell! In 14:9, Jesus affirms that the woman's action will be remembered in connection with the worldwide preaching of the gospel. But there is an even closer connection between these two sections. There is in both a prediction of Jesus' death. In 2:20, Jesus says: "The days will come when the bridegroom is taken away from them." In 14:7, Jesus asserts: "For you always have the poor with you, and you can show kindness to them whenever you wish; but you will not always have me." The apparent excess shown by the disciples' eating habits finds its counterpart in the woman's apparent misuse of her resources.

f/f': Issues related to the law (2:23—3:6/12:13–44).

In *f*, the main issue is Sabbath-keeping. While in 2:23–28, the Pharisees accuse the disciples of doing work on the Sabbath, in 3:1–6, Jesus appeals to the Pharisees' understanding of the law, as well as their common sense, by asking the question: "Is it lawful to do good or to do harm on the Sabbath, to save life or to kill?" The outcome of both confrontations is Jesus' assertion that the law is really subordinated to human beings and the Pharisees' decision to get rid of Jesus.

In *f'*, it is the Pharisees who ask Jesus a question that starts again with "Is it lawful . . . ?"[24] This time, it refers to the duty, or absence of it, of a Jew to pay taxes to the Roman Emperor. In the rest of the section, 12:18–37, first the Sadducees and then the scribes ask Jesus questions that relate to the law. One question concerns the provision of the levirate marriage and its applicability in the new age. The other refers to the great commandment. In both cases, as in the case of the question concerning taxes, Jesus bests his opponents by unmasking their real intention, which is to entrap him (cf. 12:13, 18, 28).

g/g': Jesus teaches through parables (3:20–27; 4:1–34/12:1–12).

These passages represent two of the few places in the gospel where it is said that Jesus taught in parables (ἐν παραβολαῖς). The first of these occurrences happens in 3:23: "And he called them to him, and spoke to them in parables." It anticipates the formal teaching of chapter 4, almost all of which is done through parables. That here we have a self-contained piece of tradition is suggested by the *inclusio* formed by 4:2: "And he began to teach them many things in parables," and 4:33–34: "With many such parables he spoke the word to them. . . . He did not speak to them except in parables." Then, in 12:1, we have the third instance of the formula: "Then he began to speak to them in parables."

I would argue that the symmetrical placement of these two sections on parable teaching is intentional. It is part of the overall structure of the

24. In the Greek text, the construction is the same in both instances: ἔξεστιν, which means "it is permitted, it is possible, it is proper." *BDAG*, 275.

Discipleship as the Rhetorical and Theological Center of the Gospel of Mark

work, laid out by the evangelist. They are placed on both sides of the middle section C, a section that emphasizes primarily the call to, and the cost of, discipleship.

h/h': Controversy with religious leaders *from* Jerusalem/Controversy with religious leaders *in* Jerusalem (7:1–23/11:27–33).

The narrative moves very clearly from Galilee, to outside of Galilee, to Jerusalem and finally into Jerusalem. At each point of the journey, Jesus is confronted by the religious authorities concerning issues that pertain to the law, the tradition of the elders or the temple. In these two sections, we have an example of some of those confrontations that are interspersed throughout the gospel, but that here seem to play a specific role in the pattern suggested by letters B and B'. They come at the end and at the beginning respectively of this pair and suggest, again, an intentional narrative or rhetorical device aimed at conveying clarity of meaning and purpose to those who either read or hear the gospel being read.

I hope to have been able to briefly outline the basic symmetry of letter B and B'.[25] Now, we have to concentrate on the center, C. Here, I believe, lies the main emphasis of the gospel.

Center C: (7:24—10:52)

Norman Perrin was one of the first scholars to notice that the two stories about people being given their sight in 8:22–26 and 10:46–52 "symbolically

---

25. B and B' could still be expanded further, but such a task lies beyond the scope of this chapter. It would be possible to add to this pair the following correspondences right after *h* and before *h'*:

i. Two people are cleansed/healed (7:24–37)
  j. A hungry crowd is fed (8:1–10)
    k. The disciples do not yet understand (8:11–21)
C. Ministry outside of Galilee
    k'. The crowd entering Jerusalem has the wrong messianic notion (11:1–11)
  j'. A hungry Jesus is not fed (11:12–14)
i'. The temple is cleansed (11:15–19)

By adding these correspondences one would have to move the beginning of the "Ministry outside of Galilee" (C) from 7:24 to 8:22. This would create some problems in terms of the geographical markers, but it would agree more with the ring composition that I am trying to demonstrate in this work.

enclose the section of the gospel where Jesus tries to make his disciples see the necessity for his suffering and its significance for an understanding of discipleship."[26] This was the evangelist's way of saying that real blindness is not physical but spiritual. Thus, the disciples are identified by the rhetorical structure of the section as the real blind!

Building on this helpful insight, I would like to suggest that this section has a center (something Perrin did not suggest) and this center lies on 8:34—9:1.

i/i': A blind man is cured (8:22–26/10:46–52).

If these two healings serve as symbolic pointers to the disciples' "blindness," then the first thing to be noticed is the way in which the first man receives his sight. It is a partial healing; he sees in stages. Accordingly, the disciples' understanding of who Jesus is and the meaning of discipleship is progressive. They will only "see" completely when they follow the risen Christ into Galilee. Bartimaeus, on the other hand, is healed immediately (εὐθὺς ἀνέβλεψεν) and follows Jesus on the way (ἐν τῇ ὁδῷ). Ched Myers has pointed out the symbolic nature of this story. He first informs us of the meaning of the expression "the way" in the Gospel of Mark. It refers to Jesus' ministry of constructing a new reality, a new way of life.[27] Secondly, Myers suggests that Bartimaeus is portrayed here as the ideal disciple, one who leaves everything ("So throwing off his cloak he sprang up and came to Jesus") to follow Jesus.[28]

---

26. Perrin and Duling, *New Testament*, 239.

27. Commenting on the quotations from Exod 23:20 and Mal 3:1a, which Mark uses in 1:2–3, Myers says: "Both texts function to introduce 'the way' as the central discipleship motif in the gospel. . . . Mark's citation, however, substitutes a verb not found in these texts: he speaks of the 'construction' (*kataskeuasei*) of a way. This is the first indication that what is being forged is no mere path; a new way of life is being built in the shell of the old world." *Binding the Strong Man*, 24.

28. Ibid., 382.

Discipleship as the Rhetorical and Theological Center of the Gospel of Mark

j/j': Peter's confession and misunderstanding concerning Jesus' ministry/Disciples' misunderstanding concerning Jesus' ministry (8:27–33/9:2—10:45).

These two sections relate to each other by the motifs of "announcement," "misunderstanding," and "fear." Three times Jesus foretells his death and resurrection, and three times the disciples misunderstand it. First, in 8:27–33, it is Peter who shows his ignorance by being the unwilling spokesperson for Satan. After having confessed Jesus as the Messiah, Peter learns what kind of Messiah Jesus has in mind. For Mark, Jesus is not the political Messiah of the Jewish tradition but the Son of Man of apocalyptic literature. But, even this symbol is subverted by Mark, because this Son of Man will have to face rejection and endure suffering and death before he can usher in the kingdom of God.[29] Consequently, during the visionary experience of Jesus' transfiguration, the disciples show their misunderstanding and are overcome by fear (ἔκφοβοι γὰρ ἐγένοντο).

Then in 9:30–37, we have the second instance in which these motifs appear. The narrative gives us an interesting clue regarding Jesus' concern for his disciples' proper understanding of his role as Son of Man. He is intentionally avoiding the crowds ("He did not want anyone to know it"), because he is taking time to make his disciples understand what his true identity—and theirs—was. Again, Mark tells us that they do not understand and are afraid (ἐφοβοῦντο) to ask him (9:32). Their misunderstanding shows up again in verses 33–37, when Jesus finds out that they were discussing who among them was the greatest. Jesus openly tells them that identifying with him will mean being in a position of marginality and powerlessness: they will need people's help and charity (9:41). Quite different from their own messianic dreams!

Finally, in 10:32–45, we have the third and last of Jesus' announcements concerning his passion and death, which is again followed by misunderstanding and fear: verse 32, "those who followed were afraid" (ἐφοβοῦντο); verse 38, "You do not know what you are asking."

---

29. The construction ὅτι δεῖ τὸν υἱὸν τοῦ ἀνθρώπου πολλά παθεῖν shows divine necessity.

x. Jesus' call to a suffering discipleship (8:34—9:1).

Here, we have arrived at the rhetorical and theological center of the gospel. Rhetorically, everything points to here. Theologically, everything spirals out from here. The inescapable reality of the cross not only serves as a model for Jesus' ministry, but also for the disciples—and the readers'—own ministry. In terms of its rhetorical logic, one can see how this center spreads up and down into *j* and *j'* in the following way:

A. Peter thinks the eschatological Messiah has arrived ["You are the Christ"] (27–30).
   B. The suffering Son of Man's lot is described: suffering/death/resurrection (31) [suffering/rejection by the hands of elders, chief priests and scribes, members of "this generation" (cf. 8:12)].
      C. Peter tries to save Jesus' life and is rebuked (32–33) ["And Peter . . . began to rebuke him. But . . . he rebuked Peter" (abb'a')].
      X. Jesus calls the people and the disciples to a suffering discipleship taking up one's cross (34).
      C'. Jesus affirms that the way to save one's life is to lose it for the gospel's sake (35–37).
   B'. The apocalyptic Son of Man's coming is described (38) [members of this sinful and adulterous generation are "rejected" by the Son of Man at the Parousia].
A'. Peter thinks the eschatological age has arrived ("It is well that we are here") (9:1–8).

This structure is highly instructive. Mark has used his rhetorical skills in such a way as to leave no doubt concerning his understanding of the times he believes to be living in. It is not that he does not have an eschatological understanding of history. He does. But it is slightly different from Peter's, the paramount representative of the Jesus movement emanating from Jerusalem. It is also different from the Zealots' violent perception of the end times, as we will see in chapter 4. Mark is suggesting here that the Son of Man's character is marked by rejection, suffering, and even death, not by victory and the obliteration of his enemies. In order to be able to convince his audience of this novel idea, the evangelist will deploy a number of rhetorical devices as many times, and in as many ways, as he possibly can. Here in this passage, we have one such occasion where the clear

Discipleship as the Rhetorical and Theological Center of the Gospel of Mark

chiastic structure of ABCXC'B'A' directs the reader/hearer's attention to a well-defined center, X, where discipleship is described. The surrounding letters are placed at the service of such a powerful theological and rhetorical center and the message becomes crystal clear: to be a disciple is to imitate Jesus, and to imitate Jesus is to imitate the eschatological Son of Man.

Notice the inclusive nature of Jesus' call. He is calling "the crowd with his disciples." We may assume there were women in the crowd (cf. Mark 5:24), as there were women among his disciples (Mark 15:40–41), so Jesus is calling both men and women to a suffering discipleship. He is also calling people from different ethnic backgrounds. The area of Caesarea Philippi was known for its Hellenistic ethos.[30] One may assume that there were, among the crowd, people who possessed this mixed identity. In this second call to discipleship,[31] Jesus is expanding his original vision. He is not calling only male Israelites, but also women and people of diverse backgrounds. And he calls them to deny themselves, that is, to renounce their positions and/or privileges in the structures of the society of the time and to follow him. No doubt this calling was good news for some (women, slaves, dispossessed peasants) and not so good for others (rich, landed males such as the ruler of 10:17–22). Peter seems to express the puzzlement of the group of followers when he asserts, "Look, we have left everything and followed you" (10:28).

Jesus' answer points at the new community of followers as an egalitarian group at odds with the patriarchal society of the time, since no fathers are mentioned (cf. 10:29–30). It is this group, in which honor and wealth is received—more than obtained—and democratically shared, that enables people to attain the eternal life the rich man was searching for and which his wealth and sense of honor did not allow him to achieve. The clue to eternal life, the life of the kingdom, is not grasping unto your life but letting go of it! This indeed is a paradox, as the rest of the gospel will slowly unravel. In this respect, Myers says that this represents "a specific kind of political and community practice that takes the disciples/reader into the deepest paradoxes of power. We are told that we cannot save our lives by

---

30. "Caesarea Philippi was a major Hellenistic city built in the far north of the land near Mount Hermon by Herod Philip in honor of Augustus. It had in ancient times been called Paneas in honor of the god Pan, who had a shrine there, but now there was a shrine for the emperor cult. In addition, it had been previously a site where the god Baal had been worshiped." Witherington, *Gospel of Mark*, 240.

31. Myers, *Binding the Strong Man*, 236.

preserving them, nor losing them by giving them up; that to be the 'last' is to be 'first,' and to be the 'least' is to be 'great.'"[32]

THE THEOLOGICAL CENTER OF THE GOSPEL: AN ALTERNATIVE READING OF MARK'S MAIN PURPOSE

The *inclusio* formed by the rending of the heavens at Jesus' baptism and the tearing of the temple's veil at Jesus' death constitutes such an obvious feature of the gospel that it is as if the evangelist has placed it there for the taking, as a literary bait for those who want to penetrate the labyrinth of his work. "Heavens torn" and "temple curtain" torn enclose a description of the life of discipleship that is also a tearing apart of an individual's life. The disciple is torn from his kin group, is forced to make a decision between his or her ancestral allegiances and the new prophet from Nazareth with his program for constructing a new way. Granted, as Bruce Malina has suggested,[33] that the new group of followers provides for the newcomer a fictive kin group into which the person is now welcomed as an active member. It is precisely in this tearing apart, in this losing of one's life, that true discipleship, and the life of the kingdom, is attained. The section of 8:34—9:1 points at this. The disciple then is someone who is abruptly torn from life in the dominant system and made to be part of a new family, a new group that will concentrate on fulfilling the agenda of its leader. This agenda is all about calling people to a new relationship with God, a reestablishing of the covenant, a revitalization of Israel in preparation for God's kingdom on earth, the creation of a new way of life, a new way of relating to each other.

The Gospel of Mark is then more about discipleship, that is, suffering discipleship, than it is about Christology, that is, exalted Christology; it is more about who is a true disciple than it is about who is the real Messiah, although the instruction about discipleship is given using the model, the example of Jesus of Nazareth, the Son of Man. That is why I believe that the center of the gospel is 8:34—9:1, a section that describes authentic discipleship, as well as those who embody it.

---

32. Ibid., 235.
33. Malina, *Social World*, 87.

Discipleship as the Rhetorical and Theological Center of the Gospel of Mark

By the same token, chapter 13:1–23 has at its center verse 10, the preaching of the gospel to all nations.[34] That which concerns the evangelist is the task of discipleship, not merely the description of the signs of the end. The Son of Man comes then in verses 24–27, but the main teaching is still "Keep awake" (v. 37), that is, be engaged in discipleship and mission.

Seeing the larger issue of discipleship as the center of the gospel creates a paradigm shift between this approach and studies that concentrate on the nature of Jesus' Messiahship. These studies are prompted by academic and/or theological concerns of the First World that are not as interested in the praxis of the people of God as they are in endless discussions about the true identity of the historical Jesus, or about the extent of his true words.[35] These discussions continue to produce hundreds of similar books, which only contribute to a generalized confusion about who Jesus really was. For me, and for a hermeneutic that has its roots in the Third World, more precisely, in Latin America, the question should not be limited to ontology—who Jesus really was—but should primarily address the question of ethics: how are we to live as disciples in our historical context?

An approach to the gospel from a "praxis-driven" context, or with a "praxis-driven" concern, will scan the text in search of a "praxis" center. When one does that, the unmistakable center of the gospel is 8:34—9:1: Jesus' call to a suffering discipleship. This center points to the Markan community's main concern: how to be authentic disciples of Jesus the Christ in the midst of a crisis that was threatening to destroy the very foundation of the community's national and religious life.[36] In that context, the disciple is called to resist the political agenda of the Jewish revolutionaries and to be ready to follow the gospel's agenda, taking a much more subversive and counter-cultural position. Myers describes this position as follows:

> [M]ark was convinced that only the way of the cross, not the sword, could truly overthrow the historical reign of the powers . . . ; the rebellion was, in the last analysis, a struggle for the control, purification, and defense of the temple, which Mark could in no way support. Any attempt to restore a Davidic state meant a return

---

34. Vena, "La Expectativa Escatológica," 95–97.

35. A typical example of this endeavor in the United States is the Jesus Seminar group.

36. I take the position, shared by many commentators, that the Gospel of Mark was written during the later stages of the Jewish revolt. This would place it around 66–70 CE. See Myers, *Binding the Strong Man*, 64–65; Perrin, *New Testament*, 256–57. For a slightly modified view, see Hooker, *Gospel According to Mark*, 8, and Waetjen, *Reordering of Power*, x.

to the politics of domination, and was thus counterrevolutionary (10:42f.).[37]

When we read the Gospel of Mark paying attention to its chiastic structure, we are swallowed up by the force of its compelling center. I hope I have been able to demonstrate that this rhetorical center was dictated by the historical situation of the community. In other words, that rhetoric was placed at the service of praxis and theological reflection.

Conclusion

For many years, I taught the Gospel of Mark with the growing suspicion that 8:34—9:1 lay at the very center of the whole piece. In one of the handouts I once distributed to my students, I expressed this idea when I wrote: "This passage seems to stand at the very center of the Gospel of Mark. If so, the central message of this gospel is suffering discipleship that takes place between the resurrection and the Parousia." But my thinking was intuitive; it had not matured to the point of becoming a conviction. Now it has. Now I have taken the time to carefully probe into this hypothesis. I believe the present work will demonstrate that my intuition was correct, that the Gospel of Mark speaks about discipleship that takes place at a critical moment in Israel's history in the midst of a vast array of alternative options. The community is being warned against those who are offering a violent solution to the crisis brought about by the Jewish revolt. The role of the disciple, says Mark, is not to reinstate the temple system, a system that failed the very people it claimed to minister to, but to announce the coming of the reign of God by actively engaging in the construction of that new reality.

In the Gospel of Mark, Jesus is the one who embodies authentic discipleship. The readers will then read this gospel at two levels. At one level, they will tend to identify themselves with Jesus' disciples, but as the story portrays them not understanding and ultimately abandoning Jesus, the readers will fix their attention on Jesus. This represents the second level, or the second movement. Jesus, after all, is the one who exemplifies true discipleship. He is the one who is abandoned, both by his disciples and by God, yet he does not abandon his followers. He is the one who carries the cross of discipleship all the way into the bowels of the city of Jerusalem and pays with his life in bold defiance of the powers that oppressed the people.

37. Myers, *Binding the Strong Man*, 430.

Discipleship as the Rhetorical and Theological Center of the Gospel of Mark

Thus, the reader will know at the end of the gospel, that by following the risen Christ into Galilee, he or she is given a second chance as a disciple. Now the cross must be taken at any cost. We too, as modern disciples, are given this second chance.

3

Jesus as Disciple of the Kingdom

A Christological Necessity[1]

IN HIS SEMINAL WORK, *Binding the Strong Man*, Ched Myers discusses the relationship between the oral traditions about Jesus and the decision on the part of Mark to put them into writing. Myers suggests that the reason Mark decided to do so and to write his own version of the story of Jesus was that the oral traditions were being subjected to manipulation or, as he says, "gratuitous misappropriation," due to the fact that the early Christian communities had little infrastructure and poor methods of communication, which made possible the work of irresponsible itinerant preachers and prophets. Therefore, Mark decided to fix the tradition in writing, but not without first interpreting it. "Mark could begin to normalize the tradition, in order to circumscribe the tendency to domesticate the words of Jesus inherent in orality."[2] What we have then is a story written for his community, adapting the traditions to their context. Mark is rereading the tradition and therefore "closing" its meaning for his community.[3]

---

1. In this chapter, I am relying heavily on my article "Markan Construction of Jesus as Disciple of the Kingdom."

2. Myers, *Binding the Strong Man*, 94.

3. "Mark presents his Gospel in a text both 'open' and 'closed,' affirming the dialectic between canonicity and charisma that is essential to every community committed to a 'living tradition.'" Myers, *Binding the Strong Man*, 94. For this idea of rereading as opening and closing, see especially Croatto, *Biblical Hermeneutics*, 40–50.

Jesus as Disciple of the Kingdom

Mark has in mind a certain way of "reading" the oral traditions about Jesus. This way was, in all probability, very similar to the way he treated written scripture (see below), that is, with a lot of hermeneutical freedom, combining texts (in this case oral traditions) so they would serve as an authoritative basis for the story he is telling. He is aware that there are other versions of the story but, realizing that these may not be faithful to what he perceives as the true nature of Jesus' ministry, he wants to present his own. I want to propose that in his version of the story, Jesus is depicted as the disciple par excellence. This affirmation is based on two of my findings in this book, one in chapter 1 the other in chapter 2. In chapter 1, I conclude that Mark is the first NT writer to ever use the word "disciple" ($\mu\alpha\theta\eta\tau\acute{\eta}\varsigma$). In chapter 2, I try to show that Mark 8:34—9:1, where Jesus calls his followers to a suffering discipleship, represents the rhetorical and theological center of the entire gospel. And that the real disciple in the gospel is Jesus himself. What would have been Mark's rationale for doing that? In other words, why was it necessary for him to develop an appropriate concept of discipleship and to use Jesus as the supreme example? Let me suggest two reasons, one external, and the other internal.

1. *External*. Faced with the dilemma of supporting the revolt of 66–70 CE, which propelled the Jewish people to rebel against Rome and which ended with the destruction of Jerusalem and its temple, the believers needed to have a model of discipleship that would serve as a guide through those difficult years. The issue that was at stake was whether or not being followers of Jesus the Messiah would preclude them from joining or encourage them to join the uprising. Mark senses the tension, due especially to the mixed nature of his congregation (Gentiles and Jews), and so embarks on the task of writing a story of Jesus that depicts him as the model disciple of the kingdom of God, as one who resisted evil but shunned violent confrontation. He is hoping that this will help his congregation make a decision against armed revolution while, at the same time, encourage them to fix their hope in the soon-to-arrive kingdom of God, which was to be brought about not by human efforts but by the power of God through the risen Christ.

2. *Internal*. By pointing to Jesus as the model disciple, Mark is trying to counteract a tendency in his community to organize into a more structured group where issues of power and gender inequality in the leadership were beginning to surface. Mark, who perhaps had known some of the members of the early Jesus' movement, is attempting to direct his community—which

was showing signs of accommodation to the Greco-Roman society—to engage in a counter-cultural praxis resembling that of the early movement. Therefore, he describes Jesus as the model disciple, totally dedicated to the kingdom and always subservient to God, which serves the purpose of criticizing that authority that is not dependent on the power of the Spirit. In the story, Jesus' disciples, figures of authority in the early movement as known by Mark, are portrayed as failing, as embodying a type of anti-discipleship.[4] Jesus then becomes, by default, the true disciple, the disciple par excellence. Besides that, Mark sees the Jewish revolt as a sign of the impending end, so he has no desire to foster stable communities but, rather, is intent on reclaiming an eschatological ethos similar to the one that characterized the wandering charismatics of the Jesus movement in order to present an alternative to the nationalistic messianism of the Zealots. Discipleship and prophetic engagement in society are presented as the true ethos of the group, and Jesus is shown as the one who best incarnates this ethos.[5]

As I pointed out in the introduction, this view of Jesus as the ideal disciple comes as a theological construction, not as a straight exegetical deduction, for the text in no place talks about Jesus as disciple. But I am convinced that it was Mark's intent to provide an example for his community to follow and, in that sense, it is something that is present in the text, perhaps not at the most obvious level, that of its wording, but in the level of its rhetoric.[6] Mark is saying something without actually saying it, with the hope that his audience will get it, something similar to the way in which he ends his gospel. To use an expression drawn from soccer, he leaves the ball bouncing in front of the goal keeper, waiting to see if someone will score.

---

4. I agree here with Richard A. Horsley when he asks the rhetorical question: "Is it possible that Mark's story presses a criticism, within the broader Jesus movement, of what the twelve disciples had become in the course of the first generation, as it summoned the movement back to its roots in the social revolutionary practice and preaching of Jesus?" Horsley, *Hearing the Whole Story*, 77.

5. This understanding of two situations, one external and one internal to the community, is very similar to Horsley's idea that the gospels betray a context of communication out of which they arose and which was formed by the historical social context and the community/movement's specific context. Horsley, *Jesus and Empire*, 68.

6. From the perspective of the social sciences, the Gospel of Mark is a document produced by a "high-context" society. These kinds of societies "produce sketchy and impressionistic documents, leaving much to the reader's or hearer's imagination and common knowledge. Since people in such societies believe that few things have to be spelled out, few things are in fact spelled out." Malina, *Social Setting*, 5.

On a personal basis, this view of Jesus as disciple of the kingdom comes out of an understanding of discipleship that developed over time. In my own faith journey, I moved from seeking to prepare people for the imminent end of the world to seeking social changes inspired by the principles of the gospel. This new understanding of discipleship constitutes the lenses through which I am going to read the text. It is unapologetically non-apocalyptic,[7] praxis-centered, and represents a movement from escape to engagement in the world. Such a movement, I will contend, can be seen also in the Gospel of Mark.[8]

Mark's Portrayal of Jesus as Disciple of the Kingdom

The Markan Jesus refers to himself metaphorically as the bridegroom (2:19–20) and as the sower (4:3). He describes his role in society as: one who came to serve (10:45), a prophet (6:4), one "sent" by God (9:37), anointed/Christ (9:41), and the Son of Man (2:10, 27; 8:31, 38; 9:12; 10:33, 45; 13:26; 14:21, 62). This last role is so important for Jesus that, even when in 14:62 he seems to initially accept the high priest's description of him as Christ and Son of the Blessed, he immediately qualifies it by mentioning the exaltation of the Son of Man.

All of these passages point at Jesus' self-awareness. Never does he describe himself in an exalted manner, but always with terms that point at his submission to God. Why is it then that the introduction to the gospel depicts him as the Messiah Son of God (1:1) and John as his harbinger? The only way to explain this is to say that by the time this gospel circulated among the different communities that made up the early church, it had undergone a considerable amount of theological rereadings, which added a heavy Christological layer. This can be seen not only in the introduction but also in the ending, chapter 16:9–20, as well as in other passages throughout

---

7. Apocalyptic is here understood in a traditional, literal, and futuristic manner. It refers to that biblical worldview that sees history as reaching a predetermined *grand finale* that will give way to a new creation to be enjoyed only by the elect, those who remained faithful to God or God's Messiah, Jesus Christ.

8. "For Mark, faith did not offer an escape from the world, but the divinely granted key to the meaning of the past, the present, and the future of the world. It is in that cosmic context that his report of Jesus is placed. And in the interest of that goal, he appropriates the Jesus tradition." Kee, *Jesus in History*, 140.

the gospel. This process of rereadings was due to different communities encountering different situations at different times.⁹ At that time, the gospel knew more than one format.¹⁰ As I said in the introduction, it is plausible to detect an original residue of traditions, or a first layer of Christological accretions, that go back to a very early stage, when Jesus' own perception of his ministry was still fresh in the community's memory.¹¹

In this chapter, I want to take a closer look at some pertinent passages in Mark's gospel. Let's start with the introduction and with the role that John plays in it.

Introduction (1:1–8)

The first question that needs to be asked is whether John the Baptist is preparing the way for Jesus' ministry or if he is rather issuing a call to people to prepare for God's kingdom, for the coming of the Lord God. If this is so, then Jesus is accepting a call to join forces with all those who heard John's proclamation. He is joining John's movement as another disciple in anticipation of God's coming rule. This may have been the original intention of the tradition, especially if we preserve the sense of the quote from Malachi 3:1 in its original Hebrew.

הִנְנִי שֹׁלֵחַ מַלְאָכִי, וּפִנָּה-דֶרֶךְ לְפָנָי

"Behold, I send my messenger,
and he shall clear the way before *me*."

The same idea is present in the LXX, which reads:

ἰδοὺ ἐγὼ ἐξαποστέλλω τὸν ἄγγελόν μου
καὶ ἐπιβλέφεται ὁδὸν πρὸ προσώπου μου

---

9. For this idea, see my article, "La 'otra' comunidad detrás del evangelio de Marcos," 51–66.

10. This is also true if one subscribes to the idea, well argued by Richard A. Horsley, that the gospel was performed orally in the gatherings of the movement, and that the text we have today represents just one of many memory aids used in these performances. Horsley, *Hearing the Whole Story*, 53–78. Also Tilley, *Disciples' Jesus*, 51–52.

11. Henry W. Beecher was asserting, as early as 1871, that "the gospels are children of the memory. They were vocally delivered hundreds of times before being written out at all; and they bear the marks of such origin, in the intensity and vividness of individual incidents, while chronological order and literary unity are but little regarded." Unlike Horsley and Tilley, he considered them as authentic historical documents. Beecher, *Life of Jesus the Christ*, vii.

"Behold I will send my messenger
and he will prepare a way before me."

But the quotation seems to refer also to Exodus 23:20, where it is Israel that is the object of God's concern. The angel, or messenger, will guard Israel in the wilderness.

בְּדָרֶךְ ,לִשְׁמָרְךָ ,לְפָנֶיךָ, הִנֵּה אָנֹכִי שֹׁלֵחַ מַלְאָךְ

"Behold, I send a messenger before *you*,
to guard *you* on the way."

Accordingly, the LXX reads:

Καὶ ἰδοὺ ἐγὼ ἀποστέλλω τὸν ἄγγελόν μου
πρὸ προσώπου σου, ἵνα φυλάξῃ σε ἐν τῇ ὁδῷ,

"And behold, I send my angel before your face,
that he may keep you in the way."

It is only when Malachi 3:1 is combined with Exodus 23:20 that this sense changes radically. God is not speaking anymore about a messenger preparing the way for God's self, but now God is speaking about a messenger who is to prepare "your way." In 1:3, the "you" of 1:2 is revealed: it is the Lord. Mark is citing here the LXX of Isaiah 40:3, where "Lord" refers to the God of Israel.

φωνὴ βοῶντος ἐν τῇ ἐρήμῳ· ἑτοιμάσατε τὴν ὁδὸν Κυρίου.
εὐθείας ποιεῖτε τὰς τρίβους τοῦ Θεοῦ ἡμῶν

A voice cries out: "In the wilderness prepare the way of the Lord,
make straight in the desert a highway for our God."

But for Mark, and for the early Christians, Lord (κύριος) was many times a way to refer to Jesus. Since this is a gospel about Jesus Messiah (1:1), the messenger then is John and the Lord is Jesus. But, interestingly enough, only once in the gospel (11:3) is Jesus called Lord explicitly (but see 2:28 and 12:36–37).

We can see how Mark has altered creatively his sources (Hebrew text and LXX) in order to point unmistakably to Jesus as the one whose coming John the Baptizer is announcing. Or perhaps he is quoting from memory a midrash[12] that combines Exodus 23 with Malachi 3 and Isaiah 40. The

---

12. For the way in which Mark, unlike contemporary Jewish midrashists, related his midrash to the life of a particular individual, see Samuel, *Postcolonial Reading*, 101.

fact that he precedes the quotation with the words "As it is written in the prophet Isaiah" makes us think that he is quoting an oral tradition that already had the three texts intertwined as one.[13] This tradition may have served the purpose of legitimizing John as the forerunner of the Messiah, Jesus Christ.

But surely it is Mark's redactional work that ties it all together by means of a series of catchwords and/or expressions. These are: ἐν τῇ ἐρήμῳ ("in the wilderness") in 1:3, 4; ἔρχεται ("coming") in 1:7; and ἦλθεν ("came") in 1:9. In this way, the connection between the voice of one "crying out *in the wilderness*" of the Isaiah text and John the Baptist, who "appeared *in the wilderness*," is made clear, as well as the connection between the one "*coming* after me" and Jesus, who "in those days . . . *came* from Nazareth of Galilee."

Therefore, we see how this introduction to the gospel is full of theological and literary tensions. Jesus is both disciple of John and, as the Messiah of Israel, teacher. John is both teacher of Jesus of Nazareth and disciple of the Messiah, "the one who is more powerful than I."[14] This all seems to reflect the way in which Mark has handled a tradition that was already being read Christologically. And this on two counts: first, the tradition of the voice crying out in the wilderness may originally have been applied to both John and Jesus. They were the ones who called people to get ready for the coming kingdom of God, first John and then Jesus, his disciple (cf. Mark 1:15). Their ministries seem to point unquestionably to that. Second, once Jesus' role as God's means of salvation through suffering, crucifixion, and resurrection was firmly established in the community Jesus became the one whose path John the Baptizer came to prepare. Thus, in the final edition of the gospel, it is only John who fulfills the prophecy of Isaiah, not Jesus. But this reading is one that came about late, so throughout the gospel, Jesus maintains the characteristics of a messenger of God who, due to the growing Christological awareness of the community, is nevertheless described sometimes with exalted terms.

In his desire to speak to the reality that besets his community, the evangelist struggles to convey the idea of a Messiah whose main characteristic was that of a disciple of the kingdom. This depiction would make sense to those who had started to conceive Jesus as a Suffering Messiah, for suffering is a constitutive part of discipleship in Mark (see 8:34–37). But

13. Marcus, *Mark 1–8*, 145.
14. Ibid., 151.

there may have been another reason. By starting his gospel with a quote from Deutero-Isaiah, a book that features prominently the so-called Servant Songs (42:1–4; 49:1–7; 50:4–11; 52:13–53:12), Mark may be pointing to a more intentional theological agenda. In Isaiah 50:4, the servant says

דָּבָר, לָדַעַת לָעוּת אֶת־יָעֵף ,נָתַן לִי לְשׁוֹן לִמּוּדִים, אֲדֹנָי יְהוִה

"The Lord God has given me the tongue of a teacher
that I may know how to sustain the weary with a word."

A more accurate translation of the Hebrew text would be "the tongue of *those who are taught*," (לִמּוּדִים) or those who are *discipled*. The word appears also in Isaiah 8:16, where it is translated "disciples." If, as Joel Marcus suggests, "Mark seems to have a special attachment to Isaiah,"[15] then it is at least plausible that he is aware even of those pieces of tradition that he is not consciously using.[16] Isaiah 50:4 is one of those pieces that may have been in the back of the author's mind. Even the rest of verse 4, as well as the following verses 5–6, may have contributed to Mark's understanding of Jesus as a suffering disciple of the kingdom:

"Morning by morning he wakens, wakens my ear
to listen as those who are taught (לִמּוּדִים)
The Lord God has opened my ear, and I was not rebellious,
I did not turn backward. I gave my back to those who struck me,
and my cheeks to those who pulled out the beard;
I did not hide my face from insult and spitting."

If this is correct then, in his depiction of Jesus as disciple of the kingdom, Mark is being informed by Isaiah's description of the servant. Like the servant, Jesus is willing to listen to God and to do whatever is asked of him, knowing that he is probably going to have to face trying times and even death. In Mark, as in Isaiah, the disciple is "commissioned" by God to do a task. This is precisely the word Robert Tannehill uses to speak of Jesus' role in the gospel. He says:

> The Gospel of Mark is the story of the commission which Jesus received from God and of what Jesus has done (and will do) to

---

15. Ibid., 147.
16. The only other time that Mark mentions Isaiah is in 7:6, but the portrayal of Jesus as a suffering disciple may be informed by the Suffering Servant passages (cf. Mark 10:45 with Isa 52:13—53:12).

fulfill his commission. We are probably to understand the baptism scene as the communication of this commission.[17]

If God is (co)mmissioning Jesus, then that means that God is deeply involved in Jesus' work. God acts through Jesus. Therefore, when Jesus (co)mmissions his disciples, he becomes deeply involved in their work as a co-missionary, or co-disciple. The title "Son of God," bestowed on Jesus at his baptism, is a functional and relational title and not necessarily an ontological one. Jesus is the Son of God because he has been given a task that he will fulfill as disciple, first of John and then of God, that is, as a disciple of the kingdom.

But there is another insight that Tannehill provides us with. He says that even God has a commission, or a task, in the narrative. He writes:

> The opening of Mark, with its Old Testament quotation indicating that God is sending his messenger, suggests that God also has a purpose and that his purpose lies behind the central events of the story. It is to realize God's purpose and mission that Jesus is given his mission.[18]

God is indeed engaged in the task of disclosing God's kingdom and does so through the work of messengers or agents. In the Gospel of Mark, these messengers are first John the Baptist, then Jesus, and finally the disciples. They are all (co)mmissioned by the God of Israel to prepare "a way for the Lord." In a sense, they are all disciples of the kingdom even though "Jesus is viewed as the central actor in the fulfillment of God's purpose, and so attention centers upon him."[19] My contention is that as the central actor, Jesus becomes the paradigm of discipleship.

Having described the possible Hebrew Scripture basis for Mark's depiction of Jesus as disciple of the kingdom, let us now consider some specific passages in the gospel where this idea is fleshed out.

---

17. Tannehill, "Narrative Christology," 60–61.
18. Ibid., 62.
19. Ibid., 63

Jesus as Disciple of the Kingdom

The Baptism (1:9-11)

a. The relationship between John and Jesus.

Jesus appears suddenly in the narrative as coming from Nazareth of Galilee to be baptized by John in the Jordan. The narrator has prepared us to see Jesus as one who is mightier than the Baptist and who will baptize with the Holy Spirit (1:7-8), but even so, Jesus' coming to John can only be interpreted in terms of discipleship.[20]

The connection between Jesus and John has been explored by Dale C. Allison, Jr. in terms of continuity and discontinuity. In his article "The Continuity between John and Jesus,"[21] he tries to disprove Gerd Theissen's thesis that proposes a clear distinction, or discontinuity, between John and Jesus' ministries. Theissen mentions five differences between them: eschatology, messianic preaching, imminent futuristic eschatology, baptism, and life style. In listing all of these differences, Theissen is being guided by what the text explicitly says, not by what it hides, which is Allison's point: there could be a lot of information that the text does not give the reader because of apologetical reasons. The early church did not want to portray Jesus as subordinate to John, and so there are things they did not include. One of these is the fact that, whereas in the Synoptic Gospels John is depicted as baptizing, Jesus, on the other hand, is not. The only reference to Jesus baptizing is in John 3:22: "Jesus and his disciples went into the Judean countryside and he spent some time there with them and baptized." But this affirmation is qualified right away in 4:2 by the words of the narrator: "'Jesus is making and baptizing more disciples than John—although it was not Jesus himself but his disciples who baptized.'" Allison believes that this is an apologetical qualification and that "[the]synoptic silence cannot be the last word because it is no word at all."[22]

Given the fact that it is the nature of religious documents to emphasize only those elements that are relevant and helpful to the group that produces them, one can say that much of what John said may be missing from the historical records and, therefore, the possibility exists that much or some of John's preaching may be reflected in Jesus' own preaching beyond the

---

20. The other gospels try to qualify this obvious subordination of Jesus to John by adding traditions that depict Jesus as voluntarily adopting a subordinate position that was necessary in God's overall plan. See Matt 3:14; John 1:26-27.

21. Allison, "Continuity," 6-27.

22. Ibid., 13.

scant textual evidence. If Jesus were a disciple of John, then he must have appropriated from his teacher not only practices but also ideas.[23]

Allison goes on to list those things that John and Jesus shared. Among them he mentions: the conviction that descent from Abraham does not guarantee entrance into the world to come,[24] the use of the image of a tree to talk about eschatological judgment,[25] the linkage between fire and baptism,[26] and the comparison of eschatological judgment to a harvest.[27] One of the most important commonalities between John and Jesus is the fact that both spoke of an eschatological figure who was to come, but while John never specified what figure he had in mind, Jesus spoke of the Son of Man, the one stronger than John, and perhaps believed himself to be the fulfillment of these expectations.[28]

According to Allison Jesus "creatively reinterpreted them by reapplying them to his own person and ministry."[29] All of this, plus the fact that Jesus underwent John's baptism, an act that "constitutes theological endorsement,"[30] talks about "Jesus' large indebtedness to his predecessor."[31] I would add that it shows, pretty clearly, that Jesus was indeed a disciple of John who took a slightly different praxiological route, given the specificity of his ministry.

b. The Baptism proper.

A couple of apocalyptic signs take place in connection with Jesus' baptism, which tells the reader that even though Jesus is technically John's disciple, he is no ordinary disciple! The heavens are torn apart, a typical apocalyptic feature that appears in Isaiah 63:11—64:1. As Joel Marcus has noted, there are many correspondences between these two texts: a going up from the waters, an endowment with the Holy Spirit, a ripping of the heavens and

---

23. The disciples' question in Luke 11:1, "Lord, teach us to pray, as John taught his disciples," may be a tacit acknowledgment of Jesus' indebtedness to John. See Taylor, *Immerser*, 151, and Chilton, *Rabbi Jesus*, 77.

24. Ibid., 16.

25. Ibid., 19.

26. Ibid., 20.

27. Ibid.

28. Ibid., 22.

29. Ibid., 26.

30. Ibid., 27.

31. Ibid.

a divine descent, which in the LXX version is said to be a descent of the spirit of the Lord![32] All of this reinforces the idea that Mark is consciously depicting Jesus utilizing Isaian images.[33] Also, a voice from heaven testifies to Jesus' special status: "You are my son." This is a quote from Psalm 2:7, a reference to Israel's king, which was already being interpreted messianically in early Judaism.[34] In this Psalm, God's rule, and that of his anointed, is being opposed by the rulers of the earth to no avail. Their dominion will be given to God's anointed, and the nations will have to serve him. Again, Marcus suggests that the same plot is present in Mark 1:9–15: Jesus, God's anointed, is acclaimed as God's son only to be challenged by Satan, the personification of an opposing kingship. After that, Jesus goes on to proclaim the dawn of the new era of God's dominion and to prove it by the exorcisms and healings that ensue right away (1:21–34).[35]

In typical Markan fashion, the second part of the quote comes from someplace else. "Beloved" is used in post-biblical traditions concerning the *aquedah*, the binding of Isaac (Gen 22:2, 12, 16).[36] Mark may have been aware of this tradition and so he wanted to underline Jesus' obedience to God's will, even to the point of death. "With you I am well pleased" comes from Isaiah 42:1, another servant passage, which reads:

> Here is my servant, whom I uphold, my chosen in whom my soul delights; I have put my spirit upon him; he will bring forth justice to the nations.

Again, the similarities with the Markan plot are only self-evident. The text affirms that God has put God's spirit *upon* him and, in Mark, the Spirit descends like a dove *on* him, literally "into him," (εἰς αὐτόν). The Isaiah text has επ' αυτόν, which appears also in some variants of the Markan text.[37] But perhaps "into him" would be a better choice—and the editors of *Novum Testamentum Graece* seem to agree—especially since it is said that Jesus will baptize others with the Holy Spirit (1:8). The Spirit has not just come upon

---

32. Marcus, *Mark 1–8*, 165.

33. Adela Yarbro Collins and John J. Collins affirm that "the narrative context of Mark (1:9–11) suggests an intertextual relationship with Isaiah 61." *King and Messiah*, 127.

34. Marcus, *Mark 1–8*, 166.

35. Ibid.

36. Ibid., 162.

37. Some of the most important ones are ℵ A L W Θ. *Novum Testamentum Graece*, 89.

him at that moment but, as Gundry puts it, "Jesus sees the Spirit descend and disappear into himself."[38]

After the title's claim that this is a gospel about Jesus Messiah, Son of God, the narrative goes on to describe him in a mixed fashion. John the Baptist testifies to Jesus' superiority by saying that Jesus is stronger than he and that Jesus' baptism will be superior. But the expectations created by such a description are somehow diminished when Jesus is described next as coming from Nazareth of Galilee, which given its peripheral position compared to Judea, would have been "tantamount to introducing him as 'Jesus from Nowheresville.'"[39] In an unmistakable gesture of submission, Jesus is baptized by John, making him another of many of John's disciples.

But wait, next Mark surprises us again by describing a vision that Jesus has of the heavens being ripped apart and the Spirit descending as a dove and entering him. After all, he does not seem to be just another disciple, for such an apocalyptic scenario is not something one may expect in a routine baptism by the Jordan! God's voice from heaven affirms Jesus' sonship in terms of contemporary messianic expectations based on Psalm 2, only to be followed by a quote from Isaiah 42 where the servant is willing to suffer in order to do God's bidding. And perhaps the whole citation is being informed by contemporary theological speculations linking the "beloved son" to the binding of Isaac. If Mark is describing Jesus as the Messiah of Israel, he is certainly doing it in very paradoxical terms[40] for, as the narrative will slowly unfold, this Messiah will not rule over the nations but will serve them (10:45). And he will require the same of his disciples (10:43–44).

The Temptation (1:12–13)

Jesus is driven to the wilderness by the Spirit, and there he is tempted (πειραζόμενος) by Satan. The two more common meanings of πειράζω are "to put to the test," which can have a negative or a positive connotation, and

---

38. Gundry, *Mark*, 48.

39. Myers, *Binding the Strong Man*, 128.

40. "By combining Psalm 2 and Isaiah 42, the text of Mark interprets Jesus both as the messiah and as the servant of the Lord. The close association of the two epithets has several implications. One is that the author of Mark . . . read the poems about the servant of the Lord in Isaiah messianically, at least some of them. . . . Another implication is that the messiahship of Jesus is not presented in royal and military terms; instead the idea of the messiah of Israel is reinterpreted in prophetic terms." Yarbro Collins and Collins, *King and Messiah*, 128.

"to tempt," which is always understood as an enticement to sin.[41] Like Israel in the Sinai desert Jesus has to undergo a preparation for his ministry. He has to get ready for the work ahead, which he will share with his disciples the same way that John the Baptist shared with him. But before he can even get started, after having decided to follow John into the Jordan and having received God's word of approval, Jesus has to face the reality of the dangerous path that awaits him. His will be a task of gigantic proportions. Announcing God's kingdom will set him up against human foes and cosmic forces. Satan himself shows up in the wilderness in his traditional role of a tempter and, even though Mark does not tell us about the nature of the temptation, as Matthew and Luke do, it is safe to assume that Satan is trying to make Jesus abandon his call to be a disciple of the kingdom. Perhaps Satan is trying to convince Jesus that he needs to embrace a triumphal Messiah sort of vocation, albeit one in which Jesus would first have to pay homage to the tempter himself (cf. Matt 4:1–11; Luke 4:1–13). But we do not know if this tradition was available to Mark, and so it is better to think that Mark is simply placing Satan in the desert to symbolize all the opposition Jesus is going to face in his life. There he is, at the very beginning of the ministry, as a stumbling block in Jesus' way to obedience to God.

Since, according to Mark 4:15, Satan's job is to take away the word that is sown in people's hearts, one could say that here Satan is doing the same thing. He is trying to take away from Jesus' heart the word of the gospel of God that has been sown at baptism and which he will soon begin to proclaim (1:14–15). This word will prove to be lethal for Satan, for he will be bound by the stronger one (1:7; 3:27) and eventually destroyed, as the exorcisms will symbolically demonstrate. Satan is then trying to stop the whole operation before it gets on its way. Obviously he fails, for Jesus starts proclaiming the gospel of God right away. Furthermore, the temptation that was personified in this passage by God's archenemy will later be voiced by Jesus' opponents. In 8:11; 10:2 and 12:15 the word πειράζω will occur again (cf. πειρασμός in 14:38). Mark is surely charging all these occurrences with theological significance. In the same way as Satan tried to impede Jesus' beginning of the ministry, now the Pharisees and the Herodians are trying to impede its continuation. They are the political forces standing in the way of faithful discipleship. Like Satan, they represent a stumbling

---

41. BDAG, 640.

block, a distraction, a temptation, and "it is against this temptation that he will warn his disciples on the eve of his arrest (14:38)."[42]

Among the possible backgrounds for the temptation scholars have cited the following: Adam, as portrayed in the Pseudepigrapha literature, specifically in a work from the first century CE entitled *Adam and Eve*, where Adam is exalted by God, opposed by Satan and worshipped by angels; also Abraham, being tempted by Satan in connection with the sacrifice of Isaac, the *aquedah*, a Jewish tradition found in the book of Jubilees and also in the rabbinic literature.[43] To these we need to add Hebrew Scripture traditions such as Israel being tried in the desert and the prophet Elijah being sustained by angels during forty days (1 Kgs 19:5–8).

But it is the connection with Elijah that I would like to point out specifically and this for a couple of reasons. First, Jesus may have been seen as an Elijah figure in the pre-gospel traditions. Second, Elijah is being fed by angels for forty days. Jesus is also being fed, for he is not fasting as in Matthew and Luke. Therefore, he is not hungry, as he is in Matthew 4:1–2 and Luke 4:1–2. The text says that the angels were serving him (διηκόνουν αὐτῷ) and one of the primary meanings of the verb διακονέω is "to wait at someone at table,"[44] most likely the meaning in 1:31. It can also have the more general connotation of "serve,"[45] which is probably the sense in 10:45. But, in the present context, the first meaning is to be preferred, even though one can never rule out that a more spiritualized sense is also connoted, namely that the service provided by the angels was equivalent to worship, as seems to be suggested in the already mentioned book of *Adam and Eve*.[46]

This first test to Jesus' vocation as a disciple of God is met with success, for the text tells us that right after the wilderness experience, and after John was thrown in jail, Jesus came into Galilee announcing the soon-to-arrive kingdom of God (1:14–15). With this experience, Jesus begins to learn something about the nature of his vocation, namely that it will entail opposing and even provoking the very forces of evil and its minions. And he will continue to learn through controversy and co-discipleship as he confronts enemies and calls folks into a following. But this moment will

---

42. Myers, *Binding the Strong Man*, 130.
43. Marcus, *Mark 1–8*, 160–70; Gundry, *Mark*, 58–59.
44. BDAG, 184.
45. Ibid.
46. Marcus, *Mark 1–8*, 168.

remain as a founding moment in Jesus' awareness of his vocation as one of "those who are taught" (Isa 50:4).

The Beginning of Jesus' Ministry and the Calling of the First Disciples (1:14–20)

When Jesus finally starts his ministry, he does so by preaching a message that is very similar to the one John, his teacher, preached (1:14–15).[47] There is no contradiction between the two messages or competition between the two messengers. Both are servants of God's kingdom, one announcing it, the other actualizing it. He calls people to repentance in view of the approaching kingdom of God. His role is that of one who announces, a prophet, one who has been sent to preach (9:37), an apostle, a disciple if you will. He subordinates himself completely to God the Patron and the kingdom. He preaches the gospel of God (τὸ εὐαγγέλιον τοῦ θεοῦ), not his own gospel. So, whereas for the evangelist, Jesus' ministry, passion, death and resurrection constitute "the gospel of Jesus Christ" (1:1), that is, the proclamation about Jesus Messiah, from the perspective of Jesus' own self-awareness at the beginning of his ministry the gospel he preaches is all about God and the approaching kingdom. In that sense, as Suzanne Watts Henderson affirms, it is an apocalyptic gospel. It is the "'good news' of God's coming dominion that Jesus will authoritatively proclaim."[48] The power he will manifest is God's power, which will signal and illustrate the reign that is about to dawn. This power, the narrator tells us, was unleashed from heaven at the baptism and is now residing in him or, as the Greek suggests, "into him" (εἰς αὐτόν). Again, we see how Mark makes an effort to depict Jesus as dependent on John for his vision and on God for his power.

But in order to start his work, Jesus needs to delegate responsibilities to other people. This mission is all about calling people to construct[49] a new reality, a new way (cf. ὁδός in 1:2–3 and throughout the gospel), in anticipation of the coming dominion of God. This is a task that Jesus can-

47. "The great embarrassment that the Christians faced was that it was well known that John had baptized Jesus—not the other way around! Jesus had come to John and *joined his movement*—which in the context of ancient Judaism meant that Jesus was a disciple of John and John was the rabbi or teacher or Jesus." Tabor, *Jesus Dynasty*, 135.

48. Henderson, *Christology and Discipleship*, 38.

49. The verb κατασκευάζω, meaning "to prepare" but also "to build, to construct," is not to be found in the Hebrew or the LXX text of the conflated quotations used by Mark. It "may well be an innovation of the narrator." Waetjen, *Reordering of Power*, 64.

not accomplish by himself. He needs helpers, collaborators,[50] disciples. He first calls four fishermen, three of whom—Simon, John, and James—will constitute his inner circle (5:37; 9:2; 13:3; 14:33). Jesus, very appropriately, calls them to follow him so he would make them "fish for people." Ched Myers has alerted us to the fact that the metaphor of fishing is taken from Jeremiah 16:16, where it is used to symbolize God's disapproval of Israel. It is also used in Amos 4:2 and Ezekiel 29:4, where catching fish with hooks is used as a metaphor to represent the divine judgment upon the rich and the powerful respectively. "Jesus," Myers concludes, "is inviting common folk to join him in his struggle to overturn the existing order of power and privilege."[51]

The announcement of the coming of the kingdom is a call to repentance and belief in the gospel (1:15), which will entail a change of attitude, a reordering of priorities, and a decisive commitment to the new era that, in God's economy or *kairos*, has already arrived.[52] This commitment is enacted symbolically when people are baptized by John in the Jordan. As we know, Jesus himself submits to it. But the gospel says nothing about Jesus requiring people to be baptized as a prerequisite for discipleship. Not in this gospel at least, although the tradition preserves an instance of Jesus' disciples baptizing people (John 4:1–2). One of the reasons this practice is not recorded in Mark may be John the Baptist's declaration that Jesus will baptize with the Holy Spirit, something that never happens in this narrative either. Nevertheless, the rhetorical function of this affirmation is to highlight Jesus' superiority over John.

In Mark's own community, though, this may have pointed to a conflict with an existing Baptist group that still practiced John's baptism and followed his ascetic practices, such as fasting, as it is made clear in 2:18–20. In this passage, the disciples of John are paired with the disciples of the Pharisees. This is an important clue that points at the situation of the Markan community, which may have been struggling not only with the Zealots' political messianism but also with a group of followers of John the

---

50. Henderson, *Christology and Discipleship*, 26.

51. Myers, *Binding the Strong Man*, 132.

52. The perfect tense of both "fulfilled" (πεπλήρωται) and "has come near" (ἤγγικεν) conveys the idea of "an arrival that has already taken place better than it would suit anticipation of an imminent arrival." Gundry, *Mark*, 65. Or, as I suggested in another work, "The kingdom was then present as a spiritual reality that had ushered in as an irreversible process in which evil was being overcome by the power of God as mediated through Jesus' ministry." Vena, *Parousia and Its Rereadings*, 184.

Baptist, who still believed that his baptism was relevant (cf. Acts 19:1–4), as well as with a group of followers of the Pharisees and their dietary laws (cf. 7:1–23). Members of these two groups may have been part of the Markan community, where they tried to convince some of its members about John's supremacy over Jesus and of the importance of keeping kosher. Mark may have been alluding to them in 13:21–22 and in 7:1–23. But the narrative will make it crystal clear that Jesus is the one who has to be followed. Jesus will be the model disciple of the kingdom, not John. And the Pharisees dietary laws will be overturned by a new purity law, that of the heart. John will certainly play an important role in the unfolding of the kingdom, but it will be Jesus who will inspire the community into resistance and prophetic engagement in society. The reason for this is that Jesus is the stronger one, something he will prove by his defeat of the evil powers through his exorcisms and healings and also through his defeat of death at the resurrection. Now the community can have a model that will carry them over difficult times with the knowledge that they will overcome evil and death just as Jesus did. This may be the baptism by the Holy Spirit that John the Baptist spoke about, a baptism achieved through participation as co-disciples in Jesus' Spirit-imbued mission.

The Calling and Appointment of the Twelve (3:13–19)

Jesus goes up a mountain and calls to him "those whom he wanted." Then, he appoints twelve disciples. The Hebrew Scripture echoes are obvious: like Moses, Jesus ascends a mountain which, in the Bible, is almost always associated with a place of revelation, of divine disclosure (cf. Mark 9:2–8). But unlike Moses, he does not go alone, or accompanied by a close circle of advisors. He goes with all of his followers. He calls them and they come.[53] Then he appoints twelve as representatives of this larger group. The word for "appointed," (ἐποίησεν) is important. The root is the verb ποιέω, which means "to do," "to make," or "to create" and it is used in Genesis 1. This may hint at Jesus' ministry as the starting point of a new creation.[54] That which

---

53. Joel Marcus has pointed out that "the middle voice of *proskaleitai* ('called to himself') and the pleonastic *autos* ('himself') emphasize Jesus' power of choice, which mirrors the sovereign electing power of God in the Old Testament (see e.g., Deut 7:6–8; Isa 41:8–10); in Isa 45:4, significantly, divine election is accompanied by a renaming, as in Mark." Marcus, *Mark 1–8*, 266. Again, we see Mark's preference for Isaiah to describe Jesus' identity and work.

54. Marcus, *Mark 1–8*, 262, 267.

is being created here is a new people, a revitalized and renewed Israel, as the choosing of the Twelve seems to suggest. Jesus proceeds to bestow upon some of them new names, another link with the creation story. Jesus is the new Adam, the New Human Being who, by assigning new names to these rugged Galileans, confers on them a new honor: they are to be disciples of God's kingdom, just as he is. And this all happens on the mountain which perhaps, as Herman Waetjen suggests, needs to be seen symbolically "as the *axis mundi* of the story world of Mark's Gospel."[55] With this action, Jesus is subverting the status of Mount Zion as the center of the world and Jerusalem and Judea as the centers of religious and political power.

But Jesus calls them intentionally into discipleship, into a following. The purpose is threefold: to be with him, to be sent out to preach, and to have authority to cast out demons. To be with him may imply some kind of training, both by example and by teaching. The disciples would then do as their teacher, the one who sent them, did. In this regard, Jesus presents himself as a model. He was also sent (9:37) with a mission, which included preaching and casting out demons. He now shares that mission, and that power that was bestowed upon him at baptism, with his disciples. He gives them authority over evil spirits. Only those who possess God's spirit can do that, and Jesus does not hesitate to share this power with the newly appointed disciples. As Waetjen says:

> [by] endowing them with the same authority he bears as the New Human Being to preach the good news and to exorcise demons, Jesus establishes the egalitarian character of this new people of God.[56]

But the disciples are to spend time with Jesus first. Even though they are given the power, they have to learn how to use it. They have to be with Jesus and he with them. Discipleship is born and nurtured in community for both Jesus and the disciples. When this time of preparation happened in Jesus' case is hard to tell. The most logical answer is that it happened during the time he spent with John the Baptist, his mentor and teacher, and with the community that gathered around him, from whom he absorbed the passion for God's kingdom. The text of Mark does not specify how long Jesus was part of John's group. The only time reference is found in 1:16: "Now after John was arrested Jesus came into Galilee, preaching the gospel

---

55. Waetjen, *Reordering of Power*, 96.
56. Ibid., 97.

Jesus as Disciple of the Kingdom

of God." It clearly affirms that it was only after John's forceful removal by Herod (cf. 6:17) that Jesus' ministry really began. Up until that point, he remained with his teacher in the wilderness. How long was that? If Jesus were tempted by Satan during forty days, and assuming that this should be taken literally—although it may just mean a long time—then he stayed with John at least a couple of months, maybe more, perhaps a year or so.[57] John 3:22-24 preserves a tradition that speaks of an overlap between the ministries of John and Jesus. This is absent from Mark, who wants to depict John as a forerunner, not as a partner in the proclamation of the gospel. But one could imagine a time when both prophets/disciples of the kingdom ministered side by side and, that during that time, Jesus was still absorbing from his teacher the content of the message.

But perhaps this process of becoming a disciple of God's kingdom started earlier, when Jesus was growing up, immersed in the Galilean version of the traditions of Israel.[58] Jesus coming from Galilee cannot be construed as an occasional visit to Judea, out of curiosity. Rather, it is a purposeful trip. He comes to be baptized, to become a disciple of John. Jesus must have heard of the Elijah-like prophet, and steeped as Jesus was in the Galilean rendition of the tradition—where the Elijah-Elisha cycle was given prominence[59]—he comes to the Jordan River in order to be part of an eschatological movement that would make people ready for the coming reign of God. As a Galilean, he was certainly ready to see this reign coming in fullness, doing justice for his people, who had suffered under the oppression of the Jerusalem and Judean leadership.

We also need to account for a developing awareness, that is, an adjustment of Jesus' own sense of mission as he encountered people and their reactions to his message. It is now usually accepted by scholars that Jesus' encounter with the Syrophoenician woman in 7:24-30 marks an important stage in Jesus' own consciousness as prophet/disciple of the kingdom. Here

---

57. Tabor suggests that in Luke 11:1-4, when the disciples ask Jesus to teach them to pray "as John taught his disciples," Jesus repeats to them the prayer that he had learned from his teacher, John the Baptist. If that is so, then, Jesus had to stay with John long enough to learn the prayer. Tabor, *Jesus Dynasty*, 137.

58. This is usually referred to as the "little tradition." "The little tradition expresses the values of peasants and incorporates their grasp and selective appropriation of the great tradition in a way that sustains their life, culture, and values; it is history seen from below." Herzog, *Prophet and Teacher*, 176-77.

59. Galilee had been part of the northern kingdom and so they preserved many of the traditions associated with it. Herzog, *Prophet and Teacher*, 112.

he is being forced by a foreign woman to realize that his ministry should not be limited to the "children," but that it should also include others, those who up to this point he had considered "dogs" but who from now on he will see in a new and different light, namely, as people worthy of God's liberating activity through his ministry (cf. 7:31–37 and 8:1–10; these are all Gentiles). In order for Jesus to do this, he needed to have considered Gentiles as part of God's covenantal people. This required an effort beyond anything he had done to the present; it required a change in his symbolic universe, a change in the way he perceived the God of Israel. All this constitutes part of Jesus learning what it meant to be a disciple of the kingdom.[60]

The disciples' time of preparation is clearly described in the gospel. It lasted throughout Jesus' entire ministry, during which they were able to put into practice all the things they learned from Jesus. They had an opportunity to be successful (6:30), but also to fail miserably (9:18). In the same way that Jesus' formal training finished when John was arrested and after which he went to the region of Galilee to start his ministry, so also the disciples' training finished formally when Jesus was removed from their midst and they were commanded by the young man to meet him in Galilee (16:7). And judging by the discipleship pattern we find in the gospel—namely, that after receiving power from above, Jesus starts recruiting disciples in Galilee—it would be safe to assume that the same pattern will be repeated as the disciples go back to Galilee to meet the risen Christ. Only this time, the disciples are in charge of the mission. They are the ones doing the recruiting, calling people to join the movement in preparation for the final manifestation of God's reign.

The readers of the gospel could certainly identify with this post-resurrection era for they themselves were living in it, repeating the pattern outlined by the story. The mandate to make disciples, clearly stated in Matthew, is absent in Mark, but certainly it is implied in the open-ended epilogue of Mark. But, whereas in Matthew this call to make disciples seems to serve the beginning of an ecclesiastical organization, or at least of an ecclesial consciousness, in Mark it seems to point to the eschatological moment when the Son of Man and his community will receive from God all authority and dominion according to the idea found in Daniel 7. Mark

---

60. "The people of Israel . . . are now undergoing a renewal like their original formation in the exodus and wilderness under Moses' leadership *and* the kingdom of God is now being expanded to include other peoples as well in the renewal led by the new Moses-Elijah." Horsley, *Hearing the Whole Story*, 89.

believes this moment to be at hand, and so does his audience. But more about this later.

The Parables of the Kingdom (4:1–20)

All the parables in chapter 4 of Mark are kingdom parables. The first one, the parable of the sower, is important, for it seems to portray Jesus as the proclaimer of God's kingdom. What does the sower do? He sows the word (λόγος). And what is this word? Judging by what has transpired so far in the narrative, the word is the preaching of the good news by Jesus (1:14–15, 38; 2:2), which sometimes takes the form of teaching (1:21–28; 4:1). The clearest correspondence between the sower and Jesus is found in 4:3, where it says that the sower "went out to sow." The verb is an aorist of ἐξέρχομαι. The same verb is used in 1:38 where Jesus says that he "came out," ἐξῆλθον, in order that he might preach also in the surrounding towns. So, the sower going out to sow is a metaphorical way of referring to Jesus' public activity of proclamation.

As the sower, Jesus handles the seed (the good news) and scatters (proclaims) it over different types of terrain (people). But the growth of the seed depends on people's response to the good news, not on the sower (Jesus) or even God. It depends on the quality of the earth, that is, on who people are. This is made explicit in the two parables that follow, where first it is said that "the earth produces of itself," (4:28) and then that the small mustard seed, "when sown upon the ground," becomes a large shrub (4:31–32). What is being emphasized here is the transforming power of the earth. Mary Ann Tolbert puts it this way:

> Productive earth, the good earth, produces on its own. . . . The sower does not dominate the production and does not make it happen; the sower only sows and goes about life, while the earth brings forth the harvest out of itself. . . . How some people, upon hearing the word, can accept it and bring forth fruit is unknown. They produce the yield out of themselves because of who they are, and it is precisely by bearing fruit that their membership in the good earth type is demonstrated.[61]

The first group of people does not even allow the seed to take root. The birds (Satan) eat it up before it even has time to germinate. The second

---

61. Tolbert, *Sowing the Gospel*, 161–62.

group of people is eager to receive the seed, which grows fast due to the scarcity of the soil. But the sun (troubles and persecutions) burns the new plant because it does not have a root. The third group of people is represented by those in whom the word does not produce any fruit for it is choked by thorns (cares of the world, love of riches). It is only the fourth group of people, those who are represented by the good earth, who bring about fruit in abundance.

Tolbert has suggested that these four types of soil correspond to four types of people in the story world of Mark. The first group corresponds to the scribes, Pharisees, and the Jerusalem Jewish leaders who, from the very beginning, oppose Jesus because "they themselves are Satan's feeding ground, the hard earth which the seed cannot enter."[62] The second group refers to the disciples who, when times of tribulation come, especially during the trial and crucifixion of Jesus, fall away and abandon him. In the third group, we have people like Herod and the rich man of 10:17–22 who "illustrate the fatal effect of worldly power and wealth on the word."[63] Finally, the fourth group refers to people who show faith in the face of fear and is illustrated in the three healings that follow immediately after chapter 4, namely, the demon possessed man, the hemorrhaging woman, and Jairus' daughter, all in chapter 5. The faith shown in these three events "is the human manifestation of the good earth, the kingdom of God,"[64] something that is absolutely necessary if the kingdom is to be manifested as "transforming power that produces incredible results."[65]

So the kingdom can only be experienced when people exercise faith in the face of fear and worldly temptations. It is not something that can be brought about only by a divine decision. It needs the human counterpart to set it in motion. Jesus, as the sower, is unable to guarantee the growth of the seed, that is, the manifestation of the kingdom, in the same way that he was unable to guarantee healing in his hometown of Nazareth (6:5–6). This was God's prerogative together with the individual's faith. As a disciple of the kingdom, Jesus' responsibility was only to do the will of the one who sent him, namely, to proclaim the word, to sow the seed of the kingdom. The rest was left to the faith of the individual.

62. Ibid., 154.
63. Ibid., 158.
64. Ibid., 170.
65. Ibid.

Jesus as Disciple of the Kingdom

The third parable is that of the growing grain (4:26–29). Here again, the seed represents the word, the message. Its growth is independent of the person who sowed it. Who is this person? It is someone who was given the task of sowing the seed. It is the sower/Jesus and, eventually, the disciples. Jesus is presented as being in the service of the kingdom, which he believed he was facilitating as a broker of God's power. He became a model broker, a model disciple for all disciples, ancient and modern and, as the Son of Man, the representative of God's people (see discussion below). He also becomes, following Tolbert's typology, a model for the good earth for, in the story world of Mark, there is no other who exemplifies faith in the face of fear, or trust in God in the face of adversity, better than Jesus.

The Sending of the Twelve (6:7–13)

As we recall, in 3:13–19, the disciples had been appointed so they may have authority over the unclean spirits. Here they are actually given this authority, which is the same authority Jesus had already manifested in his encounters with demon-possessed people (1:21–28; 5:1–20). They are not told to do this in Jesus' name,[66] as the early church later would do, but to exercise this authority in an autonomous way. The idea here is that Jesus shares his God-given authority with the disciples and makes them co-disciples, partners in the same mission, collaborators. He is not sending them to do anything he hasn't already done, with the exception perhaps of the anointing with oil, which is probably a practice that the early church read back into the story. He tells them to rely on people's hospitality, for they were not carrying anything with them, not even a change of clothes.[67]

---

66. John's report concerning another exorcist in Mark 9:38 includes this person's method of exorcism: it was done in Jesus' name. The disciples object to this practice because the man was not part of the group of disciples. Jesus' reply is important. He says that they should not stop him because "no one who does a deed of power *in my name* will be able soon afterward to speak evil of *me*. Whoever is not against *us* is for *us*." Jesus identifies so much with his group of disciples that he shares with them his own name, as it is made very explicit in v. 41: "Whoever gives you a cup of water to drink because *you bear the name of Christ*." It is unlikely that the disciples drove demons in the name of Jesus. This was the early church's practice after the resurrection. It is more probable that they did it the way Jesus did it, by commanding the evil spirit to come out, relying on the power that they knew resided both in Jesus and in them by virtue of Jesus' bestowing of authority as he sent them out.

67. The disciples' equipment for the journey may echo some of the Exodus themes. For instance, the staff may point at Moses' staff which, yielded God's authority to perform

But he warns them that they may not be welcomed in some places. This he already knows by experience (cf.6:1–6a). The only thing that is different here is the way the disciples should react to rejection. They should shake off the dust of their feet as a testimony against the household that rejected them. This needs to be interpreted as a sign of shame for lack of hospitality but also as a sign of eschatological judgment. The fact that Jesus never did this when he was rejected may point at a reworking of the tradition by the early church, in this case the author of Mark. Rejection may have been a common experience for members of his community and, therefore, Mark had to provide a way of coping with it.

In Mark, the place of discipleship is clearly "the house." Already in chapter 3, we find a listing of the different symbolic places that will play an important role in Mark's story. There is the synagogue, described as a place of confrontation and unbelief (1:21–28; 3:1–6; 6:1–6a; cf. 13:9); the seaside, pictured as a place for teaching (3:7–12); the mountain, described as a place of calling and commitment (3:13–19); and the house as the place for the gathering of the new community, Jesus' new family (3:20–35). In 6:7–13, the disciples are not sent to proclaim the kingdom in synagogues, as Jesus had done already three times in the narrative (1:21, 39; 3:1; 6:2), but to move into people's homes and accept their hospitality, if given.

After having been rejected at his home-town synagogue, Jesus decides to change the strategy. This sets up a new pattern for the Jesus movement, which is reflected in the practices of the Markan community. The home becomes now the center for the movement, the place where the kingdom will be experienced in an egalitarian way.[68] This is seen clearly exemplified throughout the gospel (see 1:29; 2:15; 6:10; 7:17, 24; 9:28, 33; 10:10, etc.). The importance of this fact cannot be overemphasized. It means, for the Markan community, that discipleship is to be lived in community, without concern for power or special privileges (cf. 10:41–45). Notice that in 3:34–35, Jesus calls the crowd of his followers "my mother and my brothers." Again, as Waetjen points out, this is not a rejection of his own family but "a

---

signs (Exod 4:3, 17), and the prohibition to carry a second set of clothing and to wear only sandals may also point at God's protection of the Israelites during their wilderness journey (Deut 8:4; 29:5). Henderson, *Christology and Discipleship*, 155–57.

68. "In the story world of Mark's Gospel (the home) is the symbol of the family-like character of the new Israel that he has constituted, and it stands in contrast to the hierarchical institution of the synagogue where leaders have begun to reject him and even plot his death. The new people of God will express its familyhood by meeting in house churches." Waetjen, *Reordering of Power*, 98.

declaration of a new familyhood which is constituted in a house."[69] There is no hierarchical ordering in this new family. Jesus is another disciple, one among equals, and his followers are his brothers, sisters, and mother. This is corroborated again in 10:29–30, where Jesus mentions the new people of God as a family without a father figure, which was the most pervasive symbol of authority in the Greco-Roman world. It is very plausible that this is the model the Markan community was following, or the model Mark *wanted* them to follow, and therefore he read it back into Jesus' life.

Jesus and the Syrophoenician Woman (7:24–30)

This incident represents the only clear example in Mark where Jesus changes his mind. He learns from this woman that his work of proclamation of God's reign has to be inclusive of all peoples. From now on, not only Jewish nationals, but everybody will be called to join the movement. The general call to follow him of 8:34–38, done in the highly Hellenized area of Caesarea Philippi, serves to reinforce the inclusive and multiethnic[70] nature of discipleship that Jesus is beginning to envision, as he calls "the crowds with the disciples" to a cruciform discipleship. I would contend that the impetus for this renewed call to discipleship comes from the encounter with this woman, from whom Jesus is gaining a new awareness as to who the people are that will join him in the proclamation of God's kingdom. He realizes that there is room at the eschatological table for the children and for those who are not. The distinction between children and not-children, Jews and Gentiles, the disciples and the crowd, still persists, but the difference is that now the kingdom is to include and be embraced by both groups, making one diverse reality out of two distinct ones. Of course, this reflects very nicely the situation of the Markan community, and that is why the story is narrated in such a way. It is Mark, not Jesus, who is setting the agenda

---

69. Ibid., 99.

70. Here it is important to notice Amy-Jill Levine's criticism of a Christian portrayal of Jesus' ministry as completely different from the Judaism of his time. She affirms that, on the whole, Judaism did not expect Gentiles to become Jews in order to enter into a meaningful relationship with God. She also states that the church, which is made into this ideal model of inclusiveness, still demands allegiance to Jesus Christ as the distinguishing mark of membership. Therefore both Judaism and Christianity are ethnocentric and exclusive and one has to be careful not to hail Jesus as the representative of an all-inclusive ministry. This seems to be more the prejudice of the scholar than the statement of the text. Levine, *Misunderstood Jew*, 158–59.

of Jesus' ministry. The inclusion of the Gentiles is perhaps based on some recollections of the manner in which the historical Jesus may have carried out his ministry, but the way in which it is portrayed in the gospel is the construction of the evangelist.

A couple of things need to be underlined in connection with this story. The first thing to be noticed is its rhetorical position in the gospel. It is placed between the feeding of the five thousand in 6:30–44, where Jesus feeds a Jewish crowd, and the feeding of the four thousand in 8:1–10, where the feeding takes place in Gentile territory. It is also placed between the healing of sick people on the Jewish side of the lake (6:53–56) and the healing of a deaf man in the region of the Decapolis, an area of predominantly Greek population (7:31–37). Finally, it is placed right after Jesus' discussion with the Pharisees about eating with defiled hands in which Jesus makes the assertion that defilement is more a moral/spiritual than a ritual/religious reality.[71] This rhetorical placement makes Jesus' initial response to the woman even more offensive for, as Joan Mitchell suggests, "The Jesus who had just rendered all foods clean in his dialogue with the Pharisees (7:19) vanishes; the Jesus of Mark 7:24–30 takes up the law-observant voice he has just silenced, enforcing boundaries and purveying exclusionary platitudes."[72]

Second, the evangelist's hand seems to be at work in the phrasing of the story, just as he had done in the previous pericope, where the parenthesis in 7:19 is clearly a redactional addendum to the tradition.[73] The word πρῶτον (first) may have been added by Mark, for it reflects an understanding of the mission that, even though privileging Israel as the original recipients of the message, it nonetheless makes room for the incorporation of the Gen-

---

71. This rhetorical placement betrays a chiastic structure of the type ABCC'B'A' that unfolds in the following way:

A. Feeding of five thousand people on the Jewish side of the lake (6:30–44)
  B. Healing of a Jewish crowd (6:53–56)
    C. Controversy with Pharisees on defilement (7:1–23)
    C'. Conversation with the Syrophoenician woman and exorcism (7:24–30)
  B'. Healing of a deaf man in Gentile territory (7:31–37)
A'. Feeding of four thousand people on the Gentile side of the lake (8:1–10)

For an almost identical chiasm, see Mitchell, *Beyond Fear*, 111.

72. Mitchell, *Beyond Fear*, 111.

73. Amy-Jill Levine says: "Not only did Jesus keep kosher; all of his immediate followers did as well." And she goes on to suggest that, if Jesus had declared all foods clean, the incident of Peter and Cornelius in Acts 10 and the controversy between Peter and Paul in Galatians 2 would have made no sense. Levine, *Misunderstood Jew*, 25–26.

Jesus as Disciple of the Kingdom

tiles, something that was already present in Paul's ministry (cf. Rom 1:16; 2:9–10; 3:1–2). This redactional addition would suggest that Mark thought that the mission to the Gentiles, which was being implemented in his days, was already prefigured in Jesus' own work. As a matter of fact, this was the main agenda of the church as he understood it. The church was to be engaged in the proclamation of the gospel to the nations as an activity that would precede, and even condition, the coming of the kingdom with power. In 13:10, we have another insertion by the evangelist,[74] which features also the word πρῶτον! All of this goes to say that the learning aspect of the encounter is even more evident if we conclude that Jesus did not say "first," thus acknowledging the right of the Gentiles to the bread of the gospel, but that, as in Matthew 10:5–6, he thought of his mission as being limited to the Jews. If that is the case, then the persuasiveness of the woman should be highlighted even more. It is because of her λόγος, that is, her persuasive speech driven by her desperate situation, that Jesus heals her daughter. The mutual transformation that takes place is insightfully described by Hisako Kinukawa in her book *Women and Jesus in Mark*, to which I refer the reader for a detailed treatment of this story.[75]

Finally, the argument for inclusion of the Gentiles in Jesus' mission seems to parallel Luke's argument in Acts 10 when, after being shown a large sheet containing all kinds of unclean animals, Peter is advised by a heavenly voice to eat them. When Peter refuses to do so, the voice proceeds to remind him that he should not consider profane that which God has made clean (10:15). This, of course, refers to the inclusion of the Gentiles into the church, which is going to be related paradigmatically with the example of Cornelius. Here in Mark, once Jesus has told the crowds in 7:15 that real defilement is produced by an unclean heart, not by food handled by unclean hands, the story moves to a house in the region of Tyre where a Gentile woman uses food as a metaphor for her right to receive the blessings of the messianic age, something Jesus thought was to be limited to the Jews. The theme of food links both passages but it is used in a different way in each. In Acts, the Gentiles are equated with non-kosher food, which is now allowed to be consumed by Peter, meaning by that the Gentiles are now to be considered as sacred, as God's people. In Mark 7:24–30, food is made to represent the blessings of the messianic age acted out in Jesus' ministry of exorcism, which should now include also the Gentiles.

---

74. Vena, *Parousia and Its Rereadings*, 202–4.
75. Kinukawa, *Women and Jesus*, 51–65.

Mark uses the woman as a character in the story to address the needs of his community, where Jews and Gentiles were worshipping together and participating in the weekly Eucharist. Both groups were to partake, literally and metaphorically, of the same food. Both groups were to have equal access to the blessings of the kingdom, but it was only after his encounter with the woman, that the Markan Jesus is able to model this attitude. The teacher is being taught and thus becomes an example of discipleship![76]

Peter's Confession (8:27–30)

People saw Jesus as a prophet (Elijah or one of the prophets) or even as someone who resembled very much John the Baptist. Peter thinks he is the Messiah. This affirmation does not elicit much enthusiasm on Jesus' part, but rather a prohibition to talk about him. For some reason, Jesus does not want people to know that he is the Messiah.[77] Why is that? One of the ways this question has been answered is to say that it is still too early in Jesus' career, and such a revelation could have hampered what he wanted to accomplish. Another way is to say that he is not satisfied with some of the popular expectations concerning the Messiah and, therefore, he is going to redefine it radically. I believe this last possibility is closer to the spirit of Mark, especially as it relates to the scribal conception of the Messiah as son of David (cf. Mark 12:35–37).

I would go further and say that the Markan Jesus is not thinking in traditional messianic terms (a royal and military Messiah son of David), but more in messianic terms that include the idea of discipleship. Or, as Suzanne Watts Henderson suggests, "Jesus' selective silencing can be seen as a calculated strategy, running throughout Mark's gospel, to ensure that Jesus' mission is understood within the framework of God's apocalyptic

---

76. "The Syrophoenician woman teaches the Teacher; she speaks out of her doubly marginal experience as mother/woman and Gentile to alter the voice of authority. Her word frees her daughter and opens a future for her within the Christian community. The woman's word reimagines the Christian community as a household in which Jews and Gentiles share bread." Mitchell, *Beyond Fear*, 113.

77. In traditional scholarship, this is known as the "messianic secret," first proposed by Wrede in 1901. But my intention here is to find out how it functions in the narrative, in the story. Whether Jesus or the early church said this is beyond the point for my endeavors in the present work. For a narrative understanding of the messianic secret, see Barr, *New Testament Story*, 277–78.

Jesus as Disciple of the Kingdom

incursion into the world."[78] He sees himself as a messenger (1:2), a disciple of the kingdom of God, someone who has been sent to proclaim the presence and embodiment of God's rule in human history. As a matter of fact, right after this passage Jesus talks about himself using another expression, "Son of Man," and he does so in a context that clearly speaks about discipleship. I will contend later in this work that this expression "Son of Man" can and perhaps should be interpreted through the lenses of discipleship.

But Jesus' question, "Who do you say that I am?" is *the* central Christological question of the Gospel of Mark in particular, and of the New Testament in general. It is not so much the question the historical Jesus may have asked—although this is certainly a possibility—but the question the Markan community, and every community before and after it, is asking, and Mark's story is clearly an attempt at answering it. Yet he is not alone in this endeavor. There are other groups competing to provide the "right" answer. So far we have seen a John the Baptist group represented in the narrative by his disciples (Mark 2:18–20; 6:29). We have seen a group of scribes and Pharisees who oppose Jesus throughout the story. These also have disciples who follow their legal prescriptions, such as food regulations and Sabbath observance, and whose messianic understanding Mark wants to correct (cf. Mark 12:35–37). The Zealots, implied in the description of the signs of the end in chapter 13, are another messianic group that competed with the Markan community in voicing their Christological understanding. Herod and the Herodians may represent another group, the priests and the High Priest yet another, and Pilate and the Romans another. All of these groups vie for settling the Christological question, which is comprised in Jesus' interpellation of the disciples, "Who do *people* say that I am?", albeit with different motivations. And Mark is writing his version of the answer, one among many, as his community faces external as well as internal challenges (see above).

Jesus' Call to a Suffering Discipleship (8:34—9:1)

In chapter 2, I have already expanded on the important place this pericope has in Mark's overall rhetorical and theological agenda. Here I want to emphasize again that, when Jesus is calling people to take up their cross, he is actually calling them to imitate him, the one whom the evangelist identifies in this context as the Son of Man. It is a call to follow him in the path of

---

78. Henderson, *Christology and Discipleship*, 12.

Jesus, Disciple of the Kingdom

discipleship, a path he has taken up as the representative of God's suffering people. I will explore this idea more in depth in chapter 4.

Jesus' call to a suffering discipleship includes gender and social privileges. He is calling the disciples but also the crowd, the ὄχλον. There were women among his disciples (5:40–41) and also among the crowds (5:24). This call is different from the time he picked twelve male disciples, his traditional Israelite entourage (3:13–19). Here, Jesus is expanding the vision. To the circle of disciples he adds the crowds, and he calls them all to renounce their privileges and follow him, being willing to face execution by crucifixion if needed. For that is what "let them deny themselves and take up their cross" means: say "no" to your social status and "yes" to the possibility of martyrdom for the sake of the gospel.

For those with important social standing, such as the ruler of chapter 10, this call, besides the possibility of actual, physical death, meant social death. For those with little or no social standing, this call represented the possibility of belonging to a fictive group that would give them the kind of identity they were lacking in the society of the time. This new family will be described in detail in 10:28–31. But more about this later.

Jesus, Apostle of God (9:37)

In this passage, Jesus tells his disciples, who had been arguing on the way about greatness, that God has sent him. Likewise, he now sends his disciples into the mission (3:14; 6:7). In both cases, the verb is the same, ἀποστέλλω. God sends Jesus, and he in turn sends the disciples. This makes them co-participants in the same mission from God. Just as Jesus acts as the broker or agent of God's kingdom, so also the disciples, being sent by Jesus, themselves become brokers, or agents[79] of the kingdom of God and co-disciples[80] with Jesus. In 6:30, and perhaps also in 3:14, the disciples are called apostles (ἀπόστολοι), "those being sent." This can only be so because they have been appointed by the one who is himself an apostle of God (Mark 9:37: "And whoever welcomes me welcomes not me but the one who *sent* me

---

79. Malina says that "they serve as agents of the central broker, Jesus." Malina, *Social World*, 152.

80. Tannehill suggests that in Mark's narrative, "Jesus functions frequently as an influencer, one who moves others to action." So, when Jesus calls his disciples they "should share in Jesus' mission and fate. They are meant to be co-ameliorators and co-influencers, subordinate to Jesus but sharing in his work." Tannehill, "Narrative Christology," 64–65.

Jesus as Disciple of the Kingdom

[τὸν ἀποστείλαντά με]"). Jesus is someone who replicates God's action of sending.[81] Jesus, as an apostle of God, is sending others as his envoys.

Again, here we return to an argument that we picked up a little earlier: if the quote from Malachi 3:1 in Mark 1:2 is taken from the MT, then "messenger" can refer to Jesus, for it reads: "See, I am sending my messenger to prepare the way before me." Jesus can easily be seen—and perhaps he was seen by his contemporaries (see Mark 8:27–28)—as the messenger of God, the one who announced the coming kingdom (cf. 1:15). This would certainly agree with 9:37, when Jesus talks about God as "the one who sent me." In the overall story of Mark, though, John the Baptist is the messenger to whom the Malachi quote is referring. It is he who prepares the way of the Lord, that is, Jesus. This is made clear by the quote from Isaiah 40:3 in Mark 1:3. But this redeploying of characters in the story is only possible if Mark is using the Greek translation of the Hebrew text, or if he is quoting from memory an oral tradition that was already composite in nature (see discussion above).

However, there is another layer to this story about apostleship. It has to do with apostleship and prestige, power. In the early church, apostleship had connotations of supreme authority. The church was built on the teaching of the apostles (Eph 2:20; Rev 21:14), who were regarded as the source of supreme authority. From the earliest times we see some of the apostles competing for supremacy, as the Pauline letters clearly show (cf. 1 Cor 1:12–13; 2 Cor 11–12; Gal 2:1–14), and the intimate circle of John, James, and Peter in the Gospel of Mark seems to suggest (Mark 1:29; 5:37; 9:2; cf.10:35–40). But Mark will criticize the notion that authority automatically resides with the Twelve in a number of ways, most obviously perhaps in his portrayal of the failure of all the disciples at the time of Jesus' passion. But here in 9:33–37, he does it by redefining greatness. The scene takes place in a house, Mark's setting for teaching. Jesus responds to the disciples' concern for honor ("they had argued with one another about who was the greatest.") by centering their attention on someone with the least amount of honor in the society of the time: a little child.[82] Jesus hugs the child, bringing him/

---

81. Henderson says that Jesus "emulates God's sending the son (see Mark 9:37, 12:6), thereby conveying an 'unbroken continuity' from Jesus through the original disciples to the Markan community itself." Henderson, *Christology and Discipleship*, 149.

82. "It is remarkable enough that Jesus draws attention at all to children, for they were considered nonentities. It is quite shocking that he would advance them as models for his social program." Myers, *Binding the Strong Man*, 261.

her to the center of the group. And then he utters the shocking two-part aphorism:

> Whoever welcomes one such child in my name welcomes me, and
> Whoever welcomes me welcomes not me but the one who sent me.

The word for welcoming is δέχομαι, which can be translated as "to take with the hand," "to embrace," "to receive favorably," to receive into one's family," "to provide hospitality," and so on. The logical conclusion of the aphorism, where if A corresponds to B, and B corresponds to C, then C corresponds to A, is that whoever welcomes a child in the name of Jesus, is welcoming God! Usually one would welcome a person of equal or higher honor, never someone of lower status. Here the values of society are reversed: welcoming the lowly amounts to welcoming the One with the highest honor, the God of Israel, the sending God. This means that the sent ones, or the apostles, are to live by this law of reversal. Being first can only be achieved by serving others, namely, being last. Jesus, as apostle of God and disciple of the kingdom, will exemplify this and expect it from his followers. He came (that is, he was sent) to serve, not to be served (cf. 10:41–45). True apostleship will be characterized by service and identification with the disempowered, not by authority and power. Some people in the Markan community may have been inclined to favor an authoritative kind of leadership modeled on the traditional idea of apostleship as represented by the Twelve. Mark will debunk this notion by showing how Jesus, the disciple and apostle par excellence, demonstrated the true nature of one being sent.

Jesus Calls a Man to Joint Discipleship (10:18)[83]

The story of the rich ruler provides another example of seeing Jesus as disciple of the kingdom. For Jesus, God is the ultimate reality, the only one in

---

83. This pericope follows a chiastic structure demarcated by an inclusio (εἰς ὁδὸν, v. 17 and ἐν τῇ ὁδῷ, v. 32):

A. A man runs up and kneels before Jesus (17a)
  B. Asks what he must do to inherit eternal life (17b)
    C. Only God is good (18)
      D. The commandments are listed and the man acknowledges having fulfilled them (19–20)
        E. Jesus issues the man a call to follow him (21)
          F. The man refuses the call (22)

whom true goodness resides: "No one is good but God alone," he tells the man. Here Jesus seems to acknowledge his complete subordination to God. He does not see himself as an end, but as a means to God and the kingdom. When Jesus calls the man to follow him (10:21), it can be interpreted as a call to becoming co-builders of the kingdom, co-disciples. Jesus is not the one who grants entrance into the kingdom. He is a disciple of God for, as the context clearly shows, it is only God who makes it possible for human beings to access the kingdom, and this includes Jesus himself (v. 27; cf. 14:25).

In verses 29–31, Jesus explains to the disciples the way discipleship works. This explanation is prompted by Peter's remark in verse 28, "we have left everything and followed you," probably Mark's rhetorical strategy to address some issues in his community. Some of these may have included the relationship between traditional life and the new community of believers, between the Torah and Jesus' teachings, and between persecution and eternal life.

1. Relationship between traditional life and the new community of believers.

a. Discipleship in Mark implies leaving everything for Jesus' sake and the gospel, that is, the proclamation that God's dominion[84] is soon to arrive. There are four direct calls to discipleship: to Simon and Andrew in 1:17, to James and John in 1:20, to Levi in 2:14, and to the rich man in 10:21. All of them, except the rich man, respond positively: they follow him. This needs to be interpreted literally. They leave what they were doing and join the group. From then on, they come to be with Jesus and are sent to an-

---

    E'. Jesus explains to the disciples why the man refused his call (23–25)
      D'. Disciples dismay at the thought that a law abiding person could not enter the kingdom (26)
        C'. Only God can save (27)
      B'. Eternal life is received, not inherited, by those who are willing to abandon possessions and to follow Jesus (28–30)
    A'. Many who are first will be last, and the last first (31)

84. Even though Jesus' main opponents were the religious authorities of Israel and their power base, represented by the Temple and their version of the Torah, the portrayal of God's kingdom is set against the backdrop of the Roman Empire. The kingdom of God is an imperial kingdom, one that proclaims another *kyrios* and advances other set of values. Nevertheless, it is an empire, although a benevolent one at that. Segovia, "Counterempire of God," 96–98.

nounce the coming kingdom in word and deed (cf.3:14–15). It seems pretty clear that, for these people at least, joining the group of disciples implies a radical break with their traditional village life ("We have left everything and followed you").

Following Jesus implies leaving behind the comforts of and the commitments to the patriarchal household. The kingdom being proclaimed is at odds with people's responsibilities in the current social system and calls for a reevaluation of a person's allegiances. The same idea is present in 8:34, where denying oneself needs to be interpreted as turning away from kinship and family[85] in order to join the Jesus group, which from now on will replace the family they have been part of up to this time (cf. 3:31–35). The bond between the members of Jesus' group is not biological, but rather theological. Now family is to be defined by willingness to do God's will. And Jesus makes it clear that the following is not merely "for his sake" but also for the sake of God's reign (10:29). In other words, Jesus sees himself as one who is calling people to follow him as he goes about proclaiming the gospel.[86]

But not everyone is called to this kind of discipleship. Some people are to go back to their families and towns with a renewed commitment to the God of Israel, such as, for example, the Gerasene demoniac (5:19) and the blind man of Bethsaida (8:26). They are to announce the approaching reign of God by a renewed allegiance to the covenant. Richard A. Horsley puts it this way: "The restoration of covenantal life in local communities is part and parcel of the renewal of Israel that Jesus is leading as the new Moses and Elijah."[87]

b. Discipleship entails entering into a community of disciples who share everything, thus becoming a type of surrogate family with a new authority figure. When Jesus calls the rich man to follow him, he is inviting him to join such a community, where there are no needy because they all share the same resources. But first, he has to cut his ties with the patriarchal household

---

85. Malina goes as far as to say that such a break with family "was something morally impossible in a society where the kinship unit was the focal social institution." Malina, *Synoptic Gospels*, 244.

86. Probably Jesus sees his own ministry as a journey that will end when God brings about the kingdom (cf. "on his journey," v. 17; and "on the road, going up to Jerusalem," v. 32). This is especially clear in the Gospel of Luke, where the trip of Jesus to Jerusalem is depicted as a travel narrative, added by the evangelist to Mark's outline (cf. Luke 9:51—18:14).

87. Horsley, *Hearing the Whole Story*, 107.

he has been a part of until now, something that obviously he is not ready to do.[88] As one who owns property—land, people, and animals—this man is the typical *pater familias* of his time. Jesus is asking him to renounce his position in society as a respectable head of family and join Jesus' surrogate community.

It is interesting to note that there is no mention of fathers in this new community (10:29–30). Obviously, Jesus fulfills the role that fathers had in the families of the time. But his authority is not exercised as that of a *pater familias* but more as that of a servant, a slave, or a woman (10:45). By so doing, Jesus is criticizing the patriarchal notion of authority of the time while highlighting the role of those groups that had traditionally been oppressed.[89] Whatever shape this new community took in Jesus' days, whether they formed a community of wandering preachers, or a network of households sympathetic to the movement (notice how many times in the narrative Jesus enters a house where he teaches or heals), there is little doubt that in Mark's times, it pointed to the house churches.

Discipleship becomes the business of every believer, not just that of a chosen few, as with the Twelve, who receive a harsh criticism in Mark's story. Others qualify as disciples as well, even people who are not called specifically to follow Jesus but who nevertheless decide to do so of their own volition, such as the leper of chapter 1 who, against Jesus' wishes, "went out and began to proclaim it" (κηρύσσω, 1:45); or Bartimaeus the blind man who, after being healed, "followed him on the way" (10:52); or the crowd of disciples who followed him into Jerusalem (11:9–10); or the women who "used to follow him and provided for him" (15:41).

---

88. Mark may be using this story to speak to some members of his congregation who were in a similar situation as that of this man: they were willing to be part of the community of followers but not willing to pay the ultimate price of social ostracism and suffering. They did not value the kingdom as a priceless treasure hidden in a field, or a pearl of great value, as Matt 13:44–45 suggests, for which people are willing to sell everything in order to buy that field or that pearl, but wanted to maintain their allegiance to the patriarchal system, while at the same time being part of the new community of the kingdom. With this story, Mark absolutely denies this possibility.

89. Schüssler Fiorenza has alerted us to the fact that the Jesus' group may have been just another group that "stood in conflict with the hegemonic kyriarchal structures of the Roman empire, of which hegemonic Judaism also was a part." In her work, she is critical of a historical-Jesus research that places Jesus in opposition to the Judaism of his time and makes him the charismatic hero who departs from mainstream Jewish society. Trying to depatriarchalize Jesus, without questioning the scholarly construction and popular understanding of Judaism as being patriarchal, amounts to an anti-Jewish prejudice. Schüssler Fiorenza, *Jesus and the Politics of Interpretation*, 39–40.

The demon-possessed man from the country of the Gerasenes deserves a special mention, for he wants to follow Jesus, but Jesus refuses and instead sends him to return to his friends at home, telling them "how much the Lord has done for you, and what mercy he has shown you," thus becoming a sort of apostle—since the text informs us that he goes away and does precisely as Jesus commands him (5:19–20). As in 1:45, the verb used for proclaiming, κηρύσσω, is the same used for the ministry of Jesus (1:14) and the disciples (3:14; 6:12). Therefore, the man is acting as a disciple, even though he is not allowed to "be with him" (5:18; cf. 3:14).

All of these are prototypes of discipleship for Mark because they illustrate the kinds of people who become part of the community. But still, the supreme example of discipleship, the supreme prototype, will not be one of the Twelve, or the women, or any other person with disciple-like characteristics, but Jesus himself, for Jesus is the only one in the narrative who provides the community with the most comprehensive and clearest model of how a faithful disciple is to behave. In Mark, the issue is not discipleship per se, but rather "faithful discipleship." There are many disciples in the gospel, but there is only one faithful disciple of the kingdom: Jesus.

2. Relationship between the Torah and Jesus' teaching.

As a Jew, Jesus never contradicts the law. He is an interpreter of the law and seeks to provide ways in which the law can be contextualized in people's lives. This story is a case in point. Jesus, as many other rabbis, makes a list of the commandments. He only mentions six, which summarize a person's obligation toward the neighbor. But one of the commandments, "do not defraud," is not actually in the Decalogue. Why is Jesus mentioning it? Commentators have suggested that it recalls Exodus 20:17, Deuteronomy 24:14, and Sirach 4:1. All of these passages talk about one's obligations toward the neighbor's property and to the poor. Defrauding would mean cheating them, depriving them of what is rightfully theirs. And this action starts always with the desire to possess the neighbor's property.[90] Is this what the rich man had done? Probably.

---

90. Richard Horsley says that "You shall not defraud" is a substitution for "You shall not covet," which gives it "a telling concrete application. For coveting someone else's goods, desiring to gain control of them, would lead the coveter to defraud a vulnerable person." Horsley, *Hearing the Whole Story*, 191.

Jesus as Disciple of the Kingdom

Ched Myers suggests that "the reference . . . is clearly to economic exploitation."[91] The fact that Jesus asks the man not only to sell what he owns but also to give it to the poor seems to suggest that he has exploited the poor. He is a member of the wealthy and ruling class,[92] many of whom read the law in ways that favor their economic and political status. But in Jesus' eyes, he is not as blameless as he says he is. He has transgressed the very commandments he claims to have kept since his youth and, therefore, is asked by Jesus to make restitution for what he has stolen from his neighbors.

For Jesus, the law is kept "through concrete acts of justice, not the façade of piety."[93] Eternal life is possible for those who do so.[94] But that is not so easy for the wealthy. It is actually very difficult, for they are accustomed to reading the law in a way that advances their standing in society. Here, Jesus is requiring them to read it with new eyes, namely, those provided by a commitment to the reign of God expressed in the concrete following of Jesus. Reading the law with a hermeneutic of liberation will mean that sometimes, in order to be truly upheld, the law will have to be transgressed (cf. 2:23–28; 3:1–6).[95] Following Jesus would have implied transgressing the letter of the law in more than one way. For example, Jesus asks a potential follower to disregard his obligations to bury his dead father (Matt 8:22), something expected according to tradition (cf Tob 4:3–4). But the paradox of discipleship resides in that, by transgressing the law one is actually fulfilling it, or bringing it to a fuller realization. Jesus' reading of the law comes from his Galilean background, which provided him with a lens for prioritizing the liberating elements of the Torah over the more legalistic ones.[96]

---

91. Myers, *Binding the Strong Man*, 272.

92. "Jesus is addressing the invisible ruling class of Galilee or Judea through its visible representative, and his prescription for the rich ruler applies to his class as well." Herzog, *Prophet and Teacher*, 135.

93. Myers, *Binding the Strong Man*, 274.

94. The text gives us no clue that Jesus doesn't mean this. Proper keeping of the commandments guarantees access to the life of the age to come. In this sense, Jesus' theology remains Jewish throughout.

95. Hinkelammert, *El Grito del Sujeto*, 37.

96. This can be interpreted in terms of the "great tradition" and the "little tradition." See Horsley, *Hearing the Whole Story*, 156–61.

3. Relationship between persecution and eternal life.

a. Discipleship implies the willingness to undergo persecution for the sake of the gospel. This was Jesus' fate and the fate of the Markan community as well. But it is important to note that persecution is a consequence and not a prerequisite of faithful discipleship. Otherwise, persecution could become another "commandment" that, upon fulfillment, people could use as a self-righteous way of earning their entrance into the kingdom. What is required of the disciple is not victimization but nonviolent resistance to evil for the sake of the gospel.

b. Discipleship contains the promise of eternal life, but this comes as a second step, as the consequence of faithful discipleship. The man wants to avoid the commitment of discipleship and obtain eternal life without it. In his mind, the keeping of the commandments already ensures him God's approval. After all, wasn't this the promise of God in the Torah?

In Exodus 20:6, Yahweh promises to show steadfast love to those who "love me and keep my commandments." If the man says he kept the commandments, but Jesus says he is lacking something, what could this be, if not love? That is, attachment and loyalty to the God of the covenant shown in the sharing of his possessions with the needy and in his willingness to join Jesus' group. Jesus is asking the man to recommit himself to God, not through the channels of the traditional Israelite society, but through the new surrogate family represented by Jesus' movement. What the rich young ruler is lacking is not the conceptual framing of the commandments, or the desire to keep them, but the specificity of the Jesuanic praxis. He is not ready to give up the traditional reading of the Torah for a more drastic and radical one. The Markan community, through this example, understood that the commandments did not lose their relevancy, but had to be lived out now in the context of a new praxis.

The Prediction of Future Persecutions (13:9–13)

When Jesus tells his disciples that they are going to be handed over to the authorities, both Jewish and Roman, and betrayed by their own relatives, and that they should not worry about how to respond to the accusations because the Holy Spirit will give them the necessary words to answer, he is presenting himself as a model of faithful discipleship, for all of these things are about to happen to him and have already been predicted in the

Jesus as Disciple of the Kingdom

narrative (9:31; 10:33) using the same word, παραδίδωμι, used here to refer to the believers' fate. In the same way that he is going to be betrayed by Judas (14:43–46), taken to the high priest (14:53–65), where he answers with words given him by the Holy Spirit, since his answer comes from Scripture (Dan 7:13), and finally to Pilate (15:1–15), so also the community is going to earn "the wrath of local and national Jewish authorities as well as Roman procurators and even Caesar himself."[97] Therefore, when conflict arises because of their "nonaligned radicalism," to use Ched Myers' term,[98] a conflict that is not only external but internal as well because it comes also from the kin group, the very supporting system that gives them identity, the community prepares itself for the worst. This generalized hatred is conveyed by the expression καὶ ἔσεσθε μισούμενοι ὑπὸ πάντων, which the Jerusalem Bible translates as: "You will be universally hated on account of my name."

Using the literary technique known as *vaticinium ex eventu*,[99] Mark is again constructing Jesus as a model of discipleship. These words are placed on the lips of the historical Jesus for the purpose of offering this war-torn community a rationale for its suffering. If they were being persecuted and harassed by the same authorities that persecuted and eventually killed Jesus, but whom God vindicated with the resurrection from the dead, then the community knew, in spite of all they were going through, that there was hope for their future. They knew that God was on their side, as God had been with Jesus, and that divine vindication awaited them, even if they had to lose their lives. So Jesus exemplifies the nature and goal of true discipleship: fidelity to God's kingdom in the face of opposition.

The Institution of the Last Supper (14:22–25)

In the institution of the Last Supper/Eucharist, Jesus seems to be relativizing again his role, while at the same time absolutizing God and the kingdom. His blood is poured out for many, but nothing is said about it being "for the forgiveness of sins," as is the case in Matthew 26:28. Nor is the kingdom the

---

97. Myers, *Binding the Strong Man*, 333.

98. Myers' main thesis in his book is that Mark did not want his community to align itself with any of the two power brokers of the conflict, namely, the Zealots or the Romans. The suffering and hatred came as a result of taking this stance.

99. According to Soulen, a *vaticinium ex eventu* "is a Latin phrase meaning 'a prophecy from an outcome.' In NT criticism, it is used to designate a passage in the Gospels that foretells an event that was in fact first known to and experienced by the early church and then placed back as prophecy on the lips of Jesus." Soulen and Soulen, *Handbook*, 204.

"kingdom of my Father," as in Matthew 26:29 or, as one of the criminals being crucified with him puts it, "your kingdom" (Luke 23:42), but "the kingdom of God." A number of things are interesting in this passage beyond the traditional discussion as to whether or not this was a Passover celebration.[100]

First, there is the idea of a (new) covenant.[101] The figure being used here is that of God's covenant with Israel in the Hebrew Scriptures (cf. Exod 24:8; Jer 31:31–34; Zech 9:11). One way of reading this text is that Jesus is presented as a new Moses who makes it possible for the renewed and revitalized people of Israel, represented by the twelve disciples, to attain the deliverance foreshadowed in the Exodus account. But also, that what Jesus has in mind here is the coming of a time when God will renew God's covenant with Israel following the prophecy of Jeremiah 31:31–34, where a new covenant is announced in which there will be no need for a visible, written law. But rather, that this law will be internalized, written on people's hearts (cf. Mark 7:14–23, where defilement comes from the heart, not from failure to fulfill the ritual law), and therefore, there will be no need for teachers, "for they shall all know me, from the least of them to the greatest."

Jesus describes this new reality as the kingdom of God and the way by which it is made accessible to "many" as the pouring of his blood which is enacted symbolically by the drinking of the wine. This sacrifice does not bring about forgiveness of sins, as it does in Matthew's version of the institution of the supper (cf. Matt 26:28), but the context of Jeremiah 31 suggests that forgiveness of sins is one of the ingredients of the new covenant: God will write God's law in people's hearts; they will then know the Lord without having to be taught and God will forgive their sins (Jer 31:34).

Is Mark thinking that all of this happened through Jesus life and death? Probably so, but even if this is true, he does not clarify it. He falls short of any explicit reference to Jesus' death as a substitutionary atonement, except perhaps for 10:5. For Mark, Jesus is the supreme example of one in whose heart the law of God had been written. Rather than teaching it, as the Pharisees did, he lived it out through a life of commitment (love) to God and service (love) to neighbor (cf. Mark 12:29–32).

So, how should we interpret his sacrifice? This leads us to a second point, namely, to the pouring out of his blood done for the benefit of many. This idea is already present in the Hebrew Bible in the righteous sufferer of the Psalms, in the martyrs of the Maccabean period, and even in the

---

100. See discussion in Witherington, *Gospel of Mark*, 371–76.
101. The word "new" is missing in some MSS.

Jesus as Disciple of the Kingdom

Suffering Servant of Isaiah 53, all of which had clear atonement implications. These inter-textual connections, plus the ransom of the Son of Man (the Human One) in 10:45, led Myers to conclude that Mark is portraying Jesus as the "eschatological paschal lamb," and that he is doing so by expropriating the Passover symbolic discourse of the ritual meal "in order to narrate his new myth, that of the Human One who gives his life for the people."[102]

But we do not know if this is what Mark had in mind here. As we said before, Mark seems to be interested in the Suffering Servant motif as an example of suffering discipleship (see discussion above). Besides the possibility that the traditions Mark is handling may have been layered already with atonement overtones, he may be also thinking about Jesus' sacrifice in exemplary terms: it will benefit others by showing them how a true disciple of God should behave at the time of death, thus serving as consolation for those going through similar circumstances. What seems clear is that Mark thought that Jesus believed that God would vindicate him, since he is hoping to drink wine again in the kingdom of God, a classical figure of blessedness taken from the Hebrew Scriptures (cf. Isa 25:6–8; 49:8–13).

This hope for God's vindication is what will inspire Christians to endure suffering and even death. If God vindicated Jesus by raising him from the dead, then God will surely vindicate those who remain faithful as Jesus did. But this hope for vindication is not the hope of a victim of evil. The disciple is not a voluntary victim. Jesus was not. True, he assumed the consequences of defying the powers, but this is not the same as being a passive, vulnerable victim. God's vindication can happen only to those who give their lives trying to change the established order of things.

Third, the expression "Until that day" (ἕως τῆς ἡμέρας ἐκείνης) is very similar to 13:32, "But of that day" (περί δέ ἧς ἡμέρας ἐκείνης), where it refers to the day of the Parousia of the Son of Man. Is Jesus here thinking about that final moment when the present age will give way to the kingdom of God? Probably. He was, after all, an apocalyptic.[103]

What is not so clear is whether Jesus thinks of himself as the one who will bring in that kingdom, the Son of Man of 13:24–27, or if he, as any other disciple of the kingdom, is hoping to see the day of God's deliverance without thinking of having any position of privilege in it. It is, after all, the kingdom of God, not the kingdom of his Father! And yet, by suggesting, in

---

102. Myers, *Binding the Strong Man*, 363.

103. Of course, this is debatable. See Wink's discussion, *Human Being*, 164–65.

a daring reappropriation of the Passover symbolism,[104] that the bread of the meal is his body and that the wine is his blood, he is clearly pointing to his particular role in the unfolding drama.

Perhaps, as we said before, this role was to be exemplary, showing how a disciple of the kingdom was to behave at the time of death. But my hunch is that Mark thought of Jesus as being a representative figure, one who God was using to show renewed Israel the way (ὁδός) of and to the kingdom. That way was one of solidarity among the members of God's people. Jesus' blood is poured out for many in solidarity, sharing their oppression under the powers that be. But, in this very act of sharing in his co-disciples' predicament, he is extending to them the benefits of God's blessings when, as the righteous sufferer, he will be vindicated with new life. Therefore, the way of and to the kingdom is one of giving one's life in solidarity with the oppressed of the world, who are embodied in the Markan narrative by Jesus' disciples, the named and the unnamed ones, the acknowledged and the unacknowledged ones.[105]

Jesus in Gethsemane (14:32–42)

Jesus is not ready to face his destiny, but he is willing to obey the will of God. But, will he find the courage to do so? Will he succeed or will he fail? Failure is always a possibility in the story Mark is telling, starting with the temptation in the wilderness right after Jesus received the Spirit, and now here, at Gethsemane, where it is clear that Jesus would rather find another solution to his predicament. The reader has already encountered examples of failed discipleship in the gospel,[106] and she will still find some more in the chapters ahead. But, is Jesus going to be one of those? That is

---

104. Just the hint of drinking blood was an affront for Judaism.

105. There are many characters in Mark who, even though they qualify as disciples, are not recognized as such. Some of these characters are: the Gerasene demoniac and the woman with a flow of blood (both in chapter 5), the Syrophoenician woman and the deaf man (both in chapter 7), blind Bartimaeus in chapter 10, the man carrying a jar of water in chapter 14 and, of course, the women who followed Jesus along and witnessed his crucifixion (15:40–41).

106. Mark is very clear in portraying the failure of the disciples. In this chapter Judas, the betrayer, is described as being "one of the twelve" not once but three times (14:10, 20, 43)! Mark wants to emphasize the failure of the community to remain faithful to its commitment to the mission. Jesus, as part of that community of disciples, is tempted to do the same. In the end, he finds the strength to remain faithful and becomes the example of endurance and obedience that the Markan community needs to follow.

Jesus as Disciple of the Kingdom

the question being planted in the reader's mind by this skillful storyteller. In the end, Jesus comes through. He overcomes the temptation of the flesh, his human nature, and submits to God's will: "Not what I want, but what you want." This, in a nutshell, describes Mark's notion of an ideal disciple, already anticipated in 8:35: knowing how high the price for being faithful to God's kingdom is, the disciple, personified supremely in Jesus, is willing to pay it. This may point to the situation of the Markan community, which was probably undergoing strenuous times as the Jewish revolt was forcing people to take sides. Which side was the community going to be on, that of the revolutionaries or that of the priests and aristocrats who favored submission to Rome? Not wanting to go through that which seemed unavoidable, but submitting to the will of God, made Jesus the perfect example of how a disciple needed to behave when confronted with the choice between violent revolt and passive submission. Jesus does not endorse either of the two, but will rather propose a third option: nonviolent resistance, thus setting an example for the community to follow.

MARK'S UNDERSTANDING OF THE LIFE OF DISCIPLESHIP[107]

Mark's construction of the life of discipleship is centered on the main paradox of 8:34–37,[108] which affirms that life is saved[109] when it is lost in the following of Jesus and the willingness to face crucifixion, if necessary. This can only be attainable through total and unconditional allegiance to God the Teacher, the God of the covenant. This allegiance will place the disciple in direct opposition to other authorities such as the Temple priests,

---

107. Mark is writing a fictional account based on some historical recollections and oral traditions. Myers calls it "realistic narrative," because it claims the autonomy of literature and the plausibility of historical writing. By literary autonomy, he means a story that makes use of poetic license so as to not make it a journalistic account of events. Historical plausibility means that the story is credible: its settings correlate to the world of first-century Palestine, its main characters are, for the most part, not make-believe, and its events are usually not fantastic. Myers, *Binding the Strong Man*, 104.

108. If, as I suggested earlier, the whole gospel has its center precisely at this point, then Mark's description of the life of discipleship, exemplified in Jesus' life, does indeed rotate around this rhetorical axis.

109. According to Bauer, the verb σώζω contains two main ideas. One is that of preserving or rescuing from natural dangers and afflictions; the other, saving or preserving from eternal death. In Mark 8:35, we have the two ideas combined. *BDAG*, 798.

Jesus, Disciple of the Kingdom

the Pharisees and scribes, and the Roman Empire. In the gospel's narrative, Jesus is the only one who embodies this kind of obedience. Therefore, Mark uses Jesus' example to challenge and encourage his community, for he knows that many of its members, like Jesus, are in danger of losing their lives. In Mark's depiction of the life of discipleship, a number of moments, or stages, can be detected:

Stage	Jesus	Disciples
A time of calling	1:9	1:16; 2:13–17
A moment of reception of power and/or authority	1:10–11	3:13–19
A period of instruction	Before and during his relationship to John	During their travels with Jesus
An official beginning	1:14	6:12–13, 30–31
An acknowledgment of discipleship as a combination of successes and failures as the disciples confront alternative views of God's kingdom[110]	6:1–6a; 7:24–30	7:30–52; 9:18, 28–29; 8:32–33
An acknowledgment of the main paradox of discipleship: life lost is life saved	14:32–42	Unrealized in the gospel narrative

It is very hard to tell how this description of the life of discipleship played out in Mark's community. Was there a moment identified as a "call," as in the case of Jesus and the disciples? Was there a moment when empowering for the mission was acknowledged? What was the period of instruction like for the believers? Was there a time when the members of the community officially started their lives as disciples? How were successes and failures evaluated in the community? Who determined what total allegiance to God meant in the specific circumstances of that community? Possibly, one could say that the call to discipleship was assumed when a person became part of the community, and that the empowerment to fulfill

---

110. This is nicely exemplified in chapter 6 of Mark, where around the main story of the beheading of John the Baptist, we find Jesus and the disciples both failing and succeeding in their ministries. The whole chapter could be structured chiastically as follows:

A. Jesus fails to do mighty works in Nazareth (1–6)
  B. Disciples succeed in their first missionary journey (7–13)
    C. John the Baptist exemplifies the cost of discipleship (14–29)
  B'. Disciples fail to meet people's needs (30–52)
A'. Jesus succeeds in healing many at Gennesaret (53–56)

the mission was acknowledged at the time of baptism. The period of instruction would precede baptism, during the baptismal *catequesis*, but also would follow it, in the weekly meetings when the community assembled in homes to break bread, pray, and hear the story of Jesus being read or recited out loud. As for an official start to their lives as disciples, this would follow naturally immediately after their incorporation into the community via baptism (cf. Acts 9:20). Falling back into their previous lives as Gentiles or into their traditional Jewish views would signal a failure in the life of discipleship. This could entail going back to the worship of the Greek gods, or engaging again in the emperor cult, or joining the revolutionaries in their pursuit for the establishment of a Davidic monarchy, or relapsing into legalistic practices such as food laws or circumcision (cf. Mark 7:1–23; Gal 3:1–5).

Success, on the other hand, would be accomplished by rejection, persecution, and eventually death, through which life was won. And, success or failure in the life of discipleship would be measured up by how the members of the community treated each other. If Mark 9:33–37 and 10:35–40 are any indication of internal struggles for power, then wanting to be given places of privilege, either in this life or in the next, was a sign of failure, whereas giving all you have for the benefit of other members of the community was a sign of success (Mark 12:41–44; 14:3–9).

One thing seems to be clear though, and this is that the Markan narrative, depicting Jesus as example of discipleship, served as the ideological basis for the community's attitude and response to the problems it faced, some of which were similar to the ones Jesus had faced. What were these problems? To name the more obvious, their relationship to: a) the Temple and its administration; b) the religious leaders of the day, namely, Pharisees and scribes; c) the Roman government; d) non-Jews, that is, Gentiles; e) the Torah with its ethical and ritual regulations; f) women in positions of leadership; and g) other Jewish groups such as the Zealots and perhaps followers of John the Baptist.[111]

By providing an ideological and theological foundation for addressing these problems, Mark wants his community to understand that to be a disciple of Jesus of Nazareth required a three-dimensional epistemological shift. One dimension was cultural and it played out in the centrality the narrative provided to Galilee over that of Judea in terms of the manifestation of the kingdom. The other was theological and it played out in the

---

111. These last two may not have been a problem for the historical Jesus.

centrality given to the "little tradition" over the "great tradition." And the third dimension was social. According to this, the *locus* of God's revelation was to be found with the poor and disenfranchised, rather than with the wealthy and powerful. God was on the side of the oppressed and the despised, not on the side of the wealthy and religious. The person wanting to be a disciple of Jesus of Nazareth had to be willing to surrender his/her previous *cosmovisión* (worldview) for a new one that demanded embracing a paradoxical existence where life was won through death. Jesus exemplifies this choice when he surrenders his life to the powers of the Empire only to regain it as a living and transforming presence in the life of the community.

A Preliminary Conclusion

It has been my intention in this chapter to demonstrate that the issue of discipleship lies at the center of Mark's gospel. Even though recent studies have tried to propose that that is not the case, but rather a reorganization of Israel alongside a renewal of covenantal practices is what really transpires in this gospel,[112] I maintain that discipleship can be construed as the central theme for a few reasons. One, Mark is the first document in the New Testament to utilize the word "disciple" and to expand on this notion of following Jesus. Paul, who wrote prior to Mark, does not even use the word or the concept. Therefore, the notion of discipleship is well established in the Markan community as a theological expression of the community's obedience to God through Jesus.

Two, the fact that the male disciples are depicted in a very negative light can be construed as the author's intention to teach the readers of the gospel a lesson about true discipleship. Thus, Jesus is used as the supreme example.

Finally, the leaders of the early movement, represented by the close circle of disciples formed by Peter, John, and James, are depicted as never quite understanding Jesus' actions and pronouncements, whereas women and children and marginal characters are given a place of relevance. Therefore, Mark may be pointing at a local issue as well as an issue that transcended the boundaries of his community.

---

112. For this idea, see Horsley, *Hearing the Whole Story*, 99–111.

Jesus as Disciple of the Kingdom

I am following here the work of women scholars[113] who propose that, in Mark, the female disciples fare much better than their male counterparts, for the former, unlike the latter, did not abandon Jesus and they seem to embody many of Jesus' expectations for a disciple. One could certainly go that route and prove, through a careful examination of the text, that the women were much better disciples than the men.[114] But this has already been done, and my purpose in this work is to show how Jesus exemplifies, for both women and men,[115] ideal discipleship. I am not trying to construct an ecclesiology but rather to suggest a Christology that would appeal to those women and men whose lives have been impacted negatively by kyriarchal structures of domination.[116]

---

113. See here, among others, the seminal work of Schüssler Fiorenza, *In Memory of Her*.

114. Kinukawa, *Women and Jesus*, 106, states that "the 'following' offered to everyone entails 'serving' in the sense of 'life-giving' suffering. 'Service to everybody' is inclusive and life-giving, while 'rule by power' is exclusive and not of any life-giving value in itself. In Mark, 'serving' is applied to women, from the beginning of the story (1:31) to its end (15:41). So, returning to 15:40, we can only conclude that the women depicted by Mark are the true disciples of Jesus in the sense that they are ready for devoting themselves to 'life-giving' suffering."

115. In *Jesus and the Politics of Interpretation*, 4–5, Schüssler Fiorenza introduced the helpful category of wo/men in order to indicate not only the instability of the term, but also to include men that have been subordinated by reason of class, race, country, and religion. According to this idea, Jesus would then be a wo/man. I am following this idea in my description of Jesus as the ideal disciple. As a subordinated man (a disempowered peasant from Galilee) he represents both women and men.

116. Schüssler Fiorenza, *Jesus and the Politics of Interpretation*, 4–5.

4

The Son of Man

A Collective and Communal Symbol[1]

THE EXPRESSION "SON OF MAN" has become a crux in biblical scholarship. Many of the issues connected with its use in the NT have been thoroughly discussed. Thomas Kazen suggests that this debate can be summarized in three areas: authenticity, origin, and reference. That is, if Jesus spoke about the Son of Man (authenticity), where did he get this information (origin), and to whom was he referring (reference)?[2]

Since the elucidation of this problem falls beyond the scope of this work,[3] which is more exegetical-hermeneutical, and so constructive, than historical, and therefore reconstructive, I will limit myself to a reading of the text that will see it as the product of a community struggling to understand Jesus of Nazareth's earthly ministry and how this understanding affected the way they related to Jesus Christ now. As I said in the introduction to this

---

1. Following the NRSV, I will capitalize both "Son" and "Man" when referring to the way Mark and the evangelists use the expression. I will use lower case when referring to the way Daniel uses it, meaning human being or son of humanity.

2. Kazen, "Son of Man as Kingdom Imagery," 89–90.

3. I will bypass the already too familiar debate among scholars concerning whether Jesus saw himself as the apocalyptic Son of Man playing a role that was shaped by the traditions found in Daniel 7, or if this is something added by the evangelist, that is, the church, and therefore should be taken as a Christological title, or if these sayings represent a self reference by a modest speaker, a sort of circumlocution for "I," without any eschatological implications at least for some of them. At the level of the narrative, it is clear that Jesus *is* the Son of Man, both the earthly and the heavenly one, and these references should be taken together as a whole.

work, I will take into account the historical nature of the traditions, that is, I will acknowledge that the (oral) traditions received by the evangelist preserved a memory of what the historical Jesus did and said, but that this memory had already been overlaid with a heavy dose of theologizing during the oral stage. Therefore, I will focus more on how these traditions were used by the evangelist than on whether or not Jesus thought of himself as the Son of Man.

The reason for this is that I believe it is practically impossible to know, given the very nature of the gospel traditions as theological embellishments, what the historical Jesus actually said or did. We can make educated guesses based on an informed understanding of the cultural and religious milieu of first-century Palestine, but we can never make accurate descriptions of it, much less of what a particular individual, who left no record of his life and work, may have thought. The evangelists, on the other hand, left us a story, the story of Jesus as they understood it. That we can assess, provided we never forget that we are reading a version—or versions—of the story, not the story as it really happened, for this is irrecoverable.[4]

The reading of the text that I am proposing will be guided by the following question: can the expression "Son of Man" be read through the hermeneutical key of discipleship? Can we find justification for such a reading in the text itself?[5] And if the answer is yes, then the next question is: should we not perhaps read "Son of Man" in discipleship key? How would such a reading change the shape of Christology traditionally associated with the Gospel of Mark? How would it change the way we see Mark's relevance for the church today? I suspect that this way of reading "Son of Man" in Mark would radically change the way in which we approach not only Christology, but also soteriology, ecclesiology, eschatology, and ethics, to mention just some of the traditional divisions of Christian theology. This reading assumes that the praxis of discipleship comes first, and that the Gospel of Mark reflects that praxis, rather than the other way around, namely, that the gospel serves as a formative model for praxis.

---

4. Many scholars nowadays make similar claims. See, for example Johnson, *Real Jesus* and White, *Scripting Jesus*.

5. In this section, I am going to be using Theissen's *Sociology of Early Palestinian Christianity*. But whereas his work concentrates on discovering the sociological realities of the community behind the text, I will attempt to find a model of discipleship that uses the text as its basis. My presupposition is that Mark, as an author, is rereading the traditions concerning the Son of Man and is offering this new model to his community for a specific reason.

Mark's Appropriation of the Son of Man Imagery

The Markan Jesus, the one constructed by the text, seems to refer to himself many times with the expression "Son of Man" (ὁ υἱὸς τοῦ ἀνθρώπου). There are thirteen occurrences of the expression, and they fall into three categories:[6]

a. The authoritative Son of Man (2:10, 28)

b. The suffering Son of Man (8:31; 9:9, 12–13, 31; 10:33; 10:45; 14:21, 41)

c. The eschatological Son of Man (8:38; 13:26; 14:62)

From Mark's perspective, these all refer to Jesus. Regardless of their origin they are now part of a narrative that makes them subservient to the authorial intention. Mark utilizes these references to build a Christology that is relevant for his community. Unlike Paul's, Mark's Christology is not propositional, but narrative. He is probably the first writer in the entire NT to write a story of Jesus of Nazareth, and to give it the literary form that came to be known as gospel, a sort of Greco-Roman biography. As we know, Paul, the only other canonical writer who precedes Mark, does nothing in his writings that can be compared to what Mark is doing here, both in terms of the story line (Paul does not tell us the story of Jesus) or the way key events in Jesus' life are interpreted (Paul places value and emphasis on atonement, Mark does not). Additionally, Paul never uses the expression "Son of Man," which raises the question as to whether or not he was aware of it or, if he was, why he decided not to use it.

One of the ways to assess this is to examine whether Paul ever quoted from Daniel 7, one of the possible sources of the expression "Son of Man." In appendix 3 of the *Novum Testamentum Graece*,[7] we find that there are no quotes or references to Daniel 7 in any of the authentic Pauline epistles, and that the only references to Daniel are general and vague. These are: Daniel 2:18 in Romans 12:1; Daniel 5:28 in Romans 9:28; and Daniel 9:16 in Romans 3:21. It is only the author of 2 Thessalonians who picks up an eschatological theme from Daniel 11:36, a description of the reign of Antiochus IV clothed in apocalyptic language, and applies it to the man of

---

6. They can also be divided into two categories: the earthly Son of Man, which includes both authoritative and suffering aspects, and the heavenly or eschatological Son of Man.

7. Nestle-Aland, *Novum Testamentum Graece*, 766–67.

The Son of Man

lawlessness (2 Thess 2:4). But the consensus among scholars is that this is not Paul. Therefore, we conclude that given the minimal use of the book of Daniel in Paul's writings, the idea of the Son of Man as an apocalyptic figure was not part of his eschatology. However, there is one passage in 1 Thessalonians that resembles the description of the Son of Man in Daniel 7:13-14, and it is 4:16-17. We'll come back to this passage later, when we address the issue of the Son of Man coming in/with the clouds of heaven.

Discipleship Redefined

1. Discipleship as *imitatio Jesu*/Son of Man (8:31-38).

I have argued in chapter 2 that the rhetorical and theological center of the entire Gospel of Mark could be found at 8:34-38, where the call to discipleship seems to be defined in terms of an *imitatio Jesu*. Self-denial and the taking up of the cross is something that characterizes Jesus' ministry so, in reality, Jesus is calling people to imitate him.[8] And since Jesus is identified in the context with the Son of Man, then the disciples are called to participate in the public activity and fate of this figure: to imitate Jesus is to imitate the Son of Man. Based on 1:14-15, where Jesus starts off his ministry announcing the gospel of the kingdom of God, one could say that to follow Jesus is an invitation to participate in his mission, that is, an invitation to be a co-disciple. Discipleship, then, is modeled after the earthly Son of Man, Jesus of Nazareth.

This is the third time the expression "Son of Man" has appeared in Mark thus far. The other two are 2:10 and 2:28, where the Son of Man, Jesus, is said to have authority to forgive sins and authority over the Sabbath. In both instances, Jesus' words are directed to representatives of the religious establishment—the scribes in 2:10 and the Pharisees in 2:28—and they are meant to de-authorize them as interpreters of the Torah. As self-appointed custodians of the law, they were the ones who decided when sins were forgiven or the Sabbath transgressed. Jesus expropriates their

---

8. Since individuals' personalities were embedded in the families to which they belonged, to deny oneself was equivalent to denying their closest of kin, that is, their parents, relatives, their households, their villages (cf. 6:4). The structure is chiastic:

   A. If anyone would come after me
      B. Let him deny himself
      B'. And take up his cross
   A'. And follow me

function, invoking a greater authority to do so on the grounds of being the Son of Man. What is remarkable here is that Mark has taken a heavenly figure and claimed for it authority on earth. Thus, he has made the Son of Man play a concrete role in the lives of people. Instead of being the agent of futuristic apocalyptic speculations, here he is representing and championing the community's present-day political struggle for power as they compete with other groups for the correct interpretation of the Jewish law.[9] In other words, from being a visionary figure, he has become a tangible reality. This may represent one of Mark's major accomplishments, that is, the de-apocalypticising[10] of the Son of Man expectation by making it relate to the historical Jesus and, consequently, to the community that followed in his steps.[11]

Now, in Mark 8:31–38, we encounter a new element: this Son of Man (or Human One) will suffer, die, and rise on the third day. Again, the evangelist continues to surprise his audience, for nothing like this was ever said of the Son of Man who, both in the Danielic, as well as in the post-biblical traditions of 1 Enoch and 4 Ezra, is always regarded as a triumphal figure. All of this provides the paradoxical backdrop against which one has to read the call to discipleship of 8:34–38. The disciple is someone who renounces life as understood in the society of the time and is willing to die, if necessary, for the sake of the gospel and the following of Jesus. And the irony is that, when one is willing to risk and even lose one's life, the opposite happens: life is preserved, saved—the idea here being one of vindication in the new age. Therefore, the disciples share in the fate of the Son of Man, not only in his sufferings and death, but also in his vindication through resurrection.[12]

---

9. Myers says: "The political struggle has really commenced: the Human One is wresting away from the scribal and priestly class their 'authority on earth.'" *Binding the Strong Man*, 155.

10. This is precisely the point Horsley makes in *Hearing the Whole Story*, 122–36, namely, that Mark's story is about how his movement should respond to the repressive violence of Roman rule rather than about the apocalyptic expectation of the coming Son of Man.

11. "[The] figure of the Son of man was central for the Jesus movement. His situation corresponded to their situation. Here belief and practice formed an indissoluble whole. The unity of this whole was deliberate. It formed the focal point of the idea of discipleship." Theissen, *Sociology*, 30.

12. Theissen, *Sociology*, 26 reminds us that the disciples participate also in the more positive aspects of the Son of Man's role, namely those of forgiving sins (Mark 2:11; cf. Matt 16:19; 18:18), having authority over the Sabbath day (Mark 2:23–28) and the

But the evangelist is not finished yet. There is something else here. He seems to shift gears and return to the traditional understanding of the Son of Man, for Mark 8:38 says that the Son of Man will come in the glory of his Father with the holy angels. Why this change, from suffering to victorious, from despised to glorified? There is broad agreement among scholars that his passage is based on Daniel 7:13–14, the vision[13] of one like a son of man, or a human being, coming to the Ancient of Days to receive from him power, honor, and the kingdom. In the book of Daniel, it is clear that this figure is acting on behalf of the people of God, Israel, for in the same way that the four beasts coming from the sea in 7:3–8 represent four successive kingdoms (Babylon, Media, Persia, and Macedonia), the one like a son of man of 7:13–14 represents a kingdom, the kingdom of "the holy ones of the Most High" (7:18, 22), or "the people of the holy ones of the Most High" (7:27). They are the ones who were suffering under the tyrannical power of Antiochus IV Epiphanes, and they are the ones who now, through Daniel's vision, are promised vindication and restitution to a position of power. Therefore, the Son of Man is really a symbol of the eternal kingdom and its representatives.[14]

It would be logical, then, to see Jesus here in the same way, that is, as the representative of a people, in this case, his co-disciples, those who were not afraid to give their own lives for the gospel. But there is a problem. We know that the interpretation of this passage in the first century was done through the lenses of the book of 1 Enoch,[15] especially the section called the Parables of Enoch (37–71), where the Son of Man is depicted as a heavenly figure that executes judgment over the evildoers and vindicates the righteous. In this book, the Son of Man is an agent of God's activity, not a corporate symbol for the people of God, as in Daniel.[16] But what if Mark intentionally ignored the more prevalent Enochic interpretation and returned to the traditional Danielic reading of the son of man as a collec-

---

regulations of fasting (Matt 11:18–19; cf. Mark 2:18–19).

13. Daniel's vision of the son of man is a symbolic representation of what the seer expects to happen on earth. The vision is not "historical" as will the actual giving of power to God's people be.

14. Kazen, "Son of Man as kingdom imagery," 94.

15. Nickelsburg, *Ancient Judaism*, 110.

16. Adela Yarbro Collins and J. J. Collins would disagree. They do not think that the son of man in Daniel is a corporate symbol; rather it "should be identified with the archangel Michael, the 'prince of Israel' of chapters 10–12." *King and Messiah as Son of God*, 78.

tive figure?[17] What would have precluded him from doing so? We will try to demonstrate that the evangelist, prompted by the specific situation of his community, may have done precisely that. This is part of Mark's de-apocalypticising strategy that we mentioned before, which should not be confused with the de-eschatologizing tendency seen in the later writings of the NT, whereby the new age of salvation is understood as being realized in the ministry of the church (see, for example, the Gospel of John, 2 Peter, Ephesians, Colossians, etc.). As we shall see, Mark maintains a futuristic eschatological expectation which he relates to the Son of Man and his community, but he makes some necessary adjustments to it in order to turn the negative, exclusivist, and violent worldview of apocalypticism, represented by the Zealots, into a more positive, inclusive, and peace-seeking worldview represented by his community. This community is sent to announce the gospel to the nations (13:10), not to defeat them.[18]

The question still remains whether Jesus himself subscribed to a corporate interpretation of the Danielic son of man. In the introduction to this work, I pointed out the need to comb the text of the gospel in search of a residue of Jesus traditions that are now present only in a veiled, redacted form in the gospel. I was trying to suggest that perhaps the pre-Markan traditions preserved a recollection of Jesus having thought of the Son of Man in corporate terms but, that by the time the gospels were written, an individualistic interpretation, proposed mainly in the extra biblical apocalyptic literature (1 Enoch, 4 Ezra, etc.), had taken over and had already permeated most of the theology of the gospels. If Jesus had a collective understanding of the Son of Man, it would show up at certain points in the narrative, creating tension with the more prevalent idea of an individual eschatological figure, because it would see the community of disciples as being part of it also. Thomas Kazen suggests that this last option is possible, when he says:

---

17. Here, I qualify my earlier position on the subject, reflected in my book *Parousia and Its Rereadings*, 180–82, where I conclude that Mark is rereading the son of man tradition of Daniel through the lenses of the Jewish apocalyptic writings of his time.

18. Whereas the Zealots advocated for a violent revolution that would annihilate the enemies of Israel (Rome and Gentiles in general), Mark advocates for an inclusion of Gentiles in God's kingdom (cf. 13:10 and the many mentions of Gentiles throughout the gospel). This idea agrees with Mahlon Smith's comments on his blog when he says: "In fact Mark 13 (and indeed the gospel as a whole) can be read as a Christian reaction to Jewish speculation (based on Daniel) about a heavenly Son of Man appearing in Judea to defeat the nations and restore the temple (which is just what 4 Ezra predicts)." Online: http://groups.yahoo.com/group/crosstalk/message/3487.

> [i]f we want to suggest that the historical Jesus understood and used the expression "Son of Man" in a collective sense, we should be able to trace a number of parallels in the Jesus tradition between sayings about the Son of Man, the kingdom and the disciples.[19]

Kazen goes on to give two examples in Mark, where some of the attributes of the Son of Man seem to also include the disciples. One is 2:10, where the Son of Man is said to have authority to forgive sins. The disciples too are given authority, and they are sent out to preach and heal (Mark 6:7–13). This is understood by Luke as including the forgiveness of sins (Luke 24:47) and presupposed by Matthew in his special material about binding and loosing (Matt 18:15–18). The other example is 2:27–28, where Jesus affirms the Son of Man's lordship over the Sabbath day. In reality, it is the disciples' needs that prompted Jesus to respond that human beings were created for the Sabbath and not the other way around and, because of that, the Son of Man was Lord of the Sabbath. For Kazen, this means that "to Jesus, the authority and priority ascribed to the Son of Man concerned the kingdom and its adherents, i.e., those to whom the kingdom was given, not least himself and his disciples."[20]

The *imitatio Jesu* that we are suggesting then is not a personal goal, something that each individual disciple should aspire to as a way of achieving moral perfection, but more like a communal vision, a commitment to be what they have been called to be, namely, the people of the Son of Man, those who will receive power only if they give it up. Service to others is now the new definition of power and the distinctive characteristic of the Son of Man and his co-disciples. When Jesus says in 10:45 that he has come not to be served but to serve, Mark is turning the Danielic symbolism on its head. It constitutes a true reversal of Daniel 7:14, where the son of man is served by all peoples, nations, and languages,[21] and Daniel 7:27, where the people of the holy ones—persecuted and suffering Israel—are served and obeyed by all dominions. Here Mark is clearly stating not only Jesus' mission as a disciple, but also the disciples' co-mission with Jesus: they are to serve others and, if necessary, to give their lives, as stated in 8:35–37. This giving of one's life is not something natural or even desirable. It is actually a paradox.[22] Jesus' own example in Gethsemane shows how difficult it is to go against

---

19. Kazen, "Son of Man as Kingdom Imagery," 98.
20. Ibid., 99–100.
21. Ibid., 108.
22. Myers, *Binding the Strong Man*, 235.

the tendencies of human nature. But it is the price every disciple, ancient and modern, should be willing to pay if he or she is to remain faithful to Jesus' vision of an egalitarian and just society, something his Jewish tradition taught him to call "the kingdom of God." For the Markan community, this price meant rejecting the violent solution proposed by the Zealots and to embrace the path of nonviolent resistance shown by Jesus and which could lead to death by crucifixion or imprisonment, as passages like 8:34–35 and 13:9–13 seem to suggest.

2. Discipleship and eschatological glory (10:35–40).

If the son of man in Daniel 7 represents the suffering people of Israel during the time of the Maccabees, and Mark is reading this text Christologically, then Jesus represents the new people of God, a renewed and revitalized Israel. If this is so, then, the exaltation of the son of man in Daniel and of Jesus/Son of Man in Mark is something in which the disciples, as members of the new people of God, will participate also. But in this passage, James and John seem to hold onto the traditional apocalyptic belief that Jesus, the Son of Man, is an individual redeemer figure that will come at the end of time to judge the sinners and reward the faithful.[23] So they ask for privileges in the coming kingdom. But Jesus tells them that their only privilege is to share in his suffering and death. In the same way that in 8:35 to lose one's life on behalf of Jesus and the gospel meant to save it, so also here the disciples have to be ready to make the supreme sacrifice for the kingdom if they want to be part of that people whom the Son of Man represents. To ask for special privileges is to misunderstand the nature of the eschatological kingdom, where there are no positions of privilege, but only the sharing of power—power that is given when it is given up!—among God's redeemed humanity.

But some may argue that Jesus, by admitting that he will be seated in glory, is subscribing to the traditional understanding of a triumphant Messiah, Son of God, or Son of Man. Now, let us remember that exaltation to heaven was also the hope of the righteous man of the Psalms or the martyrs of the Maccabean period, which became the basis for the doctrine of the resurrection of the dead (cf. Dan 12:2–3). At the resurrection, all the faithful would be vindicated. That is why Jesus tells James and John that they

---

23. In the story, they may be made to represent conflicting views concerning the Son of Man in the Markan community.

would suffer and die, as he was also going to, but that after that they would be vindicated and rewarded with heaven's glory. It is then possible to say that by asking to be seated with Jesus in glory, one on the right side and the other on the left side, the disciples are acknowledging the Danielic tradition of the Son of Man as a corporate entity who will exercise judgment at the end time. That is, they may not be thinking of the Son of Man coming down to earth, but rather of the people of God being exalted to heaven, that is, vindicated, which in some traditions included the idea of sharing the judgment seat, or throne, with God. We can see a residue of this idea in passages like Matthew 16:27, 19:28, and 25:31, where the Son of Man is explicitly mentioned, and in Matthew 20:21, Luke 22:30, and 1 Corinthians 6:2, where he is not.

James and John may be correct in referring to this tradition in which the Son of Man and his people are made to reign and to exercise judgment over God's enemies. But they are wrong in assuming that they can occupy a place of privilege. Jesus wants them to realize that they are part of the Son of Man's people, and that only God can determine who will be accorded privileges in the new age. And he also tells them that because he too is a disciple of the kingdom, and as such subordinated to God, he could not make a decision concerning their *post-mortem* status. As part of Jesus' subordination to God's will, seen throughout the gospel, he tells them that this petition is not his to grant; it is God's prerogative alone (10:40).

In Mark 10:33–34, Jesus had announced for the third time his sufferings, death, and resurrection. He did this by utilizing again the Son of Man imagery. On Jesus' lips, this apocalyptic figure has been transformed into a symbol for his own ministry and that of his disciples. Consequently, the readers begin to read this symbol in discipleship key in such a way that any time that the expression "Son of Man" appears, they suspect that it has something to do with their own praxis.[24] In the case of the Markan community, these sufferings would come for being faithful to a nonviolent understanding of the kingdom in the midst of alternative visions that called the believers to an armed revolution against Rome. But their suffering would give way, as in Daniel 7, to their vindication, which was anticipated in Jesus' resurrection.

---

24. Again, Theissen says: "Above all in the figure of the Son of man, early Christian wandering charismatics were able to interpret and come to terms with their own social situation." *Sociology*, 27.

As Paul would put it, Jesus is the ἀπαρχή (first fruits), after which come those who belong to him at his coming (1 Cor 15:23). Even though the apostle is working with a different eschatological framework, one that imagines a *coming* of Jesus to earth, he still recognizes that Jesus was raised as part of a people of whom he is the forerunner, the first fruits. His death and resurrection had set in motion the final resurrection and the kingdom, because for Paul, Jesus is presently reigning (1 Cor 15:25). He is the Lord of the universe (Phil 2), but his reign is a spiritual one, felt only by the believers in the church. One day, though, this reign will be manifested to all and will encompass the whole of creation (Rom 8). This will happen when death, the last enemy, is destroyed and the dead will rise at the final and universal resurrection. It is then that Christ will hand over the kingdom to God, "so God may be all in all" (1 Cor 15:28).

The differences with Daniel are obvious. Whereas in Daniel, the son of man *receives* the kingdom *from* God, in Paul, Christ *hands over* the kingdom *to* God. In Daniel the holy ones of the Most High will possess the kingdom for ever (7:14, 18, 27). The context suggests an earthly kingdom. In Paul, the believers are said to share in Christ's glory (1 Thess 4:16–17) and God's kingdom (1 Cor 15:23). The context clearly points to a heavenly kingdom. Even if, in 1 Thessalonians 4, Paul is presupposing Daniel 7, he is clearly reversing the symbolism, for here as in Mark 13:26, the Lord descends from heaven, and the believers who are still alive are taken up *in clouds* together with him. But more about this in the next section.

The Final Coming of the Son of Man in(to) Glory Redefined

After having discussed the plausibility that Mark is interpreting the Danielic Son of Man figure as a collective symbol that stands for the suffering people of God, I would like to concentrate now on that most salient feature of this figure, namely, his coming in or with the clouds of heaven. I would like to propose as a preliminary hypothesis, subject to verification in the text of the Gospel of Mark, that those passages in which the Son of Man is coming in clouds (see Mark 13:24–27; 14:62) refer primarily to the vindication of the suffering people of God and not so much to a coming of Christ at the Parousia.

Strictly speaking, and from a narrative's point of view, Jesus does not have to come back in victory from heaven, because he is already present among the disciples as the risen one who will meet them in Galilee. In

The Son of Man

the gospels of Matthew, Mark, and John, Jesus never leaves the community. There is no ascension narrative in any of these gospels. There is only a passing mention of it in John 20:17 and a possible echo of Moses' death at mount Nebo in Matthew 28 (cf. Deuteronomy 34). How can Jesus then come back from heaven if he never went there in the first place? Of course, this assumes that the Gospel of Mark ends at 16:8,[25] and that verses 9-20 constitute an addition (late second century) that tries to bring Mark into harmony with the story as it became known in the early church.

1. The origins of the doctrine.

The doctrine of the victorious return of Christ to earth to exercise judgment upon his enemies and to vindicate the righteous was developed by the early church following ideas already present in the apocalyptic literature (Enoch 37–71; 4 Ezra, etc.). These concern the coming of an agent of God, an anointed one and thus *messiah*, at the end times, but also ideas found in the prophetic writings of the Hebrew Scriptures concerning a future coming of the God of Israel, without the presence of any agent, which would have saving but also judicial consequences for Israel and the nations. This rereading of apocalyptic and Hebrew Bible traditions[26] came to fruition in the doctrine of the Parousia, whereby Jesus was expected from heaven as the agent of God's judgment at the last day. Since the early church identified Jesus Christ with the Lord, it was only natural that the day of the Lord of the Hebrew Scripture prophecies (cf. Zeph 1:7-18; 2:2-3; 3:8; Joel 2:1-11; Zechariah 14; Malachi 4; etc.) would become the day of the Parousia of Jesus Christ. Theologically, but also sociologically, this was done in order to explain to the world Jesus' shameful death and to bring consolation to those who were suffering for their faith. This is especially notorious in the eschatological passages of the Synoptic Gospels, in the book of Revelation, in 1 Thessalonians 4:13—5:11 and in 1 Corinthians 15:20-28.

Chronologically speaking, the Apostle Paul is the first writer in the NT to actually write about the παρουσία of Jesus Christ and to use this

---

25. There is general consensus among NT scholars that 16:8 is the gospel's true ending. Rather than trying to justify such a posture, we direct the reader to the pertinent bibliography. See, for example Hooker, *Endings*, 11–30, and Perkins, *Mark*, 729-32. For a different opinion, see Witherington, *Gospel of Mark*, 40-49. This issue also is addressed in chapter 5 of the present work.

26. Vena, *Parousia and Its Rereadings*, 109, 271.

word in a technical way. The Synoptic Gospels, except by Matthew 24:3, 27, 37, 39, do not use this expression with eschatological connotations. This tells us that very early in the life of the nascent Christian communities, as early as 49 or 50 CE at least, which is the probable date for 1 Thessalonians, the belief in a coming of Jesus Christ from heaven to usher in the end of the age, or the kingdom of God, already existed. Paul did not invent this idea but he certainly fleshed it out. As a Pharisee who had an apocalyptic worldview, it was relatively easy for him to connect Jesus' resurrection with the beginning of the final resurrection of the dead, which set in motion the chronology of the end times. For him, it was just a matter of time, a very short time indeed, before the Lord would return from heaven to take the believers with him. So short did he anticipate this time to be that he thought he was going to be alive when this happened (cf. 1 Thess 4:13–18). This kind of eschatology was prevalent in the Pauline communities of the first half of the first century, although not everyone would agree with the apostle in every detail. Proof of this is the church in Corinth, where there were people who subscribed to a more existential, or realized, view of eschatology (cf. 1 Cor 15:12–34).

When we move on to the Synoptic Gospels, and especially to the first of the three, Mark, we find that even though the expectation of Jesus' return to earth is preserved, it is nonetheless qualified in a number of ways. First, the term for coming is not the noun παρουσία but the verb ἔρχομαι. And instead of the Lord (κύριος), we find the Son of Man (ὁ υἱὸς τοῦ ἀνθρώπου), which is sometimes used interchangeably with kingdom of God (ἡ βασιλεία τοῦ θεοῦ), as is the case in Luke 9:27; 17:20–21; 19:11; 21:31; 22:18. Sometimes they are even used together (see Matt 16:28; cf. Mark 9:1).[27] Second, the sense of immediacy present in Paul is toned down by affirming that the gospel must be preached first to all nations (Mark 13:10), that no one knows when the end will be (Mark 13:32), and that a number of signs must happen before the end, something Paul never envisioned (Mark 13:3–27).[28] All of these qualifications may be due to a desire to counteract an excessive emphasis on the end times promoted by Paul and his communities. By the time Mark writes his gospel, Paul had been dead for at least five years (if Mark wrote before 70 CE; more if he wrote after the fall of Jerusalem). The Parousia had not happened as the apostle had anticipated it and, even worse, his witnessing of it, as assured to the Thessalonians, had

27. Ibid., 176.
28. See my discussion of this very issue in *Parousia and Its Rereadings*, 194–208.

The Son of Man

not happened either. An adjustment of the eschatological expectation was in order, but also a redefining of some of the major symbols by which that expectation was conveyed—mainly that of Jesus as Son of Man.

2. The Son of Man as a symbol for God's people.

The tendency in the interpretation of NT eschatology has been to take the coming of the Son of Man as equivalent to the coming of the Lord at the Parousia. In other words, Synoptic eschatology has been read through the lenses of Pauline eschatology. Therefore, the Son of Man has usually been interpreted as an individual figure, an agent of God's judgment, Jesus Christ. But what would happen if one were to regard the Son of Man sayings in the gospels, especially in Mark—who was the first writer in the NT to use such a title[29]—as a symbol for the people of God, and his coming in clouds as the moment when God establishes God's reign, bringing justice to those who suffered for their obedience to Jesus and the gospel?

In Mark, Jesus' prediction that the one who loses his life will save it, and that suffering, when it happens for the sake of Jesus and the gospel, will be rewarded with eternal life, connects, theologically, with the book of Daniel where the faithful Israelites who suffered under the Antiochian persecution of the second century BCE are promised vindication. Add to this the use of Son of Man imagery, and we have a clear reappropriation, or rereading, of Daniel 7 done from a similar political context: Antioch IV Epiphanes equals the Roman Caesar (cf. 13:14 where the desolating sacrilege, which in Dan 9:27, 11:31, and 12:11 seems to refer to Antiochus' profanation of the Jerusalem temple, may point at the Roman presence in the temple);[30] the saints of the Most High of Daniel 7:18, 21–22, 27 find their parallel in the faithful followers of Jesus, in this case the Markan community;[31] and the son of man of Daniel 7:13 becomes, likewise, a corporate figure who represents God's suffering people.

Jesus' resurrection as the Son of Man anticipates the vindication of God's people, since he is their representative. His resurrection means that

---

29. The only four other times that "Son of Man" is used outside of the gospels is in Rev 1:13 and 14:14; Heb 2:6; and Acts 7:56.

30. Vena, *Parousia and Its Rereadings*, 192.

31. In Daniel 7, the saints or the holy ones of the Most High are the angelic host raging battle against the forces of evil but they represent the people of God, as 7:27 clearly shows.

the righteous have been vindicated; God has been faithful to God's promises. The disciples now know that by meeting the risen one in the Galilean mission front, they would continue a project of liberation that was set in motion by Jesus' ministry and guaranteed by his resurrection from the dead, and which will culminate with the actualization on earth of the kingdom of God. They are co-disciples with Jesus who now, having been raised, is going ahead of them to Galilee. Given the fact that there is no ascension narrative in the short ending of Mark, which we take as the original one, the only explanation for such a meeting is that Mark thinks God is about to establish the kingdom on earth and, therefore, the moment of the vindication of the suffering people of God is about to occur. That did not preclude Mark from believing that a general resurrection of the dead would happen in connection with this giving of power to God's disempowered people, for this was the belief of many Jewish people at the time.

Mark just locates the actualization of God's kingdom in Galilee, mediated by the Son of Man and the people he represents. After that, and following Daniel's theology, the kingdom of the new people of God, the suffering disciples of Jesus, will last forever on earth (Dan 7:14, 18, 27). This would be the fulfillment of everything Jesus' ministry stood for, the liberation from every oppression and evil. In this way, Mark opposes the ideology of groups like the Zealots or the Essenes, who envisioned a new age brought about by their own intervention in the warfare that would ensue at the end between the forces of evil (the Romans) and the righteous (themselves). It also relocates the place of the kingdom's appearance, from Jerusalem, the site of traditional Judean/Davidic expectations, to Galilee, an area that was considered marginal at best and racially and religiously mixed at worse. So Mark is not only de-apocalypticising the expectation of the coming kingdom, but he is also de-centering it. He accomplishes all of this by going back to a corporate understanding of the Son of Man imagery that finds its roots in the book of Daniel, and also by consciously opposing the traditions found in the books of 1 Enoch and 4 Ezra, where the Son of Man is an individual, angelic figure who enacts God's judgment at the last day.

3. The Son of Man goes to God (Ascension redefined).

As in the text of Daniel, so also in Mark the Son of Man does not come down to earth, but goes to God and receives the kingdom. And when does such a thing happen in Mark? Well, it doesn't. Jesus never goes to

The Son of Man

God in a visible way as he does in Luke-Acts. But in 9:1-8, we have a glimpse of it in visionary fashion. Here, at the transfiguration, the disciples have a preview of the Son of Man's future glory to which he will have access through the resurrection. And the whole scene is preceded by the affirmation that this is a vision of the kingdom of God coming with power. Notice the words in the Greek: see (οἶδα), power (δύναμις), kingdom (βασιλεία), God (θεός), Son of Man (ὁ υἱὸς τοῦ ἀνθρώπου), glory (δόξα), cloud (νεφήλη). Compare that with the LXX of Daniel 7:13-14: I saw (ἐθεώρουν), clouds (νεφελῶν), son of man (υἱὸς ἀνθρώπου), kingdom (βασιλεία). Like Daniel in the past, so also Peter, James, and John have a vision of the future triumph of the Son of Man. As in Daniel 7:13, here Jesus is presented to God, for it is God's voice that testifies to his special status as beloved son. The voice utters from God's throne in heaven, and Jesus is standing in front of it. Elijah and Moses, two prophets of the past who were transposed to heaven without tasting death, are with him. Jesus will also be raised from the dead and exalted to heaven, although this last element, the ascension, is not so clear in Mark, as we shall see.

The setting is a high mountain, the traditional place for epiphanies, but the idea here is not that heaven has come down to earth, but rather that the disciples are given a glimpse of heaven at the moment the Son of Man receives the kingdom from God. It is a vision of heavenly things, which assures the disciples that things on earth will be affected by this vision. Therefore, even though the coming of the kingdom with power, which implies the giving of dominion and authority to the people of the Son of Man, does not happen in the narrative, it is foretold through the vision as something that will happen in the near future. The resurrection will enable this power and authority to be bestowed on Jesus, the Son of Man, and the kingdom will follow shortly, in Galilee, where the disciples, according to the evangelist's belief, will see its actualization on earth. This is especially warranted by the lack of an ascension narrative in Mark. It is very possible that Mark thought that this was going to happen during his lifetime and in connection with the destruction of Jerusalem (cf. Mark 9:1; 13:28-32).

4. The Son of Man comes *in* and *with* clouds (Parousia redefined).

But I know what the reader may be thinking: what about Mark 13:24-27? Isn't this a clear description of the coming of the Son of Man, Jesus Christ, to earth at the end of times? And the answer is yes and no. The tradition preserved by Mark is based on Daniel 7:13-14, but it is already reinterpreted through the lenses of the traditions found in the books of 1 Enoch and 4 Ezra, where the Son of Man becomes an individual who comes to earth to establish the messianic kingdom. Mark, or the tradition he is utilizing, changes the Danielic quote to make it read as if the son of man comes down to earth "in clouds" (ἐν) instead of "with clouds" (μετὰ) as is the case in Daniel.[32] So Mark does include a tradition that seems to speak clearly about the coming of the Son of Man to earth.

But the problem is that Mark's narrative strategy deconstructs this reading because what is missing is that moment that makes it possible for Jesus to return to earth, namely, the ascension. Thus, even though the coming of the Son of Man is announced, it does not necessarily mean that it would be *to earth* but, as in Daniel, *to God*, to receive the kingdom. I am suggesting that it is plausible that Mark understood this as being preannounced at the transfiguration and actually happening at the resurrection. By virtue of his resurrection, Jesus as the Son of Man is given power and authority in a representative way, but the kingdom is not yet given to the people of the Son of Man until he meets them in Galilee, after the resurrection. That moment would mark the glorification of the Son of Man together with his people. It is the glory that Daniel 7:14 talks about, which is manifested by the fact that the greatness of all the kingdoms of the earth is transferred to the people of the holy ones of the Most High, who thereafter are served and obeyed by all (Dan 7:27).

Mark plays with this symbolism but modifies it too, for it is the Son of Man and his people who serve the nations, not the other way around. But this service is not subservient, and therefore oppressive, but liberating. It is the kind of service that Jesus rendered during his ministry, as he went about releasing people from the limitations imposed on them by an evil system that preyed on them.

Following this line of thought, let us turn to 14:62. In this passage, Jesus answers the high priest's question: "Are you the Messiah, the Son of the Blessed One?" with "You said that I am."[33] And he adds right away: "And you will see the Son of Man seated at the right hand of Power, and coming with the clouds of heaven." This is the same quote from Daniel 7:13-14 that had been used in 13:26 except that this time the Son of Man is seated

---

32. See my discussion of Perrin's treatment of this idea in *Parousia and Its Rereadings*, 180-81.

33. The MSS evidence for this reading is as follows: θ ƒ 13 565.700 pc.

The Son of Man

at the right hand of God (cf. Ps 110:1) and comes "with" (μετὰ) the clouds of heaven! From this use of Hebrew Scripture passages by Mark, who is not only trying to preserve some authentic oral traditions about Jesus but also to construct a Christology suitable to his audience, we can surmise the following: Jesus is affirming his role as Son of Man, the Human One, the representative of God's suffering people. He anticipates his own vindication as well as that of his followers. This is described as sitting at the right hand of the Power to whom he will come with the clouds, i.e., through the resurrection and posterior glorification[34] in Galilee when the kingdom would be given to him and his people.

The historical moment that Mark's community is living would point at this understanding of the kingdom. They should disregard the messianic claims of the revolutionaries, who were trying to establish God's reign by force, and rather look forward to the day, which may be coming soon, when Jesus, the risen Son of Man, would receive from God power to rule and would share it with his co-disciples. This is the moment when the disciples, who lost their lives for the sake of Jesus and the gospel (the message of the kingdom), will save it. At that moment, their vindication will take place. To say more than this would be to import insights from other gospels or from other authors, like Paul. We contend that this reading is especially warranted by Mark, although there are elements for a similar reading in the other gospels.

That Mark does not preserve an ascension tradition may be due to the fact that this is the first of the canonical gospels to be written. Paul, who wrote about the same time, from 49/50 to 66 CE, speaks about the resurrection of Christ, but not about the ascension. In 1 Corinthians 15, he speaks of Jesus as being raised and calls him the man of heaven as opposed to Adam, the man of dust. This, plus Paul's own experiences with the risen Christ, presupposes that Jesus is presently in heaven from where he will return at the end of time (cf. Phil 2:3–11; 1 Thess 1:10; 4:16).

But there is no systematic development of the idea of the ascension as in Luke. Paul does not preserve any tradition that talks about Jesus going up to heaven. As a matter of fact, when he quotes traditional material, as in 1 Corinthians 15:3–7, he mentions Jesus' atoning death, his resurrection, and

---

34. Malina explains glory and glorification as terms that belong to the honor and shame code. He affirms for example that "'glory' is bestowed honor that is publicly displayed for all to see." In this sense, the glorification of the Son of Man and his people in Galilee would be an earthly event witnessed by everyone. Malina and Rohrbaugh, *Synoptic Gospels*, 151.

his post-resurrection appearances but says nothing about the ascension. We suggest the possibility that the ascension tradition developed when the church felt that the giving of power and dominion to God's people had become a non-event and, therefore, needed to explain it theologically. The best way out of this conundrum was to affirm that Jesus had been taken up to heaven from where he would eventually return to restore all things, that is, to establish God's kingdom and to vindicate the faithful. We see this developed especially in Luke-Acts (Luke 24:50–53; Acts 1:6–11), which was written much later than either Paul or Mark.

This reading of the text assumes that the interpretation of the Son of Man as an eschatological redeemer figure was not the first or the only one present in the early church. Rather, this interpretation may betray a process of theologizing and rationalization due to the lack of fulfillment of the promise of the vindication of God's suffering people. In other words, when the giving of power and dominion to the people of the Son of Man, Jesus, did not happen, the early Christian communities had to come up with a different scenario. Therefore they resorted to an individualistic reading of the Danielic son of man passages viewed through the lenses of the book of 1 Enoch and 4 Ezra. Then they created the traditions of the ascension of the Son of Man to heaven from which he would return in due time to restore all things (cf. Acts 1:6–11).

5. The convergence of the discipleship and Son of Man motifs in Mark's narrative.

There are at least three places where these two motifs converge in Mark: 2:10, 28; 8:34–38 and 16:7 (cf. 13:26; 14:28, 62). The first instance is Mark 2:10 and 28, where authority to forgive sins and authority over the Sabbath is given to the Son of Man, Jesus, who as the model disciple represents God's people. For Mark, this is his community. They are the people of the Son of Man who now, after Jesus' death and resurrection, are responsible for carrying on the redemptive task of healing, exorcising, forgiving, and reinterpreting the law in liberating and life-affirming ways.

The second instance is Mark 8:34–38: Jesus' call to suffering discipleship, which is really a call to imitate him, the Son of Man (see chapter 3). As the Son of Man, he embodies discipleship, for he came to serve and not to be served, and to give his life as a ransom for many (10:45). As the community follows him, they too become instruments of redemption for the many (see chapter 6). In the specific context in which the Markan community

The Son of Man

found itself, most probably the Jewish revolt of 66–70 CE, this meant having to face the high cost of not aligning themselves with the revolutionaries or with the Romans, and being willing to sacrifice themselves in order to save others. Following the logic of the martyrdom theology born during the Maccabean period, the so-called expiatory power of martyrdom,[35] the community becomes a source of redemption for the rest of the people of Israel.

The third instance is Mark 16:7 (see also 13:26; 14:28, 62). In these passages, the expressions ὄφεσθε and ὄφονται are used. This is Parousia language. The verb has been used by the evangelist to refer to the coming of the Son of Man in 13:26 and 14:62. Now he uses it in connection with the appearing of Jesus to the disciples in Galilee. The message is clear: the risen Lord, the Son of Man, will join the community of disciples as an abiding presence and power, reissuing the mission again from Galilee. It will be a presence—another meaning of the word παρουσία—that will be experienced and witnessed by all (13:26; 14:28).[36]

The advantage of this interpretation is that while it maintains the eschatological nature of God's kingdom, it does not necessitate a coming of Jesus at the Parousia to gather the elect, understood as those who believed in Christ. But if Jesus is the representative of God's suffering people on earth, that is, all those who suffer under the oppressive forces that oppose God's kingdom, and if his resurrection announces beforehand the final vindication of the faithful, this last event will happen when God brings the kingdom and the new age starts. Mark may have thought that this was going to happen in the future, although not as soon as Paul maintained, and so in his writing he does not include the ascension of Jesus.

Jesus is still around, as the risen one who symbolizes the vindication of the disciples of the kingdom, of all who suffered for the sake of the gospel. His presence in Galilee points at a moment of truth that, according to the evangelist, will soon unfold as God's final liberating act. Given the suffering that the community is probably facing, this idea constitutes a true theodicy.

---

35. 1 Macc 6:44; 4 Macc 17:20–22.

36. The narrative fulfills the purpose of historicizing the community's spiritual experience of the risen Christ. "How is it that we are sensing in our midst the presence of the risen Lord?" a member of the community would ask. And Mark would answer: "Because he promised he would go ahead of the disciples to Galilee. It's all here, in the story." So the narrative of Jesus meeting the disciples in Galilee becomes an etiology for the experience of the risen Lord in the community.

Conclusion: The Sociological Reason for Mark's Christology

Mark is telling his community who this Jesus they believe in is. He is constructing a Christology. To them, says Mark, Jesus is not the Son of God, for this is how the demons relate to him.[37] He is not the Christ either, that is, the Messiah from Davidic lineage, for this is the way some people saw him during his ministry, and Jesus discouraged them. And now there are some people in the community who still want to see him through these lenses, and Mark is trying to discourage them also. For Mark, Jesus was and is the Son of Man, the Human one. In developing this role, he is using a corporate idea similar to the one found in Daniel 7. Jesus is the representative of the community. Whatever he did, the community is also to do. Whatever happened to him will also happen to the community. And the reason for this is that, as the Son of Man, Jesus best exemplifies discipleship in the kingdom. His fellow disciples will not only follow him while he is still on earth, but also they will share his sufferings, death, resurrection, and vindication at the moment when he, as the Human one, receives the kingdom from God and establishes it on earth.

Since, in the Gospel of Mark, Jesus never ascends to heaven, this can only mean that he is still around, spiritually alive in the midst of the community. Surely enough, the risen Christ in chapter 16 issues a command to his disciples through the young man at the empty tomb saying: "Meet me in Galilee." He does not tell them: "Wait for me." He tells them: "Come and see me in Galilee." The difference between these two ideas is enormous, and it creates two very different types of communities: one that awaits Jesus from heaven while consolidating itself socially and theologically; the other that follows and commits itself to ministry to the world. I am suggesting here that Mark's Christology creates the latter type of community. This Christology is especially granted by the gospel's ending, which, in Myers' words, is "the hardest ending of all: not tragedy, not victory, but an unending challenge to follow anew. Because that means we must respond."[38]

I contend that, to many people today, this understanding of Jesus as disciple of the kingdom is more congenial and more practical. Perhaps the

---

37. Interestingly enough, in 15:39, the centurion at the foot of the cross, more than representing the Gentiles' belief in Jesus as savior, is expressing the demons' opinion of Jesus as enemy!

38. Myers, *Binding the Strong Man*, 401.

word is not practical but realistic. "That's what I preach!" said a minister friend of mine who used to be one of my students. I also heard a believer say in my congregation: "This speaks to my reality." And she continued: "I can't intellectually manage the Trinity, but I can manage this idea of Jesus as the model for discipleship, which we try to implement, empowered by the Holy Spirit, in order to announce God's kingdom."

Such an understanding of Jesus as disciple of the kingdom does away with gender, class, ethnic, and cultural distinctions for discipleship, and is defined as an egalitarian, non-hierarchical praxis into which we are *all* called. The Human one, as a collective symbol for all of God's people, sets the bar high: he rejected the titles his contemporaries wanted to ascribe to him—Messiah, Son of God, Son of David, and King of the Jews, all of which were heavily influenced by a male and hierarchical view of the world—and chose to identify himself as the son of humanity. He rejected nationalistic and metaphysical titles in favor of a more corporate, popular self-designation. He chose to be a disciple of God and the kingdom, not God's representative on earth. He represented God's people, not the Godhead. He was fully human. He showed this in many ways: he made mistakes, he knew fear, he had physical needs, he accepted the care of others, especially the women of the group, he changed his mind, etc.

We made him fully divine by saying that, if in the incarnation God had become fully human, then it is possible for a human being, Jesus, to become fully immersed in the divine. But he never said that. He only pointed at God and the kingdom and called us to follow him as co-disciples into the Galilees of our world. It is a fairly simple call that the church has obscured and complicated by superimposing on it aspirations of power and selfish and exclusive interpretations of what it means to be the people of God. Jesus as disciple of the kingdom and our representative reminds us that the only responsibility we have is to be faithful to our call and to follow him as co-disciples in the construction of God's reign on earth. I believe that when we do that we will discover the true meaning of *ekklesia*.

5

The "Other" Community behind the Gospel of Mark

IN THIS CHAPTER, I WILL try to show how a different community from the one that wrote the first Mark left its Christological imprint on the gospel by adding to chapter 16 several verses that are usually known as the "long ending." This long ending, comprised of verses 9–20 of chapter 16, has been subject to the merciless work of text criticism, which has deemed it to be unauthentic.[1] This section is not an original piece of the gospel, text critics say. It was added during the second century, many years after the original Mark was finished, with the purpose of bringing Mark's shocking end into harmony with the rest of the canonical gospels.

Many of us, students of the biblical text, have accepted these conclusions uncritically. We think, since there is plenty of evidence for the short ending of Mark, that this must be the real one. We are convinced that this ending agrees very much with the gospel's general tenor.[2] True as this may be, I still feel compelled to ask: What makes an ending original? Who decides what is original, and what is not? Is it possible that there is more than one original ending; that is, that for some second-century believers, the long ending was *the* original ending?[3] Furthermore, I would ask, what may have been the reason for this addition? What sort of community would have

---

1. See Hengel, *Studies in the Gospel of Mark*, 168n47.
2. For a different take on Mark's end, see Witherington, *Gospel of Mark*, 49–51.
3. Recent scholarship has suggested the strong possibility that the Gospel of Mark was meant to be a script, or "libretto," for an oral performance of Jesus story and that each of them would vary according to the circumstances of the performer. If that is the case, then, one can argue that the long ending of Mark represents one of those performances. Horsley, *Hearing the Whole Story*, 67.

been interested in hearing the message conveyed by verses 9–20? Was that community in continuity or at odds with the group that produced the first version of Mark? Did that community have a Christological agenda that the longer end of the gospel advanced? And if so, has this addition changed the meaning of the gospel message as it is presented in the short version? These questions will guide our investigation in the following pages. My hope is to find a way to redeem this long (forgotten)[4] end and bring it back into the conversation concerning Markan studies,[5] especially as it may provide another layer to the argument I am making in this book—namely, that Christology is a construct that betrays a community's self understanding as it tries to cope with the realities of the post-resurrection era, something that is true not only for the first century but also for the twenty first.

The Ending of Mark

Manuscript Evidence

According to Bruce Metzger,[6] there are four endings to the Gospel of Mark: the short ending, verse 8; the intermediate ending, between verse 8 and verse 9; the long ending, verses 9–20; and the long ending expanded with an addition after verse 14. For the purpose of this chapter, I will concentrate only on the long ending.

Verses 9–20 are missing in the two earliest codices, Sinaiticus (ℵ) and Vaticanus (B), both from the fourth century, and in many early manuscripts. On the other hand, this long ending is present in a great number of witnesses, including many of the minuscules and most of the Old Latin

---

4. Brevard S. Childs suggests that the importance of the long ending has been usually disregarded by modern critical scholarship. Childs, *New Testament as Canon*, 94.

5. William R. Farmer gives five reasons for the existence of the long ending without opting for any of them. They are: (a) after having finished the gospel at 16:8, the evangelist himself writes verses 9–20; (b) the author of Mark uses traditional materials, which he then redacts and incorporates into his gospel; (c) verses 9–20 already existed in that form before the evangelist wrote the gospel; he utilized them with little or no modification; (d) the long ending was written by a late author who consciously tried to imitate certain characteristics of Mark's vocabulary and syntax while at the same time developing his own conceptual usage of certain terms; and (e) verses 9–20 represent a late composition having no linguistic or conceptual relationship with the rest of the gospel. Farmer, *Last Twelve Verses of Mark*, 107–9.

6. Metzger, *Text of the New Testament*, 226.

Jesus, Disciple of the Kingdom

witnesses to the gospels, as well as the Coptic and Syriac.[7] In some MSS, it occurs after the short ending with indications that this section has been added later. Eusebius and Jerome, in the fourth century, believed the gospel ended with verse 8, since all the Greek MSS known to them lacked the long ending. Nevertheless, Irenaeus, who was writing in 180 CE, assumes verses 9–20 to have been penned by Mark, and Tatian, a disciple of Justin Martyr, includes the long ending in his *Diatessaron* (circa 140 CE). This proves that these verses were added very early.

The most common solution to this riddle has been that the author or authors of verses 9–20, aware of the existence of the other gospels, wrote this section at the beginning of the second century. There is one MSS from the tenth century that attributes these verses to the elder Aristion, who lived circa 100 CE, a contemporary of Papias and allegedly a disciple of John the Apostle, but this tradition is not very reliable.[8]

Internal Evidence

The long ending of Mark uses a vocabulary that does not belong with the rest of the work. In this regard, Danove asserts:

> These twelve verses include sixteen examples of words not found in 1:1—16:8, five examples of words which appear earlier but are used in a unique sense, and four unique phrases. Though some divergence in vocabulary and usage may be explained by the difference in the subject matter under consideration, on the whole this study indicates significant problems concerning the continuity between 1:1—16:8 and 16:9–20.[9]

There are also considerations of style. Verse 9 follows abruptly after verse 8, with the introduction of Mary Magdalene as a new character in the story without recognizing that she had been mentioned a few verses before. Also, there is a lack of transition in the syntax. In verse 8, the subject of the verb ἐφοβοῦντο is the women. Suddenly, we are told ἀναστὰς δὲ (having risen), which is a clear reference to Jesus. All of this, says Metzger, is sufficient evidence to prove that this section is of a secondary nature.[10]

---

7. Metzger, *Text of the New Testament*, 227. See also Danove, *End of Mark's Story*, 120–21.

8. Hooker, *Mark*, 389; Metzger, *Text of the New Testament*, 227.

9. Danove, *End of Mark's Story*, 121.

10. Metzger, *Text of the New Testament*, 227.

The "Other" Community behind the Gospel of Mark

Reason for Addition

The long ending is a *pastiche* of passages from Matthew, Luke, John, and Acts.

16:9–11	John 20:11–18; Luke 8:2; 24:11
16:12–13	Luke 24:13–35
16:14	Luke 24:36–43; John 20:26
16:15–17	Matt 28:18–20; Luke 24:47, 48; Acts 2:4, 43; 5:12; 8:6; 10:46; 19:6
16:18	Acts 28:3–6
16:19	Luke 24:50, 51; Acts 1:9–11
16:20	Acts 14:31

According to Edward Schweizer, all of the signs mentioned in verse 17 are found in Acts (2:1ff.; 3:1ff.; 9:32ff.; 14:8ff.; 16:16ff.; 19:13ff.; 28:3ff.), except the drinking of poison without harm. But something like that is reported by Papias (130–140 CE), who says that someone by the name of Justus Barsabbas (cf. Acts 1:23) drank a poisonous potion and did not die. This account appears in Eusebius, *Church Fathers* III 39:9. He also believes that the fact that these charismatic gifts are promised to all believers betrays a time when the church was not yet institutionalized, but rather showed a high degree of flexibility.[11]

Obviously, the editors/authors of verses 9–20 felt that the abrupt ending of Mark was not fitting as the conclusion of Jesus' story. Consequently, efforts were made to bring the end of Mark into theological harmony with the other gospels. This was done in spite of the fact that consensus was not reached, and it has not been reached,[12] as to the question of whether Mark really ended his gospel at verse 8 or if the real ending was lost.[13] At any rate, the general feeling was that something had to be done. And they did.

Rather that proposing a single, lonely author as responsible for the addition, I prefer to imagine a community behind it. That is, that even if these verses are the work of a single scribe, he is responding to the needs of a specific community, his own. I would suggest that the community to which this text was targeted was one that emphasized the gifts of the Spirit

---

11. Schweizer, *Good News*, 377–78.

12. The modern discussion about Mark's ending continues. See Black, *Perspective*.

13. This is Childs' opinion. He also says that this being the case, how this happened is irrelevant. The important thing is that the original ending does not exist anymore. Childs, *New Testament as Canon*, 94.

as a way of counterbalancing, perhaps, an initial disappointment with the delay of the Parousia. These people believed that the risen Lord was present in their midst and this made for a different understanding of eschatology.

Our editor worked with a text of Mark that finished at 16:8 and constituted the founding document of a primitive Markan community that lived through the events of the Jewish revolt of 66–70 CE,[14] and which anticipated or witnessed the destruction of the temple by the Romans in 70 CE. This group of believers lived in a time of heightened apocalyptic expectations brought about by the revolutionary movements that operated throughout Palestine. As well, they had a communal sense of eschatological immediacy prompted by their understanding of the role of the preaching to the Gentiles in the timetable of the end. In other words, they probably assumed that the acceptance of the gospel by the nations was one of the final signs before the end. This they surmised from passages such as Mark 13:10, etc.

Already the original author of Mark had to make adjustments to the eschatological expectation of his community, given especially the increasing political pressure from the Jewish revolutionaries, the Zealots, coupled with the extreme apocalypticism of some people inside the church. He clearly affirmed that the task of the church at that historical juncture was to continue the mission initiated by Jesus,[15] a mission that included the nations as recipients of the good news, until the Son of Man, following the Danielic vision, would be given the kingdom from the hands of the Ancient of Days. The women that came to the tomb early on the first day of the week received the mandate to go to Galilee to meet the Risen Christ who, for Mark, was the Son of Man. The fear that these early disciples experienced may have been a combination of awe, real fear for their lives as followers of a crucified, but now risen-rebel (how do you explain that to the Romans who did not believe in resurrection?), and the realization that perhaps the time of the eschatological coming of the Son of Man was fast approaching. These three factors—an experience of the numinous, the threat of imperial police repression, and the imminent end of their world—were enough to instill fear in the bravest of human beings. On this note, the short ending of Mark finishes.[16]

14. For a date during the Jewish war, see Vena, "La expectativa escatológica," 85–101.

15. It is difficult to know if Jesus had the Gentiles in mind from the very beginning, or if this was a progressive awareness. His encounter with the Syrophoenician woman in chapter 7 seems to suggest that, up to that point, the Gentiles were not part of his mission. This woman, then, needs to be given full credit for making Jesus change his mind.

16. To see how this ending may have obeyed rhetorical practices of the time, see Bryan, *Preface to Mark*, 120–21.

The "Other" Community behind the Gospel of Mark

THE FUNCTION OF THE LONG ENDING OF MARK

The short ending of Mark came to be regarded as problematic already by Matthew and Luke, who freely added to it when incorporating their versions of the Resurrection appearances. In a similar vein, although perhaps unaware of the existence of Mark, John wrote his own conclusion to Jesus' story. Therefore, and as Metzger has suggested, the New Testament contains not four, but five accounts of the post-resurrection events: Mark's short ending; Mark's long, canonical ending; Matthew's ending; Luke's ending and John's ending.[17] The question we want to ask now is not historical, but rhetorical and theological: what was the function of the long ending in the gospel as a whole? What kind of Christology did it convey? And what sort of community did it betray?

Rhetorical Inclusio

Even if we acknowledge the secondary nature of the long ending, we have to recognize that this was not done without attention being given to the gospel as a whole. The author is consciously making additions to an already-existing document or script of the story. He is completing the document. His is a rereading, a final version of Jesus' story, or, in the words of Robert Fowler, a "resisting reading."[18] Thus, the long ending of Mark serves as a bookend to the gospel, a rhetorical *inclusio* to the beginning of Jesus' ministry in chapter 1. We suggest the following structure, which constitutes a sort of diptych:

Mark 1:1–15	Mark 16:9–20
A pre-Easter beginning (v. 1)	A post-Easter beginning (v. 9a)
John the Baptist's proclamation is received with demonstrations of repentance (vv. 2–8)	Mary Magdalene's announcement is received with unbelief (vv. 9b–13)
Jesus' baptism as preparation for ministry (v. 9)	Believers' baptism as preparation for worldwide mission (vv. 14–16)

---

17. Metzger, *Text of the New Testament*, 229.

18. A resisting reading is defined as a reading against the grain of a given document. Fowler takes this concept from feminist writer Judith Fetterley. Fowler, *Mark and Method*, 73, 75n30, and 79.

Jesus, Disciple of the Kingdom

Mark 1:1–15	Mark 16:9–20
Holy Spirit confirms Jesus' call (vv. 10–11)	Signs confirm believers' call (vv. 17–18)
Jesus tempted in the wilderness (vv. 12–13)	Jesus enthroned in heaven (v. 19)
Jesus starts proclaiming the good news in Galilee (repent/baptize and believe) (vv. 14–15)	Disciples start proclaiming the good news everywhere (believe and be baptized; vv. 16, 20)

Beyond this symmetry, there is another parallelism between Jesus' ministry and the disciples' ministry, this time between 1:21–28, 32–34, and 16:17–18:

- We are told in 1:21–28 and 32–34 that many unclean spirits and demons (δαιμόνια) were cast out by Jesus. Similarly those who believe will cast out demons (δαιμόνια) in Jesus' name (16:17).
- While Jesus delivers a new (καινή) teaching in 1:27, the believers will speak in new (καιναῖς) tongues (16:17b).
- Finally, as Peter's mother-in-law is healed, Jesus "took her by the hand (χειρός) (1:29–31). In the same fashion, the missionaries of the post-resurrection era "will lay their hands (χεῖρας) on the sick," and they will recover (16:18b).[19]

The theological rationale behind this editorial addition is clear: in the same way as Jesus was empowered by the Holy Spirit to carry out a ministry of proclamation that was legitimized by the deeds of compassion that accompanied it, so also the disciples are being empowered by the Risen Christ to engage in a worldwide mission legitimized by the miraculous signs that accompany it.

Theological Harmonization

The long ending serves also the purpose of bringing the whole gospel into theological harmony with the rest of the canon. As I already mentioned, it is very clear that the author or authors of this section borrowed freely from the other gospels and Acts. Part of this harmonization is to address the issue of "unbelief" in the post-Easter community (the words πιστεύω

---

19. Bas van Iersel, *Reading Mark*, 216, has called attention to the similarities between this section and the rest of the gospel. He finds similar language in 6:5 and 6:13.

and ἀπιστία appear seven times: 16:11, 13, 14[2], 16[2], and 17). However, there is nothing in the short ending of Mark that suggests unbelief. The idea is more one of fear. But one can be fearful and still believe or, even better, one can be fearful because one believes! One could even argue that the fear of the women was produced by their belief that the *eschaton* had been set in motion with the resurrection of Jesus. By the same token, one could argue that the community that produced the long ending, as well as the communities that were responsible for similar accounts in Matthew, Luke, and John, were really dealing with a lack of belief produced in part by the physical absence of the historical Jesus and the delay of the Parousia. They needed to be reassured of Christ's presence in their midst as the Risen Lord, or the enthroned one of 16:19–20 (cf. Phil 2:5–11; Rev 1:12–20), precisely because the *eschaton* had not happened as promised. Emphasis on belief was necessary, because people were perhaps leaving the community in disappointment. In fact, belief needed to be supplemented with baptism, a rite that would ensure proper membership in the community and the assurance of the constant presence of the Enthroned One among them. The first version of Mark would encourage believers by saying that "the one who endures to the end will be saved" (13:13). That was good for a time, when the end was believed to be in sight, but now that the Parousia had been removed indefinitely from their eschatological horizon, another kind of encouragement was needed. It is the presence of the Risen Christ that is promised now and the assurance that the Lord Jesus, although enthroned in heaven (16:19), is working with them (συνεργοῦντος) and confirming their ministry through the signs described in 16:17–18, as they carry out the message of the good news. Which brings us to the next issue: has the meaning of the proclamation of the gospel changed in the addition to Mark?

The Meaning of the Preaching of the Gospel in the Enlarged Mark

A Non-canonical Structure

There are eight references to the preaching of the gospel or to simply preaching in the Markan text that includes 16:9–20. Four of them refer to the preaching during Jesus' earthly ministry and four to the preaching of the post-Easter Christian community. There seems to be a thematic correspondence between the first four and the last four occurrences, which would point at the redactional work of a late editor, whose intention was to reflect theologically on the implications of the gospel for his community. This rereading of the Markan text was prompted by some specific issues that had arisen among his audience as they were faced with the task of being disciples of Jesus Christ in a time of profound political and social changes, a time when traditional expectations were being challenged and a new consciousness of being a community of believers in the Jewish Messiah in the Greco-Roman world was slowly emerging.

There seems to be a chiastic structure that unfolds as follows:

a. Jesus comes to Galilee preaching the gospel of God (1:14)
   b. Jesus reaffirms his mission to preach (the gospel) (1:38, 39)
      c. Jesus chooses twelve disciples to be sent out to preach (3:14)
         d. Jesus sends the Twelve and they begin to preach (6:7, 12)
a'. Jesus affirms the divine necessity to preach the gospel to all nations (13:10, δεῖ)
   b'. Jesus reaffirms the worldwide scope of the preaching of the gospel (14:9)
      c'. Jesus sends the eleven disciples to preach the gospel to all creation (16:15)
         d'. The disciples go out and preach everywhere (16:20)

The relationship between abcd and a'b'c'd' seems to be as follows:

a. The preaching of the gospel is affirmed as an activity that follows Jesus' coming to Galilee (1:7, 9, 14)

a'. The preaching of the gospel to all nations is affirmed as an apostolic activity that precedes the eschatological coming of the Son of Man (13:10). The disciples continue Jesus' ministry of proclamation, which is sandwiched between two comings (ἔρχομαι) of Jesus: one *to* Galilee as the son of a carpenter (1:14; 6:3), the other *from* heaven as the Son of Man (13:26–27).

b. The centrality of the preaching of the gospel in Jesus' ministry in Galilee is reaffirmed.

b'. The universal scope of the preaching of the gospel is reaffirmed.

c. The Twelve are chosen to preach the gospel to the surrounding villages: a mission limited in time (cf. Mark 6:30) and local in nature.

c'. The eleven receive the commission to preach to the whole creation: a mission only limited by the *eschaton* and universal in scope.

d. The disciples go out and preach in the region (καὶ ἐξελθόντες ἐκήρυξαν).

d'. The disciples go out and preach everywhere (ἐκεῖνοι δὲ ἐξελθόντες ἐκήρυξαν πανταχοῦ).

This diptych may reflect how the final editor understood the pre and post-Easter preaching. In abcd, contained in chapters 1–12, the ministry of the good news extends itself from Galilee to Jerusalem. It reflects Jesus' own understanding of his mission and that of his disciples: it was a local mission, limited to Palestine, which would finish sometime after his passion, death, and resurrection at the Parousia of the Son of Man in Galilee. In a'b'c'd', contained in chapters 13–16, the preaching of the good news is extended to the whole world and includes all the nations: it becomes universal. It reflects the understanding of the mission that the early church developed as a reaction to the delay of the Parousia and the unprecedented fact of Gentiles coming to be part of the people of God.

The extended Gospel of Mark seems to be saying that the mission of the church in the post-Easter era (a'b'c'd') is a continuation but also an adaptation of the mission of the earthly Jesus and his disciples (abcd). This mission is still a divine imperative (cf. 1:14, τὸ εὐαγγέλιον τοῦ Θεοῦ and 13:10, δεῖ, which connotes divine necessity) that needs to be carried out at this time as a prelude (13:10, πρῶτον) to the eschatological end. The suggested structure, abcd and a'b'c'd', is canonical and does not necessarily belong to the original text of Mark (or the Markan *Vorlage*). As we have already pointed out, a number of late redactors reworked the gospel theologically, adding verses 9–20. This would certainly support the hypothesis, developed in another work,[20] that when the Parousia did not happen as expected, some of the later Christian communities gradually stopped thinking eschatologically and began to develop a missionary consciousness. Verses 9–20 paint the picture of a church that is immersed in the work of proclamation without any obvious concern for the *eschaton*. Salvation is not related to the coming of the Son of Man from heaven, but to the act of believing and being baptized (cf. 16:16). This description agrees more with a Lucan or Johannine understanding of history than with Mark's ambivalent posture towards the end-times. The signs (σημεῖα) that in 13:4ff were related to the end times, are now related to the believers' ministry of proclamation (16:17, 20). Whereas in chapter 13, the signs are to be regarded as landmarks to the Parousia, itself the last sign before the *eschaton*, in chapter 16 they are

---

20. Vena, *Parousia and Its Rereadings*.

understood as divine confirmations for the work of the believers: they are instruments of evangelization and proof of the Risen Christ's presence among the believers (16:20). All of this points at a conscious rethinking and reworking of the eschatological timetable.

In this section, as in chapter 13,[21] the proclamation of the gospel occupies a central position. John Breck has shown the basic chiastic structure of these verses.[22] The difference with chapter 13, though, seems to be that, whereas in 13:10 the proclamation of the gospel to all nations is seen as a prelude to the Parousia, as an interim activity of the believers, in 16:15, it is regarded as the central activity of the post-Easter community aided by the Risen Lord through miraculous signs. There is no mention of the end times. Eschatology has been modified. Salvation and condemnation happen now, in the act of believing or not believing,[23] even though one may assume that the final realization of this status lies in the future, due to the fact that "the element of time . . . is more important in the future than in other tenses."[24] But the future tense in Greek can also convey the idea of punctiliar action. At any rate, the main emphasis of the future passive here (σωθήσεται, κατακριθήσεται) is on God's action. It is God who will save or condemn.

A Non-apocalyptic Praxis

In the pre-Easter situation, the preaching of the gospel anticipates the coming of the Son of Man from heaven. In the post-Easter situation, the preaching of the gospel follows the Risen Christ's commissioning of the disciples and points at the co-mission of the church and the enthroned Lord. There is no indication that this proclamation anticipates the Parousia. Therefore, the long ending of Mark serves the purpose of legitimating the praxis of a non-apocalyptic group. This community is not a fearful community that avoids talking about the events that transpired at Easter because they sense that the final days are upon them, but rather a doubting community that therefore has to be commissioned by the Risen Christ to preach the gospel

---

21. See my treatment of the centrality of the proclamation of the gospel in Mark 13 in *Parousia and Its Rereadings*, 202–4.

22. Breck, *Shape of Biblical Language*, 164.

23. Something similar happens in the Gospel of John: belief or the lack of it is the final eschatological determinant in someone's eternal destiny.

24. Brooks and Winbery, *Syntax*, 86–87.

to the whole of creation (cf. 13:10 and 14:9; also Matt 28:17, where the element of doubt is clearly mentioned). This is not a fearful community, but a skeptical one. Because of their disbelief, they have to be promised the continuous presence of the Enthroned Christ. Thus, they are sent to heal the sick, cast out demons, and manifest the fruits of the Spirit. They are promised that they will experience freedom, as well as the divine confirmation of their ministry, in the act of proclamation. They are not paralyzed by fear, but by incredulity and, therefore, need to be given encouragement by means of a tangible promise. Thus the function of the σεμεῖα (signs) is that of an observable phenomena that will constitute the objective proof of the presence of Christ in their midst.

It is very interesting to notice how the long ending avoids the word "disciple" when referring to Jesus' followers. In 16:7, the young man had told the women to "tell his disciples and Peter that he is going ahead of you to Galilee." In 16:10, Mary Magdalene "went out and told those who had been with him." Why not, for the sake of continuity, use the same expression as in 16:7, "his disciples and Peter?" We are not sure, but this avoidance of the term "disciple" is puzzling and continues throughout the section: "two of them" (v. 12), "the rest" (v. 13), "the eleven" (v. 14), "those who believe" (v. 17), "them" (vv. 19, 20). In a similar fashion, Paul avoids the term "disciple" when referring to himself or to the believers (see discussion in chapter 1). We concluded in that chapter that the reason for this avoidance is that, for Paul, Jesus was the Risen Christ, the Lord of the universe, who was coming to judge the world at the Parousia, which in his view was about to occur. He did not concentrate on Jesus' teachings, which would have necessitated disciples to preserve and transmit them, but on the significance of his death and resurrection, which needed apostles to proclaim it and people to believe in it. Thus, the terms he used addressed this reality: "saints," "the called," "the faithful," "co-workers" and, especially in 1 Thessalonians, "believers" (1 Thess 1:7; 2:10, 13). Do we have a similar situation here in the extended, longer ending of Mark? That is, for this community, the main task was to proclaim the gospel as the offer of salvation and eternal life through the belief in the atoning sacrifice of Christ on the cross, a very Pauline understanding of Jesus ministry *vis-à-vis* a Synoptic understanding of it. For one thing, there is an obvious emphasis on believing. As we said above, the expression appears seven times in verses 9–20, which may be pointing at a crisis of belief in the community that the writer/s is trying to address. There is also a connection with the Pauline tradition, not only in the use of the term "believers," but also in the reference to speaking in tongues and handling poisonous snakes (cf. Acts 2:4; 10:46; 28:3–5). And Jesus is described as the Risen Christ, assumed throughout the entire section with third-person personal pronouns and, at the end, as the Lord Jesus, an expression that never appears in Mark![25] On the other hand, "Lord Jesus" and "Lord Jesus Christ" appear countless times in Paul.

The other point of contact with the Pauline tradition is the concept of the Risen Christ "appearing" to people. As we know, Paul tells the Corinthians that Christ had "appeared" to a number of people, including himself (1 Cor 15:5–8). The verb Paul uses is ὁραω, which means, among other things, "to see," "to notice," "to become visible," "to appear."[26] In its passive form, ὤφθη, it implies a visionary event: he was seen by people. This we surmise by the fact that he tells the Corinthians that he was the last to whom the Risen Christ appeared, and we know that Paul had a visionary experience of Christ on the road to Damascus (Acts 9). Mark, on the other hand, uses two verbs, φαίνω (v. 9), which can mean "to appear," "to make one's appearance," "to show oneself" [27] and φανερόω (vv. 12, 14), which can mean "to show or reveal oneself," "to be revealed," "to appear to someone."[28] It is then clear that, whereas for Paul the appearances of the Risen Christ were visionary experiences, for the evangelist they were actual occurrences.

Therefore, we conclude that this addition reflects the work of a community that felt the need to harmonize the end of the gospel with the other gospels and with Paul's understanding of eschatology and mission, but not without first rereading it theologically. The Risen Christ is now enthroned in heaven, but his return is not promised, as in Acts 1:11, or expected very soon as in all of Paul's authentic letters, only assumed. But it is not even mentioned! In the meantime, the church is engaged in the work of proclamation, while the Risen Lord (or is it God?) "worked with them and confirmed the message by the signs that accompanied it" (Mark 16:20).

---

25. Perhaps the closest Mark gets to using this expression is in 11:3, when Jesus instructs his disciples to tell the owners of the colt he was to use in his entry to Jerusalem the "The Lord needs it and will send it back here immediately."

26. *BDAG*, 577–78.

27. *BDAG*, 851–52.

28. *BDAG*, 853.

THE SOCIAL POSITIONING OF THE TWO COMMUNITIES

The two communities represented by the short and the long ending were counter-cultural in their own way. The community of the short ending, by affirming the nearness of the *eschaton* while engaging in an "interim" evangelical preaching, was *eschatologically* counter-cultural. The apocalyptic proclamation of the coming of the Son of Man from heaven to usher in God's kingdom relativized and questioned the worldwide existence of the Roman Empire, as well as its presence in Palestine. The community of the short ending assured its members of the short-lived nature of the empire (cf. 13:31). They were to preach and live out the good news of the kingdom of God as a prelude to the final and cosmic appearance of the Son of Man (13:24-27).[29] The only engagement with the society of the time was one of announcing the presence of an alternative commonwealth on earth, which was characterized by suffering discipleship (8:34-35). In turn, this reality was going to give way to God's universal kingdom.[30] People were invited to be a part of this group of suffering chosen ones, the ἐκλεκτοί of 13:27, in watchful anticipation of that day (13:32).

The community that produced the long ending, by affirming the necessity to preach the message in a situation that would continue to be

---

29. Since the writing of the article that I am partially reproducing here, I have changed my mind as to the eschatological understanding of the Son of Man in Mark. As I hope to have demonstrated throughout this work, I now believe that Mark had a corporate understanding of the Danielic son of man. The fact that there is no ascension narrative in the short ending of Mark seems to suggest that the evangelist understood the beckoning of the disciples to Galilee as a call to continue the mission started by the historical Jesus, with the hopes that as they did that God was going to establish the kingdom promised in the Hebrew Scriptures. Mark's eschatology is not necessarily "apocalyptic," although it uses apocalyptic traditions such as the one found in Daniel 7, but his community lives on the verge of a soon-to-happen, God-driven eschatological event. In that sense, the community of the short ending differed from the one represented by the longer ending in how it faced the realities of life in the Greco-Roman world. For the former, the end of the Empire was near (13:28-32), perhaps within a generation. But for the latter, the end had been postponed by the ascension and enthronement of the Risen Christ. The community is then left to do the work of proclamation for an indefinite period of time (16:20). Obviously, the believers had experienced the disconfirmation of their eschatological expectation and had to come to terms with it.

30. I still maintain this idea, only that now the kingdom does not need a coming of the Son of Man from heaven because he is already present, as the Risen Christ, empowering the mission of the community. God will manifest God's kingdom through the Markan community, not through the cosmic coming of a divine messenger.

"in-this-world," was *ecclesiologically* counter-cultural. Salvation was attained within the community, through faith and baptism. These believers did not stress suffering for the sake of the gospel as their theological center,[31] but rather a victorious kind of living, free from the demonic powers of the age, possessing a new language that liberated them from the imposed *lingua franca* of the Roman Empire[32] and free from sickness and disease. These were three of the most prevalent forms of alienation in first-century Palestine—namely, the ever-present reality of Roman occupation that affected every aspect of a person's life, especially the economic and spiritual side of it; the burden of a language that carried with it the connotation of centuries of colonization; and the presence, especially among the poor, who did not have access to proper medical care, of all kinds of sicknesses and infectious diseases that made life unbearable. The expanded end of the gospel then offers to those who believe and are baptized the opportunity to be part of an alternative community on earth, where salvation is not only promised but actually lived out as liberation from political, economic, cultural, and physical oppression.

Finally, both communities offered an alternative in-group for those lost in the totalitarian globalization of the Greco-Roman culture with its militarily imposed *pax romana*. The first community, living perhaps the horrors of the war between the Jewish rebels and the Romans, found in the gospel the necessary encouragement to endure the harassment of both the Zealots and the imperial army, but also the consolation of a soon-to-happen vindication, especially when some of its members lost their lives as willing but involuntary martyrs (cf. Mark 8:34–37). The second community, removed from the war and its consequences, now saw life in the world with different eyes. Now it was time to coexist in a still-hostile world, one which did not seem to have arrived at its divinely decreed ending, at least not for the time being, for neither the establishment of God's kingdom on earth through the proclamation of the gospel, nor the Parousia of the heavenly Son of Man had yet happened. Rather the time had stretched toward an unforeseen future which, although still in God's hands, [33] allowed

---

31. See Vena, "Rhetorical and Theological Center."

32. Greek was a tool for colonization. All of the peoples that constituted the Roman Empire had to use it in order to relate to each other and to the central imperial administration. It was the language of domination. On the other hand, tongues were the language of the Spirit. It empowered believers and gave them a new identity. They were no longer subjects of the Roman Caesar, but of the Risen Christ.

33. Ancient societies were present-oriented, and reality meant only the experienced

The "Other" Community behind the Gospel of Mark

for the establishment of faith communities in which belief was confirmed by baptism. We have here the beginnings of the soon-to-appear Orthodox Church, where eschatology began to be displaced by ecclesiology.[34]

Mark's Christology in Historical Perspective

Christology is always grounded in historical realities. It changes when the context changes. It adapts to new circumstances. Any new Christology is always a rereading of a previous one. It builds on it more than it cancels it. It gives new life to communities, new perspectives, new hope. This is certainly the case with Mark, where it is possible to detect a Christological development as the Markan community went through different phases.

1. Mark understood the Son of Man as a corporate, collective symbol for the suffering people of God. In the gospel, these are those who have followed Jesus, risking their lives for the sake of the gospel. This group includes the Twelve and the rest of disciples and followers. During Mark's time, the members of his community were the ones who constituted God's suffering people, a suffering brought about by staying non-aligned in the face of the Jewish-Roman war. The evangelist believed that God would bring the kingdom in Galilee, where the disciples in the story are sent to meet the risen Christ (Mark 16). Galilee, being as it is the bedrock of the Zealot's revolution, provides the community with a paradoxical site for mission, where life lost will mean life saved.

2. Because of this belief, Mark had to adjust the eschatological expectation of the community by making room for the preaching of the gospel before the arrival of the kingdom, which he saw as the giving of power to the suffering people of God. In the story, Jesus' disciples are warned of future persecutions and harassment in the hands of both Jewish and Roman authorities (Mark 13). Therefore, they are the ones who, like

---

world and experienced time. There was no true past or true future as we understand it. There was only the present, the perceived world of actual experience, and what for us would be the future was simply the outcome of a given activity, the forthcoming. But there was also that which fell outside the horizon of the experienced world. This was imaginary time, which covered everything that did not exist in the present. Thus, for the early followers of Jesus, the kingdom of God was forthcoming (cf. Mark 1:14–15), but for the evangelists it was moved into imaginary time known only to God (cf. Mark 13:32; Matt 24:36). In the NT, we see how the forthcoming becomes future and the experienced becomes imaginary. Malina, *Social World*, 188–93.

34. See my argument in *Parousia and Its Rereadings*, 257–70.

the people of Israel in Daniel 7, are promised vindication. In that sense, they represent a (re)new(ed) Israel. In the referential world of the readers, these disciples correspond to the members of the Markan community who were called to proclaim Jesus Christ as the true Messiah/disciple of the kingdom *vis-à-vis* other claimants to that status, namely, the self-proclaimed messiahs of the Jewish revolt. The proclamation of the gospel had to precede the arrival of the kingdom with power and, in a sense, it conditioned that arrival, since this proclamation was a divine necessity that had to occur first (πρῶτον δεῖ).

3. What Mark expected never happened, so the next generation of believers in the Markan community had to add a new ending to the story, one that would harmonize with the way it was told in the other gospels, whose audiences also had experienced the disconfirmation of the Parousia. Therefore, Jesus is presented as an individual agent of God's salvation, who will return from heaven to exercise judgment upon the unbelievers and to rescue the elect. This coming down from heaven needs an ascension narrative, which the community appropriately provided (Mark 16:9–20).

We see in this progression how Christology adapts to the changing times. First, Mark suggested that the Parousia, announced by Paul and other early communities, was not as imminent as previously imagined. Nor was it going to happen in the *way* it was previously imagined. The final eschatological event, when God establishes the kingdom, would not move from heaven to earth, but rather from earth to heaven. The new age would have heaven-like qualities, because God would vindicate the righteous, dead and alive, ushering in the final resurrection and giving power to God's people still alive. Mark then inserted into this eschatological framework the concept of mission, the preaching of the gospel to the nations which, in order to be carried out, necessitated disciples, followers. He identified Jesus with the Son of Man of Daniel 7 and, accordingly, understood it as a collective symbol that, although standing for the whole community, served at the same time as a model for discipleship. Therefore, the identities of the Son of Man, Jesus, and the community are intertwined. Jesus is the Son of Man, but the community is also the Son of Man. Jesus represents them, and they share in his authority and power. And he expects the kingdom to be given to God's suffering people soon, in Galilee. Since this never happened, the next generation of believers had to go back to a more individualistic understanding of Jesus' role as Son of Man. They adjusted their eschatology one more time, making it coincide with the other gospels which, following the prevalent tendency of the early church, saw Jesus coming from heaven in judgment.

Conclusion

Back to the question of origins. Why is it so important for scholars to find out what the exact text of the original Mark was? Isn't it because of the desire to recover the original version of the story?[35] Doesn't this have to do with a desire to equate truth with origins or beginnings, that is, what is original is true, what is first is more reliable? The intent of the original author is what counts, they would say. This approach disqualifies the work of later communities and authors by saying that these all depart from the truth, that they are apocryphal, spurious, and not authentic. It follows then that rereadings and resisting readings are all subjective, non-scientific, biased, inauthentic, suspect, deviant, and false.

This chapter has tried to prove that behind the long ending of Mark stands a community, not a lonely scribe who used his pen as an instrument of orthodoxy. This community was not preoccupied with issues of doctrine, but with living in the uncertain times of the post-resurrection era, with the realization that their expectations concerning the end had been radically and forever modified. They resisted the reading of the first version of Mark, not because they found it heretical, but because they found it outdated and irrelevant. This community provides us with an example of theological rereading and Christological inventive. It compels us to do the same, to read the gospel anew in an ever changing world, to relive the story and, in turn, make it livable for others. That is the work of any Christologist, exemplified masterfully by the writer of the second gospel and his community.

---

35. As Manuel Villalobos asserts, quoting Werner H. Kelber, "No such thing ever existed in oral speech." Villalobos, *Abject Bodies*, 167.

6

The Soteriological Aspect of Jesus' Discipleship

REFERRING TO JESUS AS DISCIPLE of the kingdom does not mean restricting his ministry to that aspect only. Because the NT portrays him mainly as Savior and Lord, for Christians—and for Christian theology—Jesus cannot be *just* a disciple. But denying him some sort of a disciple status is not a possibility either. The historical Jesus, however we understand him to have been, given the post-resurrection bias of all the writers of the NT, must have regarded himself as an instrument for the actualization of God's kingdom, although he perhaps never considered himself to be the only agent of such reality. His coming to John to be baptized seems to bear witness to that fact: he wanted to join a movement already in progress. He came to place himself under John's authority, to learn from him. He became a disciple of the baptizer as a prelude to his own consciousness as disciple of the kingdom of God. It is this apparent contradiction between being a disciple and yet more than a disciple that I want to explore in this chapter. And, especially, how his understanding of being a disciple of God's kingdom connected with God's saving activity, that is, with soteriology.

JESUS AND THE KINGDOM: THE VOCATION OF DISCIPLESHIP

In the *Global Bible Commentary*, Pablo Richard writes:

> Jesus' historical project, the kingdom of God as manifested in his liberating actions is, for us, more important than the historical

The Soteriological Aspect of Jesus' Discipleship

Jesus himself. . . . It is noteworthy that Jesus identified the kingdom of God not with the Davidic monarchy, not with the sanctity of the temple, and not with the fulfillment of the law, but with the lives of the poor.[1]

Jesus' understanding of the reign of God was not theoretical, but practical. He *lived* more than *preached* the kingdom, although preaching he did. But his preaching was always based and supported by his actions on behalf of the marginalized of his society. He started off his ministry proclaiming the gospel of God, the kingdom message. But before he did that, he was already committed to it. He grew up in Galilee listening to the Torah through the "little tradition" preserved and cherished by the peasantry,[2] so by the time he arrived at the banks of the river Jordan to become a disciple of the baptizer, his mind was already made up. He was going to embrace John's dream and make it his own. But he was going to do it as a Galilean, as a teacher of the "little tradition" and as a disciple of God.

Jesus must have had a notion of God's kingdom that was informed by the situation of the Galilean peasants. Part of this situation was heavy taxation, both by Herod Antipas (one of the sons of Herod the Great) and the Romans, land ownership issues, and food production. How was his self-understanding as disciple of the kingdom affected by these realities? Following Pablo Richard's idea, it is clear that his Galilean context is to be credited for the rejection of the Davidic monarchy as the seedbed of the Messianic expectations. The same can be said about his criticism of the temple system done from the perspective of someone living at the religious and cultural margins of Israel.[3] And his own attitude toward the law, as I said, was one of a teacher of the "little tradition," the peasants' oral version of the Israelite, text-based tradition.

N. T. Wright has said the following about Jesus' self-understanding:

> Jesus' beliefs, therefore, remained those of a first-century Jew, committed to the coming kingdom of Israel's God. He did not waver in his loyalty to Jewish doctrine. But his beliefs were those

---

1. Richard, "Jesus: A Latin American Perspective," 341.

2. See Horsley, *Jesus and Empire*, 61–63.

3. "The Jesus movement saw the principal obstacle to the realization of God's kingdom in Palestine to be the temple and the class structure that it supported. . . . Because the class domination of the priests rested principally on a deep-seated ideology, the strategy of the Jesus movement was one of ideological attack." Pixley, *God's Kingdom*, 72.

of a first-century Jew who believed that the kingdom was coming *in and through his own work.*[4]

According to Wright, these beliefs were: a) monotheism, the belief that there existed only one God, YHWH; b) election, the conviction that this God had chosen Israel to be God's special people on earth; and c) kingdom, the belief that upon the return of YHWH to Zion, there was going to be a final defeat of evil that would prompt Israel's real return from exile. Wright would go on to affirm that Jesus "embraced this Jewish hope, making it thematic for his own work."[5]

The fundamental difference between Richard and Wright is that, whereas Wright tries to answer the question of Jesus' own identity in relationship to the kingdom as an eschatological reality, Richard tries to answer the question of Jesus' own identity in relationship to the eschatological community of the kingdom that was being called into being through his work. Whereas for Wright the person of Jesus is important, for Richard, it is Jesus' project that is central to his ministry. What Jesus thought about himself[6] is not as important as what he thought his mission was going to be during the eschatological time he assumed to be living in. I would contend that he thought of himself as being a disciple of God, an organizer and teacher of the peasantry, in preparation for God's eschatological kingdom.

My understanding of Jesus as disciple of the kingdom somehow qualifies N. T. Wright's affirmation that Jesus believed that "the kingdom was coming in and through his own work." I would say that Jesus believed that his actions were symbolic of what God was going to do in Israel very soon. He thought that God was about to bring God's kingdom, which included the vindication of God's oppressed people and the judgment of the powerful. Therefore, his mission was to call people to co-discipleship. He spearheaded a movement, a community of disciples of God's kingdom, and he considered himself one of them. He may have believed that he had a special and real, although not unique, connection with God, an awareness that sustained him throughout his ministry. But he never understood himself as

---

4. Wright, *Jesus and the Victory of God*, 652 (emphasis added).

5. Ibid.

6. "We are not interested here in Jesus' 'messianic consciousness' or in his private understandings. Many generations of research in these themes have led to contradictory results. Our interest is focused instead on the historical project borne by Jesus and his Galilean movement, as it is told in the gospel narratives." Pixley, *God's Kingdom*, 72. As a liberation theology scholar, Pixley agrees completely with Pablo Richard.

The Soteriological Aspect of Jesus' Discipleship

"the" Messiah of Israel. He never claimed to be a divine being or one equal to God, not even the eschatological Son of Man. He always referred to this figure in the third person, as if he were talking about someone else. The only claim he made about himself, at least in the Gospel of Mark, was that he had been sent by God (Mark 2:17; 9:37), and that his status was that of a διάκονος (Mark 10:45). I would further suggest that those instances where he seems to be referring to himself as the Son of Man (Mark 2:10, 28; 8:31; 9:9, 12, 31; 10:33, 45; 14:21) are theological constructions already present in the traditions that Mark was handling, or perhaps even the evangelist's own contribution. One thing is sure though: Mark is the first NT writer to have used the expression "Son of Man" to refer to Jesus. He is followed by Matthew and Luke, and the expression is used independently by John and the author of the book of Revelation. He is also the first author in the NT to have used the expression "disciple" and the concept of discipleship (see chapter 1).

The Gospel of Mark is one among many versions of the traditions about Jesus, and the question to be asked is if the theme of discipleship in general, and that of Jesus in particular, was something the evangelist superimposed on the traditions available to him or if there were already elements in those traditions that made it possible for him to construct a Christology in which discipleship, and not lordship or messiahship, became the main emphasis and therefore the driving force and focus of the community. I would suggest that both things were happening; namely, Mark's interest in the discipleship motif provided the lenses through which he read the traditions (mostly oral), and that the traditions themselves contained the remains of what had been, perhaps, the true consciousness of the historical Jesus, but now it was buried under a heavy layer of exalted, post-Easter theology. Furthermore, Mark found that the concept of disciple and discipleship were already present in the Greco-Roman society, and so he put them at the center of his gospel. In contrast to all the other disciples, who are depicted as failing, Jesus is shown as being faithful to the demands of the kingdom. Jesus does what disciples are expected to do and so becomes an example for them, although he is never called a disciple in the gospel.

More than an *archetype*, Jesus becomes a *prototype* of discipleship, that is, what discipleship of the kingdom looked like in its first-century Palestinian context. I am not saying that his divine being manifested itself in his taking the form of a disciple, that sonship was expressed through discipleship, for that would be another way of saying that the *logos* became

Jesus, Disciple of the Kingdom

flesh, that this time he became a disciple of the kingdom. Then we would be "worshipping" Jesus the disciple, instead of "following" Jesus the disciple. And we would be making discipleship into an ontological category rather than into a praxiological necessity. No, I am saying that discipleship was his vocation, the path that he as a human being chose to follow, and the limits he imposed on his ministry. He never wanted to be more than that. Unlike some of his contemporaries, he never entertained any personal messianic dreams. His only dream was the kingdom and doing God's will.

Jesus' Discipleship and Soteriology

The minute we start talking about Jesus as disciple, some people, especially clergy and scholars,[7] feel uncomfortable. This was best exemplified by one of my colleagues who, playing the devil's advocate, said: "If Jesus is the disciple, who then is the teacher?"[8] We seem to have gained a disciple but lost a savior! So the question of Jesus as model of discipleship as it relates to soteriology is pertinent.

Does Jesus as an example of discipleship enable, facilitate, and mediate salvation? And if so, what is the role of the cross? Is the death of the disciple par excellence redemptive, like the Suffering Servant of Isaiah, or the Righteous Sufferer of the Psalms, or the Maccabean martyrs? Can discipleship and suffering servanthood be equated or related? Can this category be also applied to the Markan community, and not only to Jesus?

In chapter 3, I tried to demonstrate that the fact that Mark is quoting from Deutero-Isaiah may be pointing at an intentional theological agenda, namely, that in his depiction of Jesus as disciple of the kingdom, he is being informed by Isaiah's description of the Servant, especially when the Servant

---

7. A senior biblical scholar once warned me about scholarship that assumes unapologetically its social location. He said that this scholarship, once it has seen its day, will pass away. "Beware of all this ideological stuff," he told me. The funny thing is that he was unaware of his own ideology. Being, as he is, a white male trained in the European historical critical methods, he assumed he did not have any ideology, that his take on the text was universal, neutral, and objective. He and I agreed on the importance of respecting the text but, whereas I foregrounded my social location and assumptions, he did not even acknowledge his own. We were talking about the same thing, biblical research, how to handle the text, but we were speaking different languages. We shared some common methods, but since I complement historical criticism with cultural, post-colonial, feminist, and liberationist theory, he did not know how to engage me at that level.

8. Ken Vaux's comment.

The Soteriological Aspect of Jesus' Discipleship

is described in Isaiah 50:4 as having the tongue of a disciple. If this is true, then, how does that play into Mark's description of Jesus as a model for discipleship? Is he consciously thinking of the Servant? Is he doing a rereading of the Servant Songs through the lenses of a militant discipleship? If so, how are the suffering of the Servant, the suffering of Jesus, and the suffering of the disciples—the community—related? The following chart may help us in deciding this:

Suffering Servant	"Tongue of a disciple"	Suffering: Israel in exile
Jesus	Disciple of John/God	Suffering: the cross
Community	Disciples of Jesus	Suffering: persecutions during Jewish revolt

In Isaiah 53:10, the Servant's life is made an offering for sin, an idea that may go back to the Levitical sacrificial system (cf. Leviticus 1–7). Isaiah 53:11 says that "the righteous one, my servant, shall make many righteous and he shall bear their iniquities." And 53:12b reiterates, "Yet he bore the sin of many, and made intercession for the transgressors." Severino Croatto[9] believes that this is a metaphor for the destruction of 586 BCE, and that the servant represents captive Israel, whose suffering has a redemptive effect on the many, possibly the rest of the nation of Israel, both at home in Judah and in the dispersion. He connects Mark 10:45, "For the Son of Man came not to be served but to serve, and to give his life a ransom for many," with the Servant Songs by saying that the idea of the many is already present in Isaiah (cf. 52:14, 15; 53:11b, 12ab), where it refers to the Diaspora on whose behalf the suffering of captive Israel is done (cf. 48:20a with 20b). Redemption, then, is accomplished by a community that accepts its role in God's saving activity.

In the essay to which I made reference in chapter 3,[10] I contend that Mark's understanding of the Son of Man goes back to the book of Daniel, where it represents the suffering people of Israel under Antiochus Epiphanes. In my opinion, Mark saw the Son of Man, Jesus, as a representative figure for God's suffering people on earth, which in the gospel are those who follow Jesus in defiance of dangerous social and political pressures. Even more, Mark may have done this rereading of the Danielic son of man through the lenses of Isaiah 53, because in his gospel, Jesus' work of representation has redemptive connotations. He has come not to be served

---

9. Croatto, "Estudio Exegético-Homilético," 10.
10. Vena, "Markan Construction," 86–87.

(i.e., worshipped, adored, etc.), but to serve the many, that is, God's suffering, captive people. It is on behalf of them that the Son of Man will give his life as a ransom. In turn, the community would suffer likewise and thus become itself a source of redemption, ¹¹as it opened its doors to receive those who followed the teachings and the vision of Jesus, the Son of Man. Like captive Israel in Isaiah, and the suffering people under Antiochus, the Markan community, doubly oppressed for being Jewish *and* Christian, participated in God's redemptive act of gathering the elect from the four corners of the earth at the end of the age (cf. Mark 13:26–27 with Isa 48:20; 49:5–6). This community was engaged in preaching the gospel to the nations (Mark 13:10 with Isa 49:6b), in continuity with the gospel preached by the disciple / Son of Man when he was on earth (Mark 1:15). Mark wanted his audience to understand that this redemptive activity is accomplished through the suffering caused by a militant, radical discipleship that is expressed as nonviolent resistance. As in Isaiah 53, it is redemptive suffering, not redemptive violence, that will bring about God's kingdom. By so doing, the evangelist was reversing the traditional myth of violence as a means of salvation, the concept of holy war proposed by the Jewish revolutionaries of Mark's time, as well as the Roman concept of *pax romana* through military conquest.¹²

When, in Mark 8:34–38, Jesus invites people to follow him taking up their cross, he is inviting them to participate in God's redemptive activity. It is through losing one's life that salvation (redemption) is obtained, not the other way around. And this is so, because preserving one's life would have meant, for the group of Jesus' followers, avoiding the shame of the cross, which in turn would have been tantamount to being ashamed of Jesus and the gospel ("my words"). What would it have meant for the Markan community to "want to save their life," if not avoiding the persecution brought about by the war? And what would it have meant to "lose their life for my

---

11. Commenting on Mark 10:42b–45, I have written in another work: "Perhaps the most important difference between Mark and Matthew is the way in which Matthew introduces the saying of the Son of Man giving his life as a ransom for many. He writes '*just as* the Son of man came not to be served' instead of the Markan '*for* the Son of man came not to be served.' The significance of this could be that for Matthew, Jesus as the Son of Man is the example of a true servant-leader that the disciples need to imitate. For Mark, it seems as if the disciples co-participate in Jesus' redemptive activity by extending to people the ministry of the servant-leader. Whereas in Matthew, the affirmation conveys the idea of an option of lifestyle, in Mark, it is clearly an unavoidable consequence of belonging to the community of the Son of Man." Vena, "Gospel Images," 7.

12. Borg and Crossan, *First Paul*, 104–8.

The Soteriological Aspect of Jesus' Discipleship

sake and for the sake of the gospel," if not willing to stay non-aligned and to practice nonviolent resistance, thus bringing upon themselves the ire of both the Romans and the Jewish revolutionaries?

The verb "to save" (σώζω), having the connotation of preserving or rescuing from natural dangers and afflictions, appears here in 8:34–38, in 3:4 and in 15:30–31. It also occurs in 10:26 and 13:13, meaning "to save or preserve from eternal death" or to "bring Messianic salvation, bring to salvation."[13] These two meanings of the verb "to save" are not as opposite as they may seem at first glance, one referring to metaphysical, a-historical realities, the other to physical, historical ones.

In Mark, to preserve or to rescue physical life and to save life in the sense of eternal damnation are interconnected. The rich young ruler is asked, in order to obtain the salvation of the age to come, to give up his possessions, which had given a secure and solid foundation to his world. Against popular understanding, Jesus does not see a direct and positive correlation between prosperity (historical salvation) and divine blessing (eternal life). Quite the opposite; he sees this relationship as inverted. One precludes a person from attaining the other. Consequently, the disciples in the narrative are asked to give up their personal safety if they want to be saved when the Son of Man brings in God's new age. And the persecuted community reading, or hearing, the gospel was encouraged to persevere to the end if they wanted to be saved (13:13). Mark's paradoxical message then is this: the best way—or perhaps the only way—to ensure eternal life is to be willing to risk or even lose life, as dictated by the values and norms of society, for the sake of the gospel, that is, for implementing a new vision of what life should be according to the standards of God's kingdom.

In 15:29–32, Jesus is derided by those passing by, mocked by the chief priests and scribes, and taunted by those who were crucified with him. These three groups of people invite Jesus to *save* himself by coming down from the cross. But the readers perceive the irony of such a statement, for it is precisely by being willing to die for the sake of the gospel, as Jesus did, that one attains salvation. Mark's community was encouraged by Jesus' example of faithful discipleship to live out their own discipleship during the strenuous time that they were living through. They realized that it was part of their call as disciples of the Son of Man to be channels of redemption to the wider society. Soteriology then is redefined. It is not the feat of a personal, individual savior but the task, the call of a community that

13. BDAG, 798.

incarnates and channels God's redemptive work in the world. Like the Suffering Servant of Isaiah, and like Jesus the model disciple of the kingdom, the Markan community, through its suffering for remaining faithful to its gospel based vision of reality, mediated God's salvation, which for that particular group of people meant only one thing: the deliverance promised by the soon-to-arrive kingdom (Mark 14:25: "... until that day when I drink it new in the kingdom of God"). By being part of such community, where possessions were shared and family roles redefined, where persecutions for the sake of the gospel were accepted and even welcomed, people came to be "saved," that is, they experienced a foretaste of God's realm. Mark 10:29–30 summarizes it well:

> Truly I tell you, there is no one who has left house or brothers or sisters or mother or father or children of fields, for my sake and for the sake of the good news, who will not receive a hundredfold now in this age—houses, brothers and sisters, mothers and children, and fields, with persecutions—and in the age to come eternal life.

If, for Mark, Jesus was the model disciple of the kingdom, then the community was a prototype of the kingdom, a reduced-scale model of God's realm.

Mark's Community and Soteriology

But Jesus does not call people to passive suffering, to resignation. He calls them to resistance. The suffering is for the sake of the gospel, for living out the values of the kingdom, for taking a concrete political stand *vis-à-vis* the current mood of the times. It is not masochism, but calculated risk-taking. Embodying the values of the kingdom means to live out the gospel in the wider society *knowing* that the price for doing so may be high, as it was for Jesus. But this embodiment carries with it the promise of life, which traditionally has been understood as the promise of going to heaven with Jesus.

I would like to suggest that that is not the message of the Gospel of Mark. In this gospel, the new age has nothing to do with heaven and everything to do with this world. The risen Christ is to be found in Galilee, the place from which Jesus came to start his discipleship, an area characterized by deep contrasts between the poor and the rich, the place from which the Zealots' revolt started, a place of marginality and *mestizaje*,[14] where

14. Virgilio Elizondo defines *mestizaje* as "the generation of a new people from two

The Soteriological Aspect of Jesus' Discipleship

the effects of the empire's globalizing project of exploitation and economic exclusion was felt the hardest. The age to come, that is, the conferring of power to God's disempowered people, was going to manifest itself precisely in the midst of such a situation, in the everyday life and reality of marginal Galilee. Here is where the community was to find and exercise its redemptive vocation and thus experience God's liberation, for it was only by being willing to serve as channels of redemption that the community was going to be "saved."

Therefore in Mark, soteriology is linked to the following of Jesus, which produces a marginal kind of living. No one can be saved who does not embrace Jesus' program of rebuilding society along kingdom values that privilege the poor and the ostracized over the rich and the powerful and that choose nonviolence over imperial repression or revolutionary aspirations as the method for implementing God's realm.

The image with which the Gospel of Mark ends is one of active following both on the part of Jesus and the disciples:

> But go, tell his disciples and Peter that he is going ahead of you to Galilee; there you will see him, just as he told you. (16:7)

One could say that Jesus, now as the risen Lord (cf. 14:28), is following God's lead in bringing God's realm in Galilee. He is going ahead, moving, leading the disciples toward an eschatological encounter that will reusher the mission. But anytime Jesus leads the disciples there is fear involved, and Jesus, or the divine messenger, has to assure them of God's sustaining presence. In Mark 10:32, for instance, Jesus is leading (προάγων) the group toward Jerusalem and the reaction is amazement (ἐθαμβοῦντο: they were amazed) and fear (ἐφοβοῦντο: they were afraid). Why were they amazed and afraid? The context suggests that Jesus' demands of his group that they should be willing to give up material possessions for the sake of the gospel, which included the supporting system of their families, made them react with amazement and fear, as they weighed the implications of such

---

disparate parent peoples," a new ethnic group with cultural as well as biological characteristics. He describes Galilee during the time of Jesus as an area "peopled by Phoenicians, Syrians, Arabs, Greeks, Orientals, and Jews. In this mixed, commerce-oriented society, some Jews had allowed their Jewish exclusivism to weaken, but others became more militantly exclusivist. Some of the *goyim* (non-Jews) converted to Judaism and intermarried with Jews. Some religious ideas of other groups were also assimilated, as is evident in the case of the Essenes. A natural, ongoing biological and cultural *mestizaje* was taking place." This natural *mestizaje* "was a sign of impurity and a cause for rejection." Elizondo, *Galilean Journey*, 16, 51.

a lifestyle. But fear is connected specifically with their going up to Jerusalem. The narrative will explicitly uncover, in verses 33–34, what is going to transpire there, namely betrayal and death. That is why they are afraid; Jerusalem was going to be the place of martyrdom for Jesus, the model disciple of the kingdom, and quite possibly also for his followers!

Previously, in the narrative, there had been instances where Jesus' lead of the disciples resulted in fear and reassurance. One such instance is the walking on water of chapter 6; the other, the transfiguration account in chapter 9. In 6:45, Jesus "made his disciples get into the boat." The verbs used here are ἀναγκάζω, which can mean "to compel, to force," or "to invite (urgently), to urge (strongly)"[15] and προάγω, which in this context seems to mean "to go or come before someone."[16] In response to Jesus' urgent invitation to cross over, the disciples find themselves in the midst of a compromising situation battling against an "adverse wind." Jesus comes to them walking on the sea, and they think he is a ghost. They are terrified (ἐταράχθησαν), and so Jesus has to reassure them that it is him, not a ghost, and that they should not be afraid (μὴ φοβεῖσθε). The disciples' experience can be classified as eschatological, inasmuch as it seems to involve otherworldly realities ("they thought it was a ghost"). Their terror is not directed at the earthly sea situation—although it certainly was a disturbing one and the text alludes to it by saying that they were "straining at the oars"—but at the sudden irruption of a spiritual presence coming as it were from the other, eschatological, world.[17] Similarly, in 4:41, the uneasiness of the disciples is directed at the possibility of perishing, and is not described as fear in the eschatological sense but as cowardice, timidity.[18] It is only when they realize that Jesus has done something that only God is described as doing in the Hebrew Bible (cf. Ps 104:6–7; 106:9) that their fear takes on an eschatological dimension: "And they were filled with great awe (φόβον μέγαν) and said to one another, 'Who is this, that even the wind and the sea obey him?'"

The other example[19] of fear directed toward eschatological realities is Mark 9:2–8, the account of the transfiguration. Here, we are told that Jesus

---

15. BDAG, 52.

16. BDAG, 702.

17. Jesus' presence is eschatological also because he is doing something that according to the Hebrew Scriptures only God can do, namely, exercising power over the sea (cf. Job 9:8; 38:16).

18. BDAG, 173.

19. Notice the verb in passive, μετεμορφώθη, indicating God's action. Jesus did not change his appearance by himself. It was God's doing. Jesus was the object of the action, God the subject.

The Soteriological Aspect of Jesus' Discipleship

"took with him Peter and James and John, and led them up (ἀναφέρει) a high mountain," where "he was transfigured" in front of them and had a conversation with two figures from the past, Elijah and Moses. The reaction of the disciples is again one of terror (ἔκφοβοι), so the heavenly voice has to reassure them of Jesus' presence in their midst as the only authoritative discourse they should listen to.

And then, of course, we have the classical ending of Mark 16:8, "So they went out and fled from the tomb, for terror (τρόμος) and amazement (ἔκστασις) had seized them; and they said nothing to anyone, for they were afraid (ἐφοβοῦντο)." Why are the women afraid now that they know that Jesus has been raised? Wouldn't this fact have produced the opposite, namely, assurance and confidence in God's deliverance? Why fear and why now? The pericope may reflect the situation of the Markan community caught up as it was between the resurrection and the coming of the kingdom, but still immersed in the drama of the Jewish revolt.

The sudden outburst of the other world into the present one instills in the disciples great terror and fear, and the only thing that seems to overcome this eschatological fear is the realization that behind that other-worldly reality stands the figure of the historical Jesus. We see this in every passage studied above. Even when history is subsumed in/by eschatology,[20] eschatology is still rooted in and explained by history. The Risen Christ, who through the young man (νεανίσκον) invites the disciples to join him in Galilee, is none other than Jesus of Nazareth (16:6), who was crucified, a victim of Rome's imperial repressive apparatus, and now a martyr and model for the nascent community.

The Gospel of John ends also with a following theme: Jesus and the disciples walking by the Sea of Galilee. These two early communities, Mark's and John's, did not incorporate into their traditions an ascension motif, although one may say that the Gospel of John talks explicitly about Jesus going to the Father (cf. John 14:3, 12, 18–19, 28; 16:22; etc). But even in these passages, Jesus does not go away to heaven in a visible way, as he does in Luke-Acts. He goes to the Father, but comes back quickly, compelling the disciples to follow him (21:19). Both gospels end with a "following" motif, not with a "going-to-heaven" one. Even Matthew is lacking an ascension narrative[21] for, in this gospel, Jesus sends the disciples to a worldwide mis-

---

20. Ched Myers has suggested that the clothes worn by the young man at the tomb stand for martyrdom. Myers, *Binding the Strong Man*, 399.

21. The fact that Matthew incorporates in his narrative the tradition of the son of

sion from a mountain (cf. 5:1 and 17:1), assuring them of his presence until the end of the age. In that sense, we can speak also of a following motif in Matthew, for the disciples are told to go to and make disciples of all nations.

Conclusion

In Mark, entrance into the kingdom is predicated upon following Jesus. This is clearly seen in the account of the rich ruler (Mark 10:17–27). And following is a response to Jesus' call to discipleship, the same way he responded to God's call issued from the banks of the river Jordan. The one who calls to participate in the construction of the new age is God, but God does it always through human agents—John, Jesus, the community. Each one of these agents plays a soteriological role in God's plan of renewal and redemption. Each one is a co-participant, a co-disciple as it were, each being taught by and learning from the previous one, but also from the only one who is good, the Supreme Teacher, God. For Mark, salvation is not something that will occur in the future in a heavenly realm, but something that will occur here, on earth, as people are brought together into a community of discipleship that becomes a prototype of God's kingdom.

People are saved when they are willing to risk everything for the gospel message. By so doing, they become liberated from the pressures and conditionings of society and are in a position to resist its seduction. They are free to announce and construct God's kingdom. They model an alternative society, which anticipates proleptically the one that is in the process of being formed. This community is redemptive, because it contains in itself the seed of the kingdom that promises new life to the world, as the evangelist so appropriately describes with the parables of the kingdom in chapter 4.

---

man coming with the clouds of heaven (24:29–31) and the judgment of the nations (25:31–46) implies the author's acknowledgment of a tradition that speaks of a temporal absence of Jesus from the world while the church is engaged in preaching the gospel to the nations. This absence can only be accounted for if Jesus was taken to heaven as Luke-Acts suggests. But Matthew never develops this concept, so there is a tension throughout his gospel between Jesus' enduring presence ("I am with you always") and his coming at the end of the age. See Boring, "Gospel of Matthew," 457–58.

Conclusion

Mark's Christology
A Model for the Contemporary Church

I WOULD LIKE TO SUGGEST that the model being proposed in this book tries to bridge the gap between what, in my opinion, are the two most popular Christological views, the *Christus Victor* model, that proclaims the Risen Christ as the eschatological judge at the Parousia, and the Suffering Servant model, that emphasizes the atoning nature of Jesus' death.[1] Jesus as disciple of God's kingdom bridges and democratizes both ideas, giving to God's people the power to judge and the privilege to suffer for the gospel.

First, the judgment is given to God's people, who are represented by the twelve apostles (cf. Matt 19:28; Luke 22:30). By making the Danielic son of man into a corporate figure, Mark has transferred the power to rule from an individual to the community which now exercises this right through voluntary service to humankind (Mark 10:45). The powers that be are judged in the very fact of being proven wrong by the resistance and the sacrificial service of the community of disciples. Thus, judgment gives way to a new social reality, God's kingdom, which is equally acknowledged by both oppressors and oppressed.

Second, the suffering is done by God's people, the community of disciples. In this way, victimization disappears and is replaced by voluntary

---

1. These two views or models correspond broadly to what Charles T. Hughes describes as the Chalcedonian two-nature Christology and the Kenotic Christology. Both Christologies emphasize that Jesus is true God and true human being but, while the first affirms that God assumed human nature as Jesus, thus being born as the God-man, the second proposes that God became a human being by a process of "kenosis" or self-emptying. Hughes, *Pluralism*, 155.

suffering for the sake of the gospel. Atonement is thus redefined. It is not the feat of a lonely Messiah, who dies to satisfy the anger of an offended deity, but the task of a community whose call is to resist the powers in solidarity with the weak and oppressed, whom the powerful have offended by treating them as less than human. The power to liberate through service is given then to the community of disciples who, by so doing, imitate Jesus, the ideal disciple of the kingdom. Therefore, suffering is not self-imposed as redemptive, but expected as the consequence of faithful discipleship.

An Evaluation of the Model

In my introduction to this book, I stated that this model of Jesus as the ideal disciple of the kingdom has to prove that it can coexist peacefully with four areas of concern proposed by Elisabeth Schüssler Fiorenza in her book *Jesus and the Politics of Interpretation*. These four areas relate specifically to historical-Jesus research, but they can also be applied to the model I am proposing in this book. These areas of concern have to address: a) whether or not it reinscribes the anti-Judaism inscribed in the gospels; b) whether or not it contributes to the liberation or oppression of women and other minorities around the world; c) whether or not it criticizes the ideologies of colonization and domination that often use the biblical text as justification for their colonial agenda; and d) whether or not it promotes a politics of exclusivity, inferiority, prejudice, and dehumanization when it comes to cultural or religious identity formation.[2] In this chapter, I will try to address each one of these concerns. This evaluation will be done through observation and recapitulation of what has already been said in the book at large. It is offered as a starting point for further investigation and probing.

Anti-Judaism

Against the possibility that this model may reinscribe the rampant anti-Judaism inscribed in the gospels, I have to say that this reading of Jesus as disciple of the kingdom goes against such view. Even if one acknowledges that the gospels as theological documents reflect the early church's stance against a certain kind of Judaism, namely Pharisaic Judaism, still the reading that I propose goes against such possibility. The Jesus constructed by

2. Schüssler Fiorenza, *Jesus and the Politics of Interpretation*, 59–60.

my reading is the one who, in Mark 8:34–38, calls both Jews and Gentiles to follow him as co-disciples of the kingdom. If this passage constitutes the rhetorical and theological center of the gospel, as I have tried to prove, then this is the main message of the gospel. Discipleship is offered to and exercised by a mixed community. You don't have to be Jewish or Gentile to join the movement. Besides that, if we place the community during the difficult years of the Jewish war, we see how other passages in the gospel[3] speak of a call to nonalignment, neither with the Zealots nor with the Romans. Also, the Markan Jesus' stance on the role of the law, which could be interpreted as criticizing its validity in people's lives—see, for example, 2:23–28, 3:1–6, 7:17–23—needs to be seen as a criticism from inside Judaism, from Jesus' own type of Judaism informed as it was by his Galilean background and traditions.

Oppression of Women and Minorities

Perhaps the most problematic aspect of presenting Jesus as the exemplar of discipleship is his gender: he is male. Women who read this book may feel excluded from this model for it is very clear throughout my argument that I want to make Jesus, not anybody else, the model disciple. But the attentive reader should have noticed how I have qualified this idea. I said more than once that it is a disempowered, landless, poor Galilean who is presented as the model disciple. Fiorenza would put him in the category of wo/men she talks about.[4] Besides, I pointed out that even when making Jesus the disciple par excellence, the characters who come closer to this ideal are women and marginal personages (see below for further discussion).

When talking about the centrality of suffering in Jesus' depiction of the life of discipleship, some may think that I am glorifying suffering to the detriment of those people whose reality is permeated by it. But in constructing this model, I have clarified more than once that suffering comes as the result of our commitment to building a better society, not from our position in society. Therefore, this model does not justify suffering, but suggests that it may be the cost we have to pay for a future without suffering, for a world in which equality and justice will be the norm, not the exception.

---

3. See, e.g., 10:41–45; 12:13–17, 35–37; 14:48–49; etc.
4. Schüssler Fiorenza, *Power of the Word*, 6n21.

Critique of Colonization and Domination

Does the proposed model criticize colonization and domination? Is Jesus being depicted as a spokesperson for the dominant view of society, in this case, Jewish society? Does his ministry as a disciple of God aim at dominating those who have a subservient role in society, such as women and marginal characters? In my treatment in chapter 3 of Jesus' conversation with the Syrophoenician woman in Mark 7:24–30, I propose that this is a turning point in Jesus' consciousness. After this encounter, he realized that non-Jews had equal access to God's dominion. The narrative has prepared the reader for this *"aha"* moment by inserting it between two different feedings, one on Jewish and the other on Gentile territory, and two healings, one of Jewish people and the other of a deaf man in a predominantly Greek region. Rhetorically, as well as theologically speaking, this pericope makes a lot of sense and drives home the point of a Jesus who as disciple of the kingdom is willing to learn from a woman who then becomes his teacher, since it is her word and not her faith (see Matt 15:28) that compels Jesus to change his mind. Far from presenting Jesus as the colonizer, this model illustrates what happens when even a person of privilege, such as the Jewish Jesus of Mark, is willing to let the broader agenda of God's dominion dictate his actions. His example would have motivated the Markan community to do the same, even as they struggled with understanding the relationship of Gentiles and Jews in their midst, as the Jewish revolt moved from threat to concrete reality to retaliation by the Roman army.

In Mark 10:45, Jesus is presented as an example of *diakonia*. As the Son of Man, he represents the whole community, and so the expectation of service is placed on each individual member. But those who are elevated are not the usual suspects, the landed aristocracy of the Greco-Roman world, but rather the low-status members of society, women and minorities. Therefore this model, far from promoting domination and colonization, advocates for equality among all members of the community and proposes a model for human existence that is based on mutual and voluntary service.

Exclusivity in Relationship to Cultural or Religious Identity

Does my model claim or promote exclusivity in relationship to cultural or religious identity? Does the Jesus who is proposed as a model for discipleship demand that his followers be only Jewish, or minister only to Jewish

Conclusion: Mark's Christology

people, as is the case in Matthew 10:5-6? Does the model promote among contemporary people the notion that discipleship applies only to "Christian" disciples? Or is the model inclusive enough, even at the level of the text, that it allows for a contextualization that goes beyond the boundaries of Christianity to encompass other religions and human groups? I believe that all these concerns have already been addressed in the book, but let me make a summary of my findings. There are elements hidden in the Markan text that point at a historical Jesus who seems to have been opened to different interpretations of the Jewish law, but also to how his own ministry of liberation was to be regarded by people. If we take the question he posited to his disciples in 8:27-30 as coming from the lips of the historical Jesus and not just a rhetorical device used by the evangelist, then Jesus was concerned about what people thought of him and his ministry. The fact that he ordered the disciples not to tell anybody about him does not necessarily mean that he agreed with Peter's confession, but rather that he was still processing what his involvement in the coming kingdom would be. When, in 8:33, Jesus rebukes Peter for his desire to make him into a victorious kind of Messiah by avoiding suffering and death, it shows Jesus' increasing awareness that his role in the eschatological unfolding of God's program was going to include hardships and possibly death. He immediately ties his own fate with that of his followers and the Son of Man, making this passage the theological centerpiece of the whole gospel, where he comes to terms with his own call as a suffering disciple of the kingdom and, at the same time, calls others to follow him as co-disciples. If that is the case, then he was not claiming an absolute and exclusive role as Messiah, but perhaps a more inclusive and participative role as one of many disciples of God who were to announce the coming kingdom, extending healing and liberation to the oppressed people of Palestine.

In the next chapter, Mark 9:38-41, we find Jesus approving of the work of an exorcist who was not part of his group, thus sanctioning for the Markan community the value of alternative ministries of liberation. The only criterion for validity is being for or against the Jesus movement. This gives contemporary disciples not a small amount of elbow room to negotiate with other Christian and non-Christian groups' programs that would empower not only the church, but also humanity in general.

The other example that comes to mind is the already discussed passage of Jesus' conversation with the Syrophoenician woman, where Jesus acknowledges the wisdom coming from the lips of a representative of another cultural and religious group, thus opening the door to modern disciples for ecumenical and interreligious dialogue.

The Significance of the Model for the Contemporary Church

Since Christology and theology are always context driven, Jesus as disciple of the kingdom is congruent with Latin American liberation theology's emphasis on the importance of following Jesus, that is, the importance of praxis. This context is different from the prevalent U.S. context of individualistic religion and ontological theology. Whereas European and North Atlantic theology attempts to answer the question of *who God is*, Latin American and third-world theologies try to answer the question of *how God acts*. While the latter is praxiological (being a disciple), the former is ontological (the being of God).

In Latin America, we know God as we walk the path of discipleship. In this path, we follow the example/model of Jesus of Nazareth whereby he becomes for us the disciple par excellence. But, as I said above, this identification is praxiological more than ontological. More than an archetype, Jesus is a prototype of discipleship, that is, the specific form or embodiment that discipleship took in first-century, Roman-dominated Palestine. Our task today is to realize the contours of discipleship in our present world.

The church today is called to incarnate and to channel God's redemptive work in the world. How do we do that? Specifically, how do we do that without glorifying suffering? The question is pertinent and, although difficult to answer, an attempt needs to be made. We live in a culture of self-gratification, where more for less seems to be the norm: more prestige, more economical benefits, more stuff for less effort, money, and emotional involvement. But as we know in our society, only a few can attain this level of self-gratification. For the majority, especially for those who have been relegated to the physical, cultural, and emotional margins, it is always less for more: less prestige, less economical benefits, less status for more and longer workdays, more frequent harassment, discrimination and explicit, as well as implicit, manifestations of individual and institutional racism. So, when these people come to passages such as the ones we are discussing in this book, they don't want to hear anything about suffering and dying, for that's all they know.

Conclusion: Mark's Christology

I would like to suggest some ways in which the contemporary church may function as a channel of salvation, as a redemptive community. In this endeavor, I will use Mark's community as an example. Mark's context was marked by a heightened *apocalyptic fervor* (Jewish revolt), *ethnical enmities* (Jews and Gentiles in his community), *gender issues* (leadership in his community was becoming ostensibly male and hierarchical), and *imperial harassment* (Rome accused the Christian communities of collaborating with the rebels).

Apocalyptic fervor. This was mitigated by relocating the place where the kingdom was going to be manifested (not in Jerusalem but in Galilee) and by redefining who the agents of this kingdom were going to be. Certainly not the self-appointed messiahs mentioned in Mark 13:21–22, but the Son of Man and his persecuted and suffering community, the company of faithful co-disciples who, through nonviolent means, were going to receive the vindication that their suffering deserved.

Ethnic rivalries. These were addressed by showing that the Son of Man represents all of God's people, both Jews and Gentiles, as the general call to discipleship of 8:34–38, done in the highly Hellenized area of Caesarea Philippi, seems to suggest. This, plus Jesus' positive attitude toward Gentiles throughout the story, can be seen as Mark's narrative strategy to mend ethnic rivalries in his community, a situation that was aggravated by the Jewish revolt. Jesus' example as the model disciple of God's kingdom would have sent a clear message to Mark's community as to what their attitude toward those of different ethnic backgrounds should be.

Gender issues. Women play an important role in the narrative, outshining the male disciples on many occasions, such as, for example, during Jesus' passion, death, and resurrection, where the absence of the male disciples is contrasted with the faithful presence of the women throughout the ordeal. The message to the Markan community is clear: women are as qualified to be disciples as men, perhaps even more qualified, as the emphasis on the need for *diakonia* among the disciples seems to suggest (Mark 10:42–45). This may be addressing a growing problem in the early church between what was rightly perceived as an open attitude towards the leadership of women, manifested by Jesus and Paul, and a desire to concentrate power in the hands of the adult males of the community, which became the norm in the church from the second century onward.[5] Here, at the beginning of the second half of the first century, the problem was beginning to surface. Mark tried to deal with it by means of a story that privileges women over men as disciples and followers of Jesus.

Imperial harassment. This was expected anytime a revolt was in full swing, as was the case with the Jewish-Roman war of 66–70 CE. The small congregations of Jesus' followers must have felt the pressure from the government to remain faithful to the emperor in the midst of the extensive recruitment done by the rebels. Mark's message in this sense is quite clear: the community would have nothing to do either with the Roman military machine (5:1–20) or with the royal-political messianism of the revolutionaries (the Messiah is not the son of David, 12:35–37!). They were to remain unaligned, waiting, and working for the manifestation of God's kingdom in Galilee, ironically the bedrock of the Jewish revolt.

The different contexts of the church in today's world will dictate the kinds of (re)appropriations of the biblical text that are plausible or possible. Writing as I am from a North American, U.S. context demands that I take into consideration some of the particularities of this reality for my reading of Mark's gospel. Even a cursory look will show that this reality is marked by analogous, although not identical, issues to Mark's community: apocalyptic rhetoric and worldview emanating from both official and non-official sources, ethnic/racial prejudices and misunderstandings both in society and in the church, gender-related issues, especially when it comes to leadership roles in the church, and imperial harassment represented by the vociferous pro-war and anti-immigration rhetoric emanating from the White House, especially during the George W. Bush administration (2001–2009) and materialized soon afterwards in concrete legislation. The Markan model of a redemptive community may have something to say about these four contexts.

First, the Markan model helps us to combat the apocalyptically imbued discourse of many U.S. conservative administrations, such as Reagan

---

5. April D. DeConick suggests that, by the time the gospels were written, the role of women, especially Mary Magdalene, was being remodeled so the male disciples became the heroes and leaders of the movement. She asserts, "The remodeling of Mary's traditional story occurred at a time when women's roles in some of the churches were being called into question because of the social and cultural implications of their leadership. Although women were still permitted in leadership positions within the churches, their power and prominence were already beginning to wane as the dominant social and cultural hierarchy was threatened, aroused, and asserted in the mid- to late-first century." DeConick, *Holy Misogyny*, 134.

and Bush, for being disciples of Jesus Christ will always be at odds with that kind of mentality. This discourse included the justification of war in the name of our "manifest destiny" to be representatives of what is good and just (democracy, Christianity, the western way of life, capitalism) over against what is evil and unjust (totalitarian regimes, Islam, Islamic societies, communism and/or socialism).[6] When the real test of true discipleship becomes not so much how faithful one is to a supposedly spiritual gospel of deliverance from earthly things, but rather how faithful one is to resisting a rhetoric that invokes divine sanction while at the same time hides a clear political and expansionist agenda (this was the case of both the Roman Empire and the Jewish revolutionaries), then Mark's depiction of Jesus as the exemplar disciple of the kingdom and the representative of God's redemptive community, is absolutely crucial for our present praxis.

Second, despite the acknowledgment that we live in a highly pluralistic and diverse society, the latest anti-immigration rhetoric coming from both official and non-official sources, as well as specific legislation that has been passed, is proof that ethnic and racial prejudice and misunderstanding are still commonplace in American life. The proliferation of bibliographies and resources of all types that address the reality of the multi-ethnic nature of our society is met with an incredible lack of awareness and/or sensitivity by the general public. Theory and practice do not seem to go hand in hand, as more and more ethnicity and race become stumbling blocks for people's interactions. When transferred to the church, this attitude is seen in the existence of segregated communities and/or segregated worship services. Jesus as the exemplar disciple of the kingdom of God models the right attitude towards diversity: he was willing to learn from a Syrophoenician woman in the region of Tyre, he ministered among those who were not ethnic Israelites (chapter 5), he fed four thousand people in a largely Gentile area of Palestine (chapter 8), thus making it clear that his ministry was to be inclusive.

Third, when faced with the current issues of women, gays, and lesbians in roles of leadership in the church, the model provided by Mark of a Jesus who described himself in terms of the service only women and slaves were supposed to provide in that society (Mark 10:45), is crucial for our

---

6. In his book *Orientalism*, Edward Said demonstrates vehemently that the East has been construed by the West as "lamentably under humanized, antidemocratic, backward, barbaric, and so forth." Said, *Orientalism*, 150. The natural consequence of such construction is that the study of the Orient and its cultures becomes "a Western style for dominating, restructuring, and having authority over the Orient." Said, *Orientalism*, 3.

Jesus, Disciple of the Kingdom

present praxis. This model of Jesus as disciple does away with gender and class distinctions,[7] for here a disempowered male peasant from Galilee is presented as the example of one who leads through service, thus debunking the cultural assumptions of the time, which expected the leadership roles in the church to be assigned to aristocratic males (cf. Luke-Acts, Pastoral Epistles).

Fourth, imperial harassment is seen today in the pro-war and anti-immigration rhetoric that pervades the media-driven public opinion. Even Bible-believing Christians are drawn into the justification of these attitudes, which go clearly against the spirit of the gospel of Jesus Christ because they promote patriotism—the worship of the nation as god—and xenophobia—the hatred of the other. Jesus' stand against violence of any sort exemplifies the only legitimate site and attitude for discipleship. As we know, Jesus was not a Judean but a Galilean Jew, and his views of the Torah, God, and Israel as God's people betrayed this marginal origin. He adhered to the "little tradition," a version of the Torah that developed independently from the control of Jerusalem and its leadership, who represented the "great tradition." This version of the Torah preserved the memory of prophets such as Elijah and Elisha, which served the Galileans well in their criticism of Jerusalem and its ruling classes. One of these criticisms was directed against Davidic messianism, the restorationist vision that tried to re-legitimate the temple state under the exegetical premise that the Messiah was David's son.[8] Actually, said Jesus, he was his Lord (cf. Mark 12:35–37). This allowed Jesus to propose a nonviolent and anti-war agenda, which later served the Markan community to oppose the Zealots' revolutionary plans. The irony of the whole thing is that while the Jewish revolt originated in Galilee and served the agenda of Galilean peasants who found in the revolution a way out of their oppression, Jesus' proclamation of the kingdom of God also originated in Galilee, but proposed a nonviolent way of attaining that liberation. In our contemporary, present-day discussion on violence, being a disciple of Jesus Christ will entail opposing any kind of rhetoric that encourages or justifies the destruction of human life, including the latest debate on gun control prompted by the massacre of twenty six people, twenty of them children, killed by a gunman at an elementary school in Newtown, Connecticut.[9]

---

7. For a completely different view, see Liew, "Re-Markable Masculinities," 93–135.

8. Myers, *Binding the Strong Man*, 319.

9. The Second Amendment is a typical example of a law that was conceived for

Conclusion: Mark's Christology

I am convinced that the church as a redemptive community is called to inhabit a liminal space, a space of marginality, as Jesus did,[10] from where God's reign can be envisioned as a possibility through a life of discipleship. This vision is constructed in solidarity with the poor, a term which should not be relegated to the economically deprived only, but which should include all those who have been pushed to the physical, cultural, and emotional margins of society. It is in the margins, in the periphery, in the "wilderness," to use a Markan motif, where God's salvation is enacted through the agency of a redemptive community. Jesus as disciple of the kingdom provides the church with a model that privileges social transformation through political praxis over escape from the world to a heavenly realm.

A Final Word

In chapter 6 of the present work, I quoted Pablo Richard when he said: "Jesus identified the kingdom of God not with the Davidic monarchy, not with the sanctity of the temple, and not with the fulfillment of the law, but with the lives of the poor."[11] Let me now finish with the words of another Latin American author, this time Jorge Luis Borges:

> Ser pobre implica una más inmediata posesión de la realidad, un atropellar el primer gusto áspero de las cosas: conocimiento que parece faltar a los ricos, como si todo les llegara filtrado.[12]

Jesus was poor. He belonged to a family of marginal artisans whose place in society was even lower than that of peasants.[13] Poverty was his

---

another time and that needs to be revisited, reread, just as Jesus and the Markan community reread the Jewish law to make it relevant for a new situation.

10. Jesus was criticized for pretending to have a right to lead when in reality he was, perhaps, the son of an illiterate carpenter. He inhabited a liminal space. So did his disciples, for Jesus' call to follow him separated them from their kin, their villages, and a life of submission to the control of the colonial power of the Roman Empire. Jesus and the disciples carried out a ministry that was geared toward those at the periphery, who found themselves in between realities because they were deemed deviant, impure, or counter-cultural.

11. Richard, "Jesus: A Latin American Perspective," 341.

12. "To be poor implies a more immediate possession of reality, a charging against the first rough taste of things, knowledge that the rich seem to lack, as if everything would reach them filtered" (translation mine). Borges, *Obras Completas*, 129.

13. Bruce Malina offers the following comment: "By Jesus' time such craftsmen were

"first rough taste of things," as Borges says.[14] When I try to imagine[15] Jesus as disciple of the kingdom, I cannot separate from this idea the fact of his marginality and poverty. The two things go together. I can't imagine a rich Jesus. That would be an oxymoron in itself. Discipleship and marginality go together. That is why it is so difficult for people to envision a Jesus disciple. It is much easier, and comforting, to see Jesus as Master and Messiah, as Lord, for at least if you are poor and marginalized you have the hope of having him on your side. You expect him to rescue you from your situation. But if the Lord is a poor peasant, then there is no hope that he can help you, for he couldn't even help himself, hanging as he was from that Roman cross. Yes, we dislike a Jesus disciple, we deem it a heresy, a bad exegetical move, a hermeneutical catastrophe, or, as an editor put it to me, "a potentially fatal exegetical conundrum,"[16] for apparently there are no warrants for it in the text. We forget that the authors of the text were in a position of privilege compared to the earliest members of the movement, and that "everything would reach them filtered," even their understanding of who Jesus was.

And yet, I dare to think it. I dare to think of Jesus as disciple of the kingdom of God, a companion in the journey he once started himself, leaving us an example to follow. Jesus as not a "Lord-to-be-obeyed," because that would have implied, in the patron-client understanding of the time, leaving untouched the status quo that condemned the poor to the margins, but as an "example-to-be-followed,"[17] an empowering and revolutionary model that nurtured in itself the seeds of a new society.

---

often itinerant, especially those living in villages or small towns. Like all itinerants who did not stay home to protect their women and family honor, they were considered persons 'without shame.'" Malina, *Synoptic Gospels*, 212.

14. "Archaeologists have conducted excavations of Nazareth to help determine what it must have been like in Jesus' day. By all accounts, life was fairly grim. There is no evidence of any public building (synagogue, town building), of a paved street, of imported goods, of any luxury items of any kind. The hamlet appears to have depended almost entirely on local agriculture for survival. Estimates vary, but it appears that the habitable part of the village took up less than ten acres in Jesus' day. The best estimates at the population put it at anywhere from two hundred to four hundred people, total. The housing was primitive: hovels and peasant homes built over small caves, made of hewn field stones piled on one another, insulated with mud, clay, and dung mixed with straw, with roughly thatched roofs and dirt floors." Ehrman, *New Testament*, 269.

15. For the role of imagination in a historical reconstruction of the biblical text, see Schüssler Fiorenza, *Wisdom Ways*, 135–61.

16. E-mail conversation with Neil Elliott.

17 This idea is again taken from an e-mail conversation with Neil Elliott.

Conclusion: Mark's Christology

If Jesus is above all a model for discipleship, then Christianity is much more for the "here and now" than for the "there and after." And the gospels become the primary documents for implementing the following of Jesus. The rest of the New Testament provides examples of how the early communities contextualized and implemented the following of Jesus. His life is then a prototype, a model for discipleship. Therefore, much of the apparatus of the institutionalized church, built on the fundamental premise of Jesus as personal savior and eschatological judge, needs to be reevaluated. Salvation is not accomplished by a single individual figure, but by a redemptive community, a community of disciples, empowered by the spirit of God.

Likewise, the eschatology of the early church needs to be seen as a theological construct that was necessary and/or unavoidable at the time, at least for the orthodox branch of the church, but which has to be understood primarily in a metaphorical way if it is going to be relevant in the twenty-first century. It needs to be reevaluated also and reappropriated, so that its liberating force can be unleashed beyond its mere literal meaning. As long as eschatology functions as a utopian ideal, and not as an objective reality, it can affect the course of history by encouraging changes in today's world. On the other hand, if we limit eschatology to its literal-historical dimension, without acknowledging its metaphorical-theological one, it becomes a legitimizer of the status quo, enslaving rather than liberating people. In other words, unless we de-historicize and de-literalize eschatology, it becomes historically irrelevant at best and oppressive at worst.

As the church, we need to experience discipleship "unfiltered," as Jesus did, without the privileges, ascribed or acquired, that we usually assume. Rather, we should assume the privileged place of marginality, for it is from there that God's kingdom can be really experienced. Otherwise, how would one explain Jesus' answer to the rich man: "You lack one thing; go, sell what you own, and give it to the poor, and you will have treasure in heaven; then come, follow me" (Mark 10:21). And especially his comment to the disciples: "How hard it will be for those who have wealth to enter the kingdom of God" (Mark 10:23). Entering the kingdom is predicated on sharing one's wealth with the poor and following Jesus on the path of discipleship. Both things go together, becoming poor or, to put it in other words, being in solidarity with the poor, being willing to live in the wilderness, to inhabit in solidarity the liminal and *queer* spaces of the marginalized in order to build together with them a redemptive community, a community of disciples that nurtures in its midst the liberating presence of the model disciple of the kingdom, Jesus of Nazareth.

Jesus, Disciple of the Kingdom

According to the Trinitarian theology of the church, the seeds of which are already present in the canonical writings, Jesus is now with God but also with us through the work of the Holy Spirit. That is why he can inspire us in our walk of discipleship, not only as part of the Godhead, but also as part of that great cloud of witnesses the author of Hebrews talks about. It is my hope that this book may point at ways in which this call to co-discipleship can be not only exegetically legitimized but also practically implemented.

Bibliography

Allison, Dale C., Jr. "The Continuity between Jesus and John." *JSHJ* 1 (2003) 6–27.
Anderson, Janice C., and Stephen D. Moore. *Mark and Method: New Approaches in Biblical Studies*. Minneapolis: Fortress, 1992.
Barr, David. *New Testament Story: An Introduction*. 3rd ed. Belmont, CA: Wadsworth, 2002.
Bauer, Walter, et al. *Greek-English Lexicon of the New Testament and Other Early Christian Literature*. 2nd ed. Chicago: University of Chicago Press, 1979.
Beck, Robert R. *Nonviolent Story: Narrative Conflict Resolution in the Gospel of Mark*. Maryknoll, NY: Orbis, 1996.
Beecher, Henry W. *The Life of Jesus, the Christ*. New York: Ford, 1871.
Belo, Fernando. *A Materialistic Reading of the Gospel of Mark*. Maryknoll, NY: Orbis, 1981.
Bird, Michael F., and Joel Willitts. *Paul and the Gospels: Christologies, Conflicts and Convergences*. London: T. & T. Clark, 2011.
Black, David Alan. *Perspective on the Ending of Mark: 4 Views*. Nashville: Broadman & Holman, 2008.
Borg, Marcus J., and John Dominic Crossan. *The First Paul: Reclaiming the Radical Visionary behind the Church's Conservative Icon*. New York: HarperOne, 2009.
Borges, Jorge Luis. *Obras Completas* 5th. ed. Vol. 1, *1923–1949*. Buenos Aires: Emecé, 2010.
Boring, M. Eugene. "The Gospel of Matthew: Introduction, Commentary, and Reflections." In *The New Interpreter's Bible: A Commentary in Twelve Volumes*, edited by Leander E. Keck et al., 8:87–505. Nashville: Abingdon, 1995.
Breck, John. *The Shape of Biblical Language: Chiasmus in the Scriptures and Beyond*. Crestwood, NY: St. Vladimir's Seminary Press, 1994.
Broadhead, Edwin K. *Teaching with Authority: Miracles and Christology in the Gospel of Mark*. JSNTSup 74. Sheffield: JSOT, 1992.
Brooks, James A., and Carlton L. Winbery. *Syntax of New Testament Greek*. Washington, DC: University Press of America, 1979.
Bryan, Christopher. *A Preface to Mark: Notes on the Gospel in Its Literary and Cultural Settings*. New York: Oxford University Press, 1993.
Burkett, Delbert R. *The Son of Man Debate: A History and Evaluation*. SNTSMS 107. Cambridge, UK: Cambridge University Press, 1999.
Childs, Brevard S. *The New Testament as Canon: An Introduction*. Valley Forge, PA: Trinity, 1994.
Chilton, Bruce. *Rabbi Jesus: An Intimate Biography*. New York: Doubleday, 2000.
Cone, James H. *God of the Oppressed*. San Francisco: Harper & Row, 1975.

Bibliography

Cook, John G. *The Structure and Persuasive Power of Mark: A Linguistic Approach.* Atlanta: Scholars, 1995.

Croatto, J. Severino. *Biblical Hermeneutics: Toward a Theory of Reading as the Production of Meaning.* Maryknoll, NY: Orbis, 1987.

———. "Estudio Exegético-Homilético 043–Octubre 2003." Unpublished Bible Study Series. Buenos Aires: Instituto Universitario ISEDET.

Crossan, John Dominic. *The Historical Jesus: The Life of a Mediterranean Jewish Peasant.* New York: HarperSanFrancisco, 1991.

Danove, Paul L. *The End of Mark's Story: A Methodological Study.* Leiden: Brill, 1993.

DeConick, April D. *Holy Misogyny: Why the Sex and Gender Conflicts in the Early Church Still Matter.* New York: Continuum, 2011.

Ehrman, Bart D. *The New Testament: A Historical Introduction to the Early Christian Writings.* 5th ed. New York: Oxford University Press, 2012.

Elizondo, Virgilio P. *Galilean Journey: The Mexican-American Promise.* Maryknoll, NY: Orbis, 1983.

Esler, Philip F. *The First Christians in their Social Worlds: Social-Scientific Approaches to New Testament Interpretation.* London: Routledge, 1994.

Farmer, William R. *The Gospel of Jesus: The Pastoral Relevance of the Synoptic Problem.* Louisville: Westminster John Knox, 1994.

———. *The Last Twelve Verses of Mark.* Cambridge: Cambridge University Press, 1974.

Fatum, Lone. "Gender Hermeneutics: The Effective History of Consciousness and the Use of Social Gender in the Gospels." In *Reading from This Place: Social Location and Biblical Interpretation*, edited by Fernando F. Segovia and Mary Ann Tolbert, 2:157–68. Minneapolis: Fortress, 1995.

Fleddermann, Harry T. *Q: A Reconstruction and Commentary.* Biblical Tools and Studies 1. Leuven: Peeters, 2005.

Foster, Paul. "The Pastoral Purpose of Q's Two-Stage Son of Man Christology." *Bib* 89 (2008) 81–91.

Fowler, Robert M. "Reader-Response Criticism: Figuring Mark's Reader." In *Mark and Method: New Approaches in Biblical Studies*, edited by Janice Capel Anderson and Stephen D. Moore, 59–94. Minneapolis: Fortress, 1992.

Geddert, Timothy J. *Watchwords: Mark 13 in Markan Eschatology.* JSNTSup 26. Sheffield: JSOT, 1989.

Greene, Colin J. D. *Christology in Cultural Perspective: Marking Out the Horizons.* Grand Rapids: Eerdmans, 2004.

Gundry, Robert H. *Mark: A Commentary on His Apology for the Cross.* Grand Rapids: Eerdmans, 1993.

Gutiérrez, Gustavo. *A Theology of Liberation.* 2nd ed. Translated by Caridad Inda and John Eagleson. Maryknoll, NY: Orbis, 1988.

Hansen, G., editor. *Los caminos inexhauribles de la palabra (Las relecturas creativas en la Biblia y de la Biblia): Homenaje a J. Severino Croatto.* Buenos Aires: Lumen-Isedet, 2000.

Heikki, Raisanen. *The "Messianic Secret" in Mark: Studies of the NT and Its World.* Translated by Christopher Tuckett. Edinburgh: T. & T. Clark, 1990.

Heil, John Paul. *The Gospel of Mark as a Model for Action: A Reader-Response Commentary.* Mahwah, NJ: Paulist, 1992.

Henderson, Suzanne Watts. *Christology and Discipleship in the Gospel of Mark.* Cambridge: Cambridge University Press, 2006.

Bibliography

Hengel, Martin. *Studies in the Gospel of Mark*. London: SCM, 1985.
Herzog, William R., II. *Prophet and Teacher: An Introduction to the Historical Jesus*. Louisville: Westminster John Knox, 2005.
Hinkelammert, Franz J. *El Grito del Sujeto: Del teatro-mundo del evangelio de Juan al perro-mundo de la globalización*. San José, Costa Rica: DEI, 1998.
Hooker, Morna. *Endings: Invitations to Discipleship*. Peabody, MA: Hendrickson, 2003.
———. *The Gospel According to Mark*. Peabody, MA: Hendrickson, 1997.
Horsley, Richard A. *Hearing the Whole Story: The Politics of Plot in Mark's Gospel*. Louisville: Westminster John Knox, 2001.
———. *Jesus and Empire: The Kingdom of God and the New World Disorder*. Minneapolis: Fortress, 2003.
Hughes, Charles T. "Pluralism, Inclusivism, and Christology." In *Jesus Then and Now: Images of Jesus in History and Christology*, edited by Marvin Meyer and Charles Hughes, 155–69. Harrisburg, PA: Trinity, 2001.
Hurtado, Larry H. *Mark*. New International Biblical Commentary. Peabody, MA: Hendrickson, 1995.
Iersel, Bastiaan van. *Reading Mark*. Edinburgh: T. & T. Clark, 1989.
Jennings, Theodore W., Jr. *The Insurrection of the Crucified: The "Gospel of Mark" as Theological Manifesto*. Chicago: Exploration, 2003.
Johnson, Luke T. *The Real Jesus: The Misguided Quest for the Historical Jesus and the Truth of the Traditional Gospels*. San Francisco: HarperSanFrancisco, 1996.
Juel, Donald H. *A Master of Surprise: Mark Interpreted*. Minneapolis: Fortress, 1994.
Kazen, Thomas. "Son of Man as Kingdom Imagery: Jesus between Corporate Symbol and Individual Redeemer Figure." In *Jesus from Judaism to Christianity: Continuum Approaches to the Historical Jesus*, edited by Tom Holmen, 87–108. Library of New Testament Studies 312. London: T. & T. Clark, 2007.
Kee, Howard C. *Community of the New Age: Studies in Mark's Gospel*. Philadelphia: Westminster, 1984.
———. *Jesus in History: An Approach to the Study of the Gospels*. 2nd ed. New York: Harcourt Brace Jovanovich, 1977.
Keenan, John P. *The Gospel of Mark: A Mahayana Reading*. Maryknoll, NY: Orbis, 1995.
Kelber, Werner. *Mark's Story of Jesus*. Philadelphia: Fortress, 1979.
Kingsbury, Jack Dean. *Conflict in Mark: Jesus, Authorities, Disciples*. Minneapolis: Fortress, 1989.
Kinukawa, Hisako. *Women and Jesus in Mark: A Japanese Feminist Perspective*. Maryknoll, NY: Orbis, 1994.
Krantz, Jeffrey H. "Crucified Son of Man or Mighty One? Mark's Chiastic Gospel Structure and the Question of Jesus' Identity." PreachingPeace.org. February 2013. No pages. Online: http://www.preachingpeace.org/2010/04/06/mark_chiasm/.
Kuthirakkattel, Scaria. *The Beginning of Jesus' Ministry According to Mark's Gospel (1:14–3:6): A Redactional Critical Study*. Rome: Pontifical Biblical Institute, 1990.
Levine, Amy-Jill. *The Misunderstood Jew: The Church and the Scandal of the Jewish Jesus*. New York: HarperOne, 2006.
Liew, Tat-siong Benny. "Re-Markable Masculinities: Jesus, the Son of Man, and the (Sad) Sum of Manhood?" In *New Testament Masculinities*, edited by Stephen D. Moore and Janice Capel Anderson, 93–135. Semeia Studies 45. Atlanta: Society of Biblical Literature, 2003.
Lindars, Barnabas. *Jesus, Son of Man*. Grand Rapids: Eerdmans, 1983.

Bibliography

Lohr, Charles H. "Oral Techniques in the Gospel of Matthew." *CBQ* 23 (1961) 403–35.

Mack, Burton. *The Lost Gospel: The Book of Q and Christian Origins*. San Francisco: HarperSanFrancisco, 1993.

———. *A Myth of Innocence: Mark and Christian Origins*. Minneapolis: Fortress, 1991.

Malbon, Elizabeth Struthers. "Echoes and Foreshadowings in Mark 4–8: Reading and Rereading." *JBL* 112 (1993) 211–30.

———. *Mark's Jesus: Characterization as Narrative Christology*. Waco, TX: Baylor University Press, 2009.

Malina, Bruce J. *The Social World of Jesus and the Gospels*. London: Routledge, 1996.

———. "Social-Scientific Method in Historical Jesus Research." In *The Social Setting of Jesus and the Gospels*, edited by Wolfgang Stegemann et al., 3–26. Minneapolis: Fortress, 2002.

Malina, Bruce, and R. L. Rohrbaugh. *Social-Science Commentary on the Gospel of John*. Minneapolis: Fortress, 1998.

———. *Social-Science Commentary on the Synoptic Gospels*. Minneapolis: Fortress, 1992.

Marcus, Joel. "The Jewish War and the Sitz im Leben of Mark." *JBL* 111 (1992) 441–62.

———. *Mark 1–8: A New Translation with Wntroduction and Commentary*. Anchor Yale Bible 27. New York: Doubleday, 2000.

Mateos, Juan, and Farnando Camacho. *Marcos: Texto y Comentario*. Córdoba: El Almendro, 1994.

Metzger, Bruce. *The Text of the New Testament*. New York: Oxford University Press, 1979.

Miller, Dale, and Patricia J. Miller. *The Gospel of Mark as Midrash on Earlier Jewish and New Testament Literature*. New York: Mellen, 1990.

Mitchell, Joan L. *Beyond Fear and Silence: A Feminist Literary Approach to the Gospel of Mark*. New York: Continnum, 2001.

Myers, Ched. *Binding the Strong Man: A Political Reading of Mark's Story of Jesus*. Maryknoll, NY: Orbis, 1995.

Nickelsburg, George W. E. *Ancient Judaism and Christian Origins: Diversity, Continuity, and Transformation*. Minneapolis: Fortress, 2003.

Painter, John. *Mark's Gospel: Worlds in Conflict*. Edited by John Court. New Testament Readings. London: Routledge, 1997.

Patte, Daniel. *Ethics of Biblical Interpretation: A Reevaluation*. Louisville: Westminster John Knox, 1995.

Perkins, Pheme. "The Gospel of Mark: Introduction, Commentary, and Reflections." In *The New Interpreter's Bible: A Commentary in Twelve Volumes*, edited by Leander E. Keck et al., 8:509–733. Nashville: Abingdon, 1995.

Perrin, Norman, and Dennis C. Duling. *The New Testament, An Introduction: Proclamation and Parenesis, Myth and History*. 2nd ed. New York: Harcourt Brace Jovanovich, Inc., 1982.

Pixley, George V. *God's Kingdom*. London: SCM, 1981.

Rengstorf, K. H. "Manthano, Mathetes." In *TDNT*, edited by Gerhard Kittel and Gehhard Friedrich, translated by Geoffrey W. Bromiley, abridged in 1 vol., 552–62. Grand Rapids: Eerdmans, 1985.

Richard, Pablo. "Jesus: A Latin American Perspective." In *Global Bible Commentary*, edited by Daniel Patte et al., 337–41. Nashville: Abingdon, 2004.

Robbins, Vernon K. *Jesus the Teacher: A Socio-Rhetorical Interpretation of Mark*. Philadelphia: Fortress, 1984.

———. *The Tapestry of Early Christian Discourse: Rhetoric, Society and Ideology*. London: Routledge, 1996.
Rossing, Barbara R. *The Rapture Exposed: The Message of Hope in the Book of Revelation*. New York: Basic Books, 2004.
Said, Edward W. *Orientalism*. New York: Vintage, 1979.
Samuel, Simon. *A Postcolonial Reading of Mark's Story of Jesus*. London: T. & T. Clark, 2007.
Schnelle, Udo. *Theology of the New Testament*. Translated by M. Eugene Boring. Grand Rapids: Baker, 2009.
Schildgen, Brenda D. *Crisis and Continuity: Time in the Gospel of Mark*. JSNTSup 159. Sheffield: Sheffield Academic, 1998.
Schröter, Jens. "The Son of Man as the Representative of God's Kingdom: On the Interpretation of Jesus in Mark and Q." In *Jesus, Mark, and Q: The Teaching of Jesus and Its Earliest Records*, edited by Michael Labahn and Andreas Schmidt, 34–68. London: T. & T. Clark, 2004.
Schüssler Fiorenza, Elisabeth. *But She Said: Feminist Practices of Biblical Interpretation*. Boston: Beacon, 1992.
———. *In Memory of Her: A Feminist Theological Reconstruction of Christian Origins*. New York: Crossroad, 1983.
———. *Jesus and the Politics of Interpretation*. New York: Continuum, 2001.
———. *The Power of the Word: Scripture and the Rhetoric of Empire*. Minneapolis: Fortress, 2007.
———. *Wisdom Ways: Introducing Biblical Interpretation*. Maryknoll, NY: Orbis, 2001.
Schweizer, Eduard. *The Good News According to Mark*. Atlanta: John Knox, 1977.
Scott, M. Philip. "Chiastic Structure: A Key to the Interpretation of Mark's Gospel." *BTB* 15 (1985) 17–26.
Segovia, Fernando F. "The Counter Empire of God: Postcolonialism and John." *PSB*, n.s., 27 (2006) 82–99.
Sobrino, Jon. *Christology at the Crossroads*. Translated by John Drury. Maryknoll, NY: Orbis, 1978.
Soulen, Richard N., and R. Kendall Soulen. *Handbook of Biblical Criticism*. 3rd ed. Louisville: Westminster John Knox, 2001.
Stanton, Graham N. *The Gospels and Jesus*. Oxford Bible Series. New York: Oxford University Press, 1989.
Stock, Augustine. "Hinge Transitions in Mark's Gospel." *BTB* 15 (1985) 27–31.
Swartley, Mark. "The Role of Women in Mark's Gospel." *BTB* 27 (1997) 16–22.
Tabor, James D. *The Jesus Dynasty: The Hidden History of Jesus, His Royal Family, and the Birth of Christianity*. New York: Simon & Schuster, 2006.
Talbert, Charles H. *Reading John: A Literary and Theological Commentary on the Fourth Gospel and the Johannine Epistles*. Macon, GA: Smyth & Helwys, 2005.
Tannehill, Robert. "The Gospel of Mark as Narrative Christology." *Semeia* 16 (1979) 57–95.
Taylor, Joan E. *The Immerser: John the Baptist within Second Temple Judaism*. Grand Rapids: Eerdmans, 1997.
Theissen, Gerd. *Sociology of Early Palestinian Christianity*. Philadelphia: Fortress, 1978.
Tilley, Terrence W. *The Disciples' Jesus: Christology as Reconciling Practice*. Maryknoll, NY: Orbis, 2008.

Bibliography

Tolbert, Mary Ann. *Sowing the Gospel: Mark's World in Literary-Historical Perspective.* Minneapolis: Fortress, 1996.

Ulansey, David. "The Heavenly Veil Torn: Mark's Cosmic *Inclusio.*" *JBL* 110 (1991) 123–25.

Vena, Osvaldo D. "Gospel Images of Jesus as Deacon: Upsetting the Hierarchies of His Culture." *NAAD Monograph Series* 14 (2003) 1–16.

———. "La Expectativa Escatológica en el Evangelio de Marcos. Análisis Literario y Estructural de Marcos 13." *RevistB* 56 (1994) 85–101.

———. "La 'otra' comunidad detrás del evangelio de Marcos." *Cuadernos de Teología* 21 (2002) 51–66.

———. "The Markan Construction of Jesus as Disciple of the Kingdom." In *Mark: Texts @ Context Series*, edited by Teresa Okure et al., 71–100. Minneapolis: Fortress, 2011.

———. *The Parousia and Its Rereadings: The Development of the Eschatological Consciousness in the Writings of the New Testament.* Studies in Biblical Literature 27. New York: Peter Lang, 2001.

———. "Paul's Understanding of the Eschatological Prophet of Malachi 4:5–6." *BR* 44 (1999) 35–54.

———. "The Rhetorical and Theological Center of Mark's Gospel." In *Los caminos inexhauribles de la Palabra*, edited by Guillermo Hansen, 327–45. Buenos Aires: Lumen/Isedet, 2000.

Vermes, Geza. *The Changing Faces of Jesus.* New York: Penguin Compass, 2002.

Villalobos Mendoza, Manuel. *Abject Bodies in the Gospel of Mark.* Sheffield, UK: Sheffield Phoenix, 2012.

Waetjen, Herman C. *A Reordering of Power: A Socio-Political Reading of Mark's Gospel.* Minneapolis: Fortress, 1989.

Weeden, Theodore J. *Mark-Traditions in Conflict.* Philadelphia: Fortress, 1971.

Wefald, Eric K. "The Separate Gentile Mission in Mark: A Narrative Explanation of Markan Geography; The Two Feeding Accounts and Exorcisms." *JSNT* 60 (1995) 3–26.

White, L. Michael. *Scripting Jesus: The Gospels in Rewrite.* New York: HarperOne, 2011.

Wilson, Robert R. "2 Kings." In *HCSB*, rev. ed., edited by Harold W. Attridge, 519–59. San Francisco: HarperSanFrancisco, 2006.

Wink, Walter. *The Human Being: Jesus and the Enigma of the Son of Man.* Minneapolis: Fortress, 2002.

Witherington, Ben, III. *The Gospel of Mark: A Socio-Rhetorical Commentary.* Grand Rapids: Eerdmans, 2001.

Wright, N. T. *Jesus and the Victory of God.* Vol. 2 of *Christian Origins and the Question of God.* Minneapolis: Fortress, 1996.

Yarbro Collins, Adela, and John J. Collins. *King and Messiah as Son of God: Divine, Human, and Angelic Messianic Figures in Biblical and Related Literature.* Grand Rapids: Eerdmans, 2008.

Author Index

Allison, Dale C., Jr., 83–84

Barr, David, 102n77
Bauer, Walter, 25, 117n109
Beecher, Henry W., 78n11
Belo, Fernando, 14n41
Bird, Michael F., 20n1
Black, David Alan, 147n12
Bonhoeffer, Dietrich, ix, xi
Borges, Jorge Luis, 185–86
Boring, M. Eugene, 173–74n21
Bryan, Christopher, 148n16
Burkett, Delbert R., 35n29

Childs, Brevard S., 145n4, 147n13
Chilton, Bruce, 15, 84n23
Collins, John J., 35n29, 85n33, 127n16
Cone, James H., 6n19, 8n26
Cook, John G., 54n3
Croatto, J. Severino, 53n1, 74n3
Crossan, John Dominic, 16n48, 36n33
Crossley, James G., 20n1

Danove, Paul L., 146
DeConick, April D., 182n5

Elizondo, Virgilio P., 170–71n14
Esler, Philip F., 4

Farmer, William R., 21n3, 145n5
Fatum, Lone, 9–10
Fowler, Robert M., 149

Gill, Athol, x, xi
Gundry, Robert H., 86
Gutierrez, Gustavo, 2

Henderson, Suzanne Watts, 89, 102–3, 105n81
Herzog, William, R., II, 4n12
Hooker, Morna D., 71n36, 133n25
Horsley, Richard A., 49, 76n4–5, 78n10–11, 108, 110n90, 126n10
Hughes, Charles T., 175n1

Johnson, Luke T., 123n4

Kazen, Thomas, 122, 128–29
Keener, Craig S., 13
Kelber, Werner H., 161n35
Kinukawa, Hisako, 101, 121n114
Krantz, Jeffrey H., 55–56

Levine, Amy-Jill, 99n70, 100n73
Liew, Tat-siong Benny, 184n7

Mack, Burton, 40n39
Malbon, Elizabeth Struthers, 16–17
Malina, Bruce J., 15n45, 70, 104n79, 108n85, 139n34, 185–86n13
Marcus, Joel, 38, 81, 83, 85, 91n53
Metzger, Bruce, 145–46, 149
Mitchell, Joan L., 100
Myers, Ched, ix, x, 8n27, 14n41, 38n34, 54, 58, 66, 69–72, 74, 90, 111, 113, 115, 126n9, 142, 173n20

Author Index

Neville, David, x, xi

Patte, Daniel, 7n24
Perkins, Pheme, 133n25
Perrin, Norman, 57n17, 65–66, 138n32
Pixley, George V., 14n41, 163–64n3 and 6

Rengstorf, K. H., 29–33
Richard, Pablo, 162–64, 185
Robbins, Vernon K., 17

Said, Edward W., 183n6
Samuel, Simon, 79n12
Schüssler Fiorenza, Elisabeth, 2n8, 6, 7n23, 8n28, 9, 22n6, 25n8, 109n89, 115–16, 176, 186n15
Schweizer, Eduard, x, xi, 147
Scott, M. Philip, 55–56
Segovia, Fernando F., ix, xi
Smith, Mahlon, 128n18
Sobrino, Jon, 1n2, 2
Soulen, R. Kendall, 113n99
Soulen, Richard N., 113n99
Stanton, Graham. N., 50

Tabor, James D., 93n57
Tannehill, Robert, 16, 81–82, 104n80
Theissen, Gerd, 14, 83, 123–126, 131
Tilley, Terrence W., 1–2, 8n29, 78n10-11
Tolbert, Mary Ann, 95–97

Ulansey, David, 59

van Iersel, Bas M. F., 150n19
Vena, Osvaldo D., 6n21, 35n29, 49n44, 53n1, 128n17, 138n32, 148n14, 154n21
Villalobos, Mendoza Manuel, 161n35

Waetjen, Herman C., 71n36, 92, 98–99
White, L. Michael, 123n4
Willitts, Joel, 20n1
Wilson, Robert R., 30
Wink, Walter, 35n29, 115n103
Witherington, Ben, III, 114n100, 133n25, 144n2
Wrede, William, 102n77
Wright, N. T., 163–64

Yarbro Collins, Adela, 35n29, 85n33, 127n16

Scripture Index

OLD TESTAMENT

Genesis
19:24–26	43
22:2	85
22:12	85
22:16	85
32:26	8

Exodus
4:3	98
4:10–12	30
4:17	98
20:6	112
20:17	110
23	79
23:20	79
24:1	23
24:8	114
24:9	23

Numbers
11:16	23
11:17	23
11:24	23
27:15–17	29

Deuteronomy
8:4	98
24:14	110
29:5	98
34	133

Joshua
1:2–5	29

1 Kings
19:5–8	88

2 Kings
2:5	29, 30
2:7	29
2:9–12	29
2:12	29, 30
2:14	30
2:15	29, 30
3:11–12	29
13:14	29

1 Chronicles
25:8	29

Job
9:8	172
38:16	172

Psalms
2	51, 86
2:7	85
71:17	12

Scripture Index

Psalms (cont.)

8	35
104:6–7	172
106:9	172
110:1	139
119:102	12
143:8	12
143:10	12

Isaiah

2:11–22	44
6	15
13:6–19	44
25:6–8	115
40	79
40:3	79
42	86
42:1–4	81
48:20	167, 168
49:1–7	81
49:5–6	168
49:6	168
49:8–13	115
50:4	81, 89, 167
50:4–11	81
50:5–6	81
52:13—53:12	81
52:14–15	167
53	115, 167, 168
53:10	167
53:11	167
53:11–12	167
53:12	167
54:13	12
63:11—64:1	84

Jeremiah

1:31–34	114
16:16	90
31:34	114
32:33	12
36:4–8	29

Ezekiel

1	15
29:4	90
30:1–4	44

Daniel

2:18	124
5:28	124
7	38–39, 48, 94, 124, 130–32, 135, 142, 157, 160
7:3–8	127
7:13	35, 36, 113, 135
7:13–14	18, 48, 125, 127, 137, 138
7:14	129, 132, 136, 138
7:18	127, 132, 135, 136
7:21–22	135
7:22	127
7:27	127, 129, 132, 135, 136, 138
9:16	124
9:27	135
11:31	135
11:36	124
12:2–3	130
12:11	135

Hosea

11:13	12

Joel

1:15	44
2:1–2	44
2:1–11	133

Amos

4:2	90
5:18–20	44

Scripture Index

Zephaniah

1:2—2:13	44
1:7–18	133
2:2–3	133
3:8	133

Zechariah

9:11	114
14	133

Malachi

3	79
3:1	78, 79, 105
4	133
4:5–6	26

APOCRYPHA/ DEUTEROCANONICAL BOOKS

Tobit

4:34	111

1 Maccabees

6:44	141

4 Maccabees

17:20–22	141

Wisdom of Jesus Son of Sirach (Ecclesiasticus)

4:1	110

NEW TESTAMENT

Matthew

3:14	83
4:1–2	88
4:1–11	87
5:1	173–74
5:11	40
5:13–16	31
8:18–22	35
8:20	41
8:22	111
9:6	38
10:1–2	22
10:5–6	101
10:5–15	31
10:15	43
10:24	21
10:25	21
10:32	42
10:33	42
11:18	41
11:18–19	127
12:8	38
12:32	42
12:40–41	41
13:24	45
13:37	45
13:41	45
13:43	45, 46
13:44–45	109
15:28	178
16:13–21	38
16:19	126
16:21	38
16:27	39, 131
16:28	134
17:1	173–74
17:9	37
17:12	37
17:22	37

199

Scripture Index

Matthew (cont.)

18:15–18	129
18:18	126
19:28	131, 175
20:18	37
20:21	131
20:28	37
23:15	22
24:3	134
24:26–28	44
24:27	43, 134
24:29–31	174
24:30	39
24:36	159
24:37	43, 134
24:39	43, 134
24:40	44
24:43	48
24:44	42
25	46
25:1	45
25:14–30	31
25:31	45, 131
25:31–46	174
25:40	46
25:45	46
25:46	46
26:20–25	38
26:24	37
26:28	114
26:29	114
26:45	37
26:64	39
28	27, 133
28:16–20	45
28:17	155
28:18–20	147

Mark

1:1	77, 79, 89
1:1–8	78
1:1–13	57, 59
1:1–15	149, 150
1:2	103, 105
1:2–3	18, 89
1:3	80
1:4	80
1:7	80, 87, 152
1:7–8	83
1:8	85
1:9	57, 58, 59, 80, 118, 152
1:9–11	57, 59, 83
1:9–15	85
1:10–11	118
1:12–13	57, 60, 86
1:13	61
1:14	110, 118, 152, 153
1:14–15	87–89, 95, 125, 159
1:14–20	89
1:14—2:12	57, 62
1:14—7:23	62
1:15	19, 27, 80, 90, 105, 168
1:16	92, 118
1:17	107
1:20	107
1:21	98
1:21–28	95, 97, 98, 150
1:21–34	85
1:27	150
1:29	98, 105
1:29–31	150
1:31	88, 121
1:32–34	150
1:38	95, 152
1:39	98, 152
1:45	109, 110
2:2	95
2:10	38, 77, 124, 125, 129, 140, 165
2:11	126
2:13–17	118
2:13–22	57, 63
2:14	107
2:15	98
2:17	165
2:18	22, 34
2:18–19	127

Mark (cont.)

2:18–20	90, 103
2:18–22	34
2:19–20	77
2:23–28	34, 111, 126, 177
2:23—3:6	57, 64
2:27	77
2:27–28	39, 129
2:28	38, 79, 124, 125, 140, 165
3:1	98
3:1–6	98, 111, 177
3:4	169
3:7–12	98
3:13–19	91, 97, 98, 104, 118
3:14	104, 110, 152
3:14–15	108
3:20–27	57, 64
3:20–35	98
3:27	87
3:28–30	42
3:31–35	108
3:34–35	98
4:1	95
4:1–20	95
4:1–34	57, 64
4:3	77, 95
4:15	87
4:26–29	97
4:28	95
4:31–32	95
4:41	172
4:45	9
5:1–20	97, 182
5:18	110
5:19	108
5:19–20	110
5:24	69, 104
5:37	90, 105
5:40–41	104
6	118
6:1–6	98, 118
6:2	98
6:3	152
6:4	77
6:5–6	96
6:6–13	31
6:7	104, 152
6:7–13	97, 98, 118, 129
6:10	98
6:12	27, 110, 152
6:12–13	118
6:14–29	118
6:17	93
6:20	22
6:29	34, 103
6:30	94, 104, 152
6:30–31	118
6:30–44	100
6:30–52	118
6:45	172
6:53–56	100, 118
7:1–23	57, 65, 91, 100, 119
7:14–23	114
7:15	101
7:17	98
7:17–23	177
7:19	100
7:24	98
7:24–30	93, 99–101, 118, 178
7:24—10:52	65
7:30–52	118
7:31–37	94, 100
8:1–10	94, 100
8:11	87
8:11–12	xi
8:22–26	57, 66
8:26	108
8:27–28	105
8:27–30	102, 179
8:27–33	57, 67
8:31	37, 38, 50, 77, 124, 165
8:31–33	56
8:31–38	125, 126
8:32–33	118
8:33	179
8:34	xi, 108
8:34–35	130, 157

Scripture Index

Mark (cont.)

Reference	Pages
8:34–37	80, 117, 158
8:34–38	23, 99, 125, 126, 140, 168, 169, 177, 181
8:34—9:1	57, 66, 68, 71, 72, 75, 103
8:35	44, 117
8:35–37	129
8:38	39, 42, 77, 124, 127
9:1	134, 137
9:1–8	137
9:2	90, 105
9:2–8	91, 172
9:2—10:45	57, 67
9:9	37, 124, 165
9:12	37, 77, 165
9:12–13	124
9:18	94, 118
9:28	98
9:28–29	118
9:30–37	67
9:31	37, 50, 113, 124, 165
9:33	98
9:33–37	105, 119
9:37	77, 89, 91, 104, 105, 165
9:38	97
9:38–41	179
9:41	77, 97
10:2	87
10:5	114
10:10	98
10:17	108
10:17–22	96
10:17–27	174
10:18	106
10:21	107, 187
10:23	187
10:26	169
10:27	107
10:28–31	104
10:29	108
10:29–30	99, 109, 170
10:29–31	107
10:32	108, 171
10:32–45	67
10:33	37, 77, 113, 124, 165
10:33–34	50, 58, 131
10:35–40	105, 119, 130
10:38–39	34
10:40	131
10:41–45	98, 106, 177
10:42	72
10:42–45	168, 181
10:43–44	86
10:45	37, 77, 81, 86, 88, 109, 124, 129, 140, 165, 167, 175, 178, 183
10:46–52	57, 66
10:52	109
11:1—14:13	62
11:3	79, 156
11:9–10	109
11:27–33	57, 65
11:30–33	xi
12:1–12	57, 64
12:6	105
12:13–17	177
12:13–44	57, 64
12:15	87
12:29–32	114
12:35–37	102, 103, 177, 182, 184
12:36–37	79
12:41–44	119
13	153, 159
13:1–14	57, 62
13:1–23	71
13:1–31	57, 62
13:3	90
13:3–27	134
13:4	153
13:9	98
13:9–13	112, 130
13:10	27, 101, 128, 134, 148, 152–55, 168
13:13	151, 169
13:14	135

Mark (cont.)

13:21	43
13:21–22	91, 181
13:24–27	42, 71, 115, 132, 137, 157
13:26	18, 39, 77, 124, 132, 138, 140, 141
13:26–27	152, 168
13:27	63, 157
13:28–32	137, 157
13:31	157
13:32	115, 134, 157, 159
13:37	71
14:1–9	57, 63
14:3–9	119
14:9	152, 155
14:10	116
14:17–21	38
14:20	116
14:21	37, 77, 124, 165
14:22–25	113
14:25	107, 170
14:28	140, 141, 171
14:32–42	57, 60, 61, 116, 118
14:32—16:8	59
14:33	90
14:37	61
14:38	87, 88
14:41	37, 61, 124
14:43	116
14:43–46	113
14:48–49	177
14:53–65	113
14:62	39, 77, 124, 132, 138, 140, 141
15:1–15	113
15:29–32	169
15:30–31	169
15:33–39	57, 59
15:39	142
15:40	121
15:40–41	69, 116
15:41	109, 121
16	153, 159
16:6	173
16:7	57, 58, 59, 94, 140, 141, 155, 171
16:8	133, 148, 173
16:9	156
16:9–11	147
16:9–20	77, 133, 144–48, 149–51, 155, 160
16:10	155
16:11	151
16:12	156
16:12–13	147
16:13	151
16:14	147, 151, 156
16:15	152, 154
16:15–17	147
16:16	151, 153
16:17	151, 153
16:17–18	150, 151
16:18	147, 150
16:19	147, 151
16:19–20	151
16:20	147, 152–54, 156, 157

Luke

3:16	41
4:1–2	88
4:1–13	87
5:24	38
5:33	22
6:5	38
6:13	22
6:22	40, 42
6:40	21
7:19	41
7:34	41
8:2	147
9:1—18:14	44
9:10	22
9:22	37, 41
9:26	39
9:27	134
9:44	37, 41
9:51—18:14	108

Scripture Index

Luke (cont.)

9:56	46
9:57–62	35
9:58	41
10:1–24	23
10:12	43
11:1	27, 84
11:1–4	93
11:30	41
12:1	42
12:8	42
12:10	36, 42
12:13	42
12:32	42
12:39	48
12:40	42
12:46	42
13:35	41
14:10	46
14:26	21
14:27	21
14:33	21
17:20–21	134
17:22	43
17:22–37	43
17:22—18:8	44
17:24	43
17:26	43
17:30	43
18:1–8	44
18:8	41
18:31	37, 41
19:10	47
19:11	134
21:27	39, 47
21:31	134
21:36	46, 47
22:14	22
22:18	134
22:21–23	38
22:22	37, 41
22:30	131, 175
22:43	61
22:48	46, 47
22:69	35, 39
23:42	114
24:10	22
24:11	147
24:13–35	147
24:36–43	147
24:47	129, 147
24:48	147
24:50	147
24:50–53	45, 140
24:51	147

John

1:26–27	83
2:2	21
2:11	21
3:22–24	93
3:32	21
4:1–2	90
6:45	12
8:31	21
9:27	21
9:28	21
13:13	12
13:35	21
14:3	173
14:12	12, 173
14:16	12
14:18–19	173
14:26	12
14:28	173
15:8	21
16:4–15	12
16:22	173
17:13–15	31
20:11	147
20:17	133
20:26	147
21:19	173

Acts

1:6–11	45, 140
1:8	12

Scripture Index

Acts (cont.)

1:9–11	39, 147
1:11	47, 156
1:22	23
1:23	147
1:24–26	23
1:26	21
2:1	147
2:4	147, 156
2:43	147
3:1	147
5:3	23
5:12	147
6:1	21
6:7	21
7:56	35, 135
8:6	147
9	156
9:1	29
9:2	23
9:10	21
9:20	119
9:32	147
9:36	21
10:15	101
10:46	147, 156
13:52	21, 29
14:8	147
14:20	21, 29
14:31	147
15:2	23
15:4	23
15:6	23
15:22	23
15:23	23
15:28	23
16:1	21, 29
16:4	23
16:16	147
18:25	23
19:1–4	91
19:6	147
19:9	23
19:13	147
19:23	23
21:4	21, 29
21:16	21, 29
22:3	26
22:4	23
24:14	23
24:22	23
28:3	147
28:3–5	156
28:3–6	147

Romans

1:1	25
1:7	25
1:16	101
1:16–17	26
2:9–10	101
2:16	26
3:1–2	101
3:21	124
3:26	14
5:15–21	49
5:18–19	49
8	132
8:30	25
9:28	124
12:1	124
13:11–12	26
13:11–14	22
16:1	25
16:2	25
16:3	25
16:5	25
16:7	25
16:8	25
16:9	25
16:10	25
16:11	25
16:12	25
16:13	25
16:14	25
16:15	25

Scripture Index

Romans (*cont.*)

16:17	25
16:21	25
16:23	25
16:25	26

1 Corinthians

1:1	25
1:2	25
1:9	25
1:12–13	105
1:24	25
4:9	25
6:2	131
9:5	25
12:28	25
15	49–50
15:3–7	139
15:5–8	156
15:7	25
15:8–10	22
15:9	25
15:12–34	134
15:20–28	133
15:23	22, 43, 49, 132
15:25	132
15:28	132
15:47	49

2 Corinthians

11–12	105
12:1–4	15

Galatians

1:17	25
1:19	25
2	24
2:1–14	105
2:6	26
3:1–5	119

Ephesians

2:20	105

Philippians

1:14	22
2	132
2:3–11	139
2:5–11	151

1 Thessalonians

1:7	155
1:10	139
2:10	155
2:13	155
2:19	22, 43
3:13	22, 43
4	132
4:13–18	134
4:13—5:11	133
4:14	48
4:15	22, 43
4:16	139
4:16–17	48, 50, 125, 132
4:17	35
5:2	48
5:4	48
5:23	22, 43

2 Thessalonians

2:4	125

Hebrews

2:6	35, 135
5:8	11

Revelation

1:12–20	151
1:13	35, 135
14:14	35, 135
21:14	105

www.ingramcontent.com/pod-product-compliance
Lightning Source LLC
Chambersburg PA
CBHW070317230426
43663CB00011B/2165